Journalism Matters

Peter W. Cox

Co-Founder of *Maine Times*

Tilbury House  Publishers
Gardiner, Maine

Tilbury House, Publishers
2 Mechanic Street
Gardiner, Maine 04345
800–582–1899 • www.tilburyhouse.com

Quotes from Walter Lippmann's published writings, 1913, 1940, and 1954,
courtesy of the Yale University Library.
Introduction by Sue Scheible courtesy of the *Patriot Ledger*, Quincy, MA.

First printing: February 2005.

10 9 8 7 6 5 4 3 2 1

Library of Congress Cataloging-in-Publication Data
Cox, Peter W.
 Journalism matters / Peter W. Cox.
    p. cm.
 Includes index.
 ISBN 0-88448-268-5 (pbk. : alk. paper)
 1. Cox, Peter W. 2. Journalists—United States—Biography. I. Title.
 PN4874.C765A3 2005
 070.92—dc22
                            2004025574

Designed on Crummett Mountain by Edith Allard, Somerville, Maine.
Editorial, layout, and production work by Jennifer Bunting and Barbara
Diamond.
Text printing and binding: Maple Vail, Kirkwood, New York.
Cover prepress and printing: John P. Pow Company, South Boston.

This book was printed on Rolland RPT Offset, a recycled paper with 30 percent
post-consumer waste, and classified ECF.

For Anna and Olivia

Contents

Foreword

Sometimes you're lucky in life and just when you need it, someone helps you find a new path. I was nearly twenty-three when good friends guided me from my first disappointing career choice, early childhood education, to journalism.

In the summer of 1975, my college classmate Eunice Theodore Cox suggested I come up to Maine, where her husband, Peter W. Cox, was the enterprising editor of a small daily newspaper, the *Bath Daily Times*. Eunice had worked as a reporter before her marriage and said, "Why don't you give it a try?"

Every year as September approaches, I remember that autumn of 1967 as an especially exhilarating time. Peter was the perfect coach and mentor, with his infectious enthusiasm and visionary ideas about the role of a newspaper in improving people's lives and challenging a community to look at itself. He was kind and constructive, rewriting and sharpening my leads, and when I left Maine two months later, I carried a file of freelance clippings.

Within a year, Peter went on to co-found *Maine Times* with John Cole. It was a ground-breaking statewide weekly with an alternative viewpoint and a strong environmental focus. Eunice, who had two small children, also worked there as a writer and editor. The first issue was October 4, 1968, and the paper was soon winning national awards and media praise.

Peter led the paper from 1968 until 1986, when he sold it and pursued his other passions for influencing public policy, education, and gardening. He started and helped fund a mentors program at the University of Maine, served on the boards of the Maine Civil Liberties Union and Portland Art Museum, and guided the resurrection of Wolfe's Neck Farm, a foundation in Freeport focused on agricultural reform and a growing natural beef operation. (He also returned to the paper briefly in the 1990s.)

Now age sixty-seven and diagnosed with incurable esophageal cancer, Peter has defied the odds, survived grueling treatments, and written his memoirs. He is a complex and fascinating man with an intriguing family history. He comes from a privileged middle-class background and the cast of characters includes many well-known and impressive people. For me, however, he is the most interesting—with his restless intellectual curiosity and an ability, even a drive, to ask insightful questions and challenge opinions, including his own. Each chapter has reminded me in different ways of what is important in choosing one's life work and values—and how both Peter and Eunice have influenced and helped young people.

He leads off each chapter with a quote from Walter Lippmann, the author and journalist who was a syndicated columnist and family friend. The first chapter is titled, "What My Father Never Told Me," and the Lippmann quotation comments on how society segregates young from old and how that segregation "breaks the connection by which the new generation takes possession of experience and improves upon it."

Peter grew up eventually suspecting but never knowing that his father, Oscar Cox, was Jewish and had grown up Jewish. He knew that his father's parents had come from Russia in 1903 and of his father's many accomplishments—Cox drafted the legislation that became the Lend-Lease Act, which enabled the United States to arm its allies during World War II. But it was only years after his father died of a stroke at age sixty-two that Peter learned about the role he played in getting Franklin Delano Roosevelt to change his attitudes toward the annihilation of the Jews and establish the War Refugee Board.

After describing his painstaking unveiling of the past, Peter writes that he doesn't feel any sense of betrayal or hurt that his father never spoke of his Jewish background. It was, however, very important to him, part of his identity. He writes, "In the milieu [his father] created, by the standards he instilled in me, what is important about who you are is not social or ethnic. According to my father's teachings, who you are is your accomplishments and most important, how you conducted your life ethically."

He describes how his father stimulated family dinner table discussions over current issues, loved "awful jokes" and shaggy dog stories, and challenged Peter and his brother with puzzles and education-as-games. Peter credits his own lifelong interest in searching for unconventional solutions to new problems to those talks.

Peter does what, I believe, a good memoirist should. He pays tribute to those who influenced him—even the second-grade teacher who loved birds—and sprinkles in anecdotes and vignettes from his early life. He revisits his decisions and actions with a fresh critical eye. He explains the principles that have guided a long and distinguished career in journalism and public policy.

As another college classmate, Anne Biesemeyer Bailey, observed, despite all the pain and anxiety such an illness brings, both Peter and Eunice have been able to devote this time to researching and writing a memoir of lasting interest.

When you may be near the end of your life, Peter has said, people start giving you awards. He has received many. But this, I think, may be his finest and most lasting tribute.

Sue Scheible
The Patriot Ledger
Quincy, MA

Part 1

THE TRUE RELATIONSHIP is, so to speak, vertical—father and son, teacher and pupil, thinker and disciple, master and apprentice. In this relationship, experience is transmitted to the young and vitality is renewed in the mature. We have substituted a horizontal relationship in which we segregate the young in youth movements and the aged in old-age movements, and then call it progress. As a matter of fact this segregation is most reactionary, in that it breaks the connection by which the new generation takes possession of experience and improves upon it. This segregation of the generations prevents the young from growing up, and it means that when they become old in years, they remain immature in mind and character.

—Walter Lippmann, "Today and Tomorrow" column, February 17, 1940

One

What My Father Never Told Me

A few years ago, I gave the cum laude address at Hebron Academy and my theme was that the students should talk with their parents who had lived through some of the most significant history of all time—from World War II and the McCarthy era through Watergate to the present. I said any of their parents could give them a clearer picture of what the 1950s were actually like than could any textbook or nostalgic re-creation. I also noted that they received many of their values from us, just as we received ours from our parents. And it is always good to know where our values came from and whether they are still appropriate today.

I've learned that who my own father was is important to me; it is part of my identity. In the milieu he created and from the standards he instilled in me, I know that what's important about who you are is not social or ethnic. According to my father's teachings, who you are comes from your accomplishments and, most important, how you conduct your life ethically.

My father was reticent about his personal life—not unusual for a man born in 1904 to parents who had arrived from Russia only a year earlier—and it has taken me years to fill in the details. But my father was proud of his public accomplishments, and the one he was proudest of was the Lend-Lease Act, which enabled the United States to arm its allies during World War II. He drafted the bill and then worked with the agency the rest of his government career. Even the little I knew, while growing up, of my father's experiences in Lend-Lease produced several clear goals for me: achievement at an early age, a desire to affect public policy, and a belief in collaborative effort.

But my father told me nothing about another accomplishment, one that linked his private and public lives. It wasn't until years after his death that I learned about the role he played in getting President

Franklin Delano Roosevelt to change his attitude toward the annihilation of the Jews of Europe and to establish the War Refugee Board. My father had never told me that he was Jewish, himself.

I knew none of this as a child growing up because it would have opened a vast area of his life my father preferred not to discuss. Somehow, at some point, I sensed he wasn't telling me something important. By the time I was in college, I began to suspect my father was part Jewish, but I never asked him specifically. It was already too late. A wall of family convention had been too carefully constructed to breach.

Only when I went to my uncle's house, after my father's burial in 1966, did I receive confirmation. When I arrived that evening, I learned that my uncle was at the synagogue, saying Kaddish for my father.

My father dwelt on the edges of published history but was at the heart of policy formation. A contemporary newspaper columnist referred to him as the most important person in government that you never heard of. During World War II, he prosecuted the Nazi saboteurs who slipped into the country in submarines. That trial would form the basis for George W. Bush's proposal for military tribunals for enemy combatants sixty years later. He participated in the debate on whether to intern Japanese-Americans on the West Coast. He participated in the conferences to set up the International Monetary Fund and the United Nations. He was a key player in bringing America's industrial capacity to war levels. He drafted the legislation for the G.I. Bill of Rights.

But most of what I know about his participation in these events I discovered much later, after his death, when I read about them, sometimes as a mere footnote in the biography of a more famous person. Through picking up tidbits, I became sensitized to where he might have been even if he wasn't mentioned. That's why one of my inner alarms went off in 1991 as I was reading Alan Dershowitz's biography, *Chutzpah*.

In his book Dershowitz took up the cudgel in the trend to charge the American establishment with the abandonment of Europe's Jews to the Holocaust. In this case, the villain was Felix Frankfurter, Supreme Court justice and adviser to President Roosevelt. Dershowitz, a Harvard law professor with a reputation for defending radical causes, was describing a 1943 meeting between Frankfurter and Jan Karski, a Catholic in the Polish underground, who had come to the United States to reveal what he had seen in the Warsaw Ghetto and the concentration camp at Belzec. It was one of the first credible eyewitness accounts of the systematic extermination of the Jews by the Nazis. After Karski told his story, Frankfurter replied: "I cannot believe you." Frankfurter did not mean that he thought Karski was lying, only that what he was describing was inconceivable. As a consequence of his disbelief, Frankfurter said, he could not relay Karski's message to Roosevelt. This was not a new story to me, but what I learned for the first time in the Dershowitz account was that the Karski-Frankfurter meeting had been arranged by "the ambassador of the Polish government-in-exile," no name provided. I knew who it had to be: my friend, Ambassador Ciechanowski.

I still have, in the simple frame my mother put it in, a fading, handwritten card that says, under the title, L'Ambassadeur de Pologne: "Jan Ciechanowski, Ambassador Extraordinary and Plenipotentiary of the Republic of Poland to the United States, presents his best Easter wishes to his very dear Friend, Peter Cox, and asks him to accept the gifts of a railway train and a ship in token of his sincere friendship. Washington, 1942."

I was only five at the time but I particularly remember the ship, which I played with at length in the bathtub. My special friendship with Ambassador Ciechanowski continued through the war years; our lengthy conversations when he was calling for my father and I answered the phone became a family joke.[1]

This connection piqued my interest in what Dershowitz had to say about the meeting. As had become fashionable by 1991, Dershowitz flayed Frankfurter for his inaction, part of the abandonment charge that contained two major components. The first was that many American Jews did not try as hard as they could to save Europe's Jews from Hitler. Regardless of the chances of success or the depth of their knowledge about the emerging Holocaust, inaction was portrayed as cowardice or, worse, being unwilling to risk their own personal posi-

1. In a 1942 letter to my father, Ambassador Ciechanowski noted: "I was very touched by the sweet personal reaction of Peter Cox with whom I had a charming conversation over the telephone yesterday. I hope to see him soon."

tions to help a minority to which they belonged. America at the time was significantly anti-Semitic, and most Americans were not concerned about the Jews in Europe.

The second charge was that thousands, perhaps millions, might have been saved if the U.S. government, even as late as 1943, had bombed the concentration camps and the rail lines leading to them, an available option. This latter contention is seriously flawed because it is based on the myth of precision bombing. One reason the Allies bombed so many civilians during World War II was that they could not be more accurate, and precision bombing effective enough to damage the camp complexes without killing inmates would have been impossible in 1944. Any bombed rail lines would have been quickly repaired. Although the military policy that was followed—winning the war as quickly as possible—may have been the only realistic one, that debate will never be resolved.

As word of the concentration camps began to leak out in the early 1940s, many Jews, including my father, spoke of the non-Jewish victims and the Jewish victims together, making the point that this was a crime against humanity. They wanted to avoid the accusation of special pleading since isolationists had long argued that the Jews had drawn the United States into the war and that Roosevelt was already overly sympathetic to Jewish interests.

My father had been intimately involved with those accusations during his work to get the Lend-Lease Act through Congress in 1941, a major confrontation between interventionists and isolationists. As the war drew to a close, Henry Morgenthau, secretary of the Treasury and the most visible Jew in the administration, suggested destroying Germany's industrial base after the war and reducing it to an agrarian state. At the time, his position was attacked as Jewish revenge.[2]

But Dershowitz contended that Frankfurter and others went from fear of special pleading to fear of compromising their own special positions and consequently abandoned their fellow Jews for narrow and selfish reasons.

In his memoir, Arthur M. Schlesinger, Jr., offers a more nuanced

2. In some of the newspaper reports of the time, my father was cited as promoting the Morgenthau view, but he either changed his mind or was not a firm believer in reducing Germany to an agricultural state because he became a strong supporter of the Marshall Plan.

explanation, pointing out that what Frankfurter was really expressing in 1943 was that the concept of such a massive genocide was inconceivable.[3] Schlesinger notes that until the concentration camps were exposed in gruesome photographs after the war and the Nazi perpetrators put on trial at Nuremberg, knowledge of the gassing of millions of civilians was still abstract. People had read about charges of the massive killings in the newspapers, but they had not made the sort of connection that was easier a mere three decades later when the evening television news brought to every living room in America Vietnamese monks setting themselves on fire in protest of our policies or a naked girl fleeing napalm.

By the time I read Dershowitz's book, I not only knew that my father was Jewish but I knew from a 1982 *New York Times* article by Lucy Dawidowicz that he had taken action on behalf of European Jewry. I had by then been to the Roosevelt Library at Hyde Park and found evidence that he had been instrumental in the formation of the War Refugee Board, whose accomplishments may have been exaggerated over time, but which nonetheless had represented a sincere attempt to take meaningful action. So I wrote to Karski, then teaching at Georgetown University, to ask if he had ever run into my father. He replied that he had not and that was that. So much for the Ciechanowski connection.

But two years later I received a letter from E. Thomas Wood, who was writing a biography of Karski and had access to his files and correspondence where he had found my original inquiry. In his letter to me, which said that Karski was mistaken when he said he had not met my father, Wood explained that Karski met so many people during the two years he toured the United States in his attempt to alert the public to the Holocaust, he could not possibly remember them all. But Wood's research showed that my father had been at the meeting—July 5, 1943—at which Frankfurter had made his statement of disbelief, and the meeting had indeed been arranged by Jan Ciechanowski, who had also invited Benjamin Cohen, a longtime Roosevelt intimate.[4]

3. Arthur M. Schlesinger, Jr., *A Life in the 20th Century* (Boston: Houghton Mifflin, 2000).
4. Ciechanowski had chosen shrewdly. All three were Jews. Frankfurter was a confidante of the President and had influence throughout the bureaucracy via former students he had placed in their jobs. Cohen, along with Tommy Corcoran, had been the most prolific drafter

Professor Wood wrote me: "My research indicates that this meeting with Oscar Cox was quite significant...your father was unusual among American Jews in positions of power, in that he took a strong stand early in the war concerning reports of atrocities against the Jews of Nazi-occupied Europe. His position contrasted starkly with the reticence of Jews like Felix Frankfurter and Walter Lippmann.

"I enclose a few documents from the FDR Library concerning your father's efforts to establish a U.N. War Crimes Commission and to alert other leaders to Karski's revelations about the Holocaust.

"I am sure you are proud of the courageous stand that your father took at a time when Europe's Jews were crying out for help and many of America's Jewish leaders felt obliged to lie low. History should judge Oscar Cox generously."

Karski's obituary in the *New York Times*[5] reported that Karski subsequently had a secret meeting with President Roosevelt, the probable result of a memo my father, in response to his encounter with Karski, wrote Harry Hopkins, urging such a meeting.

Although Karski believed he had failed to move Roosevelt to significant action during that meeting, John Pehle, who became head of the War Refugee Board, was quoted by the *Times* as saying Karski's visit with Roosevelt convinced the president to establish the board, for which my father had already helped draft the order. Pehle said Karski's mission—and his ability to get to the President—"changed U.S. policy overnight from indifference to affirmative action."

It is difficult to describe the emotional impact Professor Wood's letter had on me. Even though while growing up, I had not known my father was Jewish and I had adapted to middle-of-the-road Protestantism, derived from my mother's having been a Presbyterian, by 1993 I was proud of my Jewish heritage. A decade earlier I had confronted my mother, accusingly asking her why she and my father never told me I was half Jewish, when that fact would have been enough to lead to my death if I had been born in Germany. She began her long letter in reply with the explanation that Judaism passes along

of legislation in the New Deal. My father was at the time a friend of Ciechanowski's, but more important a special aide to Harry Hopkins, Roosevelt's chief of staff. I have no doubt my father participated in the selection of attendees.
5. 14 July 2000.

the female line and technically I was not Jewish and ended by saying I should improve my thinking, a clear rebuke of my raising the issue.

Today, someone not being told they are Jewish is rare but not unheard of, but when anti-Semitism was more firmly intrenched, it was more common.[6] Knowledge of the Holocaust also caused some reluctant Jews to identify themselves out of solidarity and the feeling it would be ignoble not to stand with the victims. I suspect that in many cases, there develops a complicity between the parent who doesn't tell the child and the child who begins to suspect and doesn't ask. My case strikes me as worth recording for several reasons: My father split his life—he was active in trying to help the Jews of Europe while disassociating himself from his own Jewishness. My brother claims he always knew and the different perspective that knowledge gave us on key events in our lives is striking.

I believe my father's decision not to self-identify as Jewish—but not to actively deny it either—had more to do with his children than with himself.

In the major references to my father's actions to help save the Jews of Europe—by David S. Wyman in *The Abandonment of the Jews*, by E. Thomas Wood in the Karski biography and in Lucy Dawidowicz's *New York Times* article,[7] there is no issue of his denial of being Jewish. Dawidowicz does not mention his being a Jew but then she does not mention the background of many of the people she describes. Wood refers to him as "more active in Jewish matters than most of the numerous other Jews in the administration."

My father attempted to aid Europe's victims by pursuing two avenues. The first was the establishment of a United Nations Commission on War Crimes, an idea he had taken to Ciechanowski before the meeting with Karski. His belief was that publicly declaring that genocide was a war crime and that its perpetrators would be prosecuted after the war would act as a deterrent to some of those participating in the slaughter. We now know that such a hope was futile.

The second was a plan he worked out with his colleague Milton

6. For my generation, however, it is a large club. Those who were not told they had a parent or more distant linear relative who was Jewish range from former Secretary of State Madeline Albright to presidential candidates General Wesley Clark and John F. Kerry.
7. *New York Times Magazine*, 18 April 1982.

Handler for an interagency board to facilitate the rescue of war refugees.[8] This plan took off when Treasury Secretary Morgenthau, whom my father had come to Washington to work for, picked it up. It quickly evolved into the War Refugee Board, which became a reality in early 1944. My father and Handler had originally proposed funding of $25 million but this never came about and the board's usefulness was limited by its inability to save many of those who had not already been killed by this time.[9] The most notable success came when the War Refugee Board enlisted the government of Sweden to help it in Hungary and the Swedes recruited the businessman Raul Wallenberg who was able to extend his protection over some 30,000 Hungarian Jews.

Wallenberg disappeared after the war and is believed to have died in a Russian prison. He has become one of the outstanding symbols of a heroic effort by gentiles to save the Jews.

Dawidowicz also said that some Lend-Lease funds were used to help refugees. While Lend-Lease was a major topic of discussion at home, there was never any mention of my father's efforts to save war refugees.

Although nothing Jewish was ever discussed at home, I was not isolated from my Jewish relatives who, while totally mainstream culturally, still practiced the religion to varying degrees.

My paternal grandfather died before I was born but when I was very young, we used to visit my grandmother in Portland, Maine, where my father was born and brought up. I vaguely remember her speaking with an accent although it was not enough to raise questions beyond the fact she had immigrated from Russia, which I was told.

Today, the very fact that the family had fled Russia at the turn of the century would have alerted me to their background. This was the time of the great Eastern European exodus of Jews suffering under the pogroms. But as a child, I knew no history and none of this occurred to me.

My grandmother often showed my brother and me a picture of her relatives, dressed in formal clothing, white tie and tails, with sashes and medals across their chests. The image was one of accomplished

8. One of the three board members would have been Leo Crowley, then head of the Foreign Economic Administration, for whom my father worked. Roosevelt approved the board concept but did not appoint Crowley.
9. Most of the funding ultimately came from Jewish agencies.

and well-to-do people, and while it would be natural to inquire why such prosperous people would want to flee their homeland, it is not a question one asks at the age of seven or eight. Indeed, I am sure that if today I walked into her upstairs apartment, overlooking Deering Oaks Park, I would notice artifacts that told me she was Jewish, since, according to my aunt, my grandmother Sarah was religious. But at that age, if I had seen a menorah on the mantel, I wouldn't have known what it was.

In many American families in the late 1940s, the time of my youth, children were negatively sensitized to ethnic differences. Native-born Americans looked down on the foreign born. They would have known that a family down the street was Irish or Italian (and they would have known the derogatory terms Mick and Spic), but the emphasis in our family was just the opposite. We were taught that ethnic background didn't matter. What mattered was that we were all Americans and therefore all equal. The exception to this egalitarian principle that could not be overlooked was Negroes, as blacks were then called. I went to grade school in Arlington, Virginia, and Washington, D.C., both of which were segregated. My graduating class at Western High School, had I not gone off to private school, was the first to be integrated, the class of 1955.

I played with black children when I visited my maternal grandparents in Bryson City, North Carolina, and I played with them after we moved to Georgetown, when I was in the third grade. While I had a gnawing sense of injustice that they could not share the playground, I took segregation as a given. Although I recall from a young age the feeling of indignation when I saw a black person forced to the back of the bus in Washington, it was only later, after many kitchen conversations with Lillian Speech, who worked for us for years, that I began to understand what it must be like to live under the daily insults that blacks suffered. People scoff at the idea of the privileged little boy who develops his racial conscience at the knee of his family's black servant, but without this contact, many a privileged little white boy would have remained unsensitized. And the teaching was not automatic. I did not have the same relationship with my grandparents' eternal maid, Lily, as I had with the volatile and outspoken Lillian.

The first time I recall any sense of personal outrage at anti-

Semitism was when my brother and I were taking tennis lessons from Buddy Goeltz at Columbia Country Club, just outside the District limits in Bethesda. My best tennis playing friend was Johnny Harris who also took lessons from Buddy. Johnny was a year older than me but we were both still younger than fifteen which meant we competed in the Boys division against one another and we were among the top players in our division in Washington. More important, we practiced with and played one another for as much as four hours a day during the summer and even though we were competitive, neither of us would have wanted to win at the other's misfortune.

The year I was thirteen and Johnny fourteen, the qualifying tournament for the nationals at Kalamazoo, Michigan, was held at Columbia Country Club and Buddy was the tournament director. This was Johnny's last year in the Boys and only the finalists would qualify for Kalamazoo but Buddy faced a dilemma. The number one seed would clearly be Donald Dell, a year younger than me, but destined to be a two-time national Boys champion. Both Johnny and I expected to lose to him.

If Johnny and I were seeded number two and three, the number two person would be assured of reaching the finals before meeting Donald, therefore qualifying for the nationals, win or lose. Since Johnny and I were almost dead even competitively, we went to Buddy and asked that he let us play in the semifinals to determine who met Donald in the finals.

Buddy replied that while our suggestion might seem fair, it was against the rules. The number three and four seeds would be drawn from a hat to see which semifinal each fell into.

So Buddy made the arbitrary decision that I would be seeded number two and the luck of the draw put Johnny in Donald's semifinal. Johnny lost to Donald in the semifinal as did I in the final.

I don't recall if Johnny qualified for the nationals in another way; I think he did. But I do recall that his sense of being treated unfairly persisted despite the fact Buddy followed the rules, setting an example of what he had taught us.

I don't know if Johnny could have felt I was favored instead of him because he was Jewish but that certainly could have been the case. Either before or after that tournament, I had had a disturbing conversation with Buddy about Jews being allowed to join the club where we played.

You must understand how much I respected Buddy, for whom the game of tennis was an analogy to life. You would succeed at tennis and at life if you mastered the essentials, if you worked hard, and if you used your brain. And you always played fair—winning was not everything.

Sometime during that period—I was under Buddy's close direction for about three years from the age of ten through thirteen—Buddy and I were discussing the fact that Columbia Country Club did not allow Jews to be members. I was critical of the policy, but Buddy defended it, saying at one point, would I want to belong to a club where Johnny Harris could be a member? I knew Buddy liked Johnny so there was only one reason for his exclusion.

I was outraged that he would say such a thing, but I was also disillusioned. I recall that I had the presence of mind to say I would be honored to belong to any club with Johnny, but I also recall that I was fighting back tears as I said it. I am not sure the tears were directed at the injustice to Johnny; they may have been caused by the fact that someone I loved and adored as only a child can love and adore a special teacher had said something that I knew viscerally to be so wrong.

Was my reaction heightened by the fact that somehow I knew, even subliminally, that I shared with Johnny a background that would have also disqualified me to become a member of Columbia? I don't think so. My brother told me many years later that he always knew our father was Jewish and he never would have had the interchange with Buddy that precipitated his comment about Johnny.

That conversation had begun when Buddy asked me why we didn't join the country club and I replied that my father would never join an organization that discriminated against Jews.

That my father had told me such a thing, without telling me he was Jewish, is indicative of the complexity of his position. (It could also be viewed as humorously absurd, like Groucho Marx's comment that he wouldn't want to belong to any club that would allow him as a member.)

In the past my father had broken traditional barriers. When, immediately after law school, he obtained a job at Cadwallader, Wickersham, and Taft in New York City, he was the first Jew to do so. According to Lloyd Cutler, one of the founding partners in my father's firm and later President Jimmy Carter's attorney, Taft had been openly critical of Louis Brandeis being named to the U.S. Supreme Court. But after the war, when Lloyd, who had a similar Jewish background, and who had openly discussed Jewish issues with Oscar, joined the Metropolitan Club and suggested that Oscar do so as well, my father told Lloyd that he didn't "want to take the chance." Lloyd attributed the difference in attitude to being fifteen years younger than my father.

But despite the fact he had reason to fear he would be rejected if he sought to join Columbia Country Club and taking the position that he would not seek to join a club that excluded Jews, my father still let us play tennis there. I believe that in his mind he made the distinction that it was all right for us to take lessons at a facility that discriminated because Buddy was considered the best tennis teacher in the city and my father always wanted his children to have the best. Regardless of his visceral feeling, to have said we couldn't take lessons from the best coach in Washington would have been to allow his Jewishness, and not our potential talent, to define our lives.

My brother, on the other hand, may have harbored a certain degree of bitterness and his knowledge may have affected his attitudes as he grew up. Besides being a second son, I have come to believe that being oblivious about being the possible victim of prejudicial slights was a factor in my markedly more sanguine personality. While I have always prided myself in being internally an outsider, I have believed my empathy with the outsider to be the result of my upbringing, not the fact that I was an outsider myself. So while I was blithely taking lessons with Buddy almost every summer day for three years, oblivious to my inclusion among the unwanted, my brother was constantly aware of our status.

I don't want to exaggerate. Except for that one confrontation with Buddy, I do not recall any other anti-Semitic incident involving my tennis career. There may have been some indicators that a person more sensitive than I would have picked up, but there was nothing blatant. Blacks were still conspicuously absent. Arthur Ashe, who would break the color barrier, was a few years younger than us and my friend Donald Dell was to become his good friend and consultant, indicating that some of us were ahead of the curve. There were other players I knew to be Jewish, especially in hindsight, but this was not an issue, at least not among the players with whom I was friendly.

Who was Jewish and who wasn't had not played a memorable role in my life until I went off to Exeter at the age of fourteen. Exeter was as close to a meritocracy as I have ever experienced, and fourteen-year-olds there seemed to be aware of everything. One of my earliest friends, Mike Hobson, was particularly sensitive on the subject of anti-Semitism. He had the credentials. His mother, Laura Z. Hobson, was nationally known for her novel, *Gentlemen's Agreement*, and the Academy Award-winning movie made from it. Even in that novel, which was a treatise against the exclusionary practices of hotels in the 1940s, the protagonist is a gentile journalist pretending to be a Jew, presumably to make the character more appealing and free from the then common anti-Semitism. Gregory Peck played the role in the film.

I had encountered anti-Semitism before but even after Exeter, it did not threaten me personally. For some reason, the summer after my high-school graduation, I wrote in the journal I kept sporadically an entry about Paul Samath, a schoolmate in sixth grade. Paul lived on Dent Place, halfway between my house and Fillmore Elementary School, and sometimes, after school, I would go to his house where he would perform magic tricks for me, but I did not socialize with him at school where I joined the pick-up baseball and football games while he retired to a corner of the playground, hoping to avoid confrontation. Paul was one of those awkward-looking kids with thick glasses that magnified his eyes and a crouched Groucho Marx way of walking. I am sure I was one of the few boys with whom he felt at all comfortable, but our relationship was isolated from the rest of my life. He was a friend I did not share with my other friends.

Noting that Paul was afraid to join in the square dances at school—I assume I used the term afraid because Paul had told me he was—I wrote, at age seventeen, about this boy I had befriended when I was twelve: "Dent Place children were strongly prejudiced against the Jewish, and Paul was a Jew." I sounded like some sort of detached sociologist.

Although it had nothing to do with my father's ethnic status, I did receive one bit of surprising information during an Exeter English class with Mr. (Robert) Bates. He described having met a fascinating man who had escaped a pogrom by hiding in the family stove while everyone else was either murdered or carried away. This man had emigrated to America and had become a tremendous success, founding the Playtex girdle company. "Are you talking about Abe Spanel?" I asked in disbelief. "Yes, you know him?" Mr. Bates replied.

My image of Abe Spanel was much different, based largely on my remembrance of his wood-paneled station wagon parked on 35th Street in front of our house. One day he showed my brother and me the special work he had done on his glove compartment, redesigning it to hold a vast array of pills. We joked about his hypochondria.

Abe Spanel was a benign, slightly humorous figure in my life. At the time, he was a client of my father's and had made a great success through his mildly scandalous advertising, showing women making leaps in their latex Playtex girdles. (My father and he later parted company when my father felt one of his key executives had done something unethical and Abe sided with the executive.)

When I relayed to my father the story Mr. Bates had told, my father gave a skeptical reply and quickly moved on to another subject.

By the time I was in college, I noticed some of the more obvious indications of my father's heritage, such as the fact my grandfather's name was Jacob and my grandmother's maiden name was Sarah Trianowski. Because I knew my father to have been the first child born in the United States, I surmised they had come from Russia just after the turn of the century, amid one of the great periods of Jewish emigration. (Only years later did I learn that my grandfather's family name had been Karakofski.) So at some stage I developed the theory that my father must have been half-Jewish and that because of a split in his family, he had chosen not to follow any religion. (He did occasionally attend Presbyterian services with my mother, especially in North Carolina, where my grandfather was a church elder and mainstay.) As I grew older, curiosity alone should have compelled me to ask my father about his background but I did not. By the time I reached college, that I was half Jewish had not been a significant factor, and the new awareness that came out of the Holocaust literature was still a decade in the future. I don't know where not knowing enough to ask was superseded by not wanting to ask.

I was as good a keeper of family secrets as the next person and so I also never discussed, either within the immediate family or outside it, that my father had diabetes. He took an insulin shot every morning, usually administered by my mother, and he watched his diet. My brother Warren and I had seen the shot administered and we accepted as routine our own periodic tests for diabetes. But this was purely a family matter.

After my father's death at age sixty-two in 1966, from a diabetic-related stroke, there was a memorial service in Washington at Georgetown Presbyterian Church and a burial service at the cemetery in Kennebunk. My wife Eunice and I, alone among the family, were invited afterward to my Uncle Morris's house in Portland. When we arrived, there were no men present and when I asked where they were, I was told they were saying Kaddish for my father.

So if my uncle was an observant Jew, what was my father? The question had only one obvious answer.

Today we lose sight of the gradual escalation of Holocaust aware-ness and its meaning. Not until the 1970s and '80s did the literature become widespread and, as I read, I, like so many others, began to change my mind about what it meant to be Jewish. One could no longer be neutral. Assimilation was fine to a point, but to deny one's Jewish identity was to deny kinship with the victims/heroes of the Holocaust.

Even before the era of new awareness, I was probably more aware of the facts about the Holocaust than most Americans. The year I graduated from college, 1959, I spent the summer in Europe and visited Dachau.

Here is how I described it in my journal entry at the time:

"The ovens look like large bakeries. The calmness of the place is frightening. The birds are singing in the small pine trees planted in memory of the dead, but fifteen years ago there were the groans of men instead of the birds, and the heat of the sun would have been increased by that of the ovens and the smell must have made the work going on there even more obvious. There are monuments for the thousands of unknown dead, and an execution mound has a blood ditch behind it so that the ground would not become too soggy. Now the mound is covered with ivy and the plaque explaining its former use is surrounded by ageratum and begonias. The flags of the various countries whose Jews died there adorn the walls but are marred by 'Sue from Hamtramck, Mich. was here, 1958.' Families come and explain to their children the meaning of these cooled ovens; this remains the symbol of the depths to which humanity can sink." Even though written with the detachment of a twenty-one-year-old literary wannabe, my journal reflected some understanding of the enormity of what had happened.

I was affected by the gradual evolution of attitude toward the Holocaust that followed World War II. I read William L. Shirer's *The Rise and Fall of the Third Reich* shortly after it was published in 1960 and it clearly described The Final Solution. However, it put the extermination of Europe's Jews in the context of Hitler's overall policies, which included killing millions of Slavs as well. While the policy of eradicating the Jews was the pinnacle of Hitlerism, it was also depicted as part of a larger crime against humanity that included non-Jews. That same year, I saw the movie *Exodus*, the widely popular initial presentation of the Jews as heroes rather than victims. The blue-eyed Paul Newman was the transcendental Jew, someone so handsome and appealing that no one could have a negative reaction to him. And his love interest, Eva Marie Saint, certainly didn't look Jewish. In the Jew/gentile crossover, the Jews win hands down. Newman has classic good looks and later in his career does exceptionally well portraying over-the-hill Irish Catholics.

Knowledge of the Holocaust is said to have practically eradicated anti-Semitism in America, but the classic Jewish film heroes were not identifiable as Jews and some of the most popular Jewish actors, such as Cary Grant, had changed their names to hide their backgrounds. *Exodus* carried on the tradition from *Gentleman's Agreement* where the protagonist is, after all, not really a Jew but only a journalist posing as a Jew. The message was that Jews were just like gentiles except for the fact they were a persecuted race. As the son of an assimilationist, I was brought up believing the same thing.

I don't think the Eichmann trial that same year had such an impact on me, possibly because I had already read enough to know what happened and possibly because in 1961 I had taken a job as editor of the *Adirondack Daily Enterprise* and my life, as a twenty-three-year-old, was consumed by myriad issues, both local and national. But I kept on reading, first the popular novels, then some of the more gruesome memoirs. Gradually, I began to identify myself as more Jewish.

In the early 1970s having returned to Maine, I was playing in a tennis tournament in Deering Oaks Park, across from Park Avenue where my grandmother had lived. After a day's matches, Rob and Annette Elowitch invited my wife, Eunice, and me to come by their parents' house for a swim. I had hired Rob as the first movie critic for *Maine Times* when we began publication in 1968 and we had become good friends, so the invitation was nothing unusual.

The Elowitch house was in a section of town near Temple Beth El and after we had been there a while, other people, most of them our parents' generation, began to show up. They were all extremely friendly and when I asked Rob where they had come from and why they were there, he replied that they had come to see Oscar Cox's son. These were people from the Portland Jewish community who had known my father's family and who, if they had not known him personally, knew all about him and his successful career in Washington.

Oscar grew up Jewish. According to my Aunt Rose, he had a bar mitzvah and they spoke Yiddish in their home. Rose said her primary language was Yiddish until she went to school. She said my grandfather was a major property owner in Portland and acted as an arbitrator/judge for people in the Jewish community who had a dispute. When I told her Oscar had never told us he was Jewish, she was surprised and she made it clear she did not want me to write about it. In her opinion, his hiding his Jewish heritage from his children was shameful.

Why did my father do it? Why did he at least collaborate in the myth he was not Jewish?

Rummaging through old papers, I found his freshman year transcript from MIT—he went to MIT for a year before transferring to Yale—where school officials had listed his nationality as "Hebrew." One thing I do know about my father is that to be described as anything other than American would have grated with him.[10]

He made the decision that he would not allow the fact he was Jewish define him and he would not let it define his children. I am not even sure his not telling us was a conscious decision.

It may be that for my father not telling us he was Jewish was no more a clear-cut decision than his not telling his mother and siblings that he had diabetes. While both were of great importance in his own life, they were of no relevance to the way he wanted others to define him.[11]

It turns out my father didn't tell me in much detail about a lot of other things either, things I know he was extremely proud of. For instance, he loved music and his association with musicians. Paul Hindemith was not just a client but a friend and when Hindemith wrote music for two of my father's poems, my father was absolutely euphoric.

I knew that he had in some way helped Aaron Copland. I recall Copland at our house, greeting me very warmly and telling me how much he appreciated my father. When I was at Exeter, Copland sent me an autographed recording of *Appalachian Spring*, I am sure at my father's instigation.

Only when I read Vivian Perlis's 1989 biography of Copland did I get a deeper feeling for what had taken place. Copland had come to my father to represent him in hearings before the McCarthy Committee.

Put quite simply, my father never told me many things that would have interested me, and when there was the opportunity, I never knew enough to ask.

---

10. With this in mind, I particularly enjoyed an anecdote by Henry Morgenthau in *Mostly Morgenthaus* (New York: Ticknor & Fields, 1991). At the age of five, the author comes home to tell his mother another child has asked him his religion and asks what he should have replied. She thinks for a moment and says: "If anyone ever asks you that again, just tell them you're an American."

11. Writing for the *Los Angeles Times* syndicate (23 February 1997), Alexander Stille commented about Secretary of State Madeline Albright's not identifying herself as Jewish after learning her father was a Jew, that it was ridiculous for a person of her accomplishments "to have a lifetime of professional achievement suddenly judged through the lens of religious affiliation." He also noted the similar reaction of the noted Italian Giorgio Bassani, author of *The Garden of the Finzi-Continis*, who refused to identify himself as a Jew, saying this attitude reflected "a deep reaction to having had a label imposed on him that profoundly limited his choices in life."

I don't feel any sense of betrayal or hurt that my father didn't tell me he was Jewish. And by the 1960s, when times had changed so dramatically from when he started down his path of reticence, the barrier to revealing the past had gone up. He was no more in a position to volunteer the information than I was to ask, even though I had enough clues by then that I should have.

It has been the immigrant tradition to blot out the unpleasant experiences of the past, but many of the experiences my father had that I would have liked to have shared were not unpleasant. The only explanation is that there is no easy explanation.

Finally, I am sure my father was inwardly proud of what he did to help Europe's Jews during the Holocaust. But I also like to think he is like the Italians the journalist Nicola Caracciolo interviewed, Italians who had hidden or otherwise helped their Jewish countrymen escape the Nazi racial laws. Their response to being lionized for their actions was: Why? Didn't we just do what any human being was obligated to do?

Two

How a Group of Thirty-Somethings
Won World War II

L end-Lease is a name familiar to every high-school student whose
history course reached World War II before running out of time,
yet few could tell you what it actually did. Not only did it make arms
and supplies available to our cash-strapped allies, Lend-Lease was at
the center of a web of little-known agencies that expedited war procurement from top to bottom. Additionally, Lend-Lease brought
together a small group of men whose influence spread throughout the
government at the time and remained their link in later life. They
were, in their own way, a band of brothers and my father was its drum
major. Nothing could have been more exciting and more rewarding to
a young man from Maine, still in his thirties.

Prior to Lend-Lease becoming law on March 11, 1941, nine
months before Pearl Harbor made the United States an actual com-
batant, my father had been involved in other preparations for the
upcoming war. He had dealt with Great Britain which was rapidly
running out of money and therefore the ability to pay cash for arms
from the United States, the only way we could supply them without
breaking our self-imposed neutrality. As a Treasury Department attorney, he worked on the deal where we traded old destroyers to England
for military bases in their territories off our East Coast, from New-
foundland to the Bahamas. He also worked to standardize armaments,
most notably the caliber of military rifles, that were then slightly different, with the British using 30.3-caliber rifle shells while the U.S.
used 30-caliber. And he was involved in a deal to sell military airplanes to the French, an opportunity to jump start that industry prior
to the U.S. entry into the war. Before the United States became a
belligerent, both the British and the French had capitalized munitions
factories in this country and therefore subsidized an armament capa-

city that would be desperately needed only months later.

The actual drafting of Lend-Lease has been written about from varying viewpoints and it is clear that many others besides my father were involved in the process. The concept of finding a way to aid Great Britain as it was going bankrupt and as Winston Churchill was privately pleading with President Roosevelt for help came from the President himself. He articulated the philosophical context in a press conference, where he described lending one's garden hose to a neighbor whose house is on fire. Roosevelt said you don't ask to be paid for the hose at such a time because protecting the neighbor's house may prevent the fire from spreading to yours. Instead, you ask for the hose back after your neighbor has used it. Roosevelt said the money was irrelevant. We needed to help our neighbors, and worry about the cost later.

There has been arcane discussion of whether the precedent for Lend-Lease was the Pittman Act, a similar measure for providing armaments to Latin American allies, drafted only a few months previously, or whether my father's discovery of an 1892 statute was the crucial element. I am not a historian and have worked almost entirely from secondary sources, but the truth seems to be that the answer is both. Lend-Lease derived from the Latin American plan with the new twist that we would not do what we did there, which was to loan the recipients the money to pay us for the supplies.[1] Instead, we would lend them the materiel directly, without a lot of concern about whether we would ever get it back. Churchill's memoir, *Their Finest Hour*, confirmed the conventional wisdom that my father had been the spark behind Lend-Lease. Excerpts were printed in *Life* magazine in 1949, when *Life* was the dominant national circulation publication, and thus Churchill's declaration underscored the repeated assertion that Lend-Lease had been the work of one person, my father.[2]

Churchill wrote about the drafting: "It seems that the idea [of leasing armaments to the British rather than demanding cash] had

---

1. This procedure, through the World Bank, was never implemented because Lend-Lease came into effect before any arms shipments were consummated. This replacement does indicate how the two measures were different.
2. 14 March 1949.

originated in the Treasury Department, whose lawyers, especially Oscar S. Cox, of Maine, had been stirred by Secretary Morgenthau. It appeared that by a Statute of 1892 the Secretary for War "when in his discretion it will be for the public good" could lease Army property if not required for public use for a period of not longer than five years. Precedents for the use of this Statute, by the *lease* of various items, from time to time were on record.

"Thus the word *lease* and the idea of applying the lease principle to meeting British needs had been in President Roosevelt's mind for some time as an alternative to a policy of indefinite loans which would soon far outstrip all possibilities of repayment. Now suddenly all this sprang into decisive action, and the glorious conception of Lend-Lease was proclaimed."

Churchill would later describe Lend-Lease to Parliament as "the most unsordid act in the history of any nation," a phrase that never caught on as did Arsenal for Democracy.

In his book on Lend-Lease, Edward Stettinius fleshes out the drafting story, still giving my father primary credit and relating Oscar's role to earlier efforts to arm the allies.[3] What happened is indicative of the freewheeling way Washington operated in those days and the get-it-done attitude my father reflected.

After the bill had been shown to a broad array of interested parties, both in the administration and in Congress, and their concerns had been met, the revised draft was presented to Roosevelt.

Stettinius wrote: "When Morgenthau handed [Roosevelt] the bill, the President read it slowly and carefully. After he had finished, he said that it provided for the aid which he had determined to give in the most direct and clean-cut fashion possible. He wanted it brought back to him as soon as possible, initialed [by key cabinet members].

"The next day [Treasury General Counsel Ed] Foley and Cox started around Washington for final clearance on the bill. There was another rapid series of conferences; a few more changes were made by the State Department and the War Department. But by five o'clock in the afternoon Secretary Morgenthau and Foley were back at the White House with a bill that everyone agreed on. It bore all the initials the President had asked for.

3. *Lend-Lease: Weapon for Victory* (New York: Macmillan Company, 1944).

"'This is really a fast piece of work for Washington,' the President said with a grin as the draft was handed to him, 'and I'm not one to be outdone.' He read the bill through carefully, asked a few more questions, and then initialed it himself."

Obviously, the bill was a highly collaborative effort in which my father played a central role but attributing it to a lone innovator meshes perfectly with the American ideal of individual invention. The result was that this became a title for my father, the author of Lend-Lease, and it stood him in good stead during his remaining years in government.

The actual wording of the bill is incredibly broad. It says that "the terms and conditions upon which any such foreign government receives any aid . . . shall be those which the President deems satisfactory, and the benefit to the United States may be payment or repayment in kind or property, or any other direct or indirect benefit which the President deems satisfactory." It had accomplished the President's goal "to eliminate the dollar sign," and left in its place the President's declaration that we had been repaid by some indirect benefit. Although tallies of the return benefits were kept, simply helping us win the war could have been enough repayment.

Fighting the bill was the isolationists' last gasp and that legislative battle, in which my father was involved particularly as an adviser to Representative Sol Bloom, chairman of the House Committee on Foreign Affairs, was to color my father's attitudes for years to come. The isolationists, led symbolically by the national hero Charles Lindbergh, feared Lend-Lease would pull the United States into the war, an event Pearl Harbor was soon to accomplish. But they were correct that Lend-Lease effectively made America a partner of Great Britain in the war, a partnership that would soon spread to the Soviet Union when Germany attacked it.

After setting off a national debate over America's role in the impending European war, Lend-Lease passed the House by 260 to 165 and the Senate by 60 to 31, with significant dissent. Two years later, when the war was underway, there was almost unanimous approval in both houses when the measure came up for reapproval.

Lend-Lease quickly became the instrument for pooling all Allied resources. Australia contributed food for U.S. soldiers fighting in the

Pacific. England provided lodging and food for airmen. Termed "reverse lend-lease," the pooling of resources reflected the underlying philosophy that this was a joint effort with no quid pro quo in monetary terms. Each participating country would give what it could and take what it needed with the United States supplying the lion's share, especially in armaments as it had the production capacity no one else possessed. Although the United Nations did not formally exist, Lend-Lease represented a degree of international collaboration the United States never again attained.

In retrospect Lend-Lease was a radical concept and one not to be repeated. A small, civilian agency would determine what armaments were produced on the basis of where the most dire need lay. Although the military still determined its own needs, what remained of our allies had a huge influence on prioritization as they were fighting the war for us by proxy in the first months. Today, the military determines everything and we sell our allies—and some of our future enemies—armaments through "private" transactions.

During its short life of less than four years, Lend-Lease expended more than $42 billion (at least $420 billion in today's dollars). At the same time, it was constantly credited with being extremely efficient, especially by the *New York Times'* conservative columnist Arthur Krock. Lend-Lease achieved its initial success with only 561 employees in Washington and another 40 representatives spread around the world to serve 43 countries. By the time it came under the jurisdiction of the Foreign Economic Administration, FEA had more than 4,000 employees.

The first administrator of Lend-Lease was Harry Hopkins, who was Roosevelt's confidante, chief of staff, and trouble-shooter. During these years, Hopkins was actually living at the White House and Oscar was to become his special assistant. Hopkins would remain as the chief conduit for getting the often dire news about rearmament to the President, and my father, who had limited direct access to the President, used this channel for other information, most notably Jan Karski's report on the extermination of the Jews of Europe.

Hopkins also headed the small group of cabinet-level officials who became the war cabinet and was one of the few early New Dealers to make the transition from the focus on the economy to a focus on the war effort. Roosevelt's old Brains Trust, recruited to deal with the Great Depression, gradually faded in importance. A lower profile group, working under Hopkins in a loose manner, took over the task implicit in Lend-Lease: if we were to provide armaments for the Allies, if we were truly to be the Arsenal for Democracy, who would make sure we produced as much and as quickly as possible?

The reality was that when Lend-Lease became law and even when it received what was then the massive appropriation of $7 billion, the munitions and armaments our allies needed were not available. In the cases of both Greece and Yugoslavia, armaments were ordered but were not ready for delivery before those countries were overrun by the Germans.

When Germany invaded Russia in June of 1941, only three months after Lend-Lease became law, Russia was in desperate need of arms America could not supply, even if there had not been strong Congressional sentiment that Russia would lose quickly and anything we sent would therefore fall into the hands of the Germans.[4] This gap was largely filled by Great Britain which diverted some of its own armaments to a country that was in a more critical situation, thus establishing a precedent that was to drive Lend-Lease. No matter who had been designated as the recipient of arms as they were produced, they could be redirected to whoever was in the most urgent need. A year later America did have the arms coming off the assembly line, and Russia was to become one of the major recipients of Lend-Lease aid.

While the U.S. could not fulfill the demand for armaments at first, it quickly filled other needs through Lend-Lease, most notably demanding and receiving an increase in agricultural production that allowed us to ship food to Great Britain while increasing the supply domestically. In another case, Lend-Lease came to the aid of the famous Flying Tigers, the American airmen who were flying out of China against the Japanese even before Pearl Harbor. The Tigers could not get enough planes in the air for lack of spare parts. Lend-Lease stepped in, paid for the parts, and rushed them by air freight across the Pacific, thus putting the Flying Tigers back in the air.

4. Strong anti-Communist feelings also played a role in our reluctance to supply the Russians at that time.

Because it was the agency buying the supplies and also deciding who received those supplies, Lend-Lease took on a role that would today be coordinated at the cabinet level. Lend-Lease was the key agency fighting the war logistically if not militarily.

Time magazine described Oscar as helping to administer Lend-Lease, adding "he scrapes up supplies, gets them shipped as often as he can."[5] The informality of the language is an accurate reflection of the informality of the arrangement.

In some cases Oscar held a title; in others he did not. But he was connected with a series of agencies, some with names so similar it is easy to confuse them, whose goal it was to make sure the right things were being produced and were going to the right people to win the war. In the early days, this meant scrounging, sometimes taking what had been designated for one recipient and delivering it to another. In these jobs, Oscar reported primarily to Harry Hopkins.

A state department liaison official at the time, Donald C. Blaisdell explained that "all of the interdepartmental committees . . . were centralized under Oscar Cox. This is one of the cases where they used an innocuous name to veil a very important, significant, strategic operation. They called it the Office of Lend-Lease Reports; this was like the Manhattan Project a little later on . . . Oscar Cox headed up the Office of Lend-Lease Reports. His office was the contact between all the purchasing agents of the British Government and other governments in this country for supplies under the Lend-Lease program."[6]

Although he never carried any Lend-Lease title except general counsel, Oscar was cited by Drew Pearson, in his nationally syndicated Washington Merry-go-Round, as running Lend-Lease and Pearson said Oscar was "the brains behind Ed Stettinius in the Lend-Lease Administration."[7]

For years, the noted Washington civil liberties attorney Joseph Rauh prodded me to write the history of my father's war efforts, claiming that he did more to thwart Hitler's efforts than almost any other

---

5. 10 August 1942.
6. Oral history interview, Truman Library.
7. 16 January, 1945. Stettinius, a former president of U.S. Steel, succeeded Hopkins as administrator of Lend-Lease and subsequently became secretary of state.

single individual.[8] I had always thought he was referring to Lend-Lease alone, because our ability to supply the Allies with munitions was certainly a major element in the war effort.

The missing link was war production and my missing knowledge was my father's role in ratcheting up war production through various agencies that came into being at the same time as Lend-Lease.

Supreme Court Justice and behind-the-scenes operator Felix Frankfurter had become involved in drafting Lend-Lease because he wanted to save Great Britain;[9] through him, Phil Graham[10] and Joe Rauh also became involved. They, as well as my father, moved on to starting a war industry. As was typical of the time, overlapping jobs were held simultaneously. So my father became general counsel to the Office of Production Management which was charged with getting war production up to necessary levels and with setting priorities. With a total commitment to winning the war, they let little stand in their way and tended to jump right to the top where they had access rather than work through the normal bureaucracy.

Bruce Allen Murphy in *The Brandeis/Frankfurter Connection* relates an anecdote about how the triumvirate of Cox, Rauh, and Graham worked:

"Together these individuals cracked whips over the heads of government officials. While others, concerned about the checks and balances in the constitutional system, would wring their hands and apologize that there was nothing they could do to mobilize for war, this dual agency [the Office of Emergency Management for which Oscar was also general counsel], just as the president wanted, pushed aside those obstacles, performing its task with incredible zeal. For example, there was the day in mid-1941, just after the German invasion of Russia, when a lawyer named Abe Feller got into a discussion with Cox, Rauh and Graham on the operations of the Lend-Lease program.

8. In a letter of condolence to my mother on my father's death, Rauh said: "One of the great experiences of my life was to be with Oscar in the prewar year of 1941. There are few if any who did as much as Oscar to stop the march of Hitlerism in those days of confusion and defeat."

9. Bruce Allen Murphy, *The Brandeis/Frankfurter Connection* (New York: Oxford University Press, 1982), pp. 220 et seq.

10. Graham later became publisher of the *Washington Post*. Both Graham and Rauh were hired by Oscar to work for Lend-Lease.

He mentioned that he had seen a sentence in *Time* magazine detailing the losses in materiel by the Russians during the previous week's fighting with the Germans. Everyone gasped when they realized that the Russians had lost more tanks, planes, and guns in one week than the United States would produce in a single year—even if all production schedules were met (which, of course, was not happening). Cox attached a copy of the article to a memorandum to Harry Hopkins, telling him that the military had to be instructed to step up their requisitions for supplies."

With the prodding of Lend-Lease staff, including George Ball,[11] Oscar wrote a memo to Hopkins urging him to set up a War Cabinet to handle the logistical problems. Written on Office of Emergency Management stationery, he cited the failure to deliver 100 promised cargo planes to the Chinese and said there had to be people in place to make sure the President's wishes were carried out. Oscar and his cohorts, using Hopkins as a conduit, were constantly pointing out that even modest production goals were not being met and they constantly butted heads with industrialists who said they could not do what was asked for legal reasons.

These procurement agencies also metamorphosed as the war continued. While my father stayed with Lend-Lease and became the figure around whom its exceptional staff[12] coalesced, Lend-Lease came under the control of the Office of Economic Warfare which in turn became the FEA in 1943; in 1945, my father was to replace Leo Crowley as head of FEA while Crowley stayed on as head of the increasingly important Export-Import Bank.

Concurrently, my father was assistant solicitor general and the trouble-shooter for those who were having difficulty with existing law in getting things done. In one case, L. M. C. Smith, with whom I was later to become involved in Maine,[13] came to him with such a problem. He wanted to use federal prisoners to make war materiel, but a

---

11. Ball was to become an undersecretary of state under Lyndon B. Johnson and the most outspoken in-house opponent of the Vietnam War.
12. Among those not elsewhere mentioned were Gene Rostow, who became dean of Yale Law, and Walter Thayer, who became publisher of the New York *Herald Tribune*.
13. Smith was an early backer of *Maine Times* and with his wife the creator of Wolfe's Neck Farm in Freeport.

law passed under Teddy Roosevelt forbade it on the grounds prison labor should not compete with the private sector. My father's reply: "I'll take care of it."

In one of his rare speeches, my father told fellow attorneys that their job was to remove barriers to the war effort rather than to erect them, a position that brought him much criticism from the conservative press but that was typical of his personality and his actions.[14] He was still in his thirties and had already been personally praised by the President for his "can-do" attitude.

I think it was how my father integrated these multiple roles in getting the war effort moving that lay behind Joe Rauh's statement. And it was this multiple activity that led *Fortune Magazine*[15] to say that Oscar Cox was "the rising man of the New-Deal-to-be-reborn." The top position *Fortune* mentioned for him was general counsel to the State Department, a post that outranked assistant secretaries. He was cited by the *Chicago Tribune*[16] as heading upward, along with special assistant to the president Sam Rosenman and legendary operative Ben Cohen but there is an implication that none of them ever went any farther because they were Jewish. The *Tribune* said: "[The plan] was rejected when it was considered that Rosenman, Cohen and Cox might provoke outbursts from race baiters." Despite being accused of having an administration infested with Jews, Roosevelt's only Jewish cabinet member was Morgenthau. It was the famed anti-Semite Henry Ford who approved of Morgenthau's serving in that position because he thought Jews had a special talent in handling money.

Oscar, despite his other jobs, stayed with Lend-Lease, following it to the Federal Economic Administration (FEA) which was in charge of the broader economic warfare program. When the war ended and Lend-Lease was discontinued, my father left government. He had hoped the United States would use the structure Lend-Lease had created to help rebuild Europe after the war.

Although Oscar had clearly been disappointed when Lend-Lease was abruptly shut down, his Lend-Lease experience was to be the basis

14. 13 August 1942.
15. March 1943.
16. 18 February 1945. The *Tribune* was an arch conservative paper and the article cited Supreme Court Justice Frankfurter as plotting all the appointments.

for his private practice after the war. Not only did he pick up such clients as Kaiser Industries in this country—Henry J. Kaiser had been described as Roosevelt's favorite industrialist and Kaiser's merchant ship production was a key element of Lend-Lease—but he also took on many European clients, subsequently helping to negotiate joint ventures between American and European companies, including Fiat and North American Aviation and Olivetti and Underwood.

Of course, Oscar never lost his love for government work and kept in touch throughout his life. Despite his financial success as an attorney, he would have given it up in a second for what he coveted most, an ambassadorship, preferably to Italy where after the war he had many friends and contacts. It never happened.

Three

Frightened People Do Frightening Things

Two important decisions in which my father participated leave
me with misgivings half a century later. The two incidents have
particular resonance today because each reflects current policies.
They have affected my perspective, and they are classic examples of
where we can learn from history. For me, it has been a personally
tinged history.

I do not condemn my father for what he did. In neither case did
his specific action lead to the consequences I now question. There
were too many other players in the chain of events to blame him.
However, one need not assign blame to see what turned out to be
mistakes, by others or by oneself, and unless we admit mistakes there
can be little hope of not repeating them.

I will not try to justify his positions, only to put them in context.
For a long time and in many instances, I have been bothered by the
habit of the pure of heart and thought to proclaim they would have
acted so differently had they made the decision that occurred so many
years ago in such different circumstances. This purity of hindsight and
the obliteration of context colors criticism of everything from Thomas
Jefferson's failure to put the abolition of slavery into the Constitution
to the dropping of the atomic bomb on Hiroshima.

The two incidents were the internment of Japanese-American
citizens after Pearl Harbor and the trial of Nazi saboteurs by military
tribunal rather than civil courts.

Shortly after the attack on Pearl Harbor, a simmering hysteria
began to boil on the West Coast with the belief that local Japanese
aliens living there were potential spies and saboteurs. Aliens were
quickly rounded up and were kept far from military installations, but
the effort did not stop there. First-generation immigrants who were
still Japanese citizens, Issei, were targeted next. Then came their chil-

dren, Nisei, born in the United States and therefore American citizens.

Writing in the *Washington Post*, Joe Rauh, in supporting reparations for what he termed "the severest blow [this nation] ever inflicted upon the civil liberties of its people," noted "it is hard now, forty-five years later, to reconstruct the panic that set in immediately after that attack...."[1] He concluded that "frightened people do frightful things."

Rauh then recounted his participation, what he called his own "minor role," in tandem with my father, in the matter. They, along with Ben Cohen, were called into consultation by Attorney General Francis Biddle. Rauh wrote that Cohen foresaw that West Coast hysteria could lead to concentration camps unless measures were taken to stem the panic. In his analysis of their position, Rauh wrote, "While others were demanding internment, on the one hand, or no action whatever, on the other, Mr. Cohen, with whatever assistance he could derive from Cox and myself, tried to forge a consensus around ways and means of avoiding internment, such as curfews, limiting access to military installations, and the like."

I will take Joe Rauh's word this was their intention. Other accounts are more equivocal.

As Attorney General Biddle tells the story, he admitted that the internment of the Issei as non-citizens was legal but opposed any action against the Nisei.[2] His adversary was General John L. DeWitt, the commander of the West Coast, who with the help of subordinates painted a picture of disloyalty and sabotage by the Nisei, based on myth.

The arguments against the Nisei resonate today: "It is better to do it now than to wait until an attack occurs," the military argued in favor of its pre-emptive strike. This was further reinforced by the irrational and therefore irrefutable claim that "the very fact that no sabotage has taken place to date is a disturbing and confirming indication that such action will be taken."

Biddle waffled. In the end, he refused to have the Justice Department take part in any internment but he indicated that if the military did so, he would not oppose the measure.

---

1. 29 April 1986.
2. Francis Biddle, *In Brief Authority* (Garden City, NY: Doubleday & Co., 1962).

In Biddle's own words: "The decision had been made by the President. It was, he said, a matter of military judgment. I did not think I should oppose it any further.[3] The Department of Justice, as I had made clear to him from the beginning, was opposed to and would have nothing to do with the evacuation. Two days later the President signed the evacuation order."

Two books on the subject reach somewhat different conclusions. Page Smith says Biddle was "almost fanatical in his determination to resist any infringement on the civil rights of U.S. citizens."[4] On the other hand, Peter Irons reached the conclusion that Biddle effectively waffled and that by accepting an interpretation that evacuation could be justified constitutionally, even if he refused to have the Justice Department participate, he was leaving an opening for the military to step in and do the job.[5] Biddle recognized that presidents, including Franklin Roosevelt, do not give much attention to the niceties of civil liberties during wartime.

I cannot escape the conclusion that the opinion of my father's group was worse for the Nisei than that of Biddle's own people, James Rowe[6] and Edward J. Ennis, those whom Rauh referred to as wanting to do nothing. As with the interpretation of how strongly Biddle opposed internment, the two books I have cited treat my father's role somewhat differently.

Smith continues his depiction of strong opposition by Biddle:

"Francis Biddle, well aware of the way the wind was blowing, had asked three New Deal attorneys who were not members of the Justice Department[7]—Benjamin Cohen, Oscar Cox, and Joseph Rauh—for an opinion on the constitutionality of the exclusion or evacuation of groups considered a threat to national security. Benjamin Cohen was one of Roosevelt's closest and most trusted advisers, a member of the New Deal inner circle, and Cox and Rauh were golden boys of the

3. James Rowe, on Biddle's behalf, had just made an impassioned argument against intern-ment.
4. Page Smith, *Democracy on Trial* (New York: Simon & Schuster, 1995).
5. Peter Irons, *Justice at War* (New York: Oxford University Press, 1983).
6. Rowe continued in Washington as a key player for years and is cited many times by Lyndon Johnson's biographer, Robert Caro. Johnson thought Rowe was a political genius, and Rowe was a key figure in convincing Johnson not to run for a second full term.
7. Oscar would later join the Justice Department under Biddle as assistant solicitor general.

administration. On February 10 the three announced their opinion: 'So long as a classification of persons is reasonably related to a genuine war need and does not under the guise of national defense discriminate against any class of citizens for a purpose unrelated to the national defense, no constitutional guarantee is infringed.'"

Read carefully, that opinion becomes an invitation to the military to take charge.

Irons, who asserts in his book that this is precisely the rationale the military used for internment, goes into more detail on the same memorandum and his account has left me with a more critical attitude toward my father's role.

Rowe and Ennis had opposed any evacuation of American citizens without a specific charge and they had cited the situation as driven by hysteria in the face of a lack of any concrete evidence of sabotage by the Nisei. They were also aware of other factors driving public sentiment, such as the competition between native farmers and the highly successful Japanese immigrants.

Without contradicting Joe Rauh's statement that he and my father were looking for a way to prevent incarceration by proposing solutions short of internment, such as voluntary relocation, the actual memorandum, as quoted by Irons, is disturbing.

First, they try to strike a constitutional balance: "It is well to remember that unnecessarily harsh action is not justified just because the legal power to take such actions exists. On the other hand, it is important to bear in mind that action truly necessary for the national safety cannot lightly be assumed to be barred by constitutional constructions which would make our Constitution in time of war either unworkable or non-existent."

They went on to make the statement that is repeated today—that the Constitution is not a license to commit suicide. When the protection of civil liberties runs head on into national safety, safety may prevail. The memo said, "In time of national peril and any reasonable doubt, [the question] must be resolved in favor of action to preserve the national safety."

This is certainly a logical and legally sound position but it cannot stand in a vacuum. It leads to the next question: Was there really a national peril represented by the Nisei or was it just hysteria as Rowe and Ennis contended? In hindsight, we know it was hysteria but the most important characteristic of public hysteria is that it is never identified as such at the very moment it is most powerful and therefore drives public policy.

While in the context of the times I can understand the equivocating in the memorandum—I would have liked to see it set a stronger standard for taking away a citizen's rights than "reasonable doubt"—I am dismayed by something else they said. "Since the Occidental eye cannot readily distinguish one Japanese resident from another, effective surveillance of the movements of particular residents suspected of disloyalty is extremely difficult if not practically impossible."

My father was saying that he could not tell people of Japanese heritage apart. They all looked the same to him. And because they all looked the same, they must all be treated as suspect. Long before we had the term "racial profiling," this was racial profiling raised to the extreme, and regardless of the context of the time, it is impossible to defend.

"Rowe and Ennis, whose constitutional objections to evacuation the outside lawyers had dismissed, reacted to the memorandum with scorn," Irons wrote. "Rowe attributed authorship of the opinion to Oscar Cox. 'He was a great dabbler,' Rowe later said, 'and he may have gotten Rauh and Cohen to do it. It was none of his damn business.'"

Irons says that memorandum "salved Biddle's constitutional doubts" and therefore was a key element in his acquiescing to the President's harsher decision.

Rauh, of course, maintains that the intention of the memorandum was not to open the door it did, the door to internment. In his 1986 Op-Ed piece, he tells one more story:

"We did not take our defeat lightly even then. I recall entering Mr. Cohen's office one evening in early 1942 to be greeted with a newspaper article containing a picture of a little Japanese boy on a train headed for an internment camp leaning out the window waving an American flag. Mr. Cohen had tears in his eyes, and I guess I wasn't too far behind."

I do not question their genuine regret after the fact. But the trick of making sound policy is to foresee as many of the consequences as possible and not to be driven by the hysteria of the moment.

Another event in which my father played a key role was the trial of the eight Nazi saboteurs who landed on the coast from submarines in June 1942.[8] There was never any doubt as to their guilt. They were carrying the equivalent of more than a million dollars in cash as well as explosives and maps of key strategic installations. Some were American citizens; all had been in this country and not only spoke good English but had connections so they could fade into the land-scape. They had phony identification papers. They had been trained in sabotage at a special school in Germany.

There were also several other uncontested facts. They might never have been caught had not two of their members turned them all in. Those two men maintained that they had never intended to carry out the sabotage but since they had been spotted on a Long Island, New York, beach, there is at least room to speculate that their going to the FBI was related to a fear of being caught. None of the men had taken any overt action to commit sabotage; there had not been enough time before they were caught.

Upon hearing the news of their capture, President Roosevelt was clear in his desires. He wanted swift action and he wanted the death penalty. His reasons were multiple: to act as a deterrent to any other potential saboteurs, to impress on the Germans how effective our defenses were, and to allay any fears among the public.

In his memoir, Biddle gave his version of the legal dilemma:

"Probably an indictment for attempted sabotage would not have been sustained in a civil court on the ground that the preparations and landings were not close enough to the planned act of sabotage to constitute attempt. If a man buys a pistol, intending murder, that is not an attempt at murder. The broad federal law covering conspiracies to commit crimes applied, but carried a penalty grossly disproportion-ate to their acts—three years, as I remember. However, they could be charged before a military court with penetrating in disguise our line of defense for the purpose of waging war by destruction of life and property, for which under the law of war the death penalty could be inflicted."

8. I deal with other aspects of the trial in Chapter Four, page 50.

Although the U.S. Supreme Court later upheld the use of the military tribunal, the justices were acting under severe political pressure as well, and a good argument can be made today that the saboteurs could have been tried in the civil courts, albeit without hope of the death penalty. On the other hand, for the same policy reasons as with the Japanese-Americans about protecting the nation in time of war, there are solid arguments for using the military tribunal so long as basic rights, such as legal representation, are preserved and the Germans did receive excellent legal counsel. The trial itself, rather than indefinite incarceration without being charged, and aggressive legal representation for the defendants differentiate this case from the current practice.

I have commented on the trial in a later chapter but here I am concerned with my father's desire to please his powerful and charismatic boss. His participation was always invited and his goal was to overcome barriers for the President. Using his legal talents to expedite the delivery of munitions to our wartime allies and finding ways to overcome civil liberties considerations are, unfortunately, different.

A condolence letter sent to my mother in 1966, from Arthur Palmer whom I have been unable to identify, tells the story of my father's role in using the tribunal. It is meant to praise him. Palmer wrote:

"When the eight German spies who landed in Long Island were apprehended in...1943,[9] Mr. J. E. Hoover announced that he would try them before the Federal Court in New York. Oscar had antennae that made this seem inadequate and within a matter of hours ascertained (on a Sunday) that the maximum federal statutory penalty would be two years in jail and a modest fine. The federal statutes simply were not geared for such an improbable event.

"Drawing on the action that was taken to try to punish the assassins of Lincoln, Oscar proposed for consideration a similar course, namely, a proclamation by the President denying the trespassers access to the courts, as being enemy aliens in time of war, and establishing a military commission to try them. Under this procedure, if proper, the maximum penalty was execution.

9. He is incorrect. It was a year earlier.

"The discussion prospered and Oscar submitted the appropriate papers to President Roosevelt.

"The action proposed was most unusual, and it appealed to the President's imagination: he seemed to reflect the feeling of many of his advisers who did not want the U.S. to appear before the world as unprepared and unable to deal with the matter at hand in a prompt and decisive manner.

"The President said to Oscar that he liked the plan, and if Oscar could have the one-page summary in front of the bundle of papers initialed by the Attorney General, and the secretaries of State, War, and Navy, then he, the President, would put the plan into effect. Oscar went to each of these four important men and got those initials during the course of a part of one afternoon. I observed his conference with the Attorney General and the Secretary of War. The conferences were short, and were in each instance dominated by Oscar's quiet, almost gentle, but incisive description of the problems and his suggested solution to it. He answered questions easily and he was effectively convincing. I sat in the car outside the offices of the other two as he obtained their initials.

"At this time, Oscar was thirty-four years old.[10] I do not recall any other instance of seeing a more outstanding demonstration of initiative, leadership, and effective action by anyone of similar years.

"As you know, the plan was successful; the saboteurs were tried and executed, and promptly, but in a manner that was consistent with U.S. standards of justice and fair play."

Former Attorney General Biddle agreed with that last paragraph, writing in his memoir: "The defendants had been given every right afforded by our law and were represented with unusual ability and perseverance by lawyers assigned to them by the country to which they had come in order to wreck war plants. It was an extraordinary example of justice at its best—prompt, yet fair—in striking contrast to what was going on in Germany."

While I agree that the six who were executed were bent on espionage, I do have reservations about the secrecy of the trial and the long sentences of the two who turned them in.[11] President Truman

10. He was thirty-eight.
11. Life for one, thirty years for the other.

commuted those two sentences in 1948. What leaves me uneasy about the tribunal and therefore my father's key role in creating this particular venue was the length of time involved. I also fear the precedent may be misused.

The first saboteurs landed on June 13, 1942. On July 8, less than a month later, they had all been arrested and the trial had begun. Testimony and argument were finished three weeks later, on July 28, and they were all found guilty. On August 8, after the hurried Supreme Court ruling but before a written decision had even been issued, six of them were executed. One month from capture to execution. Can justice be so swift?

While even in hindsight I do not condemn my father's position and I can particularly understand the excitement of a thirty-eight-year-old who has come up with another solution—Lend-Lease being the first and in so many ways similar, all the way to the obtaining of key signatures in a short time—for the President of the United States. But I can also see the flaws and the potential for abuse. That the defendants were so aggressively represented was something of a fluke and strong legal representation was not part of the tribunals as they were proposed in 2002, using the precedent my father's action had set.[12] Nor would I have had much confidence then or now in the secrecy surrounding the tribunals, a secrecy that even Biddle admits was to keep from the public the fact that two of the saboteurs had turned the others in, although he puts a much more benign interpretation on that logic than I do. He claims we had to protect our sources; I would suggest the goal was to protect the FBI's reputation of high competence.

Pleasing one's superior, especially when that superior is the President of the United States, by finding a way for him to do something he has decided to do on emotional grounds without careful thought about future consequences, is intoxicating. It may also produce a terrible hangover.

---

12. The U. S. Supreme Court subsequently forced the Bush Administration to allow legal representation.

Four

Growing Up in the McCarthy Era

There is nothing I can complain about regarding my family life as I grew up. I suffered no deprivation, emotional or physical. Before I developed an awareness of the larger world around me, I lived a made-for-the-movies life of middle-class privilege. It was the intrusion of that larger world that made my childhood worthy of reflection.

In 1950, when I was twelve, World War II was still the dominant event in American life. Despite the fact that my father's brother Ben had been killed in the Pacific, I was generally unaffected by the war while it was happening. It was the war's aftermath that was so important, because that's when the culture of suspicion began. Despite hundreds of books on the subject, the popular rendition of the 1950s is some sort of *Happy Days* sitcom nostalgia. For a child growing up in the '50s, the situation was much more complex and much more difficult to describe. There were few clear manifestations of the suspicion and those seemed exotic, such as the blacklisting of Hollywood screenwriters for previous left-wing activities. For the normal person, the suspicion was not a single event; it was woven into the fabric of everyday life. And the partner to suspicion was conformity. Anyone who did not meet the norm, anyone who stood out in any way, was suspect.

What people today seem to forget about the McCarthy era is that while the senator from Wisconsin found no previously unknown communists anywhere, the fear he engendered caused thousands to be fired for the vaguest of reasons. After McCarthy's top aide, Roy Cohn, raised suspicions about Americans working abroad, the Voice of America "in a whirlwind purge of its ranks, fired 830 employees, just to be on the safe side."[1]

Nowhere were the rules more quickly drawn and recognized as

---

1. Thomas Powers in the *New York Review of Books*, 12 February 2004, page 23.

crucial than in Washington where careers were in jeopardy for what people had recently done in good faith and for what had previously elicited praise.

To my knowledge, my father was never a target but when I look back, I realize he could have been. As the key person in the continued activities of Lend-Lease, he had overseen the transfer of billions of dollars in military aid to the Soviet Union. Our house was full of Russian cigarettes with their long filters and bitter tobacco, a redundant and wasted gift from the diplomats with whom he dealt. Fortunately, the aid we gave Russia as our military ally never became an issue although it did come close.

In 1953 the nationally syndicated right-wing columnist Westbrook Pegler fired the first blast of innuendo against my father but didn't go anywhere with it.[2] He had found a man named John W. Hanes who had been in the Treasury Department and had made disparaging remarks about Harry Dexter White, a favorite of those charging Roosevelt administration officials with being communist spies.

Pegler's tenuous speculation was typical of the kinds of charges that flew in those days and if he had simply repeated them enough times, they could have caused trouble. He wrote: "I asked [Hanes] whether he remembered Ed Foley and Oscar Cox, attorneys in the Treasury, who secretly drew up the lend-lease program in the form of a congressional bill between a Friday night and a Monday morning in an office in the Treasury building. Yes, he remembered them but only as New Dealers, perhaps socialistic in their extreme, but not communists or sympathizers with treason.

"Long after the war, when Foley and Cox were positively identified as the secret authors of lend-lease, reference to the record of a senatorial committee under Hiram Johnson, of California, showed that these two and Morgenthau stood silent when they knew the Senate was trying to find out who actually wrote lend-lease so that Congress could learn the 'legislative intent.'[3] Morgenthau actually testified

2. The version of the column quoted was printed in the Bridgeport (CT) *Post*, 27 Nov. 1953.
3. Congress was well aware of who had written Lend-Lease and what its intent was. In an October 15, 1945, insertion in the Congressional Record, eight years prior to the Pegler column, Representative Sol Bloom of New York praised Oscar upon his retirement from government service. He identified Oscar as "principal author" of Lend-Lease and went into detail about its contents and the amount of aid offered.

and doggedly evaded the question. The committee never did learn the truth.

"This deal, under Averell Harriman, Ed Stettinius, and Harry Hopkins, cost the American taxpayers many billions of dollars, much of it for expensive machinery such as railroad diesels and other rolling stock, factories, and miles of heavy copper cable, all for Russia's postwar industrial strength, which is now being used to build up her might for war against the United States."

The aura of secrecy Pegler uses to indicate something was being hidden is, of course, ridiculous. Writing the Lend-Lease Act had been my father's calling card for years. The real issue for Pegler was that Lend-Lease had helped the Russians, then our ally, now our foe.

Had Pegler had the ambition to do any research, he could have added detail to his picture of complicity with the enemy, citing such things as the Lend-Lease dinner in which the Russians, led by legendary Soviet Ambassador Andrei Gromyko, feted the top Lend-Lease officials, my father among them.[4]

Another massive recipient of Lend-Lease aid, was Nationalist China, and while the cry of "Who lost China to the Communists?" became the downfall of principled diplomats, the fact that much of the Lend-Lease aid that went to Chiang Kai-shek was squandered or used against Mao rather than against the Japanese was something the right wing chose to minimize or cover up entirely.

Years later I learned that my father had written the introduction to a consumerist book called *Guinea Pigs No More* and may even have been associated with the Lawyer's Guild, just the kind of associations that could have caused trouble had anyone taken the time to dig them up. No one did. But that is how close he stood to the epidemic.

The dangers that lurked in one's past were a subject I couldn't avoid, even at the age of thirteen. I knew from overheard conversations that it was unwise to join organizations that might later fall out of favor. One must constantly weigh one's career against taking unpopular views. People who took those unpopular views were to be admired but there was always discussion of how vulnerable the person was who took a public stand for a tainted person or position. Dean

4. 7 October, 1943. Vodka and caviar were served.

Acheson had been right to stand up for Alger Hiss, no doubt about it. But how many people could have afforded to have done so? Acheson could do it. Others couldn't.

At least this is what I heard at home.

Just after Hiss had lost his perjury trial in January of 1951, Secretary of State Acheson was asked to comment. In his biography of Acheson,[5] James Chace tells how many of those close to Acheson suggested he avoid the issue and when he said he was going to quote from the Bible, one of his key aides said, "Well, that's fine. Wrap yourself in the Bible."

Acheson did quote Matthew about showing Christian charity to those in difficulty but the highlighted quote was, "I do not intend to turn my back on Alger Hiss." Congressman Richard Nixon, the chief Hiss prosecutor, attacked Acheson for his remarks; even Acheson's friends said he should have distanced himself more from Hiss the person while standing on principle. Fortunately, President Harry Truman backed his secretary of state but a month later, before a Congressional committee, Acheson felt compelled to say he would never knowingly tolerate any disloyal person, read communist, in the Department of State. It was powerful evidence that even those who had reached the highest levels were not immune and would, in some form or another, be forced to pay obeisance or pay the consequences.

Acheson did not sink as far as later critics of the great Red Hunt would; he did not say their cause was important and ferreting out communists in government was crucial. Many who believed the national mood was one of hysteria had repeated that mantra. Acheson stands almost unique in that he didn't feel compelled to condone the witch hunters' goal while criticizing their methods, and for this he remained one of the right's icons of treason. In most cases, even its critics started by endorsing the Red Hunt and in doing so, strengthened it. While there were undoubtedly spies in America, their threat to immediate security—with the exception of the nuclear spies—was minimal.

I still felt free to take Hiss's side in the back seat of the car with my friend Donald Dell as we drove to tennis tournaments, but I soon

5. James Chace, *Acheson* (New York: Simon & Schuster, 1998).

learned to be careful just where I said what. Conformity flowed throughout society, filling every corner, and we felt it as well on the playground. Buzz cuts were in for boys. Girls dressed so similarly they might as well have worn uniforms. We played baseball and football and went to the Calvert Theater on Saturdays to see Randolph Scott westerns. Kids who looked funny (strange, not ha ha) or acted funny—they didn't play baseball and football and go to the Calvert on Saturdays—were shunned, marginalized at school, and never invited to parties in sixth grade. No one ever told me what to do, how specifically to conform, or even advised me on the necessity of conforming. It was unnecessary.

Today's conformity is different. Children still dress in the uniform of their group or the group they seek to join, but ever since the '60s, there has been an outlaw-culture element, ranging from long hair to facial piercing and cargo pants. In the '50s, the conformity was uniformity. No one chose to stick out; or if they did, it was at their own peril.

I had learned to compartmentalize my life. I had friends I played sports with every afternoon at Georgetown Playground, and I had friends I visited at their homes after school, where we would share comic books or hobbies. Although everyone read comics, the discussions I had with my more clandestine friends were not the same as I had with my sports friends.

I was not only a little ashamed of my more offbeat friends, I knew that they could be held against me, not just then but in the future. In a society where children still thought seriously about what they would grow up to be and do, we understood that whatever you did could come back to haunt you years in the future. One of the reasons we were convinced not to shoplift was because being caught would go on your permanent record, and stealing could keep you out of the army.

An understanding of the necessity to conform followed me through life and I was always acutely aware of nuances of dress and speech. In grade school, I lived in a democratic society. Many of my friends, especially those I played sports with, came from an economic and educational stratum well below that of our family and I am certain that for most of them the perils I so clearly defined were unimagined. They fit in. So long as I fit in, there was no problem. The difference was that I was aware and later in life, when I chose to take unpopular positions in public, I knew what I was risking.

I analyzed and placed everyone. Even today, I cannot walk into a house without immediately drawing judgments by looking at the pictures on the walls and the books in the bookcases. When I interview a person, I notice clothing and speech pattern. The difference today is that I do not base any decisions on what these superficial characteristics represent; but I still notice them.

As with so many families like ours, we didn't have television in the early '50s. I only saw TV when I visited a friend's house and his family was gathered around the screen with a huge magnifying lens in front, watching Milton Berle. But in 1954 my parents, as did their friends, rented a television set so they could watch the Army-McCarthy hearings. They put the TV on a coffee table in front of the sofa in the living room, with the wires running along the floor and the rabbit ears placed on top.

Senator Joseph McCarthy was powerful but he was a boor. Europeans, and our household was always full of Europeans, looked down on America for McCarthy. At the dinner table, McCarthy was universally abhorred. Not much was said in public.

My father was critical but not contemptuous of McCarthy. He did not like McCarthy's tactics but he did not deny there was an external communist threat. However, in our household there was no talk of spies in the State Department or people in government working against the interests of the United States. Within the safe confines of our home, my father expressed disapproval of the tactics of others associated with McCarthy or riding on his coattails.

I recall my father's reading, during the summer of 1953, the printed testimony of the hearings in which J. Robert Oppenheimer, who had directed the scientists in the Manhattan Project, was stripped of his security clearance. My father sat in his expansive study in Kennebunkport, having received the new transcripts in the large manila envelope that came from Washington every day, and with his glasses on the table beside him, his nose almost pressed into the text, he carefully underlined passages. Oppenheimer was a distant figure to me. I knew he had been one of the progenitors of the atomic bomb and I did not know my father was by then close to the project's off-site director, Vannevar Bush, and that the current battle was between those who wanted to build the hydrogen bomb and those who didn't. Oppenheimer didn't and Bush didn't and James Conant, former president of Harvard, didn't. But they were on the losing side in more ways than one and Oppenheimer, whose political associations had left him vulnerable, was the victim. Even today, when there is more evidence of the communist leanings of some of Oppenheimer's friends, there is no evidence he was ever disloyal or passed on any secrets.

My recollection is that my father sympathized with Oppenheimer but also felt he had been a fool. We never formally discussed McCarthy's congressional hearings and it was only much later that I learned my father had helped defend the composer Aaron Copland when his visa was denied because of his leftward leanings.

The Copland case is instructive because it so clearly indicates both my father's sympathies and his caution.

By 1950 Copland was already one of America's foremost composers, known for his celebration of American tradition, most notably *Appalachian Spring*. But like so many others, he was linked by association with a group that was supposedly "soft" on communism and his name was included in the famous blacklist, Red Channels. For President Dwight D. Eisenhower's inaugural concert, January 18, 1953, the National Symphony, with the noted actor Walter Pidgeon narrating, was to perform Copland's *Lincoln Portrait*. But a single anti-communist congressman, Fred Busbey of Illinois, protested and the Copland piece was scratched from the program. The nation's most influential music critics protested but to no avail.[6]

Then in May, Copland received a telegram summoning him before the McCarthy committee with only three days' notice. He was given an extra day to obtain legal representation, which he did, from my father.

I can accurately project that my father was thrilled. He loved music and he had no more important self-image than as the protector of artists, especially the modern and avant-garde. Over the years, he not only represented Copland, but also Paul Hindemith with whom he

---

6. This story comes from *Aaron Copland* by Howard Pollack (New York: Henry Holt & Co., 1999) and *Copland Since 1943* by Aaron Copland and Vivian Perlis (New York: St. Martin's Press, 1989).

had a long, personal friendship, and Igor Stravinsky.

Copland said later, according to his biographer Vivian Perlis, "It was my lucky day when I walked into your office," to which my father replied, "It was our great luck."

My father begged off actually appearing at the McCarthy closed hearing, saying he was otherwise committed, and assigned that task to Charlie Glover. Charles Glover III had impeccable Republican and establishment credentials. He would be the perfect front man, my father said.

Subsequently, my father employed his own meticulous skills in going over the actual charges the McCarthy committee had made, finding more than ninety errors, and Copland was never called back. In 2003 previously secret transcripts of those closed hearings were released and they made clear that the purpose of the preliminary hearings was to determine what kind of witness a person might make in public. Those who did well in private avoided any public confrontation with the committee. Without knowing this, my father's strategy of detailed preparation with a specific reply to each accusation had proved to be right on the mark.

On the other hand, Copland's passport was subsequently denied and my father continued his association with the composer for years to handle that matter. They, too, became friends and I recall meeting Copland at our house and being struck by his warmth.

Before Christmas 1953 my father sent Copland the following note: "To you, Louise and I wish a good Xmas and New Year of even more fruitful production unhampered by the madness of the small hearts and minds." It was a nice note but in retrospect a little strange considering it was from one Jew to another.

My father's specific comments about the attacks on Copland are more revealing and reflect what I heard at the dinner table. He wrote Copland: "Non-conformists in any field—particularly the ones who are the salt of the earth—are the ones who at intermittent periods are the key targets of the political demagogues. But after someone like you has gone through the long, slow, hard road of public acceptance in your primary field—with the growth of public stature which goes with it—you tend more and more to be less and less vulnerable to unfounded political attacks."

So maybe fame and stature were an insulator, but they were not much of one. Copland, according to his biographers, had to fight for years to get and renew his passport. He may have been philosophical about his travails but it couldn't have been easy.

The party line at our house was that these matters should be taken out of the political arena and turned over to the FBI. While the certitude with which my father proclaimed J. Edgar Hoover's competence and fairness may have weakened over the years, the core belief persisted. I lost faith in Hoover long before my father did. It is a total supposition on my part, based on what I have read as the J. Edgar Hoover story has unfolded, but I believe my father must have known the FBI played a key role in the accusations made against Copland.

My father's belief in FBI director J. Edgar Hoover probably went back to the trial of the Nazi saboteurs in 1942 in which my father was one of the prosecutors. Going to pick my father up at the Justice Department at the end of the day and seeing the soldiers with their water-cooled machine guns behind the sandbags left an indelible impression on my five-year-old imagination and even though we never discussed the case, first because my brother and I were too young, then later, after we had read a brief magazine account, for "security" reasons, I had remained curious.

When my mother died in 1984 and my brother and I were sorting our parents' books, I found a copy of *They Came to Kill* on their bedroom bookshelf.[7] It was written in 1961, five years before my father's death, but after I had gone off to Saranac Lake. We would never discuss the book even though it took a strong pro-government slant on the military tribunal and the execution of six of the saboteurs.

As I opened the book for the first time and turned to the photographs in the middle, I came upon a picture of the courtroom in which my father is sitting next to J. Edgar Hoover. The text explained that Hoover was at the trial every day and as I read it, my suspicions mounted that he might have been there to make sure the world never knew they had caught the saboteurs because they had turned them-

---

7. Eugene Rachlis, *They Came to Kill* (New York: Random House, 1961). The book tells the entire story of the saboteurs, their capture, and the trial. While it never questions the military tribunal from a civil liberties viewpoint, its thoroughness raises those questions by implication.

selves in, not because of the work of the FBI. When newspaper articles began to appear in the wake of President Bush's proposal for new military tribunals in 2002, one quoted Lloyd N. Cutler, one of the assistant prosecutors and later in partnership with my father, as expressing the very same suspicion I had. Cutler had told me in an interview several years before that Hoover had "acted badly. He announced the capture of the saboteurs to garner publicity when keeping it quiet would have allowed the FBI to follow the saboteurs to their contacts." Cutler also agreed that Hoover pretended the FBI had captured the saboteurs rather than admit they had turned themselves in. Hoover lived by the aura of his agency's superhuman competence. Over the ensuing decades, I have noted many times when secrecy in the name of security has been used to hide incompetence.

When Hoover became the nation's leading anti-communist after the war, no one who had any regard for his future dared challenge him. As we learned later, Hoover fed information to Richard Nixon and Joe McCarthy but when McCarthy finally self-destructed during the army hearings, Hoover quietly stepped back from him, but only far enough to make sure he was not splattered by any of the negative reaction McCarthy had stirred up.

If my father ever lost faith in Hoover, he didn't tell me, but I do believe he was genuinely awed by his daily companion during that trial, when he, in his mid-thirties, was under the obvious tutelage of the single most untouchable person in America. Despite my total trust in my father's judgment, even in 1950 his total confidence in Hoover left me uneasy.

When McCarthy first catapulted into the national limelight, with a 1950 speech in Wheeling, West Virginia, in which he claimed to have the names of 205 communists who had infiltrated the State Department, I was only in the seventh grade and so I was not immediately aware of him.

Later, once I had become a journalist, I used McCarthy's Wheeling speech and its press coverage as an example of what was wrong with American journalism. When editors at the Associated Press read the astounding figure, they asked for verification—verification that a U.S. senator had actually used that number, not verification as to its source or its basis in fact. As long as a public figure made a statement, it would be printed as true. Over the next week, McCarthy was to keep revising his numbers downward but the press stayed with the story and McCarthy had found his issue and become a national figure.

Soon I was following McCarthyism like a soap opera, especially the antics of his twenty-something chief counsel Roy Cohn and Cohn's protégé, G. David Schine. Cohn exuded arrogance and his ability to travel the world and instill instant fear in the hearts of American officials was impressive. But Schine was strange, the rich-kid sidekick who dressed so beautifully. When Cohn started seeking favors for Schine after he was drafted, I suspected there might be something a little unusual in their relationship. But one didn't talk about such things in those days. I can read today that there were suspicions and there was innuendo but that was all. Even when Roy Cohn finally died of AIDS, he was still denying his homosexuality.

The Army-McCarthy hearings were, of course, McCarthy's downfall.[8] Roy Cohn's attempts to get special treatment for his friend Schine had led to threats that if the army did not comply, the McCarthy committee would expose their institutional laxity about security risks. To defend itself, the army prepared accusations of improper political intimidation by Cohn on behalf of the senator.

The hearings went on for more than a month, and on the East Coast, at least, they brought a whole new audience to television. (They were not broadcast on the West Coast.) My father came home early from work so he could watch more of it.

McCarthy self-destructed when he reverted to his most time-tested tactic: Guilt by association. He questioned the loyalty of Fred Fisher, a young attorney in Joseph Welch's firm. Welch, representing the army, had already told Fisher, that because his former membership in the Lawyers' Guild might be used against him, he could not work on the hearings. The two sides had made an agreement. Welch would not ask why Cohn had not served in the military—it was because of a disability—and the McCarthy side would not bring up Fisher's past affiliation.

---

8. My own impressions about the hearings remain vivid. The specifics of the testimony printed here come from *The Life and Times of Joe McCarthy* by Thomas C. Reeves (New York: Stein and Day, 1982).

McCarthy could not resist. With Cohn on the stand mouthing the word "no," McCarthy plunged forward, describing the Lawyers' Guild, a reputable organization with definite liberal leanings but on the infamous Attorney General's List, as the law firm of the Communist party. It was the classic smear and just making the connection on television would have, under ordinary circumstances, been enough to ruin Fisher's career. Photographs showing people in the presence of communist officials could be devastating.

Of course, Welch made his famous rebuttal. "Let us not assassinate this lad further, Senator. You have done enough. Have you no sense of decency, sir, at long last? Have you left no sense of decency?"

Welch's speech marked the end of the career of Joe McCarthy but it did not mark the end of McCarthyism. Even those who opposed him had validated the internal communist threat and it would take another decade, past the Cuban Missile Crisis and into the Vietnam War, for the nation to recognize the threat was external, not internal.

As the McCarthy frenzy rushed toward its climax, I had left home for Phillips Exeter Academy and migrated toward the *Exonian*, the school newspaper, where the atmosphere was as radical chic as we could have been radical chic in 1954. The *Exonian* published a spoof May Day edition, in which we reported on an upcoming but fictional communist-inspired rally at the Plimpton playing fields. This so unnerved the administration that they would not let the issue go off campus for fear the story would be taken as true and the school, already seen as a hotbed of communist sympathizers led by alumnus Corliss Lamont, would come under fire.

Although we resented the censorship and thought the principal pusillanimous for agreeing to it, we also knew his judgment was not rash. Our own motivation for the spoof was that New Hampshire was in the midst of its own mini-McCarthy era.

William Loeb, the vituperative publisher of the *Manchester Union Leader*, had anointed Attorney General Louis Wyman as his own Joe McCarthy and Wyman had been holding hearings, profusely reported by the *Union Leader*, on the communist threat to New Hampshire.

The most successful target, from Wyman's and Loeb's viewpoint, was a man named J. Willard Uphaus who had run a world-fellowship summer camp in the White Mountains. Uphaus testified before

Wyman's committee that he would tell them anything about himself but would not release to them the names of others who had participated in his camps, on the grounds that it would violate their rights of freedom of association. Underlying the confrontation was Uphaus's belief that his release of the names would subject his campers to guilt by association and would be used against them regardless of their beliefs or anything they had discussed at the summer sessions which generally focused on world peace and international government, subjects as popular on the left at the time as they were distrusted by the right. Uphaus, of course, was correct about the guilt by association as McCarthy had proved on a national level that anyone whose name was even mentioned at one of his hearings could lose his job and become unemployable.

One evening, when I was in the school library, I pulled a copy of the *Union Leader* off the rack, and was confronted with a double headline: "Get the Commie Uphaus" the 72-point banner read. Above the logo was another banner: "Go to the church of your choice this Sunday." (Loeb made a big thing of being Christian to counter the innuendo, derived from his name, that he might be Jewish.)

When Uphaus continued to refuse to give out the names of his campers, he was cited for contempt and actually ended up spending time in jail. The case went all the way to the U.S. Supreme Court where the contempt citation was upheld 5 to 4 but with a strong dissent by Justice William J. Brennan.

Fast forward to 1960. While working on Frank Coffin's gubernatorial campaign, I finally faced the lingering residues of McCarthyism where it counted. Although the campaign focused entirely on state issues, the anti-communist issue was raised and relentlessly pursued by a talented humorist named John Gould, who was also something of a political ideologue. He had turned his local paper, the *Lisbon Enterprise*, into a statewide publication for the election year and he used the platform to accuse the Democrats, and Senator Edmund S. Muskie, in particular, of being soft on communism. To those of us in the campaign, the *Enterprise* was viewed as hateful, but forty years later I had reason to re-read some of those issues. By today's standards of personal attack and vituperation, the *Enterprise* was quite tame, well within the bounds of fair comment—although I still disagreed with the viewpoint. At least, I disagreed most of the time. Gould's newspaper may have been supported by well-known right wing Republicans but, maverick that he was, Gould editorially opposed prayer in the schools. He did not march in the same lock step so many partisan journals do today.

The real test came when Coffin received a high rating by Americans for Democratic Action (ADA), the leading liberal anti-communist organization of the time. The Republican right considered the ADA endorsement tantamount to an endorsement by the Communist party itself and painted it as such, so there was always the question whether using it would backfire in a state like Maine.

The communist issue was not key in that election. Maine was still a Republican state and the Nixon-Kennedy presidential race was to help generate the largest voter turnout for decades before and after. There was the added dollop that Maine was still somewhat anti-Catholic and the Democratic ticket, from top down, was full of Catholic names, even if John Donovan, running for Congress, was in fact a Baptist.

Only a few months later, I found myself working for Jim Loeb—no relation to William Loeb and one of the founders of ADA—as the editor of his small daily newspaper in Saranac Lake, New York.

I had been there only a short time when I was asked by the local Rotary Club to speak to them about the "documentary" film, *Operation Abolition*, a last gasp of the McCarthy heritage.

The film was an account of the demonstrations against the House UnAmerican Activities Committee (HUAC) by students at the University of California at Berkeley and purported to prove the demonstrators were communist inspired. It was the work of Fulton Lewis III, a contemporary of mine I had actually run across in Washington and the son of one of the leading pro-McCarthy newspaper and radio commentators, Fulton Lewis, Jr.

The Saranac Lake Rotary had seen the film a few weeks before, knew it was controversial, and someone had had the idea to get a different perspective on it. There had been considerable coverage in the *Washington Post, New York Post* and *New York Times*, detailing its flaws, including how in some cases the lip movement of speakers did not correspond with what they were saying on screen.

I had long been a critic of HUAC and felt strongly about the issue, but I also recognized the pitfalls of my appearance at Rotary. Only twenty-three years old and new to my job, I was not about to launch an all-out attack on the film, so instead, I quoted heavily from what I considered reputable publications and pointed out where the film did not correspond with known facts. Although my sympathy with the student position was no doubt obvious, my approach was to discredit the film and not attack the congressional committee directly. I was sounding strangely like those members of Congress who said while they approved of McCarthy's desire to weed communists out of government, they disagreed with his tactics. Only with his tactics.

At one point during my presentation, I said, almost as an aside, that I had read that FBI Director J. Edgar Hoover had not endorsed the film specifically, probably because of some of the heavy-handed propaganda techniques used.

At the end of my presentation, during the question and answer period, all seemed to be going in a predictable manner until Jack Roosa, who had been the Rotary member to promote the original showing, stood up and said, "I have just one question. Why are you a communist?"

I don't recall my answer. I am sure it was some denial that I was a communist, but I had been caught in what I so abhorred, letting the charge put me entirely on the defensive. Indeed, what I had admired most about the California students, many of them from middle-class families in which their parents would have done anything to prove their freedom from communist taint, was that they had said, in essence: We don't care. Call us whatever you want. It doesn't matter to us.

Since the power of the post-McCarthy inheritors of his tactics had come from the threat their victims felt at being labeled communist, for the students to say they didn't care removed that power. Even in retrospect, I think the Berkeley demonstrations were a turning point, because others began to scoff at their accusers and refuse to defend themselves when charged. I had not yet reached that stage.

Two days after my Rotary appearance, I was sitting in my office, a raised space at the back of a long narrow room that opened on the street, with windows that allowed me to see who was coming in the front door. I noticed them immediately, two men in suits who were obviously confident of their authority.

Rose Dest, who acted as receptionist, did not even call me on the intercom. I could see her talking with them and pointing in my direction.

They walked authoritatively by the advertising department and the wire desk and up the three steps to my office. I rose to greet them and they introduced themselves as "from the director." They did not say they were from the FBI and they didn't say what director they represented, but I did not have a second's doubt.

They were there to "set me straight" on a few things, an obvious reference to my Rotary speech. While they did not say that "the director" endorsed the film and they did not quote my reference to his withholding such an endorsement, they made it very clear which side of the issue any good American should be taking. Whether my crime was debunking *Operation Abolition* or taking the director's name in vain, I don't know. I can't remember everything they said, not just because it was so many years ago, but because I could not have related the conversation five minutes later. I was petrified. I do know I was more than conciliatory; I had caved in.

They left me with a copy of *Masters of Deceit*, a treatise on the internal communist threat which bore Hoover's authorship, and suggested that I read it thoroughly before venturing any further comments on the subject. I said I would. Then they left. I doubt if the meeting lasted ten minutes.

Only later did a different reaction set in and I began to think of Arthur Koestler's *Darkness at Noon*, where the protagonist is told during a communist show trial that if he will only confess to what he has not done, everything will be all right. To confess sets you free.

By coincidence I talked with Jim Loeb that same day and his immediate reaction was outrage. I had been impressed that the FBI informer system was so effective—probably no more than good old Jack Roosa—and that they had sent agents from Albany, three hours away by car, within forty-eight hours.

Loeb was impressed by the fact they had sent two agents to intimidate his young editor over what was in essence an issue of legitimate dissent. He called them and told them so.

My father was still alive, but I am not sure I ever told him about the incident. If I did, I don't remember what he said.

I was, of course, thankful that Jim Loeb had taken up for me, and while I already harbored doubts regarding Hoover's wisdom, despite my father's position during my childhood, feeling the intimidation firsthand, and so quickly submitting to that intimidation, changed my attitude toward Hoover and the FBI.

It also changed my attitude about the entire McCarthy era because I finally realized that they derived their power to intimidate from the willingness of their victims to be intimidated. Intellectually, I admired the Berkeley students because they had dared to reject the very premise of McCarthyism—that fear of being accused would make them conform. And Jim Loeb had shown me that one could stand up to them.

When I had had my chance to do the same, I had failed.

Part 2

Individuals do not have the time, the opportunity, or the energy to make all the experiments and to discern all the significance that have gone into the making of the whole heritage of civilization. In developing knowledge men must collaborate with their ancestors. Otherwise they must begin not where their ancestors arrived but where their ancestors began. If they exclude the tradition of the past from the curricula of the schools they make it necessary for each generation to repeat the errors rather than to benefit by the successes of its predecessors.

—Walter Lippmann, Phi Beta Kappa Address, December 29, 1940

Five

Getting Educated

I don't remember her name, my second grade teacher at the James Madison elementary school. But I do remember she taught us about birds.

That was in Arlington, Virginia, in 1944, just across Chain Bridge from Washington, D.C. The community was truly suburban with large, undeveloped tracts and the songbirds were plentiful. We learned to identify not just the flashy and obvious, such as cardinals and scarlet tanagers, but also the more subtle, such as house wrens and red-eyed vireos. When, a few years later, I was sent to summer camp in Pennsylvania, where songbirds also abounded, the ability to identify an indigo bunting or a downy woodpecker thrilled me.

Now, more than half a century later, I live on the Maine coast where many of those brighter and more easily distinguished birds are scarce. I still nail orange slices to trees in a fit of optimism, but the Baltimore orioles the oranges are meant to attract are rare. On the other hand, each spring and fall a dizzying variety of warblers moves through, pursued by several types of hawks and I struggle to name them. Warblers distinguish their identity from one another by a discrete patch of yellow or white, not the garish primary colors of the scarlet tanagers that made an unusual appearance in Maine two decades ago by mysteriously falling from the sky.

On a recent spring evening I was walking in the yard, admiring the sunset, when a woodcock plopped down at my feet, almost hitting me as he descended from his spiraling flight, and I felt all the excitement I had when I was a second grader, noticing a red winged blackbird for the first time because I knew what it was.

I can't specifically remember anything else I was taught in those first two years by that wonderful woman, who connected the real world with what we were learning. What I do remember is that she taught me the pleasure to be derived from learning.

I received a similar gift from Miss Tennyson in the sixth grade. She made grammar fun. Diagramming a sentence was like doing a puzzle. Properly using an apostrophe was a matter of pride and at the age of twelve, I learned and never forgot the proper use of a gerund and how to write a proper parallel construction.

Miss Tennyson would never let bad spoken grammar slip by uncorrected; we didn't say "ain't" in school nor did we use double negatives there, although they were common on the street.

These were the years, through sixth grade, when, like other children, my desire to learn and the pleasure I derived from satisfying that desire were overwhelming. Good teachers didn't discourage us. But this period was to be followed by several years of school drudgery where any interest was systematically drubbed out of us. Few of us cared about what we were learning and few of us understood why it was important, if indeed it was. Maybe it wasn't the teaching and the curriculum, maybe it was just the confrontation with junior-high-age hormones. Maybe we should have been put out to pasture for a few years until we were ready to return to the classroom.

Even though my interest in education faced a hiatus at school, my father never let up and kept us interested by his continuation of the education-as-games model. I later learned that when he was growing up, his father had tested him and his siblings with math problems at the dinner table. This may have led to my father's lifelong interest in math and his going to MIT his freshman year, before transferring to Yale where in his junior year he won the top mathematics prize.

What I remember was mainly silly, such as "How many three-cent stamps in a dozen?" meant to trick us into saying "four." After that, he couldn't trick me with: "If a herring and a half cost a cent and a half, how much do a dozen cost?" (I never caught on to the ethnic reference to herring as a unit of trade.) There was one real puzzle: "Your mother sends you to the well with a three-gallon bucket and a five-gallon bucket and asks you to bring back exactly four gallons of water. How do you do it?"

I still use this puzzle as a test not of a person's mathematical skills but as an indication about that person's willingness to address a new problem. The vast majority don't even try to solve it. They just throw up their hands in despair. Yet it is quite easy once you begin—by filling either bucket and pouring its contents into the other bucket.[1]

My father's goal was to teach us to look for a solution even when dealing with something we had not previously confronted. What seems complex at first turns out to be simple when subjected to calm analysis. Throughout life I have found this to be sound advice. When given a specific problem to solve, whether mathematical or social, too many people withdraw and look to someone else to solve it. Sometimes this is because they think they do not know how to solve a new problem. The only problems they can deal with are those they can recognize as parallel to what they have had solved for them in the past. Sometimes this is because they believe there is one correct answer to every problem and since they do not know it at once, they assume someone else does and will supply the answer. Much of the educational experience, heightened today by the mania for uniform testing, focuses on learning the right answer rather than the process for arriving at the right answer. So you either know the answer or you don't; it is not something you can figure out. Too often, when a group is asked to solve a problem collaboratively, the majority opts out of the process and seeks a leader to provide the correct answer.

My father also liked to make us overcome our preconceptions, to be punished for jumping to conclusions, for anticipating an answer without really listening to the question, as in the problem of the three-cent stamps. One of his non-mathematical conundrums was decades ahead of its time. It went like this: "A big Indian and a little Indian are standing on a mountain. The little Indian is the big Indian's son but the big Indian isn't the little Indian's father. Explain."

In 1945 a big Indian was a male Indian and an amazing number of people were stumped by their own preconceptions; today, almost anyone would recognize the big Indian was the little Indian's mother.

---

1. If you fill the five-gallon bucket and pour off three gallons into the three-gallon bucket, you have two gallons left in the five-gallon bucket. You then pour the three gallons back into the well, empty the two gallons from the five-gallon bucket into the three-gallon bucket, leaving one gallon of capacity in the three-gallon bucket. You refill the five-gallon bucket, pour off the one gallon into the three-gallon bucket, and voilà, you have four gallons left in the five-gallon bucket. You can also do it the opposite way, filling the three-gallon bucket and pouring it into the five-gallon bucket, etc.

My father told wonderfully awful jokes and he particularly liked what were then called shaggy dog stories, long stories that had a silly or anticlimactic ending. Or so they seemed at first.

For instance, there was a man who believed he had little green bugs crawling up and down his arms so he went to his doctor for a cure. The family doctor looked him over and could see no sign of any bugs, so he sent the patient to a dermatologist. The dermatologist saw no little green bugs or any sign of skin rash, so he recommended the patient see an allergist. The allergist gave him scratch tests for every known substance but could produce no itching sensation as a result, so he recommended the patient see a psychiatrist. The psychiatrist asked the patient what the matter was, and the patient replied that he was plagued by little green bugs crawling up and down his arms, and as he spoke, the patient made a sweeping motion with his hand as if to brush them off his skin. At which the psychiatrist drew back quickly and exclaimed, "Well, don't brush the damn things on me." My opinion of psychiatrists may have been irreparably influenced by this joke.

These jokes were told so many times in our family that my brother and I needed only to repeat the punch lines to bring a smile. And there was a joke about that.[2] I fully expect these stories to be passed on to my grandchildren as part of a family tradition and a link to my father.

The jokes were told and the questions posed around the dinner table and I have come to believe that is one of the significant differences between how my generation and later generations were brought up. We ate dinner with our parents and they chose the topics of con-

---

2. A man is sent to an insane asylum and the first time he is in the day room, he listens to the other patients as they rattle off numbers. The first patient says, "Thirty-five," and everyone laughs. There is a period of silence and another patient says, "Sixty-four," and people laugh even more than they did the first time. Finally someone says, "Seventy-seven," and there is a total uproar. The new patient is baffled and when he has the chance, he asks one of the orderlies about what's happening. The orderly explains to him that all the patients have heard the same jokes so many times they have given each joke a number, and then when someone says the number, everyone thinks of the joke and laughs accordingly. So the next day the new patient is in the day room and decides to enter the social whirl, so he recalls the most popular joke of the day before and says, "Seventy-seven." He is greeted with dead silence and turns to the orderly and asks why no one laughed. "You didn't tell it right," the orderly explains.

versation so we talked about the events of the day, often public events. There was no separate youth culture and when Donald Dell and I were spending hours in the back of a car on the way to tennis tournaments, we did not discuss teen idols or pop music. We talked about the same things we had listened to our parents discussing at the dinner table—in our case, the accusations of communism leveled by Whittaker Chambers against Alger Hiss.

While political names and political topics had to be a subject of dinner table conversation between my parents, I don't recall any of it specifically until about age twelve even though prior to that age I knew who the major political players were, since I read the newspaper from the time I was able to read. I had been to the White House and I had had a grandstand seat at President Truman's inauguration in 1948 when I was eleven. The last was courtesy of Henry J. Kaiser, one of my father's clients. I did not realize then the importance of an industrialist like Kaiser who had been called in to build the Hoover Dam when no one else could and whose progressive health care plan for his workers remains a model today. I did know that Kaiser made ships—my mother christened two of them—and an unsuccessful automobile—we owned one.

One of my most vivid childhood memories is the summer we spent at the Bretton Woods conference where my father participated in discussions about the World Bank for Reconstruction and the International Monetary Fund. The year was 1944 and I would turn seven that summer.

For some reason, we had the best accommodations at Mt. Washington, an old log cabin at the base of the Cog Railway that ran up the mountain to the summit and was closed for the duration of the war. There were other log-cabin-style cottages, but ours was the largest and we had been allowed to stay there because of some connection with the owner of the railway and the surrounding property, Colonel Teague, who was reputed to be a curmudgeon and to dislike children but who was very nice to my brother and me.

The cabin had running water but was otherwise rudimentary with an ice box rather than a refrigerator. The inside walls were unfinished, chinked logs, and we slept under piles of blankets.

More important than Colonel Teague was his caretaker, Jimmy

Webb, who became one of those mythical figures in our young lives, teaching us how to worm fish for the ten-inch brook trout that flourished in the Ammonoosuc River, which poured down the side of the mountain a few yards from our door, causing a constant roar. One day Jimmy sent my brother Warren and me home with a Wonder Bread wrapper, opaque with bright polka dots, filled with illegal trout, a piece of bread carefully placed at each end in case we were stopped by a game warden. I don't recall ever seeing a game warden that summer but we boys were thrilled by our venture into the outlaw life.

We could stop in at Jimmy's house any time and be fed his home-made doughnuts, deep fried and crisp, and listen to his stories of mountain lions and blizzards. Jimmy would let us follow him on his rounds and we could see the stored railway engines and cars or inspect the other closed buildings.

For the most part, we saw little of the conferees who were meeting well below us at the hotel with its magnificent porches, although an occasional exotic hiker in a turban did venture as far up the mountain as our cluster of buildings.

Heading in the opposite direction, we made an expedition to the summit, the highest in the Northeast and famous for its winds, climbing a narrow trail until we emerged above tree line and then coming back down the railroad tracks, walking the high, vertiginous trestle called Jacob's Ladder. I do not remember being frightened—perhaps the ties were close enough together so I had no fear of falling, perhaps an adult was holding on to me. Most memorable was my mother coming up the tracks near the bottom, bringing us fresh grapefruit, a precaution against my thirty-eight-year-old father's diabetes.

While my memories revolve around such trivia and seeing moose and gathering hailstones the size of ping pong balls in tennis ball cans and trying to preserve them in our old-fashioned ice box and my brother trying unsuccessfully to trap raccoons, I have always preserved a sense that I was present at the making of history that July in New Hampshire. Even though I had nothing to do with the events that made history, being contemporaneously present at the site of a historical event left me connected in a way a later visitation to a site never would have. My father did tell us a little of what went on at Bretton Woods, as he told us a little about Dumbarton Oaks and

San Francisco, both conferences on the founding of the United Nations that he attended, but because of my presence, Bretton Woods remained a central part of my education.

More than thirty years later, totally by happenstance, I listened at Riverside Church in New York City as Michael Manley, the once radical prime minister of Jamaica, talked for more than an hour about how Bretton Woods, while its results might have been flawed, represented a high point of idealism about the responsibilities of the United States and the rich nations to help the poorer nations. Bretton Woods had remained in my consciousness and I was always hungry for more information about its significance. So that evening at Riverside Church, I remained rapt while most of the others in the audience nodded.

On the way home from Bretton Woods, we drove east through the mountains so we could visit my grandmother in Portland, Maine. Somehow we were transported in a rather grand car with a chauffeur and an operable window between the back and front. I suspect now that the car was the work of E. I. Kauffman, an important if somewhat mysterious—at least to me—figure in my father's life. Kauffman had founded Kay's jewelry stores and was active in the formation of Brandeis University. He was lavish in his gifts to us and lent my father the money to start his own law firm when he left government. I still have a cel of Goofy from a Walt Disney cartoon that E. I. gave me as a present. It is signed to me by Disney. I am sure Disney must have signed thousands of such cels but for a child it was still an exotic gift and typical of E. I.'s thoughtfulness and special place in our lives.

On the way back to Maine, we stopped at the Summit House hotel, owned by E. I., next to the famous and still opulent Poland Spring House. All I remember about it was a breakfast of blueberry pancakes before we set off for Portland again, but years later I was to learn that the Summit House was the alternative to the Poland Spring House, which still didn't allow Jews in 1944. When my father was a boy, the Poland Spring House had reputedly had a sign that read: "No Catholics, Jews, or dogs allowed."

That summer was our family's last together for a long time. The next year my brother Warren and I were sent off to Camp Pocono, near Lakeville, Pennsylvania. Run by Quakers, the camp's emphasis was on woodcraft and the counselors were all addressed as Uncle and Aunt. We lived in tents and learned how to split wood properly and light fires with tinder from the dead underbranches of hemlocks. As campers improved their skills, they were rewarded with honors, which were presented each Saturday night at a big campfire, lit with flint and steel by a chosen camper. Since the honors, much like Boy Scout merit badges, represented tested skills, they also allowed privileges. An avid canoer, I quickly reached fifth honor which allowed me to paddle anywhere on the lake, alone, when I was only about ten. These were all wood-and-canvas canoes and sitting in the bow seat, facing the stern, I liked to go off by myself in the early evening and paddle to a nearby cove where snowy egrets fed. I imagined myself an Indian boy and attempted to paddle in complete silence, feathering the paddle in the water instead of lifting it out with each stroke.

Camp Pocono fostered the Indian mystique and this is undoubtedly where I began to develop my romanticized image of what life on the frontier must have been like. Only a few years later I was to become enamored of the novels of Joseph Altsheler who wrote about the adventures of a group of teenagers in the Kentucky wilderness who lived by Indian skills. Camp Pocono and the novels were the formative influences on my earliest conservation ethic.

One of the most memorable Saturday campfires occurred when some of the counselors and older boys painted their bodies with red clay, wore loin cloths and leggings, and performed a snake dance with anesthetized puff adders and black snakes. Several of the snakes began to regain consciousness during the dance, writhing and trying to snap back at the tormentors who held them in their mouths, and who were in no position to let them go.

Such antics were common and at Camp Pocono we did many things that absolutely would not be allowed today, including a kidnapping hoax, perpetrated by the counselors. When the group did not return from an overnight trip, the sheriff arrived at camp and we were told he was investigating the disappearance of the four campers and their counselor. (The perpetrators of the hoax undoubtedly knew the sheriff was coming on some other errand and wrote that into their script.) After they had reduced all of us to abject fear, the kidnapped marched back into camp in triumph.

We had several black counselors, one of whom, Jim Dillard, I came to particularly admire after he was my counselor, and who was to be the subject of a confrontation with a racist teacher years later.

And we had Jorge Bolet, a concert pianist. We were encouraged to listen to him practice, dressed in white tie and tails and red shorts, if we took off our shoes so we would not make noise when shuffling our feet. Years later I was to attend a concert of his at Constitution Hall in Washington; I left my shoes on. I am quite sure it was Bolet who composed the camp song that had such memorable lines as:

Running, walking, even on a crutch,
You can always tell a Poconut, but you can't tell him much.
Oh, I'm a nut, you're a nut.
Once you're a Poconut,
You're nuts for life.

I don't think Camp Pocono could exist today, at least not with its emphasis on self-sufficiency and relatively high levels of danger. Teaching eight-year-olds how to sharpen their knives, split wood with a well-cared-for ax, and build fires is no longer an acceptable regimen. The dangers to which we were routinely exposed would today bring a flock of lawsuits. But the rough and tumble of Camp Pocono had no deleterious effects on me and even as small children, having lived our entire cognizant lives in the atmosphere of World War II, we liked to think of ourselves as tough.

More astounding may have been the presence of black counselors. This was the only time in my young life when I was under the direct supervision of a black man, someone I respected and looked up to.

Because of my father's attitude, I was always to have sympathy with the injustices blacks suffered in our society—*Brown vs. Board of Education*, outlawing segregation was still a decade off—but I did live in a segregated society, both in Washington and when I visited my maternal grandparents in North Carolina. As a child, I knew it was wrong for black children to be isolated in inferior schools or for black adults to have to move to the back of the bus, but I thought there was nothing I could do about it.

Nor could I totally escape the attitudes of my time. Even today, I know I have ingrained instincts that can only be described as racist. Fortunately, I know they are wrong and would never act on them, but their very existence demonstrates why we need enforced societal norms and laws. When people tell me there is no longer racism in the South, I apply my own experience. Such ingrained attitudes die slowly. But I remain optimistic. I was a major improvement on my mother's generation and my children do not harbor any of those same prejudices.

I also had my first encounters with death at Camp Pocono. My best friend that first summer, when I was eight, was Perry Gilpatrick, the son of diplomats, who died the next winter in a plane crash while traveling between the United States and Europe.

My counselor for several summers was Uncle Beak, so named because his name was Richard and there were several other Uncle Richards and Uncle Dicks but he had a protuberant nose. Everyone accepted his nickname with equanimity; he may have come up with it himself.

The peak occurrence of the summer was Gold Rush, a day-long, late-summer event that started after breakfast when counselors performed a skit of finding a treasure map. We all inspected it and set off to find the treasure, painted rocks whose colors changed annually so that no one could make his own. One year, the nuggets were silver with red spots.

Once the treasure was spotted, word spread quickly and everyone rushed to the "lode," collecting as many rocks as they could. But in these elaborate games, everything was allowed—remember the snake dance and the kidnapping. We younger campers were particularly vulnerable to robbery by gangs of senior campers who could be as old as sixteen and we had to use subterfuge to get back to the bank with our nuggets where we could cash them in for specially printed paper money.

Everyone had a little cash as a result but they would acquire more—or lose more—during the afternoon when the concessions opened. Each tent or cabin, or sometimes a group, built a concession for which they charged. The more popular the concession, the more those campers earned. The most successful venture my group ever put together was Cleopatra's barge, two canoes with a platform in the middle and a canopy over the top. We would paddle our customers around the lakefront while they drank lemonade and read comic books.

Some of the concessions developed by the oldest campers were spectacular. One year, there had been a giant swing that was suspended on ropes between two pine trees and pulled back with another rope on a pulley so that one was lifted a good 30 feet off the ground before being let go. The swing brought in big bucks.

The year I turned eleven, the oldest campers attempted to outdo even the giant swing with a ferris wheel.

They chose two huge white pines about six feet apart and climbed as high as they could where they bolted a socket to each tree to hold the axle of the ferris wheel. They then connected two long poles to the axle to form a rotational device and strung a chair from each end. Each of the two riders, one after the other, would be brought close to 60 feet in the air, then would sweep down to just a few inches above the ground as the huge poles rotated.

To construct the ferris wheel, they had to raise the apparatus into position and set the axle into its sockets. This took a number of counselors and stronger boys, operating with pulleys and ropes. Two particularly daring counselors put on the spikes electrical linemen used and climbed the pine trees to seat the axle and rotational poles once the entire apparatus was lifted to them.

Uncle Beak was one of those pulling on the ropes when the accident occurred. I don't recall if a rope broke or if some people simply let go, but suddenly the huge, heavy apparatus was falling and as I and my tent mates stood watching, experiencing helplessness and horror, one of the long poles hit Uncle Beak. He was rushed to the hospital but died within a couple of days.

For my tent mate Sammy Hinkle and myself, this was our third year with Uncle Beak as our counselor. We were fiercely loyal to him and treated him with the reverence only a pre-teenage boy can show for a college-age man. We were stunned by his death.

Camp continued—there were only a couple of weeks left. I don't think there was any consideration of sending us home, and we were given a new temporary counselor. Whenever anyone would mention Uncle Beak, I would burst into tears. Never again was the death of anyone to affect me in the same way. Perry Gilpatrick, my contemporary and fellow camper, had been far away when he died. An airplane crash was abstract. When my parents died, I was old enough to realize it was going to happen sooner or later. But Uncle Beak's accident was totally unexpected and who could have been more immortal than my college-age counselor?

I tend to be fatalistic about death and while I am touched and saddened by death, I do not dwell on it. I sometimes wonder if that early, devastating experience caused me to take such a detached attitude. I certainly applied it to myself when I was diagnosed with cancer and told I had less than a year to live, a prediction I proved untrue.

In 1945, when my parents bought a house across the Potomac River in Washington, the part of Georgetown we inhabited was not yet gentrified. On the other side of Wisconsin Avenue were the beautiful brick houses that had never lost their glamour, but we were next to the Volta Bureau for the Deaf on 35th Street and only a block from a cul-de-sac called Charles Court where black families lived in rooms stacked above one another. Soon the blacks were pushed out, the buildings rehabbed with a faint New Orleans feel, and the cul-de-sac renamed Pomander Walk.

Nearby was Georgetown Playground where on weekends we would have pickup neighborhood games only to be chased off by the police from the Seventh Precinct if we were playing with black kids. Segregation was a way of life. Similarly, one of my playmates was the child of servants in the house where Alexander Graham Bell had lived on the other side of Volta Place. I considered the boy my friend but accepted without further thought that we did not go to school together.

It was at Georgetown Playground that our sixth-grade teams from Fillmore Elementary School practiced. We had both a touch football team—I was center—and a softball team—I played second base.

Don't ask me how this was all organized. I remember no coaches or faculty present. We elected a captain—Carl Fay was captain of both. We assigned positions and, led by Carl, practiced on our own and had a regular schedule, traveling by bus or trolley to other schools or playing at home with officials who miraculously showed up, an indication of adult supervision. That year, we won the city championship in football and my brother took 8mm movies of the final game, which we all watched in a room on our third floor, before a victory dinner prepared by my mother at which she made the mistake of having candles on the table and serving carrot sticks. My teammates were soon roasting their carrot sticks in the candles.

Years later, my son Tony asked me to arrange a football game for him and his sixth-grade friends. Perhaps he was inspired by the tales of my own championship year. The boys immediately fell apart. Everyone wanted to be the ball carrier. No one wanted to block and as soon as someone did block, the other player would fall to the ground as if mortally wounded. In one generation, they had lost all knowledge of the pickup culture.

We had always played pickup football, usually tackle. (I was the fat kid who was almost impossible to bring down and while I was allowed to be the ball carrier in tackle, I was too slow to play backfield in touch.) Our official game was seven man touch, played from a single wing formation, and I was the center. I don't know who taught me the long snap with a strong spiral but I learned it and the skill stuck with me for life.

The only time our self-imposed discipline was broken was when a boy who had been at a nearby juvenile detention center, was transferred to Fillmore and he insisted to Carl Fay, aided by a knife, that he would play second base. I was temporarily moved to right field where I remained only until he was sent back to reform school. I had no negative thoughts about recidivism rates.

It was this same boy who allowed me to go one up on my Aunt Ellen Winston, my mother's sister. She was a leading figure in welfare reform, first as commissioner of welfare in North Carolina and then as national welfare commissioner under President Lyndon Johnson where she initiated the alternative of home nursing care for the elderly that still exists.

I still came home for lunch, and one spring day Aunt Ellen was visiting and requested that I remove the dirt from my upper arm before sitting down to eat. I announced proudly that I could not remove it as it was not dirt but bruises I had received in the cloak room, bruises dispensed as noogies by our classmate from the reformatory. Aunt Ellen did not demur when I expressed the hope that he would soon be returning to reform school.

At junior high we were split up. Until then, our school classes were determined entirely by where we lived and the neighborhood filled only one sixth-grade class. Because that part of Georgetown had not yet been gentrified, we had an interesting mix. We not only went to school together, we played in the streets together, having large gun battles through alleys and over the roofs of garages. On Saturdays we gathered for matinees at the Calvert Theater, eating Good and Plenty during the show, getting a lime sherbet cone next door at High's afterwards, then looking for snakes in the cemetery on the way home. I knew not to express my fear of snakes and I never seemed to find one on my own.

Gordon Junior High took students from a much larger area and we were probably tracked as well, so the neighborhood gang began to disperse. I came into contact with such exotic people as Loretta Bones, who sat next to me in art class and had an endless supply of dirty jokes.

My previous dirty joke repertoire had been developed as a crossing patrolman, one of those kids who stands on a corner with a white crossbelt and helps the smaller kids cross the street on the way to school. To ease the boredom and attract the company of the patrol leader who went from post to post, it was necessary to have a steady supply of new jokes. Most of ours were not very funny except for their naiveté and their anatomical incorrectness—you mean a boner doesn't have a bone in it? This was not a circumstance where I told any of my father's old jokes; they had to wait until I had a family of my own.

My corner was at R and 34th Streets, facing the wall that surrounded the McLean mansion where the owner of the Hope diamond lived. The diamond was cursed.

Evalyn Walsh McLean, my research tells me, died in her home in 1947 but we all knew she had been run over by a trolley car, about as gruesome a fate as we could imagine and one fitting the diamond's curse that we felt so close to. We were correct, however, in our information that she had recently died.

I did not go downtown to the museums with my school friends. I went with my brother or alone and the Hope diamond was not placed in the Smithsonian until many years later. My favorite was the National Gallery of Art, a marble mausoleum that was always cool in the summer and that I could reach by bus. I particularly enjoyed the corridors that were decorated with plants and pools and I would wander about looking at paintings, taking a lunch break in the cafeteria. These excursions, more a search for relief from the terrible humidity of pre-air-conditioned Washington than any cultural quest, set a life-long pattern for me.

I soon shifted my allegiance to the Corcoran Gallery, a somewhat musty venue in those days and nowhere near as cool as the National. On the other hand, the Corcoran had a room full of François Boucher paintings that I kept going back to. In those days, the powdered and pink nudes were racier than anything I could find in a magazine.

I stayed only a year at Gordon Junior High because our parents had decided it was time for my brother and me to go to private school. I don't understand why. While public school in Washington wasn't much in those days, neither were the private schools. Perhaps the reasons were social rather than academic. Today, the better social climate is the major justification for sending one's children to the education-ally second-rate private schools that proliferate, and it may not be such a terrible thing because without the disruptive atmosphere and anti-intellectualism that too often mar public schools, private schools may offer a better chance of learning, even if what is being offered is of low caliber.

The decisions—to go to camp, to take tennis lessons, to go to prep school, to go away to school—were always made for both my brother and me at the same time, even though there was two years' difference in our ages. So I started everything two years earlier than Warren did. Neither of us liked St. Albans, the upper-crust school that was proba-bly our parents' preference and academically the best of the private schools in Washington. It had a deadly Episcopalian and school uni-form feel. Our visit left me only with an image of dark paneling, lead-ed windows, and organ music.

Instead we were allowed to go to Landon, an institution run by an idiosyncratic headmaster. Its main attraction was its excellent tennis team. The eponymous headmaster did not like being known for his tennis team, headed by the current national junior champion, Teddy Rogers, and wanted us all to play football in the fall. He thought ten-nis was not manly enough.

Academically, Landon School was spotty. My eighth-grade French teacher barely managed to stay a chapter ahead of us and the rumor was he had been recruited by the headmaster's wife while she was on vacation. He used to say that he had inked a G on his left hand and a D on his right, so he would know the words for left and right—gauche and droit. He did not speak French to us and the classes were not conducted in French, and since he imparted nothing to us of French life or culture, he did not inspire us to want to use the language. Fortunately, I had other factors in my life, most notably my father's urging and people whom I admired who spoke French, that made me want to learn French. It was, at the time, the official international language and I already wanted to be international.

My Latin teacher was probably better. At least, he had access to the proper translations of Caesar's Gallic Wars and no one expected us to speak Latin. My Latin teacher's most memorable characteristic was that he drove his car sitting in the middle of the front seat so he wouldn't wear out the springs unevenly by sitting on the driver's side when he was alone. I suppose they didn't pay very well at Landon.

The saving grace was that in those days third-rate prep schools like Landon picked up the curricula of better schools and we had essentially the same reading list as we would have had at Exeter, reading *Silas Marner* and *The Rise of Silas Lapham* on schedule. When I did apply to Exeter, despite good grades at Landon, I failed both the French and Latin exams at the level I hoped to enter. My father tutored me in French that summer and I was able to pass a makeup exam; I went back a year in Latin but was later able to recover it. Landon had prepared me to grade level in English and math due to the standardized curriculum. This did not mean I was up to par with the other students when I transferred to Exeter. I had read much less than they and my competence in math was based on drilling and my father's help rather than a real understanding of mathematics. I clearly had not inherited his skill in the subject.

In the eighth grade, I had my first public confrontation over civil rights with Donald Collins, my English teacher and Landon's assistant headmaster. Although other students might have sympathized with me, I was the only one strongly arguing for equal rights against Mr. Collins and those who were making the case for Negro inferiority, the backbone of the genteel rationalization as to why blacks should not be allowed equal rights. Or at least, they argued, the implementation of such rights should proceed even more slowly than the snail's pace at which it was moving in this still segregated era.

While eugenics underlay the debate, no one could argue that there were not individual blacks who had demonstrated intelligence and competence on an equal level with whites. Ralph Bunche, who had just won the Nobel Peace Prize, had seen to that. I am not sure I was getting the best of the argument, but I was obviously not backing off. Consequently, Mr. Collins sought to put me down by saying that although I argued for the equality of blacks, I would never invite one to dinner at my house. I replied angrily that not only would I invite a Negro to my house for dinner, but that I had, referring to my former counselor, Jim Dillard, and I went on to point out some of Uncle Jim's finer qualities. In 1950 this was a major confrontation and I had little idea that I could do anything more for the cause of blacks. Nor did I have any knowledge of the kinds of internal rage people like Jim Dillard must have felt—it was several years before I read Ralph Ellison's *Invisible Man*. Much of my understanding of blacks derived from kitchen conversations with our own hired help, and I came to understand how broad the daily insults were and how closely these supposedly contented domestic help were following the early Civil Rights movement, something they made clear to me but would never have discussed with my mother. They always treated me gently, never expressing the anger they must have felt toward whites in general.

The real attraction of Landon was the tennis team, possibly the best high-school team in the nation at that time. Not only was Rogers number one, but Donald Dell, on his way to becoming both national boys and junior champion, was number six and he and I often played doubles, much to the chagrin of our older opponents. Donald was twelve and I was thirteen; he was short and I was fat, so together we made a short and fat team of pre-high schoolers. When we beat a couple of seniors in a match against the Hill School, their headmaster asked his students how they could have lost to such little kids.

The same years when my educational career was in a slump, tennis became the dominant learning experience in my life.

When I was ten, my parents had decided both my brother and I should take tennis lessons and had put us under the care of Buddy Goeltz. Buddy's great moment had been taking a set off Don Budge—

he had also played against Bill Tilden. Later, Buddy was to dominate the sixty-five-and-over national circuit, winning more championships than anyone before him.

Because he taught a continental grip, we tended to have weak forehands and great backhands. In fact, Teddy Rogers won his national championship almost without a forehand.

At ten, you learn a sport rapidly, especially if you practice four or five hours a day as we did during the summer. When we weren't playing with one another, we worked on the backboard and I developed a good backhand and an almost impenetrable ability to get the ball back. I became known by my opponents as a human backboard, not a term of praise but of exasperation. Because we were playing exclusively on clay, I had time to get to the ball despite being overweight.

Buddy taught us court sense and in the days before power tennis, placement strategy was everything. I still watch a match by mentally anticipating where each player will hit the next ball, more often than not disagreeing with the shot selection that depends more on power than on intelligence. We used more of the court, hitting down the line as much as cross court, hitting long and short to move an opponent forward and backward. I was considered to have excellent anticipation—a euphemism for wondering how I did so well in getting to the ball when I was so fat. In fact, it wasn't a sixth sense; it was that most of my opponents were entirely predictable in where they hit the ball.[3] My strategy was to lure an opponent into making unforced errors in an effort to end the torture I was inflicting. I was happy to stay out there all day. Others were less patient.

Because of Buddy's intellectual approach to the game, I learned to hit my opponent a variety of shots in an effort to discover his weakness and then exploit it. My goal was to reduce the other player's ability and to this day, when I play someone who is much weaker than me, I find they try too hard to win points and so make more

---

3. A good forty years later, when I was in my fifties, a young woman at the courts where I played in Maine was a strong enough player to go to the Nick Bolleteri camp in Florida. When she came home, we would sometimes play and despite her walloping the ball with lots of topspin, I was able to beat her regularly because I always knew where she was going to hit the ball and she never knew where I was going to hit it. Her lack of court instinct severely limited her career.

errors, widening the gap and making their own situation worse. By attempting to play beyond their ability, they do worse. The same could be said of how people in other situations get themselves in greater trouble by attempting to fake what they know rather than admit their limitations.

Buddy was the first to instill in me the understanding that excellence is attained only through discipline. Not only would I hit against the backboard, able to return hundreds of balls without missing, but Buddy would use his ball machine for exercises on the court, where he would mark sections with pieces of string, then have us hit a hundred backhands, fed to us by the ball machine, down the line, between the piece of string and the sideline. He made these practice sessions enjoyable enough so that I actually looked forward to them and when I would play a match, I would be happy to keep the ball going over the net exactly where I wanted while my opponents lost all patience and self-destructed.

Buddy taught us that to lose one's temper was a sure way to lose one's skill. In 1987 he wrote me on the subject: "If you cannot control yourself, how are you going to control your hand, and if you cannot control your hand, how are you going to control the racket face, and if you cannot control the racket face, how are you going to control the ball, and if you cannot control the ball how are you going to be tactical in your play." That sentence is typical of the Buddy Goeltz philosophy of sport and life.

I continued playing and enjoying tennis through high school, ending my career there by losing in the finals of the New England Interscholastics to my teammate Dick Hoehn and in the semis of the Eastern Interscholastics to Donald Dell, the last time I played him competitively. By college I had begun to lose interest and even though I played two years there, my heart was not in it. After college, I actually stopped playing and then picked it up again ten years later in Maine, but by then I was no longer my old, ignorant, nerveless self and found the extreme butterflies of the first few games distinctly unenjoyable. But recreational tennis allowed me an unfettered outlet for my competitive streak and I always had the urge to win.

Tennis brought me my moment of notoriety at Exeter. Senior year, the New England Interscholastics were played there and my semifinal opponent was Don Hicks, someone I had played several times in fairly even matches throughout New England. The day prior to our match, his older brother started taking bets on the outcome and word spread through the school. Because of rain, the match was moved inside, into the cage, where two courts were laid out on the dirt floor and students could watch from the wooden track suspended above.

Much to my surprise, half the school seemed to have come out for the match and all the other competitors were there. I did win, in three sets, but with the largest gallery I would ever face, many of the spectators stamping on the wooden track for effect whenever I made a good shot. In general, I cannot recall specific matches and I cannot remember specific points from that one but I do remember believing throughout that I was going to win, even after I had lost a set. That confidence is a crucial element in any sport.

I didn't like the fact that for years many of my Exeter classmates defined me primarily as a tennis player because of that match, but Buddy Goeltz had taught me well and my reliance on strategy and all the years of practice had paid off. His lessons about tennis and life had been effectively absorbed. I was also helped by the fact Don Hicks's brother had given me an added incentive to win, a benefit at a time when I was losing my enthusiasm for tennis as other interests began to enter my life.

During those years of heavy-duty tennis, I was also invited to sit in the family living room after a dinner party, an educational experience far beyond anything I could have received at school and one that was to determine the path I would choose in life.

At the age of twelve, I put on my blue blazer and necktie and listened quietly as the men discussed current affairs. I recall James "Scotty" Reston, the Washington Bureau Chief for the New York Times, and Alan Barth, an editorial writer for the Washington Post, and Walter Lippmann. J. William Fulbright, chairman of the Senate Foreign Relations Committee was there, as was former ambassador to Russia and presidential candidate W. Averell Harriman. I recall Leon Keyseling, who had been on Harry Truman's board of economic advisers, arguing why a shorter workweek would be beneficial. He said that leisure time was going to be the next great engine of economic growth and with a shorter workweek, people would use their leisure time productively, creating new demand for products and services.

Of course, I never said anything. I just listened. And then I read the newspapers to learn more about the subjects they were discussing, and I saw some of the same ideas show up in the columns and editorials of those I had listened to a few days before.

The living room gatherings were not just political. When I was in high school, my father pursued his interest in artists and was involved with a group called the Institute for Contemporary Arts, which invited speakers who would often show up at our house before or after their scheduled public appearances.

One such visitor was Marcel Duchamp who must have earned many a dinner with his anecdotes. He told a story, which seemed faintly scandalous at the time, about making a film of his most famous painting, *Nude Descending a Staircase*.

He described how a young woman had offered her parents' New York apartment to make the film because it had a long, sweeping staircase. They had been filming for some time and had taken a break to cook up a snack in the kitchen when they heard someone come in the front door, and the star of the film, clad only in an apron wrapped around her waist, went to see who it was—the greatly shocked owners of the apartment. He had probably told the story many times, but that night he was telling it on the couch in our living room and I have always remembered it even though it sounds much less risqué and enchanting than it did in the 1950s.

The Washington conversations continued in Kennebunkport with a steady stream of guests, some on their way farther Down East to Mt. Desert Island where many Washingtonians summered. The Lippmanns always stopped by, and we developed a ritual of journeying to the home of our next-door neighbor, Kenneth Roberts, the successful historical novelist and a wonderful raconteur. He was also very conservative and could be expected to disagree with much of what Lippmann believed. Despite their ideological differences, the two got along wonderfully, sparring with both enthusiasm and respect. They listened to one another carefully and were willing to change an opinion when the other, using facts and logic in combination, could make a point felt to be irrefutable. Those evenings left me with the belief that good conversation, particularly about public policy and by persons of opposing viewpoints, was great entertainment. What I did not realize was that the already rare phenomenon of sequential conversation—as opposed to ideological rigidity—was soon to become even more rare and today nears extinction.

After two years at Landon, I had moved on to Exeter where I received the most important part of my in-school education, the most exceptional education I was ever to receive from a school.

I have since come to the conclusion that the most memorable educational experience in a young person's life is going away from home for the first time and being, more or less, on one's own. For most people, this means college. For me, it meant Exeter.

Exeter is unlike any other high school. First of all, its campus is the size of a small college and like a college, it is a self-contained society. Not only does it have some of the best teachers to be found anywhere, but even then it had some of the best students. This was where boys—in 1953 it was only boys—who really wanted to learn went and where everyone was expected to learn. I never met a poor student while at Exeter. Some were brilliant; some were only normally intelligent. Almost all felt the peer pressure to achieve academically. Although I did not run with the athletic elite (lacrosse and hockey were the sports to play), even the jocks respected the really good students and I was never aware of anyone being looked down on for academic success, for being a grind. This is not to say there weren't outcasts. There were, especially among those who were shy and lacked social skills, but excelling in class brought universal admiration.

We knew about other prep schools and their reputations and we admitted freely, even condescendingly, that St. Paul's boys came from a higher social stratum and Groton was the traditional school of American patricians. But none was more academically challenging than Exeter. Exeter also had the greatest freedom.

During my years, there were plenty of sons of the wealthy and talented. Jay Rockefeller (John D. IV), now a U.S. senator, was in the class ahead of me; Jack Heinz, who would also become a U.S. senator, was in the class behind.[4] Mike Hobson, whose mother had written

4. Exeter was rigid about equality of treatment, and no one could leave for even a special weekend event until after classes on Saturday at noon. In 1953, when Jack Heinz's family was taking him to the coronation of Queen Elizabeth, they sent a car to pick him up and

Gentleman's Agreement, was in my class and a friend. John Pierson's father had been the golden boy in my father's class at Yale, 1927.

Although Exeter prided itself in its diversity and made a big thing of how many students came from the West Coast or from public schools, it was still dominated by children of the Eastern establishment. But within our little bubble, merit ruled, both in the classroom and extracurricularly.

Education at Exeter is built around the Harkness table, an oval table that seated approximately twelve students. The very structure forced the students to face one another and participate in dialogue. The teacher led the class and provided basic information—more data was imparted by the teacher in math than in English—but essentially the students taught one another. If a student wanted to participate in that classroom discussion, and everyone did or was highly encouraged to do so, the student had to be well prepared. Homework was not a chore; homework was the ammunition one needed to participate.

I recall a particular class in tenth-grade English with Robert Bates, a teacher we admired as an international-class mountain climber who had attempted K2 in the Himalayas.

The assignment was Joseph Conrad's short novel, *The End of the Tether,* and as we progressed, Mr. Bates kept asking us what was underlying the actions of the protagonist. He never told us and if we could not answer that day, he left the question to the next class, when we had read more of the book and might have a better idea.

At some point, I realized I did not know what a tether was or what function it served and so looked it up in the dictionary to learn it was a restraining leash for animals by which they are kept within a certain radius in a field. This made me realize that the protagonist was being restrained and that he was blind. With that understanding, everything else fell into place.

take him to Logan Airport. The car was a maroon Mercedes and it stopped in front of Dunbar Hall, one of the large dining centers. The chauffeur, in livery, got out to open the back door for Jack, age fourteen. With a good portion of the school watching, Jack waved the chauffeur off and went to the passenger side to let himself in so he could ride in the front seat with the chauffeur. When he grabbed the handle to open the door, it came off in his hand. We applauded. Jack died young in a plane crash and his widow married John F. Kerry.

But at Exeter, one did not blurt out the answer. Even though I had been there only a few months, I had picked up the protocol and I waited for Mr. Bates to ask his question again. Exerting massive self-control, I did not answer first but let some others grope for the wrong answer. At what I determined to be the right time, I offered the answer: He's going blind. As soon as I said it, everyone else realized I was correct. Such were the memorable victories around the Harkness table.

This may sound terribly competitive and in some cases it was, but one quickly became so accustomed to the give and take of the classroom that the idea of competitiveness disappeared. At least for me it did, which may say more about my enjoyment of mental competitiveness than it does about an actual lack of competition. Those classes developed in me an intellectual curiosity and a love of informed debate that I have never been able to shed. Indeed, I had a girlfriend in college who finally became so fed up with my compulsion to always discuss issues that she told me I made the lousiest small talk she had ever experienced. Then she dumped me.

Exeter's reputation for competitiveness—this was what everyone mentioned when you told them where you went to school—was not undeserved. We had three debating societies, two in direct competition with one another and they were the natural extension of the classroom, with students using all their skills to defeat one another in argument. Formal debate was a common school activity then and it was seen as a model of argumentation. Speakers for each side made an affirmative presentation to state their case, then the rebuttal debater attacked the other side's presentation, and even the rebutters were rebutted. Like other debaters, I wanted to be the rebutter. It was the most fun and it was the most prestigious. Thinking on one's feet, developing counterargument in a matter of minutes was the goal. Impartial judges scored one for logical argument and presentation. Facts not presented and arguments not made did not count. Partly as a consequence of debating, I came to believe that logic and facts marshalled in a coherent way should be how policy makers determined the proper course of action.

I was president of one of the debating societies, the Golden Branch, and as such arranged a mock trial on the issue of euthanasia.

Instead of a standard debate with exposition and rebuttal, we would stage it as a trial, with my having written the basic scripts for the key witnesses who were allowed a certain amount of ad libbing. The attorneys on both sides were on their own as one side argued for the mercy killing of the vegetable-like child and the other argued against it. They were like traditional debaters and their role was to cut to the heart of the matter.

I was gratified by the interest the debate aroused and our school paper, the Exonian, covered it as an event. The defendant, who had killed his birth-damaged child, was convicted by the jury. I was the judge. To my surprise, a group of younger students staged an abduction of the defendant to save him from his sentence, a turn of events luridly covered by the Exonian, much to my satisfaction. The abduction, based on emotion rather than logic, was closer to reality than my vision of the power of detached logic.

Everyone had his group at Exeter and mine included John Pierson, Pancho Mayer, Bill Edgar, and Moose Enders. Our meeting place was the Exonian offices where we sat around and smoked unfiltered cigarettes, sometimes choking on a Gauloise, and listened to Joe Hill songs. Our interests all leaned toward the literary and revolved around the Exonian, the literary magazine, and the Lantern Club, our literary discussion group where such people as Elia Kazan and Budd Schulberg met with us and discussed issues we raised. We had all read Schulberg, especially What Makes Sammy Run, and their movies, such as On the Waterfront, were popular at the time. Kazan had a son at Exeter and Schulberg was an alumnus.

Most of my friends were in Darcy Curwen's senior English class, considered the elite class. I did not make it into this coveted group the first time around but harassed my English teacher so much, proclaiming that I was way ahead of the other students in the class where I had been assigned, that he finally gave me the transfer I so desperately wanted. In retrospect, the teacher I left, Sheldon Leonard, was probably a better teacher than Curwen, but I wanted to be in the best class and like so much of Exeter, the other students proved more important than the teacher. We wrote 750-word "themes" every weekend, sometimes essays, sometimes fiction. We received not only the teacher's detailed criticism, but often read our pieces for the rest of the class who tore them apart. A disproportionate number of the themes written for Mr. Curwen's class were developed into pieces that appeared in the school literary magazine, the *Review*.

Although anyone who goes to Exeter writes a great deal, between course work and the *Exonian*, I was writing all the time. I was still not a good writer and did not have the graceful style some of my friends, especially Pancho Mayer, had already developed but I persevered and through practice alone, my writing gradually improved. Buddy Goeltz would have been proud of me.

My placement in Mr. Leonard's English class was as close as I ever came to being tracked into a lower level and I clearly had the determination to change the situation. My guess is that my burning desire to be with my friends and those I considered my academic peers had as much to do with Mr. Leonard's decision to back my transfer as did his belief in my talents as a student. Before he actually let me transfer, he did make some stipulations, raising his expectations for me above those he had for the rest of the class. They were goals I willingly met with extra work.

My academic career at Exeter was a success. Although I had flunked my French and Latin entrance exams, I was later able to accelerate my status in both those subjects, skipping Latin 3 so I could read the *Aeneid* with Norman L. Hatch, a legendary instructor, in my senior year. Mr. Hatch had been a lacrosse player and he liked to use a six-foot rod, designed to open and shut the tall windows, as a pointer, holding it at its base and keeping the tip steady, no easy task and an obvious indication of his forearm strength. There was an old and perhaps apocryphal story of a student botching a translation so badly that Mr. Hatch jumped out the window, an apparent suicide attempt. I believed it enough to look out the window and discover that an embankment ran up against the outside wall so the drop was no more than a few feet.

Mr. Hatch demanded exactitude and knew every available translation—called a trot—we might seek to cut corners. If you were going to use a trot, you had better alter the translation to get it by Mr. Hatch.

Similarly, I was allowed to take an accelerated year so I ended up in French 5, able to hold a literary discussion on almost any subject and having translated every word in *Madame Bovary*. I was to find, when I spent the summer in Grenoble after my senior year, that while I had a good working comprehension of literary French, I knew little of the practical French needed to order a meal or engage in other practical transactions. And nothing in my instruction prepared me for the so-called Turkish toilets, the hole in the ceramic floor, still common in France in 1955. Whenever I read of high-school learning standards that call for graduates to be "fluent" in a foreign language, I think of my excellent instruction and my lack of fluency. Not yet indoctrinated in the complacency that all the world should speak English, we had the motivation to learn foreign languages, but not the skills to overcome starting so late, in the junior-high years at best.

All of us tested well. We had plenty of practice and an overwhelming self-confidence. We didn't clutch at the idea of a test; we relished it. We were the same way about interviews and throughout life I always looked forward to the job and admissions interviews that I subsequently learned many other people dreaded. I not only liked to talk about myself and my interests, I enjoyed interviewing the interviewer.

Partly due to our superior education at Exeter and partly due to our ability to test well, I received advanced placement at Yale in both English and French, getting credit for freshman-level courses and being allowed to immediately pursue more advanced courses in both. Had I chosen, I could have simply taken the French as a distributional requirement, making it unnecessary for me to take any further foreign language at all. I did take one more French course but after my summer in Grenoble, I was more interested in learning the colloquial language than in comparative literature. I also realized that my French teachers at Exeter had been better.

On the other hand, my advanced placement in English allowed me as a freshman to take a poetry course from Cleanth Brooks, one of the founders of the New Criticism and an exceptional teacher. He taught me how to read poetry and instilled in me a lifelong appreciation of work from John Donne and T. S. Eliot.

Those were the days when a decent prep-school record and a legacy (my father was a Yale alumnus) made Ivy League entry a sure thing. About half our Exeter class went to Harvard, 25 percent to Yale, 20 percent to Princeton, and 5 percent elsewhere. This was ripe for reform and was changed a decade later. The greatest weakness at Yale, as it had been at Exeter, was the relative dearth of public high-school students, especially the unconventional. Of course, there were no women at either Exeter or Yale but as a student body, Exeter may have been more diverse than the Yale I entered in 1955.

Even though we had not been particularly close at Exeter, Don Louchheim and I decided to room together at Yale and remained good friends for life, exercising our innate competitiveness on annual ski trips.[5] We specifically asked for a quadruple room in Vanderbilt Hall and said we wanted as roommates a student from Europe and one from public school on the West Coast. It was one of the better decisions we made as the roommates Yale selected were Jon Schleuning from Oregon and Alexander "Phoebus" Mourelatos from Greece.

We had great fun with Jon whose perverse sense of humor matched ours. He was also willing to live in the chaos we preferred, a chaos that almost got us kicked out of our room. Every so often, an inspector came by to check the condition of the rooms and one time too many, we did our cleanup only after a student yelled up from the first floor that the room checker was on his way. We piled everything, mainly dirty clothes, into the double-doored closet in our bedroom and when the inspector opened the doors, he was inundated by dirty underwear. The bedroom Don and I shared was so bad it took the pressure off Jon and Phoebus; our parents received notices, much to their displeasure, warning we were about to be evicted. It mentioned the cost of our finding accommodations off-campus. Tuition, room, and board was then $3,500.

Academically, Yale is something of a blur. Freshman year I got in a major argument with the graduate student teaching our seminar in a Milton course when he said he was going to give us a true/false test on *Paradise Lost* and I told him it was a stupid way to teach. He challenged me to do well on the exam and I crammed for two days, reading the poem over and over again. The test turned out to be quotes that we were supposed to identify as correct or incorrect, sometimes with only a word or two changed to make it incorrect. If the test had

5. Don and I, and his brother Hal, have now skied together at practically every major ski area in the Western United States and Canada.

really been sophisticated, the errors would have been identifiable because they threw off the meter or used an anachronistic word. That was not the case. It did not measure comprehension. Despite the subtle differences that could be identified only by total familiarity with the poem, I did well thanks to my heavy-duty cramming. When he handed back the tests, the instructor made a point of saying that overall the class had scored poorly and he would have scaled the grades. He couldn't, he said, because one student—here he looked at me—had scored above 90 and therefore the scaling of scores would not raise the grades for everyone else. The idea was to get the other students to hold it against me for doing well on the test. They reacted with indifference.

That episode was typical of the ups and downs of my Yale academic career. If I really enjoyed a course, I studied and got good grades. More often, I took good courses and tried to get by with as little work as possible. In most cases, the standards were so high that even operating at half level I was forced to learn a good deal. One semester Don and I decided to have a contest to see who could get the best grades and we really did study, both ending up in the top 10 percent of the class. After that we felt we had proved our point and generally went back to getting by with B averages.

I chose to enter the Honors English program which meant I had to write a senior essay on my own. I chose the novels of Robert Penn Warren and had the avuncular Cleanth Brooks as an adviser. Having read through it again recently, I can report the essay was so-so. It was cleanly written but really did not have any great insights. Warren's *All the King's Men* is excellent and holds up today but was frowned on then as being too "historical," and political, a thinly disguised biography of Huey Long of Louisiana. It is a major American novel in a prose style that holds up despite its intricate imagery. His other books tend to reflect his obsession with Southern self-immolation over slavery and segregation. With my mother representing Southern genteel racism and my father a Northern abolitionist and growing up in the racially ambivalent but segregated atmosphere of Washington, I was also fascinated by the subject and this may have been a reason I liked Warren's lesser novels. In retrospect, it is easy for me to say now they were spotty, with real insights into the South but often verging on potboilers. Today his reputation rests primarily on his poetry.

But I did learn a great deal from doing the essay, just because I had to do it on my own, without the discipline of regular class assignments, and I had to organize and write a paper of more than 100 pages. This experience was one of the motivations behind my founding the Public Policy Scholars at the University of Maine decades later.

Sophomore year, we lost Phoebus who pursued a much more academic life and seemed to be working full time as an assistant to professors to pay his tuition. Jon and Don and I pinned together with Aubrey Peterson and Dick Maltby, two Exeter graduates, and stayed on the same entryway, Linonia, in Branford College for the next three years, first living in a quad and then in adjacent singles. Junior year, we lost Jon, who went back to the West Coast where he later became a successful architect.

Tennis was so disorganized at Yale that I quit after sophomore year and spent most of my time going with my brother Warren, two years ahead of me, to Smith College for dates and acting as his assistant as he raced an Austin-Healey in Sports Car Club of America (SCCA) races in New England. My senior year and his second in architecture school, Warren almost won the national championship for his class and we had a wonderful year of traveling as far as Elkhart Lake, Wisconsin, and Danville, Virginia, on the circuit.

My best academic memory is taking history of art courses with my brother, who was a history of art major. Studying with him was a major advantage, not only because of his knowledge of art but because of his knowledge of the system. The basic testing in history of art was to throw a slide on the screen and have the students identify it and explain why they had reached the conclusions they did.

Taking advantage of both my short-term and visual memories, Warren used to run me through almost every known work of the artists under study just before an exam so there was seldom a slide shown on the test that we had not been looking at the day before. Since I could recognize the artist immediately, I would turn the process around and never say I knew who the artist was because I recognized the picture. Instead, I would repeat what the professor had told us were the important characteristics of that artist and sometimes that painting and then say this analysis had made me conclude who the artist was. Obviously knowing the artist first made the process much easier and years later when I was reading about the forger of Vermeer, Van Meegeren, who painted his fakes to meet the criteria propounded by the expert Bredius, I felt certain the forger would have done well as a history of art student at Yale.

When Warren and I were taking the same history of art classes— I particularly remember Baroque Art—we had the highest grades in the class.

Unfortunately, I had a tendency to repeat the problems I got into with the Milton instructor. In modern art, taught by George Heard Hamilton, then well known and instrumental in getting Yale to buy such painters as Ad Rheinhart, whose work I found excruciatingly dull, I got similarly snippy (or arrogant, take your pick) on an exam.

One section of the test was the names of paintings for which we were supposed to name the artists. This might have been all right for *Guernica* with its important political overtones but when it came to *Composition in Blue*, I thought it a little ridiculous. I did answer as instructed. However, the final essay asked us to comment on the course and I used the opportunity to let loose about the exam and how it was indicative of teaching history of art as a cocktail party sport, allowing Yale graduates to drop names with no understanding of the art itself. Although I had aced the rest of the test—I did know the paintings by name—I received a C on the essay, with no comment. The grader was not taking my bait.

Despite my reservations about the quality of my education and my sporadic enthusiasm for study, I did receive a very different education than most students do today. Part of the difference was due to lingering traditions.

Taking Latin at Exeter was more than an exercise in memorizing a dead language. Through reading Ovid, I learned the traditional myths which, as in Homer, are not just wonderful stories but are an explanation of the relationship between god and man. Who can forget a story like that of Io, who, through the vengeance of Hera, angry that Zeus has seduced the girl, punished not her consort Zeus but the innocent girl whom she turns into a cow in her father's herd. I still feel the poignancy of Io, now trapped inside the animal, trying to make eye contact with her father in order to tell him she still lives.

When reading Virgil, I not only learned the Trojan side of the war with the Greeks and began to understand the direct linkage between our language and that of the Roman empire, I also came to understand the structure of language, how the most subtle change in case or word placement can alter meaning. Thanks to Mr. Hatch, I also learned intellectual rigor. Getting it half right was not tolerated.

In college, we read the Greek tragedies where I became familiar with the sin of hubris or overarching and therefore destructive pride. By example rather than direct preaching I came to understand that being too sure of oneself and refusing to identify the signals of one's own misperceptions can lead to disastrous results. Self-doubt, a key element in man's gradual ascendancy, has fallen out of fashion among our contemporary leaders.

We read the Bible as literature and parable rather than as gospel, an exercise that instilled in me forever the insight that whether or not either testament is God's word, it is God's word interpreted by man. Of course, one needs a basic knowledge of the Bible because it is so ingrained in our culture but it helps to recognize that contemporary references to its meaning are often interpretations that are not universally shared. We read Shakespeare, all of it. We read poetry from Horace, famous verses of which I can still quote, *Dulce et decorum est pro patria mori*, on the nobility of dying for one's country, and we read the anti-war realism of Randall Jarrell where a dead airman is washed from his ball turret with a hose.

In reading poetry we found the rest of our education pertinent. We could understand the allusions—to the Bible, to Shakespeare, to the classics in Latin and Greek, even, in many cases to events contemporary to the poetry itself—and enjoy the extra dimension they gave what we read, without having to resort to footnotes. Especially in learning to read poetry, we not only appreciated the benefits of a shared familiarity with the landmarks of Western culture, but we became careful readers.

We were assigned "great books" that I have read again on my own and appreciated even more as I grew older and had more experience to bring to my reading. Rereading *War and Peace* was a case in point;

forty years out of college I found it a compelling adventure and love story as well as a commentary on life. We read literary landmarks like James Joyce's *Ulysses* that I have promised myself ever since I would read again on my own, a task I have never accomplished. Had I not read it under supervision in college, I never would have read it.

We were exposed to the great philosophers, particularly to those whose ideas are the underpinning of American democracy, such as John Locke and John Stuart Mill. We understood Thomas Jefferson's belief that an informed electorate would make democracy possible. We understood the concept of natural law, that humankind was special and had rights neither a single despot nor a despotic majority could remove. We learned that pure democracy would allow the majority to inflict its will on the minority and that's why the concept of minority rights was codified in the first ten amendments to our Constitution.

We had great lecturers, like B. Brand Blanchard whom I heard lay out all the arguments great philosophers had made to prove the existence of God. And then, after he had convinced me, one after the other, that the proof was valid, I heard him destroy those same arguments, one after the other, until he left me with the conviction that belief in God is a leap of faith, and must be accepted as such. Just as important, he and others taught me how to question effectively because a key to learning is asking the right question.

I developed a moral and ethical code based on Western cultural traditions and I came away from school with the conviction that one could obtain the information one needed to make important decisions. Even if we could no longer meet the Jeffersonian ideal, where an individual could make sound decisions about government based on his own personal experience, I had no doubts about my ability, primarily through reading, to educate myself continually on a changing world.

Despite my realization in retrospect that college was part of a thorough education, I was so burned out with school in 1959 that I skipped graduation and took a week on my own, driving a red Simca convertible that the company gave my mother, through the Loire Valley. My French was still pretty good—everyone thought

I was Canadian—and I wandered where I wanted to go, eating salades de tomates, drinking wonderful local wines, and visiting chateaux.

As planned, Aubrey Peterson joined me after graduation and we went all over Europe together. We budgeted $10 a day and when we spent too much on good meals or other extravagances, we made up the difference by staying in ratty hotels, only a few of which seemed to be the places where prostitutes brought their customers.

Aubrey fixed us up with a double date with a couple of girls from home who were in Geneva, and since our hotel lacked facilities, we went to the beach and soaped ourselves up in the shallow water, causing the rest of the swimmers to scatter as if they had sighted a shark.

We visited museums, from the Prado in Madrid to the Kunst-historiches Museum in Vienna with its fabulous Breughels. I can still remember the Goyas in Spain even better than the 10:00 P.M. dinners washed down with pitchers of Sangria.

It was an idyllic trip. Cannes was still a fishing village and I was to be shocked on driving through only fifteen years later to see that it had developed into a congested city. Everywhere we went, we felt welcome. Americans were liked. We spoke French and attempted a few words in Italian and German. It was long enough after the war— on that first trip, in 1955, the ravages of war were all too evident in many cities, especially in Italy—so that prosperity had begun and the rubble had been removed. And it was cheap.

My own experience left me with some strong opinions on the subject of education and our headmaster at Exeter, William G. Saltonstall, had told us repeatedly that we were participating in an experiment that should be replicated in other schools. Exeter had received a major grant from the Standard Oill baron Edward Harkness to do something truly innovative, and the result had been the Harkness tables and their emphasis on peer teaching.

Years later I was to assign a *Maine Times* story on Exeter to our education writer, Jeff Fisher, who also taught English at the local high school in Maine. Jeff demurred at first, saying what happened at Exeter was irrelevant to public school because Exeter had so much money and because it had its pick of students. I countered that he should spend a couple of days there and then make his decision about whether it deserved a story. Jeff did as I had asked and when he came back, he was enthusiastic, saying he had students with whom he could institute the peer-teaching practices he had witnessed. His subsequent piece on Exeter was reprinted as a cover piece in the alumni magazine. The school told me it was the best piece they had ever read on what Exeter education was all about, a legacy of Mr. Saltonstall's telling us to spread the word about what made an Exeter education different.

I believed in education, was grateful that I had been exposed to such a good education, in and out of school, and wanted others to share a similar experience. This left me a natural education reformer the rest of my life but also out of the mainstream.

One of the disasters of our time has been how the latest educational fix so quickly becomes conventional wisdom until today we have a President, George W. Bush, who proudly told the graduating class at Yale that he was an example of how far one could go without being interested in getting a good education. His disinterest set the agenda for American education—testing, testing, and testing. This uniquely incurious President stands in direct contradiction to what I consider the best motivation for learning—curiosity.

After college, I thought about becoming a teacher but the certification requirements, most of them having to do with education courses that struck me as worthless, always put me off. Through the years, I often spoke to students or even ran a single class, successfully I thought, because I was able to communicate to the students some of my sense of enthusiasm for the material. And, thanks to Exeter, I listened to what they were saying because you cannot respond to another person's argument before you fully understand what that argument is, no matter how well or poorly they articulate it.

In 1986, after I had sold *Maine Times* and come into some cash, Ed Kaelber of the Maine Community Foundation (MCF) approached me about doing something with them. The MCF essentially held funds for donors and distributed them according to the donor's wishes. The donor, in return, did not have to do his own research on recipients or be harassed by people seeking money. I liked the idea but told Ed I thought the programs in place were too narrow, so he suggested I start my own fund. I wanted to do something with education other than enforce the status quo. I wanted to establish a model that would serve as a beacon for real change in what I considered stagnant teaching methods.

The idea I came up with was for undergraduates at the University of Maine, based on my belief that students should be able to have a meaningful academic experience before graduate school and that it should be in a public institution. I wanted the students to work on a real public policy issue, a reflection of my experience with *Maine Times*, where writing a story was like having to do a term paper in three days. Believing in the collaborative experience, and hoping that students would drive each other to do better, I wanted them to work together on projects. Finally, I wanted each team to have an outside mentor.

This final idea was the most difficult to get the academic world to understand. In the first place, academics seem to know few people in the non-academic world, even in their own fields, on a statewide basis, a trend that is getting worse. Second, they conceived of a mentor as being an expert in the subject the students were researching. I did not seek someone who tells students what to think but someone who helps them reach their own informed conclusions.[6] My closest comparison is to a Supreme Court judge asking attorneys on both sides pointed and sequential questions.

The concept of the mentor whose knowledge was informed by personal experience collided head-on with what has become the prevailing methodology in Political Science, the course umbrella under which many of the first public policy scholars fell. The accepted methodology, it seems, is to construct a questionnaire and send it out to a group of people. No personal interviews. No follow-up questions. Nothing that would taint the "objectivity" of the written survey.

This, of course, was just the opposite of what experience had taught me. Only through direct questioning, where one can see

6. In 2003 we held a seminar with teachers and students in which former governor Angus King was to participate on the second day. As we were closing the first day's session, I asked the students to think overnight about what they wanted to ask the former governor and to consider follow-up questions. One of the teachers then suggested what the students should be asking Angus, to which I replied, somewhat sharply, "No, that's your question. What I want to hear are their questions."

the facial expressions and body language of the person being interviewed, can an interviewer penetrate the natural facade. There must be sequential questions, each based on the person's last answer. Most students do not even know the rudiments of interviewing. They tend to telegraph their own preconceptions so baldly that many of the people from whom they should be getting information simply clam up.

My experience has been that people in direct interviews will tell you all kinds of things they would never say in a written response, and sometimes their expression will invite you to pursue a particular line of questioning, something you could never pick up on if you were not face to face. Happily, the teachers involved are now more interested in face-to-face interviews.

I put $50,000 into the project, the largest single contribution I was ever to make and more than I could afford. I also raised money from other sources, including the Betterment Fund and the New York Times Foundation. The program is still floundering, at least according to my standards, but I have asked former governor Angus King to take over my role in its direction and he has accepted, leaving me optimistic for the future.

My belief in using outside talent has been reinforced by a recent experience at the local middle school, at Woolwich, where my wife Eunice, who runs the computer lab there, enlisted my participation in helping eighth graders to write. The teacher, a bright young woman named Courtney Culley, welcomed my participation and we gave the students three assignments. First, they were to report on a school trip to Mt. Battie in Camden. Second, they were to review a play, *The Face on the Barroom Floor*, that the whole school was attending. And third, my particular assignment, they were to write a short story about a hero, in which they demonstrated the characteristics that made the person heroic.

With the first assignment, I learned, to my amazement, that they could all write a communicative essay. Everyone told me what happened even though there was a huge variation in the spelling, grammar, and descriptive talents. The spelling and grammar I left to Ms. Culley after noting the most common and repetitive mistakes, just what you would expect, such as confusing the homophones *there*, *their*, and *they're*. Instead, I focused on descriptive qualities, on the details some of them used effectively to give a real feeling for what the trip was like. As examples, I quoted from the students' own work.

For the second assignment, they had reviewed a play the entire school had attended. I had asked them to give me their opinion of the play and to back that opinion with specific examples. Since the play was melodrama reduced to farce, there were mixed opinions. Some took it seriously and thought it stupid. Others understood the premise and found it funny. Few wrote a coherent review, mostly because they did not understand the genre, probably never having read reviews themselves.

With this second assignment I was already beginning to separate the individuals who were superior writers and even those who were diligent. Typically, the writing would start out well, with good punctuation and spelling. Then as the students tired or became bored, the writing would deteriorate, capitalization would suffer, spelling would get bad. Most of the students were losing their motivation before the review was finished.

The final assignment really separated the students. They were all over the lot. Some just punted, giving me a few paragraphs and quitting. There were others so autobiographical as to be embarrassing. And a few were surprising.

One boy wrote about a dogfight over England during the Battle of Britain. He had such a good grasp of the technology—he knew the names of all the airplanes on both sides and even the caliber of machine guns they used—that I thought he might be plagiarizing. But some of his grammatical errors indicated that he was not, that I was simply reading a piece by a boy who was fascinated by the period and had read a great deal about it.

A girl, the obvious writing star of the class, turned in a seventeen-page error-free story, no spelling errors, no bad grammar. All it lacked was heart that could have only come from someone with more life experience. Since you can't expect too much life experience from a fourteen-year-old, what she needed was more reading, especially short stories, and I would have liked to have been in the position to make specific suggestions to her. I did let her know I would give her a reading list if she wanted, but she did not follow up and I really don't blame her.

In every case, I wrote individual comments on all the papers, as I had received at Exeter and Yale, and with the short stories, the comments were sometimes quite lengthy. Ms. Culley was most receptive, pointing out that with ninety students, the time I had put into my comments was something she simply couldn't do. (Also, as an editor for so many years, the work was easy for me and I was fast.)

I won't claim that after only three sessions I knew every student, but I did know the levels of achievement of many of them—and all without testing. I also realized what all of them needed—motivation. But motivation of different types. Some just had to be convinced that writing could be fun, that it was more than leaving a message for the repairman, although in later life that might be the extent of the demand on their writing skills. Others had to realize they had innate talent and there were rewards in developing that talent. And the top echelon needed to do more writing, more selective reading, and to be pushed into new areas. While I could be helpful on all levels, I could be most helpful with the last category because I had obviously read more widely than almost any middle-school English teacher, partially because I was so much older and partially because I had the time to read and was not correcting papers for ninety students on a daily basis.

Another fact that became obvious when I had asked the students to write fiction was how little they had read and how their model was television where there is so little character development and so much action, much of it illogical. Many of them wrote stories of great violence where the only definition of the hero was that he won. When I tried to explain to them that I didn't care if their heroes won or lost because they had not been portrayed as people I could care about, I uncovered a generation gap. I was brought up on characterization in fiction; they were brought up on action.

This experience reinforced my belief that the single most important innovation in pre-college education would be the effective use of mentors. By that I don't mean throwing someone into a class, even as my wife threw me into the writing project. I mean wise and controlled use of talented people in the community, on a person-by-person basis, adapting not only to their talents but to their schedules and commitment. Similarly, the mentors' talents would have to be carefully matched to student needs, a coordination between administrators and teachers that seems radical in today's public schools where administrators are so removed from the classroom.

For several years I had had a Little Brother, Buddy Dudley, under the Big Brothers program and it was most rewarding, if fatiguing.[7] I had tried to enlist some of my friends—the program is constantly in need of men—but they had demurred at the time commitment and the logistics. However, these same men would have participated on a more limited and directed program, such as one offered in the schools where they could participate for a couple of hours a week or a student might come to them on a regular basis.

Just as I had lined up mentors for the Public Policy program at the university, and no one had ever refused me, I was convinced I could have lined up similarly qualified mentors on the local level but these are not people who are about to waste their time. The schools would have to have a sophisticated mentor director in place to make sure such talents were not wasted for there is no faster way to lose a volunteer than to not use him/her effectively.

In a time when we seem to be directing our energies to measuring how students are doing comparatively—through standardized testing—we are neglecting how to teach them better or at least to teach them anything other than how to do better on the test. Any decent teacher can evaluate a student even more quickly than I did. By reading their writing, especially their writing about what they have read, a teacher can quickly evaluate students in a much more subtle manner than any test will reveal. The real question is to identify individual student needs and address them.

Those needs, of course, are going to vary widely and in some cases no school is going to overcome what has occurred elsewhere, particularly in the home. But what should be obvious is that no single teacher is going to be able to give the kind of individualized attention to every student that will allow each to reach the peak of his/her ability. That's where the help is needed and I can think of no better way to break the logjam than the judicious use of mentors.

---

7. The greatest reward came the day his mother told me she had been lecturing Buddy on how he should not emulate his father, who had left him and his sisters in his quest for ever-younger women. Buddy replied that because he had been with me (and Eunice) for three years, he knew how men were supposed to act.

Six

The Path to Journalism Is Paved with Clear Intention

Libby Donahue, my political mentor and surrogate maiden aunt, told me I was destined to be a journalist, not a novelist. She was correct.

She contended that novelists mull over events for years and then distill their experiences into fiction. Journalists need to write immediately about what they have seen and approach events much more literally. I fit the second category.

Long before I reached the fork in the road that separated a career in journalism from one in creative writing, I had started in the direction of journalism.

I was brought up in a time and in a family where journalism mattered. Everyone read the newspaper at breakfast and even if I focused on the comics and a columnist named Bill Gold, who dealt mainly in human interest trivia, I read the paper at breakfast as well. I also read the back of cereal boxes and the dividers in the Shredded Wheat box.

In my world, reading was the dominant source of information. I remain baffled that so few people read today and even then read only publications that reflect a viewpoint that already matches theirs. While television is the dominant source of news for Americans, only a third of the population watches the evening national news and even the small number of stories they see have been chosen for them by someone else.

We did listen to the radio for special events, a presidential address, or Edward R. Murrow, but mostly the radio was for entertainment. Almost no one had television. After school I would listen to Jack Armstrong, All American Boy, alone in my room, and Sunday evenings, when we all ate chopped liver and egg together without guests, we would listen as a family to Amos 'n Andy and Sam Spade, everyone commenting.[1] We were a family of critics.

Print was where the really serious stuff happened and the commentators were at the top of the heap. If something was to be uncovered, Drew Pearson would uncover it, and according to my father, if Pearson said it, it was probably true. Walter Winchell was unreliable trash.

I do not recall my father ever criticizing the press. To him, they were allies, the conduit through which new ideas were transmitted to decision makers and to the public in general. As a result, he devoured newspapers, retreating every morning to the bathroom where there was a speaker for the hi fi, to listen to music, smoke cigarettes, and read the *Washington Post*.

Even if I did not read the newspapers thoroughly until I was a teenager, I picked up information secondhand through dinner table conversations. And while I started with the comics, when I was interested in a topic, as I was in the Hiss-Chambers confrontation, I had only to flip a few pages to learn about it.

When I was sixteen I made my first foray into the actual practice of journalism, and the experience was the only formal training I ever had. It may have also been the best. It was certainly memorable.

The year was 1954 and I was in my next-to-last (junior) year at Exeter when I decided to "heel" for the *Exonian*, a student-run and student-controlled newspaper that published twice a week. So many students tried out for jobs at the *Exonian* that there was a screening process and the person in charge of weeding us out was Christopher (Sandy) Jencks. Exeter has always prided itself in peer teaching and there was no more stringent peer teaching than the heeling system. The upperclassmen took pride in showing their expertise and subjecting us to a boot camp regimen. To instill fear in the heelers was a sign of prowess.

Exonian journalism was rigorous and traditional. For years its editor had gone on to become the editor of the *Harvard Crimson* and the next step after that, traditionally, was a job at the *New York Times*.

---

1. I grew up disliking chopped liver, not realizing my mother could never deal with the mysteries of schmaltz. Ours was too dry and, like the herring for sale, I never grasped the ethnic significance of my father's weekly craving for the dish.

The *Exonian* office was under the main Academy Building, next to the office of the *PEAN*, the yearbook, but we of the *Exonian* considered ourselves tougher and more radical that the yearbook types. We had deadlines to meet every day and hard news to write.

As I was writing this, I checked a picture of Sandy Jencks on the dust jacket of his 1992 book, *Rethinking Social Policy*. Now a professor at Northwestern and wearing a plaid shirt, he looks absolutely benign. But fifty years ago, he scared the hell out of us. Not only would he assign the stories but after they were written, he would critique them, whether they had merited publication or not, before the entire group.

No matter what your assignment—and most of them were small, the major articles being assigned to the more experienced and already tested seniors—you worked assiduously, making sure you had written in classic pyramid style, covering the essentials in the lead paragraph. You had to be ready to answer any questions from the copious notes you had taken to write the original ten inches, and not a word longer, cuttable, sentence by sentence, from the bottom up. The lead paragraph could stand alone. Our aspiration was to master the style so thoroughly that we would one day be able, working only from notes, to call in a breaking story to the copy desk of a major newspaper and having written it so perfectly in our heads it would be printed word for word.

Another job given heelers was writing headlines to a discipline I seldom saw repeated. Depending on type size and column width, each headline has a different character count and many newspapers today allow ragged edges and jargon. Not at the *Exonian*. Every headline had to fit to the half character. In a multiple-line headline, the first line had to be able to stand by itself. Headlines had to start with a subject and could not take the easy path of starting with a verb. That was for inferior papers such as the *New York Daily News*.

When I began, I would sometimes spend an hour getting a headline right but that was expected. There were plenty of heelers to slave over a single headline, sometimes simultaneously, and have it rejected. But like doing crossword puzzles, we soon developed the vocabulary and learned the conventions. By senior year I was a facile headline writer, a talent that stood me in good stead for years to come.

Writing such headlines could be considered tedious, especially at age sixteen, but I liked doing it and appreciated the reward of discipline. If I could hit a tennis ball against a backboard for an hour, uninterrupted, I could handle headline writing. During this same period, I also enjoyed translating French poetry into English, a regular assignment in French class. There the challenge was finding the right word to fit the meaning, the meter, and the rhyme scheme.

The *Exonian* was always the most controversial organization on campus and the year Sandy Jencks and Dick Cooper were editors started off with a bang when Jencks, in his editorial in the first issue of the new school year, called a faculty/trustee report that had been completed over the summer a "nebulous blurb." The administration prevented it from going out in the mail and thus reaching alumni, parents, and presumably, trustees. We heelers admired Jencks for treating the trustees with no more diffidence—i.e., with the same contempt—than he treated us.

Although we lived in a totally cloistered world, the stories we wrote had genuine importance to us. We may have been the only ones on campus who cared about student council decisions, but we cared deeply. Our comments on the council allowed us to demonstrate our disregard for any kind of authority.

The yearbook described the 1954 *Exonian* as calculatedly controversial and as focusing on ideas. It noted criticism that sports were no longer found on the front page. The editors were accused of "yellow journalism." We wore such comments as a badge of honor.

Our senior year, under the editorship of John Pierson and Bill Edgar, we continued the tradition. Although I had not been elected to one of the editorships, I continued to find my best friends at the paper and to join in the push for what we considered reform. We criticized the student council as a bunch of dull-witted jocks and partly in consequence, I was appointed—not elected—to the council, a reinforcement of our belief in the power of the press.

When not putting out an issue on deadline and usually between 9:00 and 10:00 P.M. when underclassmen had to be back in their dorms but we seniors were allowed our extra hour to stay out, we gathered at the *Exonian* office. We smoked cigarettes and listened to Joe Hill records. Our editorials advocated the abolition of varsity sports, the Four-Year Club for students who had been there all four years, and the cum laude scholastic honor society. I can't recall why we picked such diverse groups as the subjects of our scorn, perhaps because they all represented tradition.

At the *Exonian*, we may have been policy oriented and hyper-critical—we earned the sobriquet "negos"—but we were still, at heart, kids. Despite our contempt for the traditions of others, we were bound by our own traditions and set great stock in our efforts to beat the record for speed in reporting the outcome of the Exeter-Andover football game. To do this, we took photographs in the first quarter and had them processed and scanned before halftime. The chief reporter phoned in a play-by-play account that was set in type as it was dictated. When the game ended, the story needed only a lead paragraph and a banner headline.

As the students left the stadium, about half a mile from the center of the campus, we were on the press and by the time they reached the campus, with the aid of that year's heelers forming a bucket brigade, we were handing them copies of the one-sheet *Exonian* reporting on the game. I can't remember who won the game but we had broken the record for getting the paper in the hands of readers.

We also did ambitious special editions. The year before, it had been about writers connected with Exeter, and I had successfully solicited a piece by our Kennebunkport neighbor Kenneth Roberts. The hot item for that issue was by Robert Anderson, who had just written a hit Broadway play, *Tea and Sympathy*. The set designer Jo Melziner had copied the interior of Williams House, a dormitory, for the set. The theme, a boy accused of homosexuality, was not unknown to us and, as an alumnus, Anderson used details familiar to us throughout. It seemed most of the school saw the play on Broadway. I did. With my parents.

Our special issue for 1955, a fifty-two-page magazine, was about secondary schools and my assignment was to report on my old class that was graduating from Western High School, in Washington, as its first integrated class. This was in the wake of *Brown v. Board of Education*, decided just the year before, which had declared separate schools unconstitutional.

There had been violence and the tension was running high when I visited during vacation and talked with students, many of whom I had known in grade school, and with the principal and teachers. The basic contention of my story was that the opposition was not coming from the students themselves but from a minority of parents. After I returned to Exeter, a school administration official in Washington called our principal, William G. Saltonstall, and asked that the story be suppressed on the grounds it would only fuel the disruption. Mr. Saltonstall said the decision was up to John Pierson as editor. The Washington official was a little taken aback by having to negotiate with a seventeen-year-old, but John acquiesced, another indication we were still kids and susceptible to intimidation by our elders.

I did not pursue my journalistic interests at Yale but when Jim Ottaway, who had been business manager of the *Exonian* and actually balanced the books in a professional manner, became chairman of the *Yale Daily News*, I wrote movie reviews, which provided a rationale for spending afternoons in darkened theaters watching Rock Hudson in Douglas Sirk epics rather than at the library studying.

At college I did pick up skills that would benefit any journalist, even if I did so inadvertently. As an English major, I wrote and wrote and wrote. Even if I remained stylistically unpolished, I became fast. The dominant approach at Yale was the New Criticism which was textual analysis, removed from historical or biographical context. Although I was later to turn 180 degrees philosophically, seeing literature and art as cultural history that not only had to be placed in context but that reflected the mood and development of its time, I did learn to be a careful reader. The exact meaning of words and how context altered meaning was one of the key lessons we were to reflect in our writing. It was also good training for an editor and I did not fully understand its importance until being the subject of a libel suit twenty years later.

Like all Yale freshmen taking the introductory European history course, including Bob Woodward who cites the same experience in *All the President's Men*, I had to deal with King Henry IV and Pope Gregory VII at Canossa in 1077. We were given workbooks that contained relevant original documents, in this case descriptions of the king standing barefoot in the snow when seeking the pope's absolution from his earlier excommunication. The accounts varied, with the king up to his knees in snow anywhere from a few hours to a few days.

Like all good equivocators, most of us wrote that the king had stood there anywhere from a few hours to a few days. Wrong. The point of the exercise was that we had to use common sense, no matter what the documents said, and if the king had stood barefoot in the snow even a few hours, he would have suffered severe frostbite. It can take journalists a long time to learn that just because someone in authority tells you something doesn't make it true. Yale was trying to teach us to be discerning consumers of information, not just passive receptacles.

I did spend parts of the last two summers of college working for the *Kennebunk Star*, a move that was to have much greater influence on my journalism career.

In 1957 Alexander Bacon Brook, a.k.a., Sandy, had just bought the *Star* from Perley Watson and his brother. It sold about 1,200 copies weekly, home delivered and newsstand combined, and had considerable obsolete equipment. He hired an old college acquaintance, John N. Cole, as his managing editor.

John worked there for only a couple of years, but during that time we established a deep relationship and he put his mark on the paper. He put his mark on me as well.

I practically camped out at his house, with John's first wife, Cynthia, and his two young children, Marshall and Darragh, still toddlers. John, whose Yale education had been interrupted by World War II, told wonderful stories from the days when he flew bombing missions over Europe in a B-17 and when he was a commercial fisherman on the East End of Long Island, rubbing shoulders with the literary set there, in partnership with Peter Mathiessen.[2] John said he had been given a painting by Jackson Pollack but had sold it before Pollack became famous, thus missing the chance to cash in. It should have been an omen.

In New York John had worked gathering items as a runner for a

---

2. Mathiessen, who is well known for his books, including *At Play in the Fields of the Lord*, was also in the George Plimpton *Paris Review* set. He spoke at John's funeral in 2003 and made a cryptic comment about having to love John but his driving one crazy at the same time. Afterward, I asked what he meant and he told the story of his and John's going into business together as charter fishermen. The boat belonged to Mathiessen, and so he was captain and John was first mate. But the first time Mathiessen could not be there, John told everyone he was captain and owned the boat. I told Mathiessen John had not changed over the years.

well-known gossip columnist, Louis Sobol, and he later edited a company publication in Ohio. When he arrived in Maine, he was excited by the challenge Sandy offered and accepted the low salary, living hand-to-mouth.

One Christmas holiday when he and I picked up my parents at the Kennebunk train station and drove them back to Kennebunkport, there was a hole in the floor of John's station wagon large enough so that we could see the snow on the road. I found it all romantic and Hemingwayesque.

Although John left me with the impression that he was an equal partner in the *Star*, this turned out not to be true. Sandy owned 100 percent. And while I am sure John's freewheeling journalistic style (in which the techniques of fiction sometimes overwhelmed fact) helped put the *Star* into the consciousness of local residents, it was Sandy's underappreciated hard work and two decades of standing on damn-the-torpedos integrity that led to several mergers and the emergence of the *York County Coast Star* as one of Maine's largest (circulation 15,000) and one of the nation's most distinguished weeklies.

When I first showed up on the *Star's* dilapidated doorstep and crossed the oil-stained floor to Sandy's office, I was just what they needed, someone they could hire for a pittance. I couldn't have been happier with the opportunity and would for the rest of my life put my interest in the job above how much I might be paid. They paid me by the word for what I wrote and if I could sell job printing, I would get a commission. As an added bonus, I was allowed to learn how to use some of the typesetting equipment and to help the men in the composing room as we put the paper together. The night Sandy had a new press moved in and we had to haul out the old flatbed, he needed strong backs and mine was enlisted along with those of the production crew and our well-oiled photographer.

The most memorable story of my first summer at the *Star* was about a school custodian who had disappeared, coincidentally, at the same time as someone else's wife. John covered the event as if it had been the Lindbergh kidnapping, making all kinds of suppositions, including a faked suicide, about a car going off a bridge into the Mousam River. Eventually, the story died out—the missing custodian eventually showed up in Florida—but not before John had everyone talking about the *Star*, expressing varied and not always complimentary opinions on this new brand of local journalism. They had seen nothing like it in Perley Watson's days.

I didn't just write stories and sell job printing but did other chores for which I could earn a commission, including selling subscriptions. It was on such a subscription-selling jaunt that I totaled my car, leaning over to get a pencil out of the glove compartment and hitting a telephone pole just inside my right headlight. The pole broke and fell on the roof, denting it and making the car worthless. When I called in to the office to tell them what happened, John told me to write six inches about it for the next edition.

In the *Kennebunk Star* days, John was not yet focused on environmental issues as he would be soon when he moved to the *Brunswick Record*. Sandy's own interest was good government, but in the early days he was so involved with keeping his head above water that he couldn't give it the attention he later would.

As important as my tutelage under John and Sandy were the long conversations John and I had about journalism in Maine with my father. Even though I was then slated to go to law school, I already had a keen interest in both journalism and Maine. My father loved to talk about such issues and to ask hypothetical questions. In Washington he often asked, "If you were president (or secretary of state), what would you do?" Now, the question was, "If you owned the *Portland Press Herald*, how would you change it?" Implicit in the question was the supposition that the person making the decision would exercise total control.

John and Cynthia would come over to dinner and afterward, we would sit in front of a roaring fire, brandy snifters in hand, discussing what we would do if we had unlimited resources to reform journalism in Maine. Such discussions about journalism reflected the subject's importance in the world I inhabited, and when I was in college and my college roommate's mother, Aline Saarinen, would take us out to dinner, the subject had switched to what we would do to resuscitate the terminally ill *New York Herald Tribune*.

Maine had forty weeklies and eight dailies. Since two of the dailies were morning/evening combinations and four were owned by the Gannett family, the number of divergent voices in the daily press was small. Portland and Bangor dominated, and both were committed to preserving the status quo. The weeklies tended to be desolate backwaters, promoting a Chamber of Commerce viewpoint when they expressed any viewpoint. During the next two decades, the weeklies would be seen as attractive properties for independent journalists who would improve them dramatically. What Sandy was to do at the *Star* would be repeated across the state.

At this stage, our little after-dinner group was just second-guessing, disparaging what existed without proposing any concrete alternative. Frankly, we didn't know much about the papers outside southern Maine. What drove our conversations as much as anything was that Maine for decades had been a solidly Republican state, a grip that had been broken just a few years before, in 1954, when Ed Muskie had been elected the first Democratic governor since the fluke of the Roosevelt landslide in 1932. None of us had developed a clear idea of what kinds of stories we would do. We didn't like the bland boosterism and reverence for the current power structure we saw in the papers we read. We were not able to comment on the more central issue—what stories important to the future of the state were being neglected by these papers?

By the time I entered law school, following the path that had been selected for me, I was academically burned out. I was not prepared for the kind of grinding study necessary to excel at technical courses that did not interest me, such as procedure and contracts. While I could enjoy the issues-oriented constitutional law or the case-centered torts, procedure, even with the excellent teacher I had, was not for the faint of heart.

It did not take me long to realize that I would not thrive in this highly competitive atmosphere where most of the students were willing to make any sacrifice to open the door to their futures. They had a motivation I simply did not possess.

While I was not highly motivated to study law, I did have a certain self-awareness about the predicament I had gotten into. I did not want to be a second-rate lawyer, both for my own self-esteem and for my father's sake. He loved the law and he was an exceptional lawyer. I did not think I could meet his standard. So I quit.

What I did get from my semester at law school was an appreciation that the really meaty part, important judicial opinions affecting public policy, was accessible to any intelligent reader, and for years, I turned to these opinions at all levels to develop stories the rest of the press overlooked.

Having left school and still not quite sure what I wanted to do with my life, I enlisted in the National Guard, agreeing to serve six months' active duty and six years of weekend drilling and summer camp in return for not being drafted for two years.

I had a couple of months in Washington while I waited to take my basic training at Fort Knox, Kentucky, and I spent my time drinking cheap wine I bought at the bargain bin at Eagle Wine on M Street, going to museums, and attending district court for amusement.

One trial involved a white man who was accused of making a homosexual advance to a twelve-year-old black boy. The boy had been wandering around a hospital parking lot when the man spotted him, thinking he must be up to no good. When the man stopped and asked the boy what he was doing there, the boy responded by asking the man if he would give him a ride. The man agreed but when they were pulling out of the parking lot, an attendant questioned the odd couple and the boy told the attendant the man had made an unwanted advance.

I thought the evidence was thin and that the boy probably realized he was in trouble. If he was street smart, and he obviously was, he knew his accusation would get him off the hook. The man's attorney was incompetent and never presented an alternative scenario to the accusations. The man was convicted. I didn't realize it at the time, but I was writing the story in my head, and my approach was now journalistic, not legal.

In February I went off to Fort Knox and sometime during this period, my father was approached by Sandy Brook who needed more money to keep the *Star* going.

Sandy was not pleased with the outcome. In his own memoir about the *Star*, Sandy recalls how he wrote my father that he needed $3,500 to stay afloat.[3] My father, bringing my brother along, came to

3. Alexander B. Brook, *The Hard Way* (Bridgehampton, NY: Bridge Works Publishing, 1993).

Maine that winter to talk with Sandy. "My desperate hopes were high. The meeting began cordially. I knew Peter, of course—and here was Warren. Peter and Warren were looking for something to do.[4] Oscar would invest the $3,500 I needed in return for 51 percent of Star Press, the business I had bought for $30,000 two and a half years before, and would be prepared to invest more as needed. I could remain as publisher. That I would really be working for Peter and Warren, my juniors by a dozen years, was unstated.

"I continued as civil and as attentive as my insides permitted. When it was over, I told Oscar I'd consider his offer and be back in touch. Desperate as I was, I couldn't bring myself to accept $3,500 or $35,000. Given my balance sheet the offer was fair enough, but at the time I was insulted by it."

I don't know if I would have deferred to my father and gone along with the offer, but I would have been the reluctant one in the family. I had worked with Sandy and John, and the idea of taking Sandy's paper from him would have upset me. In retrospect, of course, I can empathize even more. After the first year of *Maine Times*, the year in which we lost the most money, I was also in dire straits but still believed fervently in my future success. Sandy must have felt the same way.

That winter John left the *Star* and went to the *Brunswick Record*, leaving Sandy to continue his struggle alone. Sandy had a wonderful cantankerous streak. In response to the calls of irate readers who felt he was abandoning their pet projects for other stories, he began carrying the letters THWTB, along the dateline on page one and without explaining what it meant: To Hell with the Bastards.

My decision to join the National Guard would allow me to serve six months' active duty and then get on with my career, without fear of the draft hanging over my head. After leaving law school, I wanted to get out into the world and get on with life.

The experience at Fort Knox turned out to be a valuable one. I was anxious to finish the obligation from the first day we were herded

4. My brother was finishing architecture school at the time and had no interest in journalism. Although I had left law school, I had no interest in the *Star* and my father never told me of the meeting. I suspect this was another case of my father following his interests—he liked newspapers and would have liked the idea of owning one, especially at such a bargain basement price.

together in a cold barracks, pungent with the coal smoke that pervaded the base, and left to sleep in our street clothes on the hard floor with government-issue blankets thrown over us.

The six weeks of basic training went by quickly and were not taxing. Although I was still overweight, I lost about twenty pounds quickly, and, having been athletic all my life, I was in better shape than many of the other recruits who lived in fear of being "recycled"—if they failed to meet certain requirements, from breaking down and reassembling their rifles to completing the obstacle course or memorizing the Code of Military Conduct, they would have to go through basic training again. Some of them we physically pulled along during the final marches so that we would all complete basic together.

For advanced training, I was sent to clerk's school, where the major skills taught were typing and spelling. At the first class, the instructor announced we would be given a grammar test at the beginning and at the end of the course. I asked what score we would need on the test not to have to take the course and he answered, probably without real authority, that if I got a hundred on the test I wouldn't have to take the course. Apparently no one had scored a hundred under his regime, and he thought he was putting me down. He didn't know about my Milton instructor at Yale.

As with everything in the army, there was a pamphlet on grammar that I studied the night before the test. Exercising my well-developed, Ivy League cramming skills, I scored a hundred and the instructor was committed to letting me skip the course but made sure I received less pleasant duties. I did continue my typing, even though they did not expect us to do more than the basic forty words per minute.

Subsequently, I was assigned to troop information and fell into the hands of a Sergeant Smith, a real life version of the wheeling and dealing Sergeant Bilko. If I performed for him, he would look after me.

My two main responsibilities were doing promotional stories and giving lectures to the troops on such things as brainwashing and current affairs. The core of the promotional work was interviews with young officers, which I would send off as "hometowners" to be published in their local newspapers. I could do one in less than half an hour of interviewing and about the same time writing. Since we tracked the results, we were able to ascertain that we were getting more hometowners printed than any other regiment on base, a statistic Sergeant Smith made sure reached his commanding officer. At Sergeant Smith's instigation, I also wrote stories on his "innovative techniques," which made it into an army-wide magazine, all under his byline. The general came by one day to congratulate him on the article and Sergeant Smith rewarded me with a two-day pass to Louisville. While these chores allowed me to continue honing my writing skills, particularly to write consciously for the medium I wanted to publish what I wrote, it was, in retrospect, a lesson in the corruption of journalism.

The troop information sessions had sparse attendance. Under the circumstances it is amazing that anyone showed up because Sergeant Smith had a system, a favor for a favor. To *not* have to listen to me lecture—I didn't take this personally although one could argue that the more boring I was the more rewards we reaped—one only had to offer us something in return. We were particularly appreciated in the mess unit, from whom we received cold watermelon and steaks we could barbecue at Sergeant Smith's house or at the water skiing outings he led for us on the Ohio River. In return, the missing cooks were marked present at my lectures.

Whether I used the information in my current events lectures or not, I did spend hours each day reading the newspapers, a practice that would soon stand me in good stead.

I had to deal with the fact that Louisville was still a segregated city. My one black friend and I had to eat dinner at the Hilton Hotel, an interstate operation that did not discriminate. The more famous Brown Hotel did not serve blacks in 1960.

I also became a good friend of John English. We played tennis at the Louisville Country Club, where I became acquainted with some local girls, one of whom used to pick me up at the base in her Austin-Healey, considerably enhancing my prestige. Dating that summer—I remember dancing on a platform under oaks with moss hanging from them—was like an F. Scott Fitzgerald short story. Not much had changed since he had been writing four decades earlier.

John English also showed me some of the beautiful horse country, especially around Lexington, taking me along to visit friends, but at his house my most memorable experience was arguing with his father about black equality. Here again was the old refrain of "they are not yet ready and why are they pushing so hard?"

Those conversations convinced me that Mr. English's generation would never accept blacks as equals and the only solution was to change the laws and thus the manifestations of racism, such as segregation. Their prejudices were too ingrained and no amount of evidence or logic was going to change their minds. But I persisted, as anyone who wanted to write editorials would.

As a result of my army experience, I became a supporter of the draft, convinced that because of our obligation to serve, those of us who would later become decisionmakers had a much better view of what the military was really like and would always be skeptical of its efficiency. We had experienced firsthand the overwhelming inertia of tradition and bureaucracy, and we were keenly aware of the poor condition of the equipment we would be asked to use if we faced combat. Not only were our fatigue jackets insufficient even for the relatively mild Kentucky winters, but most of the vehicles were in a constant state of disrepair. Those among us who became mechanics did not inspire confidence. The range of those in my unit at Fort Knox was broad, including college graduates and those who complained they had enlisted only because they had been drunk at the time. One evening a sergeant asked a friend of mine why he disliked the military so much and he replied, "Could it be because my father is a general?"

Of course, I still hadn't learned to control my arrogance. One day our company's captain gave a lecture on military protocol and why it was so important to address officers as "sir." That same evening, I had KP duty and was waiting on the captain's table, saying, "Yes, sir" and "No, sir" and asking how I could be of service to "you gentlemen." The captain commented that I had listened well to his lecture and wanted me to tell the table, obviously parroting his speech of earlier in the day, why it was important that I was so respectful. So after reciting the answer he expected, I couldn't resist having the final word. I said the real reason I was saying "sir" all the time was that I was brown-nosing.

I should have had KP only about once in two weeks but the next day I found I had been assigned to KP again, this time to a job outside in the still-cold March weather. Stripped to my tee shirt, I was to reach into the coagulated grease of a large vat and search for any bone particles or other detritus that might be harmful to the pigs the garbage was being fed to.

Fortunately, the captain later confused me with a recruit named Brown who became the victim of any lingering resentment the captain had. I never told Brown how he had attained his position atop the captain's shit list.

At some point during my brief army career I had made the decision that I wanted to go into journalism. Although my mother was still disappointed that I had dropped out of law school, my father seemed to have accepted my decision with equanimity. At least, he never voiced his regrets to me.

But if I was going to consider a career in journalism, he felt I should do it with his model of preparation, by considering the options and getting expert advice. So he arranged a meeting in Washington with James Russell Wiggins, the editor of the *Washington Post*. We had lunch with Wiggins at my father's favorite restaurant, the Bistro, and my father set the stage with his questions. I suspect he knew at the time, although I did not, that Wiggins had a deep interest in Maine, where he spent summers. Wiggins was soon to retire from the *Post*, where he would be replaced by Ben Bradlee, and move to Ellsworth where he bought the weekly *Ellsworth American* and would transform it into a newspaper of stature. He also assumed the mantle of dean of Maine journalists.

Wiggins's advice was that I should not work for one of the large, established dailies—a code for the *Post* or the *New York Times*—but should go someplace where I could make my mark. I already knew that good journalists often started on small but high-quality papers. The *Berkshire Eagle* in Pittsfield, Massachusetts, was famous as one of these feeders. But Wiggins was not even suggesting this path to the big time. He was arguing for local journalism as a goal in itself, perhaps a reflection of where he was in his own life.

I found the conversation interesting, but because I had no immediate prospects it was academic. On the other hand, I did want to return to Maine to work and his advice reinforced that decision.

My active duty ended in September and I had signed on as a volunteer with Frank M. Coffin, whom I had interviewed for the *Star*. He was a Maine congressman running for governor.

Coffin had been the brains behind the 1950s Democratic resurgence in Maine. He had been elected to Congress, where he had shown outstanding promise, but was now running against John Reed who had become governor on a fluke when the incumbent, Democrat Clinton Clawson, who had succeeded Muskie as governor, had died in office. Reed, as president of the Senate, had been in line for succession under Maine law and the rumor—at least among Democrats—had been that the very strong speaker of the house, Robert Haskell, had selected Reed to be his Senate counterpart because he would never pose a threat.

The Coffin campaign formed the basis for much of my journalistic career in Maine. It introduced me to a group of extremely intelligent and dedicated people who would become my target audience for *Maine Times*. It gave me an opportunity to learn about the state that could have been achieved no other way. And it introduced me to Libby Donahue.

My job was blissfully ill defined and since they didn't pay me anything beyond a few dollars in expenses, I felt unencumbered by any restrictions on what I could do. I started out as Frank's driver, piloting Don Nicoll's mammoth Plymouth station wagon with a huge box on top that read on all four sides, "Here Comes Coffin." One of my more memorable moments came when we got caught in a funeral procession.

Frank was not one to limit anyone's ambition and I was not one to hang back, so after a few days it was decided that I should add the duties of advance man to that of driver. While Frank went to his morning coffees and walks down Main Street, I would visit the weekly newspaper office and tell the editor about Frank's positions and suggest he might want to do an interview. And just in case the editor didn't have time, I had brought along a press release geared to that particular community that Frank and I had discussed as we drove and that I had typed out on the hood of the station wagon on my trusty Olivetti Lettera 22 with its blue typewriter ribbon.[5]

5. Blue typewriter ribbons had been used at Lend-Lease, and many of those who worked there continued to use them after the war. It was a subtle link between them, and I picked it up as an homage to my father.

The next step was to do a press release on the speech Frank would make that day. Since he had the speeches only in his head, he would tell me what he intended to say and I would turn it into a news story. This quickly evolved into my "writing" his speeches, which we would then make available to any press who attended and any whose paper or radio station covered the area we were visiting.

My campaign job also gave me the opportunity to study the Maine press in much more detail. The *Bangor Daily News* was known as so Republican that Democrats entered the building only at their own (imagined) risk. The *Lewiston Sun Journal* was the Democratic bastion in a Democratic city. The *Portland Press Herald* was Republican but its chief political correspondent, Peter Damborg, was scrupulously fair. The weeklies were all over the lot but were almost uniformly dull, relying on press releases and not assigning reporters to political coverage, if they had reporters other than the owner-publisher. I became acutely aware of the poor coverage of state issues and the fact the concerned reader had nowhere to turn.

During this time I began to formulate a new idea for the statewide newspaper we had discussed in our Kennebunkport living room. What if it became the second section to weekly newspapers, starting with three that were for sale and that we would buy—in Kittery, Rumford, and Ellsworth? The first sections would be local news, the second section state news, and we would have a distribution system started that could grow without overlap.

Our base of operations for the Coffin campaign was Lewiston. Tom and Jeanne Delahanty had made available to me and any overflow their downstairs den that consisted of a bedroom, a bathroom, and a large pink room with a couch. Many late-night strategy sessions were held in the pink room, and it was here that Ben Dorsky had his heart attack. Dorsky was the state union leader and although he was ideologically a Republican, his union members were overwhelmingly Democrats and he liked to be part of the inner circle. He was on good terms with the Republican incumbent and didn't broadcast his closeness with the Democrats. The fact that Tom Delahanty had recently been appointed to the Maine Superior Court left us not wanting to publicize that any Democratic meetings were held in his basement, even though he never attended.

So when Dorsky collapsed in our midst one evening during a heated discussion, there was a moment's hesitation about whether to take him to a hospital ourselves or to call an ambulance. Fortunately, after only a minute or two and while everyone was still arguing over what we should do, Dorsky revived, apparently none the worse for wear, and the meeting went on.

Shep Lee, who was the campaign manager, told the story at my retirement party in 1986 of how one day he asked me to take a press release from Lewiston to Augusta and I suggested he have someone else do it as I was too busy. Shep went to Frank to complain that his driver was becoming insubordinate and Frank, on hearing the story, replied, "Good for him," indicating that I probably was too busy and had simply been standing up for my rights.

"At that moment," Shep said, as he retold the story twenty-six years later, "I knew we were in deep trouble."

My rapid rise from station wagon driver to general assistant was aided and abetted by Frank Coffin but it was actively stimulated by Libby Donahue. Libby, who came from a politically active family in Portland and whose mother still owned the Lafayette Hotel, had become Frank's administrative assistant in Congress in 1958 and was a fierce loyalist in a campaign full of people who greatly admired Frank for his intellect and for his personal warmth.

Libby had been a journalist and had covered the women's beat at the White House when there was a women's beat. That meant she covered Eleanor Roosevelt.

Her newspaper was the legendary *PM*, the nationwide afternoon daily that hoped to revolutionize American journalism. The publisher was Ralph Ingersoll,[6] who had been one of the major causes for the success of *Time* magazine, and its editor was James Wechsler, who would split with Ingersoll on just how left wing the paper should be. Wechsler would continue an important career at the *New York Post* in the years it was one of the nation's leading liberal voices and I would read him regularly when I arrived at the *Adirondack Daily Enterprise*.

---

6. When I went to the Adirondacks, one apartment I rented had previously been occupied by Ingersoll's former wife, Tommie. Later his stepson Bill Doolittle bought the *Adirondack Daily Enterprise* that I had edited.

Ingersoll would take a conservative turn and build a successful chain of small papers.

Libby had also been a speechwriter for Adlai Stevenson in his unsuccessful bids as the Democratic candidate for President in 1952 and 1956. My favorite picture of Libby is of her, Stevenson, Newton Minow,[7] and Marian Schlesinger.[8] It hangs in my office. Libby, I learned over the years, knew almost everyone I cared about.[9]

The friendship I developed with Libby that year lasted for the rest of her life. She would show up in Maine, unannounced, every summer with a bottle of vodka and a few steaks and would stay with us. (One late spring day in downtown Brunswick, I ran into John Donovan, a former congressional candidate and administrative assistant to Ed Muskie and then a professor of Political Science at Bowdoin. He looked at the leafed-out trees, sniffed the warm air, and asked, "Don't you think it's time for Libby to arrive?" implicitly comparing her annual, unannounced arrival to a force of nature.) Eunice, my wife, became one of Libby's favorites as well and my children grew up with a special "aunt." Libby even took a trip with us to Cervinia and later to Charlottesville. I cannot recall a moment when I did not enjoy her company.

When Libby began developing two major campaign television presentations for Frank Coffin, each lasting a half hour, she designated me her assistant. My driving duties had been turned over to someone else, everyone having accepted that I was not a reliable gofer. Since the incumbent, a drab Fort Kent Republican, John Reed, refused to debate Frank, we decided to have a one-man debate. My job was to plow through Reed's printed record, his speeches and statements, and find quotes that would state his position on issues we wanted to raise. Of course, they had to be statements with which we would disagree.

For my research I was sent to the printed legislative debate, which in those days and long afterward came out daily in the form of large

---

7. Minow later became head of the Federal Communications Commission and described television as "a vast wasteland."
8. The first wife of the historian Arthur Schlesinger, Jr.
9. In the 1970s I was riding up a ski lift in Taos, New Mexico, with a young woman in my ski school class. Making polite conversation, she asked where I was from and when I said Maine, she replied, "The only person I know from Maine is Libby Donahue." She turned out to be the fiancée of one of Libby's nephews.

sheets, called horse blankets. Because of this experience I was later to order them for *Maine Times,* allowing me to review the legislative debate of the previous day—that's how fast they came out—without having to travel to Augusta. They formed the basis for lots of short stories and quotes at the weekly *Maine Times* almost a decade later and gave readers the impression we covered the legislature much more intimately than we had time or staff to do.

The campaign hired Harry Marble, one of the most recognizable television voices in the state, to present the Reed statements from behind a curtain, seen only in silhouette, and Frank would counter them with, we were convinced, irrefutable logic and eloquence.

Television time was still cheap and you could actually expect an audience to stay with a political presentation for a half hour. Campaigns used few of the thirty-second ads that dominate today and television, while important because of its instant reach, had not yet become the overwhelming medium. After our one-man debate, the phone erupted with congratulatory calls from our supporters.

We were so elated, Libby and I started work immediately on a follow-up show. We took our theme from a statement by Reed's campaign manager that the Republican candidate would break chairs over Frank Coffin's head.

We would (with what we thought was great wit) use that statement against Reed, so we went to Portland for a day to scour the city for chairs. We found a high chair to represent Reed's infantile arguments, we found a rocking chair to represent how he had waffled on certain issues. We found more chairs that we presented to the audience as broken because they represented flawed ideas. Then we switched to a three-legged stool. Simple, sturdy, functional. This represented the Coffin platform. The three legs symbolized the three cornerstones of his campaign—but I can't remember what they were.

So, with the help of our symbolism, Frank used the chairs to reduce Reed to a shambles—so we were convinced—and then sat on his three-legged stool to expound on his own program.

The producer at Channel Six who helped us do the two shows told us the three-legged stool show was the most innovative use of television he had ever seen in Maine. Maybe so, but we could tell even from the supporters who called in to say how wonderful Frank had been that they were a little baffled by our visual cleverness. Libby, Frank, and I thought it had been devastating to the opposition.

Frank lost the election.

I don't think he lost because of that television show. He lost because the Democrats lost. Jack Kennedy trailed Richard Nixon in Maine by almost 40,000 votes. Margaret Chase Smith kept her Republican Senate seat by about 60,000. Frank lost by 17,000. And it was until then and for decades after, the largest voter turnout in Maine history. Frank had been the beneficiary of a huge number of split tickets, but it wasn't enough to stem the tide.

Besides gaining more experience in writing press releases and converting speeches into news stories, I had been called on to edit and produce the sporadically published newspaper, the *Maine Democrat*. It was my first try at putting together any newspaper from top to bottom and although it was propaganda, albeit propaganda I believed, I did get a chance to test my technical skills.

My other view of a journalistic future came in a bizarre conversation with Louis Jalbert, a state representative from Lewiston, who titled himself Mr. Democrat. One day when Frank was campaigning at the Montagnard Club, a French bar where mill workers came for an early morning pick-me-up when their shift ended, Louis pulled me into the back room full of beer crates. There he explained that after the campaign perhaps we could work together, with my gathering information about political figures, and his making sure it was not published. I was too stupefied to answer coherently.

With the election lost, winter was coming and I didn't have a job.

I talked with Ernie Chard, then the editor of the Portland papers, and he told me I was overqualified. Al Ingalls, the editor of the *Biddeford Journal*, had mercy on me and gave me work covering superior court at the York County seat in Alfred. I was paid by the story but worked consistently for the next two months, writing about low-level crime.

Relief was provided by the deputy sheriff, J. Albert Merryman, a rotund glad-hander who displayed his last meal on the garish ties he wore. One day, the only other reporter on the scene, Scott Hoar of the *Press Herald*, had had a conflict and missed a case so he came in to ask Merryman about it while I was there. Merryman announced that Scott had missed a good case and that he would have to rely on me to fill him in on the details. When asked what kind of case it was, Merryman replied it was sodomy. With what, Scott asked. Merryman paused for effect and said somberly, "a chicken."

No, it wasn't true.

With John Cole and his family already having moved an hour away, where he would edit the *Brunswick Record*, I had no friends outside work and I spent my free time at home, in the barn my brother, while in architecture school, had redesigned into a house. I watched a lot of old movies in black and white on a small-screen TV and won a bottle of Aqua Velva shaving lotion for my movie suggestions to Channel 8.

After two months of this social isolation, I cannot explain my frame of mind any better than to compare it to a passage in Evelyn Waugh's *A Handful of Dust*, which I was reading at the time.

The hero, Tony, has been lost up the Amazon and has been found by a Mr. Todd who lives among the Indians. He is delighted to see Tony and offers his protection in return for Tony's reading to him, endlessly, from the novels of Charles Dickens. Tony thinks of nothing but how he will some day be rescued, both from this wilderness and from the tedium of reading Dickens. Mr. Todd will not show him the way out but surely there will be an expedition to find him.

One morning he awakes with a terrible hangover, the result of a native brew Mr. Todd had offered him and learns he has slept for two days. Tony can't believe he slept for so long and Mr. Todd adds that because he was asleep, Tony missed their guests. What guests? Tony asks.

Mr. Todd replies: "Why, yes, I have been quite gay while you were asleep. Three men from outside. Englishmen. It is a pity you missed them. A pity for them, too, as they particularly wished to see you. But what could I do? You were so sound asleep. They had come all the way to find you, so—I thought you would not mind—as you could not greet them yourself I gave them a little souvenir, your watch. They wanted something to take back to England where a reward is being offered for news of you. They were very pleased with it. And they took some photographs of the little cross I put up to commemorate your coming. They were pleased with that, too. They were very easily pleased. But I do not suppose they will visit us again, our life here is so retired . . . no pleasures except reading . . . . I do not suppose we shall ever have visitors again . . . well, well, I will get you some medicine to make you feel better. Your head aches, does it not? . . . We will not have any Dickens today . . . but tomorrow, and the day after that, and the day after that. Let us read *Little Dorrit* again. There are passages in that book I can never hear without the temptation to weep."

It was clearly time for me to move on. I had learned from my court reporting that I enjoyed journalism on any level, so much so that I rose every morning anxious to go to work. I had found a career. Now I needed someone to hire me.

Seven

You Learn to Do Everything
Because There Is No One Else to Do It

When I arrived in Saranac Lake in February of 1961, I was twenty-three years old, a Yale English major with a pretty sophisticated understanding of language and only the most rudimentary knowledge of editing a newspaper.

In December of 1960 while I was covering domestic violence and sodomy trials in Maine, my mother was at a Washington dinner party where she learned from Roger Tubby, who had been Harry S. Truman's last press secretary and was taking a job as U.S. ambassador to the U.N. in Geneva, that he and his partner needed an editor for their paper in Saranac Lake, New York. She was convincing enough about my ability to edit a small daily that he gave her the name of his partner, Jim Loeb, who was still on the job and would be doing the hiring.

I called Jim. He asked me mercifully few questions about my experience and invited me to drive over to the Adirondacks in January for an interview.

Jim was also receiving an ambassadorship, his to Ghana. He would go from there to Peru. Jim was intellectually intense and comfortably rumpled in dress. He, along with Hubert Humphrey and Reinhold Neibuhr, had founded Americans for Democratic Action (ADA), the leading liberal, anti-Communist political organization of the Fifties.

The *Adirondack Daily Enterprise*, and its satellite, the weekly *Lake Placid News*, could not support both Jim and Roger. Indeed, the two papers could not support either of them. But they rolled up their sleeves and became small-town journalists. Roger seemed to fit into the local culture better than Jim, but I had little to do with him. Jim ultimately hired me and I developed a deep affection and admiration for him.

The key to their hiring me for $85 a week to edit their paper while they were abroad was Libby Donahue, whom I had mentioned during the job interview. Jim Loeb recalled Libby from the ADA days and remembered her as tough as nails in her evaluation of others. He phoned her for a recommendation. She told him that if he didn't hire me, he would be making the greatest mistake of his life. He was stunned. I was hired. Only years later did I tell him he would not have received a more biased recommendation from my mother.

I took the job, packed my basic belongings into my Chevrolet Corvair, and headed for Saranac Lake in February 1961. Since I did not yet have a place to stay on my first day of work, the Loebs put me up in their first-floor guest bedroom.

On the very first day of this temporary arrangement, I had risen and gone into the bathroom adjacent to my bedroom when I heard the Loebs come downstairs and begin to prepare breakfast. When I had finished shaving and turned the doorknob to leave the bathroom, nothing happened. The door did not release. There was no visible lock, no button or other device in the knob. I had locked myself in, not an auspicious way to begin my new career.

Fortunately, the hinges were on the inside. (This is a story my children loved hearing and insisted I tell their friends. The line about the hinges being on the inside always brought a visible reaction as the kids realized what I was about to do.)

So I carefully removed the pins from the hinges and lifted the door inward, making no discernible noise. As I prepared to set the now open door back on its hinges and replace the pins, Jim's wife Ellen, who had come downstairs and was now standing in the hallway, asked: "Is that the way you always go in and out of the bathroom?"

They appeared to accept my explanation that I had never before encountered a door with such a lock—it engaged when you pushed in the knob—and they did not withdraw the job offer.

Jim must have taken me to the office that morning and there I met John Waterbury, an experienced newspaperman who had been hired as general manager and who was to run the business end and oversee their inexperienced editor in the owners' absence. He was to leave after a little more than a year.

As is so often the case, the other employees at the *Enterprise* knew what they were doing and the paper could have run itself. I just had to fill in certain blanks and what I lacked in experience, I made up for in energy.

Others helped me along. I was blessed with a proofreader, Ernest Rogers, who had been a Latin teacher and had come to Saranac Lake to cure his tuberculosis. He was a good copy editor as well as proofreader and knew all the procedures in use at the paper. Since he had been reading every word in the paper for years, he also represented institutional memory. He was quick to both correct me and share his knowledge with me.

Since Jim Loeb was still on hand and John Waterbury could write on demand, it was a few days before I started writing editorials. Jim and Roger, of course, loved writing on national and international affairs and were well qualified to do so. I was less qualified.

But with the help of the *New York Times*, the *Herald Tribune*, the *New York Post*, the *New Republic*, the *Nation*, the *Manchester* (England) *Guardian*, and by taking my cues from Walter Lippmann and Scotty Reston, I was able to continue the *Enterprise* tradition. All editorials, no matter what the subject, were locally written.

Turning out 5,000 words a week as an English major at Yale had made me a fast writer. I could attend a school board meeting or a village board meeting and write the story at 11:00 P.M. so that I was ready to edit incoming copy and clip the Associated Press wire and lay out the paper and write the headlines the next morning. Those sessions writing headlines for the *Exonian* stood me in good stead and soon, under the regimen of having to produce thirty or forty headlines a day, I could create each one in a minute or two.

As an afternoon paper, our editorial deadline was around noon. This left almost two hours to finish production and complete the press run, giving us about three hours to reach our circulation area before people arrived home from work and expected to find their evening paper on the doorstep.

Morning papers have a huge circulation advantage. Even if they go to press at midnight, they still have six or seven hours to deliver to homes in their circulation area before customers get up for breakfast. This simple logistical fact is why morning newspapers have a broader circulation reach and are larger. Afternoon dailies are typically small or serve a compact metropolitan area. They have also gone out of business at an alarming rate, partly because of this limited distribution possibility.

At the *Enterprise,* work on that day's paper began at 5:00 A.M. when the sports editor came in and began to clip the Associated Press wire.

In those days the AP stories were printed on a narrow sheet of continuous paper, line for line exactly as they would appear in type. The wire feed also produced a perforated tape to be fed through a Linotype machine. In 1961 this was high technology. The perforated tape allowed the material to be set automatically on an adapted Linotype machine, at a speed of about forty words a minute, much faster than the average Linotype operator could set type manually and with fewer errors. This extremely slow process was a key limiting factor for a small daily like ours. We were always hard pressed to set in type all the stories we wanted to run that day. If there was a gap at 8:00 A.M. with nothing to be set, that was lost material. Non-utilized time on a Linotype was lost time. There was no way we could recover the type not set as we raced toward our noon deadline.

The lesson I learned that lost capacity could not be recovered and the consequential importance of good scheduling and rigorously meeting deadlines was to make *Maine Times* technically and economically feasible a decade later.

Although not much would change technically during the four years I was at the *Enterprise,* by 1970 the changes in equipment would accelerate to the point where every innovation was obsolete within a year or two. Less than a decade later, *Maine Times* was able to set type on what amounted to fancy typewriters, allowing us to double typesetting speed. The entire process of hot type, a reference to the molten metal used to create letters, became the technology of the past, used only by those larger publications that were bound to obsolescence through union contracts. Straight cold-type machines, with memory, allowing immediate corrections, became dominant. In the late '70s, we adapted to the first Apple IIe computers that allowed reporters to set and correct directly on screen and then editors to do the same. Not only were the expensive and slow Linotypes obsolete; typesetters were obsolete, and an entire layer of production and the cost associated with it had been removed. Next, we could plug into the more sophisticated but underutilized equipment our printers owned, using modems and telephone lines. This gave us unlimited typesetting capacity.

This technological revolution—moving from cumbersome molten lead to images on a screen, from seven lines a minute to unlimited capacity, was the hidden factor in allowing the birth of the alternative press in the early 1970s. Today, if I were starting a new publication, I would design it around current technology, including electronic delivery.

But as editor at the *Enterprise* in 1962, I would come in to the office at 6:00 A.M. and begin clipping material for national coverage. At 7:00, I would go out to breakfast with the men from the composing room. I don't know how many years they had been going to the same place; I simply joined the group and sat at the counter eating pancakes and sausage with the rest of them—our places were always available at the counter when we arrived.

The technical expertise I had gained during summers at the *Kennebunk Star* and elsewhere gave me some initial standing in the composing room and I was soon taught much more. My willingness to pitch in and set type if we were running late was seen as an asset. Even though I designed page one every day on a makeup sheet, I also went into the composing room to work hands-on with the shop foreman, Armand Amell, in putting page one together. When I went to the *Bath Daily Times* four years later, the shop foreman there was impressed with my hands-on ability. From the first day in Bath, I worked with Arthur Johansen to compose page one in lead, and consequently established my credentials as knowing what I was doing and developed an instant rapport with the men in the shop who tended to see the editorial side as hopelessly clueless, never meeting deadlines, and constantly making their job more difficult.

At the *Enterprise*, I quickly learned to read type upside down and backwards, to lift large segments without having it buckle (pie) in my hand, and to add lead spacing quickly to make the type fit snugly in the metal frame, called a chase, that held it. But before I acquired these skills, I, like those before me, had to be introduced to type lice.

Type lice, I was told, particularly infested old type, even type only a few days old that had been put aside for some reason. When I could not see the type lice, Armand Amell, the foreman, urged me to look more closely, even to take off my glasses as I put my nose only an inch or two above the type. When I still couldn't see the lice, he squirted some of the gasoline we used to clean ink from the type on it, then separated two blocks of type so I could examine more closely where the gasoline had collected and where the dead lice would float to the surface. Once my nose was sufficiently close, Armand slammed the type back together, splashing the gasoline into my face and eyes. It was a lesson no one was allowed to forego, an essential initiation that went back as far as anyone could remember. No one gave a second thought to the potential danger of gasoline in the initiate's eyes.

The composing room in 1961 was a total boys' club—to which I was welcomed as a member after my initiation. We told inappropriate jokes, pitched pennies, had contests on who could sit against the wall the longest. We also did things together, including drink, outside of work.

If I was lucky, I could leave the office for a few hours in the afternoon after the press run finished. I particularly coveted this time in the winter, when I would drive to Mount Pisgah, the local ski hill about ten minutes from the office, and try to learn to ski. Pisgah had lights and night skiing. In my early twenties, I could deal with the 40-below-zero nighttime temperatures in the Adirondacks. We used to say it wasn't so bad because the air was so dry. In reality, if you ever let your skin touch the shaft of the metal T-bars on one of those nights, it would stick to the metal and peel off as you tried to pull away.

Skiing had been one of the added attractions of moving to Saranac Lake, 10 miles from Lake Placid where the 1932 Olympics had been held. I did learn to ski there but with bitter cold and icy conditions, it was a far cry from an alpine paradise.

Although the position of editor of the *Enterprise* gave me a certain social standing, and my adoption by Bea Sprague, who became my surrogate mother, gave me an entree to the dinner parties with the Park Avenue set, I had a broad range of friends and acquaintances, broader than I was ever to have in any other professional capacity.

Bea was about fifty when I arrived in town and she had been a good friend of the Loebs, so it was only natural that she would adopt me. Like so many people, she had come to Saranac Lake when it was a tuberculosis center and had stayed to become the business manager for one of its best doctors' groups. She was well read, well informed, and endlessly curious. I had dinner at her house at least once a week and it was my place of refuge. I was sitting in her living room, with a plate of food on my lap, when I saw Jack Ruby shoot Lee Harvey Oswald, live on television. It was at Bea's that I met Charles Jackson, the author of *Lost Weekend*, who was recuperating at the Will Rogers Hospital.[1] No one so interesting could pass within 50 miles without Bea inviting him to dinner. Jackson regaled us with lurid tales and was openly curious about our relationship—the twenty-four-year-old with the fifty-year-old—and let us know that he would be most interested in any details we might offer. He was not invited a second time.

Bea also collected names, one of her favorites being the diplomat Outerbridge Horsey. One day she showed me a copy of *The Wind in the Willows* with the bookplate of Imbrie Buffum, a name she thought most appropriate for that whimsical book. It was further enhanced when I told her that Imbrie Buffum had been a French professor and a friend when I was at Yale.

One of our classic evenings on the Park Avenue social circuit occurred the evening we attended the first party to which the Ayvazians were invited. Fred Ayvazian had just moved to town to head the Will Rogers Hospital and it was quickly revealed that he wrote thrillers under a pen name none of us ever learned. His wife, Gloria, was very attractive—they must have been in their forties— and an obvious maverick. I spent two hours on the couch in the living room charmed and delighted by the Ayvazians, even when everyone else had left the room.

On the way home that evening, Bea turned to me and asked with a rare tone of pique in her voice, "How could you have done that?"

"Done what?" I asked.

"Sat there so blithely, having such a good time."

It seems that while I was totally enamored of the Ayvazians and having a wonderful evening, our host and hostess had been develop-

1. My pre-Saranac Lake recollection of the Will Rogers Hospital was when they used to take up collections for it at movie theaters. At that time it was still a cure center for those in the film industry who had tuberculosis. By the 1960s the residents seemed to have mostly drug and alcohol problems. It was still star-studded, and one time I was asked to share the rostrum with George Jessel, the Toastmaster General, as fabulous a speaker as his national nickname implied.

ing a major row in the kitchen that had drawn everyone but the three of us. The argument had culminated in the hostess pouring an urn of scalding coffee in her husband's lap and everyone else dealing with the consequences. Everyone except myself and the Ayvazians had had a lousy evening.

Fred Ayvazian liked to make self-deprecating remarks about his city-boy roots and would joke about the dangers inherent in living so close to such creatures as deciduous conifers—this after we had explained to him that the common tamarack tree was the only deciduous conifer.

So one evening, we all got together to make him a game dinner, with people ransacking their freezers for trout, moose, venison, ruffed grouse, and whatever else we could find. The party was to be at my apartment, and we converted the living room into a campsite with a tent and a light under cellophane to simulate the campfire. Bea, as usual, was the leader of the band and insisted on the extra detail. She went by the local taxidermist to borrow the standing black bear he kept in front as an advertisement. We placed the bear in front of the toilet, with the seat up, and his back to the door.

Unfortunately, Fred got caught in some kind of an emergency and was more than two hours late. In those days we all drank hard liquor for cocktails and by the time we began eating, I was pretty well soused. I am assuming this because when the next day one of the women guests showed up at my door, I asked what she was doing there and she said I had invited her. I didn't recall ever having done so. I announced I had a meeting in five minutes and bolted. Graciously, she never brought the incident up again.

On the opposite end of the spectrum from the Park Avenue set were my friends in the National Guard.

While I had entered the military in Washington and done my active duty at Fort Knox, I was to do the first years of my continued obligation in Saranac Lake. I came there as an E-4 and left as an E-5, basically a clerk. As such I worked primarily with the non-commissioned officer who ran the show and continued to pursue the policy I had learned at Fort Knox: do more than is required and convince your non-com he can rely on you and you will pass through with a minimum of hassle. Of course, I also practiced on the rifle range and mopped the floors with everyone else and so was on equal footing with many of the men who plowed the streets, fixed the telephones, and performed the other necessities of life in town.

One Saturday our captain was away and a young lieutenant had come down from Plattsburgh to oversee our weekend drill. At the opening meeting, he decided to warm up the troops with a Little Rastus joke. Little Rastus jokes are virulently anti-black and were told in those days by the same types who referred to black soldiers as Night Fighters or Jungle Bunnies.

The lieutenant had just launched into the preamble for his joke—they all begin: "Little Rastus was . . ."—when I stood up and said, "Excuse me sir. That joke is totally inappropriate in the U.S. military and if you insist on proceeding with it, I shall be forced to leave the room." Yes, I said shall, not will.

He was dumbstruck, to say the least, but he did stop short, abandon his joke, and go on with the orders of the day. As soon as the initial meeting broke up, I could see him talking to our top non-com, no doubt asking who the hell I was. Of course, as editor of the local newspaper, I knew I was immune from any retaliation. I do not know if I would have been so forthright had I not been so secure. On the other hand, I was outraged that the officer had been so cavalier at a time when, as the *Enterprise* reported daily, blacks my age were being beaten to a bloody pulp for having the audacity to ask to be served a cup of coffee, or, even more radically, to try to vote.

My penchant to disregard rank was not limited to the National Guard. At one point, the paper's co-owner, Roger Tubby, on leave from Geneva, was back in town at the same time Robert Kennedy, recently elected a U.S. senator from New York, was there for a political tour of the area.

Ambassador Tubby had been part of the Kennedy entourage, and he came back to the office to see what we were going to do with the story. I showed him the copy. It was pretty standard. Then I showed him the photos I had chosen. One showed Senator Kennedy with a woman doctor at the Veterans Administration hospital, engaged in a lively exchange. The other was a group shot in which Tubby was standing next to Kennedy.

I explained that I would run the lively shot on page one and the group shot inside. Roger suggested that I do the reverse.

I disagreed and when he persisted, indicating clearly that he owned the paper and it was his prerogative to make the decision, I told him bluntly that as long as I was editor, I was making such decisions. Any time he wanted to come back from Switzerland and run the paper, I would happily leave and he could choose any photographs he wanted. I didn't offer him much choice.

My undiplomatic stance reflected an attitude I always had about the newspapers I edited: I was responsible so I was in charge.

Other friends were my fishing and skiing buddies. I fished with Fritz Decker, more about whom later, and Tom Finnigan, also my prime skiing friend, but I also fished with Glen Corl—his wife, Natalie, was a skiing pal—and the inimitable Martin Pfeiffer. Both Glen and Martin worked for the Conservation Department and Martin, a bachelor, lived to fly fish. He had dilapidated skiffs stashed all over the high peaks region so they were at hand when he walked in. Because they tested ponds, the wildlife biologists knew every inlet and spring hole where trout congregated. To watch Martin throw a fly with one of his Orvis split bamboo rods was to witness ultimate grace.

Fishing with these wildlife biologists tended to put me on their side in the endless debate about who should be making decisions in the Adirondack Park. The hunters and fishermen claimed the scientists didn't know what they were talking about and that anecdotal experience, not science, was the needed criterion. In reality, the hunters and fishermen simply wanted to kill more deer and catch more fish. This same debate between science and anecdote continues to this day in Maine, not so much in the woods where consensus has been reached, but at sea where there is a crisis in the ground fishery and the commercial fishermen claim there are plenty of fish left and hope to keep harvesting them until they put themselves out of business.

The most important issues the *Enterprise* covered revolved around the Park. I had not understood its significance when I came to Saranac Lake but I soon learned. Created in the aftermath of devastating exploitation and on the basis of protecting the watershed for all of New York, including the city, the Adirondack Park pitted urban conservationists against locals seeking economic gain. Although a state rather than a national park, it was huge and it was more restrictive than the national parks, providing a model for the limitation of motorized transport. The hot button issues *Maine Times* would later confront at Baxter State Park, deemed Forever Wild in emulation of the Adirondack Park, had all been played out in the Adirondacks and it became my training ground in environmental policy as well as in journalism. The basic issue there and elsewhere was that too much access could destroy the qualities that attracted one to the park in the first place.

I was philosophically inclined to take the limited access position and in practice, I was young and didn't mind walking in. In fact, I appreciated the fact that having to hike a mile weeded out most fishermen and gave us the semblance of wilderness although there was almost no place within the park where one could not hear evidence of civilization.

Even this semblance of wilderness allowed a lifestyle that had disappeared elsewhere in the East. I spent one evening with Glen Corl and his son Doug as they negotiated with a buyer about Doug's muskrat pelts. Doug was being brought up like his father and he had his own trapline at the age of eleven. We were sitting in the basement, sipping drinks, with both Glen's and Doug's pelts laid out on the floor and the itinerant buyer striking a bargain. Glen had some more-valuable skins, probably beaver, whereas what Doug had was almost entirely muskrat. It became clear to me that there was a little dance taking place, that Glen would take less for his beaver if the buyer would give Doug more for his rats. The buyer understood and a deal was struck—after about two hours of roundabout chatting and drinking.

Glen's wife, Nat, was a wonderful skier and ran the elementary school ski program, where she occasionally enlisted my help even though my own skiing was pretty bad. Mainly she needed an extra body. The first time I took one of her classes, on a particularly cold day, I made the mistake of allowing one of the eight-year-olds to go to the bathroom, thus obligating me to honor similar requests by all the others in my class. When I went into the lodge to retrieve them after they failed to reappear, no one would admit to being in my class. As they had all been wrapped in face warmers I had no way of pinning them down and Nat joked for years about how quickly I had "lost" my first ski class.

Nat took pride in being a maverick and later married a former priest. We stayed in touch and she convinced my son Tony to attend a summer ski camp out West that changed his life. As with a number of those friends I made in Saranac Lake forty years ago, we remain close to this day.

Tom Finnigan and I did a lot of stream fishing for 10-inch brook trout where the real thrill is in finding the insect hatch that brings the fish to the surface and then finding the right fly and presenting it perfectly. To fish for trout, you cast upstream because the fish are looking upstream and thus away from you, to see what comes floating their way. With a dry fly, the lure must come back toward you no faster than the current or the fish will be spooked. But you cannot allow the fly to merely float because slack leader material will form and as soon as the fish strikes, it realizes it has been fooled and tries to spit out the fly. If you have allowed slack line, you cannot bring it taut quickly enough to hook the fish. Dry fly fishermen make much of the skill needed to make the perfect presentation, but some fish, in all honesty, simply hook themselves in their frenzy no matter how badly one casts or retrieves.

Nothing matches stream fishing, especially in the evening as the light changes the color of the water, and you can see the newly hatched insects rise and the fish suck them from the surface. You don't know how long the rise will last and you try frantically to match the hatch, then not to let your excitement cause you to cast badly and disturb the water. Even the small trout take the fly aggressively and come out of the water, often standing on their tails in an attempt to dislodge the hook. I have caught much larger fish that have caused much less pumping of the heart.

There were big fish in the Adirondacks, especially the lake trout in major ponds and the brown trout that lurked in some of the larger rivers such as the Ausable. The bait fishermen had much better luck in catching them. And not all fishermen were like those of us who cast flies, in it for the thrill of the chase. But Tom and I were. We also liked the time after fishing. We would head out after work for any one of numerous streams and fish until dark, about 8:30 or 9:00 P.M. Then, still slathered with aromatic coal tar and camphor bug dope, we would drive to Durgin's, a roadhouse run by Bea LaFountain. We would give her the trout we had kept and she would sauté them, delivering them back to us at the bar on sizzling metal platters resting on wooden trays.

Part of the ritual was imbibing a very dry martini while waiting for the trout to be cooked.

Many evenings Peter LeMay would be at the bar along with a self-proclaimed mountain man who went by the name of Hawkeye. Peter would want to argue about Hemingway or some other macho literary subject and Hawkeye would argue about anything.

There were lots of bars in Saranac Lake, as there were in such towns throughout New York with its eighteen-year-old drinking age, and each seemed to have its own ambience and clientele. Durgin's was my favorite hangout. Besides Bea, there was her son Jimmy, about my age, who may have been the most relentless skirt chaser in the Adirondacks. He worked on the theory that if you asked every girl you met to go to bed with you, and if you kept on asking, you would be amazed by how many said "yes." My wife later told me she had gone out with Jimmy at least once and that he had asked her. She said that although she refused, he had such a nice way of asking that she was not offended.

Jimmy always had someone he wanted to fix me up with and I often accepted the offer—but never successfully followed his advice about always asking.

Sometimes my accessibility and friendliness could be a bit disconcerting. I had not been in town long when I got a call after midnight, waking me, from Dew Drop Morgan, who ran the Dew Drop Inn along the river. "Ernie Stautner wants to talk to you," he said.

"About what?" I asked.

"About this House UnAmerican Activities stuff," he said.

"When?" I asked.

"Now," he said.

"Okay," I replied, expecting him to come on the phone.

"No," Dew Drop said. "Down here. Come on down. We'll wait for you."

I didn't know who Ernie Stautner was but I was already awake and I was young and Dew Drop's was only five minutes away.

When I arrived, near 1:00 A.M., the restaurant was empty and about to shut down but Ernie Stautner, who ran the local drive-in movie theater, was sitting at the bar with Dew Drop. Although small by today's standards—small that is for an all-pro lineman for the Pittsburgh Steelers—Ernie was still impressive. He had recently become a coach for the Washington Redskins.

Although Ernie and Dew Drop held opinions close to Jack Roosa, who had turned me in to the FBI, they were much more open-minded and after a couple of hours and numerous scotches on the house, we were pals even if I didn't feel so good when I had to get up after three hours of sleep and go to work.

Besides fishing together, Tom Finnigan and I also skied together. I owe the best elements of my style to following Tom down trails I should never have been on, imitating him in an effort to keep myself alive. Our favorite trip was to Stowe, where we stayed at Jennie Gale's farmhouse for $7 a night, breakfast included, and skied the front four on Mt. Mansfield. Tom, who had raced at the top collegiate level while at Middlebury, was one of the best skiers there, taking the moguls on the National like a dancer, while I crashed and burned my way down.

Saranac Lake was important to ski history and the town was full of interesting skiers. Tom Cantwell, who knew all the ski pioneers of the East, took me under his wing from day one and besides showing me around town also included me on some of his ski trips. I had the opportunity to ski with Mo Distin. He called me one evening and asked me to ski at Stowe the next day, a Sunday. I thought it was a pretty exhausting day-trip, two and a half hours each way, and he explained that we would fly and I should meet him at the airport at 7:00 A.M. I did and we opened the lifts on Mt. Mansfield.

I immediately noticed that his skis, still wooden at that time, were uneven, or at least the bindings were mounted unevenly. He admitted that they were. He said he had been changing the bindings and had only finished one but figured it wouldn't be too cumbersome. It wasn't, at least not for a skier of his ability. Mo had been a member of the U.S. Olympic team and his fluidity took my breath away. I would never be able to ski like that even thirty-five years later when I was more experienced and the new equipment made it so much easier. The ability and grace of people like Tom and Nat and Mo left me understanding just how good such skiers were in the early '60s.

One day Tom Finnigan came into the newspaper office and said he had just received a call from a friend in the Glens Falls ski club who had two leftover tickets for a round-trip charter flight to Europe for $100 each. (This was before modern discount fares and flights to Europe cost about $1,000, more than two months' salary for me.) The plane was scheduled to depart in ten days, and the person from the ski club felt it was better to get whatever he could for the tickets rather than let the seats remain empty. Part of the deal was that we would not tell anyone else how little we had paid.

I decided I could take a week's vacation and telegrammed our old family friend, Ginia Gargioni, in Turin. She told us to get ourselves to her and she would take care of the rest.

Reminiscent of my boyhood when we were always under Ginia's wing on trips to Italy, we arrived at the Hotel Nazionale where she still lived with her mother, had a wonderful meal of spaghetti and veal, and were given a car and sent off to Sestriere the next day. Sestriere had been developed by Fiat and was little more than an hour's drive from downtown Turin. Ginia had obtained a room for us at one of the two famous tower hotels, full pension, with a week's lift ticket waiting at the desk. Tom and I had the ski trip of our lives, an alpine vacation I was never able to repeat.

It was so inspiring that the first winter vacation I ever took with my family was to Sestriere. That was fifteen years later and already there had been major new development, a distinct change for the worse. On the other hand, because of a fabulous exchange rate, we stayed at the very posh Principi dei Piemonte and had wonderful service and wonderful food. The waiter would juggle the fruit for my eight-year-old son, Tony, and every afternoon my daughter, Sara, and I would be joined by a vacationing airline pilot who found it difficult to keep up with her as she, at age ten, had already become more expert in the moguls than I would ever be.

When Tom and I took that spur-of-the-moment vacation in the mid-1960s, Sestriere was almost idyllic. The sun seemed to shine every day and we hired an instructor/guide who took us from the top to the valley, a two-hour run starting in powder and ending in corn snow. We had to take a bus back up the mountain to get to the hotel again. Not only have I been unable to match this experience in

Sestriere or elsewhere in Europe, I have not even come close in the United States where I have skied at nearly every major resort in the American West. None of the American resorts, with the exception of Taos, even comes close to the ambience of Europe but skiing is also a case where improved technology and increased popularity have removed a great deal of the charm that existed in the '60s. Increased convenience and ease have extracted a price.

Down the hill from the *Adirondack Daily Enterprise* office was the Blue Line Sport Shop run by Howard Ellithorpe, who, knowing I was from Maine, used to constantly ask me what was so great about L. L. Bean. (I wanted to tell him the first thing was they wouldn't sell you a piece of junk.) Howard used to point out, quite correctly, that he had similar items at similar prices to Bean's and if you knew what you were doing you could outfit yourself well. But to meet the demand for low prices, Blue Line also had items of a quality Bean's never would have carried. Howard thought Bean's no-questions-asked return policy was ridiculous.

While at my desk one day, I received a phone call from an official at Schaeffer Brewing which ran a Biggest Fish contest. They said that Howard Ellithorpe had just registered a record-breaking lake trout from Big Green Pond and wanted to know if I had heard anything about it or could otherwise help them confirm the information. I asked when the fish had been caught, and they said two days previously.

Two days previously I had been doing a story on Little Green Pond, not far from Big Green, about its poisoning. Periodically, the Department of Conservation used rotenone to poison ponds that had become contaminated with junk fish. They killed off everything and then restocked the lakes. At Little Green, we had watched as the surface became covered with a variety of dead fish, dominated by perch, an inferior game species that competed for food with the more desirable trout. While there I had seen Howard Ellithorpe in another boat, picking up some of the larger lake trout that were still edible because the rotenone suffocated them and was therefore not harmful to humans.

I told the woman from Schaeffer about the pond poisoning and my seeing Howard. I left it to her to make any connection and I never mentioned the call to Howard. However, I felt a little better about carrying the honor of L. L. Bean and the State of Maine on my shoulders.

Although the breadth of my acquaintances and interests allowed me to learn things about Saranac Lake I would not otherwise have known, at the center of my life there were the Deckers.

Janet and Fritz Decker were almost twenty years older than I and could have been seen as members of my parents' generation. Although I was brought into their household as a member, it was not a parent/child relationship, but more like having a wise and devoted pair of older siblings.

The Decker kids weren't really that young. The eldest, Jane, was just finishing high school and going off to college. The others—Anne, John, Margaret, and Charlie—were like younger cousins to me. I liked them immensely.

Fritz was a legendary surgeon. According to Bea Sprague, who worked for his medical group, he was blessed with miraculous hands. Every patient was an important individual to Fritz, and he was known throughout the Adirondacks as the model of a caring physician.

More important to me, he loved to fly fish and to canoe. With Fritz in his early forties and me in my twenties, we made a canoe racing team, placing second to a couple of ringers—they were college-age and had spent the summer in a logging camp—in the Willard Hamner Race down the Saranac River. Fritz and I practiced hard for the event, developing our rhythm and stamina by paddling evenings after work for weeks before the event.

For Janet and me, one of our great bonding events was the arrival of Bertin, their American Field Service exchange student from Italy. She and I spent weeks beforehand learning Italian from records.

But most important, both Janet and Fritz were among that breed of people who are interested in everything and become informed about what interests them. This always makes for good conversation and whether it was at their house for dinner or paddling a canoe laden with supplies and kids out to their camp, the conversation was always fun and reluctantly concluded. Fritz was the more conservative of the two, but he was never dogmatic and I always learned from him. These were the kind of people I wrote for in Saranac Lake and they were the kind of people I was to write for in my future journalistic career—

people who didn't necessarily agree with me but who based their opinions on information and who were prepared to change their opinions should the facts warrant.

Even though I was only in Saranac Lake for four years, it is amazing how close I became to the Deckers and to others, and how spontaneous it was to renew those relationships thirty years later, after the hiatus that occurred when I came back to Maine and started *Maine Times* and my own family.

In the summer of 2002, after a wedding in nearby Potsdam, Eunice and I stopped to see the Deckers for the first time in several years. Fritz was not well. Janet seemed unchanged. Eunice is as at ease with the Deckers as I am, often having called on Fritz for a second opinion when dealing with her mother's illnesses. That evening the affection in the room was palpable.

Only a few months later, I learned I had cancer and the Deckers more than anyone took over the case—Fritz gave me good advice and Janet bucked me up—both of them putting my condition in the forefront despite Fritz's own precarious condition. He would die a year later.

In my brief four years in Saranac Lake, I also developed friends among the summer residents as well as the locals. I got to know Bruce Sundlun and his wife, Maddie, and used to spend evenings there immersed in political discussion, Bruce's favorite topic. They rented for the summer at Knollwood, a family compound where I also met and played tennis with Ellen Sulzberger and her husband, R. Peter Straus. Almost forty years later I was reading about Bruce as governor of Rhode Island and about Peter as the new stepfather of Monica Lewinsky.

The pinnacle of the summer heap was Marjorie Merriweather Post Davies May, the elderly heiress of Post Cereals (which had become General Foods) and one of the richest women in the world. She owned a glorious camp on Upper St. Regis Lake that I first approached in an electric-powered guideboat. Once it dropped me at the boathouse, I took a funicular up the side of the hill. The main house was decorated with Indian artifacts and the little pavilion where she invited people to dance on Sundays and Thursdays was lined with Fabergé eggs in cabinets, mementos of her marriage to

Joseph Davies who had been ambassador to Russia.

My father had done some legal work for her, and Mrs. May was involved in the Washington Opera with my mother. When Mrs. May learned I was working in the Adirondacks, she invited me to dinner. I was sitting among the mementos of Sitting Bull and Geronimo when Frank Trudeau arrived. Frank, it seems, had been a very good friend of Mrs. May's daughter, the actress Dina Merrill.

Frank Trudeau, like his father who had established Saranac Lake as the great tuberculosis cure center, was a doctor and was still the local aristocracy of one. His telephone number was "one," while ours at the paper was "two." He carried the Trudeau legacy and had recently married a glamorous younger woman, Ursula, from Montreal who was lively and always very friendly to me.[2] When he saw me in the room at Mrs. May's, Frank's face showed a mixture of surprise and disdain. "What are you doing here?" he asked. As I recall, I didn't have much to say for the rest of the evening.

However, I did return to Mrs. May's several times and she treated me like a young relative, often confiding to me in wry asides.

I was invited to a couple of the dance sessions to which she also invited professional instructors from Whiteface Inn in Lake Placid, both to instruct the incompetent guests, such as myself, and to dance with her. Even though she was at least in her seventies, she did a regal and fluid tango.

One evening we had been chatting between dances and the male instructor came up and started laying on the flattery about her striking good looks and graceful line. When he had finished and turned away, Mrs. May whispered to me, "There are times when I'm thankful I'm hard of hearing."

Another evening I was at her dinner table and among the guests was a museum curator, goatee and all. He picked up one of the dinner plates, inspected it carefully, and declared it "charming."

"I'm so glad you like it," Mrs. May said. "We gave it away as a premium to get people to buy Postum." Dealing with sycophancy is a talent the super rich must develop.

When I was editor of the *Adirondack Daily Enterprise* I was at the

---

2. His son is Garry Trudeau, author of *Doonesbury*.

right age and stage in my life to make these kinds of connections with people. I was young and unattached. My girlfriends tended to come from another group, most notably young women who came to the Adirondacks for summer jobs. During the winter pickings were slim, so I had plenty of time for my older friends.

I knew many different sorts of people well and I constantly had their feedback about what was happening in the community and how the newspaper was covering it, even though they seldom criticized specifically. It was more that they would tell me something I did not know, something I could not have known unless I had lived there for decades as they had, that changed the context of a story and therefore the viewpoint of our coverage. In Saranac Lake, my key critic and source of institutional memory was Bea Sprague with whom I discussed the local coverage on a regular basis.

Something I wrote in the *Adirondack Daily Enterprise* about Saranac Lake was much more likely to bring an irate reader to my desk than the same article in the Syracuse or Watertown paper, which covered the area from hundreds of miles away. As I was to learn, the more local the paper, the more accurate writing could be. I say "could" because of the counterforces at work. For the experienced reporter, fear of offending the local establishment—of which the publisher is a member—may lead to the pulling of one's punches. All of the characteristics that give the local reporter an advantage can work equally against him. Intimate knowledge cuts both ways. In the old days we journalists lived in the community and we attended the events we were reporting on and giving opinions about. Today that overlap and intimacy would be frowned upon. Journalism watchdogs tell us the same person should not be reporting on events and writing editorials about them. But on a paper like the *Enterprise*, circulation 3,700, we did not have enough staff to make this an option. I covered meetings—school board, village board, town supervisors—several nights a week and I wrote both news stories and editorials about them. There was seldom a local issue that I commented on where I did not personally know some of the people involved.

My own belief was that as editor, if I could not separate straight reporting from opinion writing in my own work, how could I be expected to identify it in others? Besides, I had total confidence in my abilities. When I was growing up, I saw Walter Lippmann and Scotty Reston making these distinctions. They had dinner with the people they wrote about. They could separate personal acquaintance from professional responsibility. If they could, why couldn't I?

Today, my local daily paper has a hard time getting the young reporters it hires to even live in one of the communities they cover. Instead, they want to live 30 miles away in Portland where there is much more social action. Their lack of knowledge and feel for the communities they report on discards an advantage we had. The strength of small newspapers is closeness to the community, the ability to evaluate much more easily than someone from away the reliability of the players, and to understand the community's history and there-fore the context in which contemporary events occur.

Local copy in the newspaper consisted mainly of reports on town and school boards, which I covered and wrote up before going to sleep. Similar reports came in from our part-time reporters in the neighboring towns, Lake Placid and Tupper Lake. Correspondents gathered club and social news, much of which was phoned in. And our photographer, Bill McLaughlin, produced a daily column—much of the information gathered during his nightly rounds of the bars—that was the most popular feature in the paper. He was a talented writer with an acid wit who was at his best when making fun of me, the young, from-away editor who thought he knew everything.

Several years after I started at the *Enterprise*, we were able to sub-scribe to the New York Times News Service and became the smallest newspaper in America to do so. Our readers wanted the columnists, especially Scotty Reston and Russell Baker. I also wanted the coverage of Southeast Asia, led by David Halberstam. At that point, AP cover-age of the emerging war, starting in Laos, was body-count journalism with very little on the internal political situation. I wanted that first reporting that attempted to explain why we were fighting the war and why we were failing.

We could not afford wire service from the *Times*, and the columns came by mail. But I was allowed to use anything from the *Times* for my payment of $35 a week—based on the *Enterprise*'s small circula-tion. Consequently, as soon as I had finished my initial clipping of the AP wire, I would go to the newsstand down the street and pick up my papers, including the *Times*. I would read a dozen stories I might be interested in, then clip one or two I wanted and had the capacity to reset, so that our readers were getting that afternoon what had appeared in the *Times* only that morning.

We didn't do investigative journalism. We didn't have the time even if we had had the talent. I did write some features about such things as the opening of a new research institute to carry on the work of the Trudeau Foundation and the AP office in Albany picked it up and sent it around the world, making sure they got clippings from as far away as Rome (Italy) and sending them to me as an incentive to do more.

The bureau chief, Earl Abramson, was actually from Maine and his assistant, Toni Adams, whom I knew only as a voice over the phone, was a taskmaster.

During my tenure at the *Enterprise*, the body of a Mrs. Douglas was discovered deep in the waters of Lake Placid, some twenty years after her disappearance, with a rope around its neck. She had been an educator (the women's division of Rutgers had been named after her), so her apparent suicide created a furor and we were supposed to report it to the world.

The story was about three days old when the weekend came and, after giving my final Friday report to Toni, I told her I would talk to her on Monday. "No, you won't," she said. "You'll call me every four hours, whether you have something new or not, just to let me know you're on the job." I don't think many bureaus worked their members as hard as Albany did; none of them would dare do so today. Now the AP, without the head-to-head competition from United Press (UPI), in many states maintains an office in the same building as the largest daily and gets copies of their stories. That's why what you see in the smaller dailies and hear over the radio and television is a rehash of the morning daily.

The one campaign I did generate was to clean up the Saranac River where it ran through town, flowing out of Lake Flower.

I wrote Ginia Gargioni in Turin and asked her to send me picture postcards with attractive riverfronts. Typical of Ginia, she took on the task as a cause and I was soon flooded with postcards not just from Italy but from all over Europe. These I printed on the editorial page for months, without comment other than where they were, but the message was clear and got through: rivers could be attractive community focal points.

The local electric company agreed to shut off the water at the dam and one Saturday morning, the river, where it ran through town, was drained, exposing old tires, junk auto parts, and three decades of miscellaneous debris. More than a hundred people, including the local assemblyman, Red Plumadore, who had little use for me, showed up in hip boots and took the burlap bags offered. Within a couple of hours the river bottom was clean and the water was turned back on. Dew Drop Morgan particularly liked the project because his best tables looked out on the river.

I was always grateful for any help I could get and one day Howard Riley, then a Linotype operator, asked if I would teach him to be a reporter, a job he was willing to perform after his full shift in the shop.

Howard was a little older than I and had grown up on a subsistence farm in a large Catholic family. He had finished high school, married, and immediately begun his own large family made up of boys whose names all began with the letter K, as in Kurt, Keefe, Keegan, Kean, Kasey, and Kelby.

Howard and I had a special affinity that continues to exist today, but although he was older and more experienced then, he didn't have the credentials to do what he wanted. So we started our own two-person writing course. I had him read the *Tribune* and the *Times* and we would discuss how they handled the same story differently. I gave him Hemingway and Fitzgerald to read and we discussed straight style. (There was very little journalistic non-fiction being done then.)

Howard took to it quickly and he was soon a competent reporter, but the economic situation at the paper was such that at first he continued setting type and did his stories in the afternoon or evening after the paper had been put to bed.

Howard was elected mayor of Saranac Lake, and became editor and general manager of the paper for nine years. He then went to Lake Placid and became a member of the 1980 Olympic Committee and then handled press relations for the games. Along with his obvious intelligence and management skills, Howard also has a wicked sense of humor, very much in keeping with the Maine sense of humor in that it is most often aimed at puncturing pretense. He later retired as village manager and visits us in Maine, as much to see my wife as to see me.

When Howard was mayor in 1964, he was also a reporter, a situation which put him in a conflict. Bobby Kennedy, then running for the U.S. Senate in New York, was visiting Saranac Lake. The mayor was to join him on the podium but before that, Howard's job as a reporter was to ask the usual questions, some of which were thought up by me and some by the AP office in Albany. At that time, many of the usual questions were not friendly, such as, "Did he consider himself a carpetbagger because he had moved to the state just to run for the Senate?" I never knew what the AP expected a candidate to say in reply to such a question—that he was indeed a carpetbagger and an opportunist? Howard did his job as reporter on the way to Kennedy's speech. After the speech, Kennedy, who had been incensed by Howard's questions, had the car leave before Howard could get in and Howard was reduced to running along beside it, calling out, "But I'm the mayor."

After I had been at the paper for about a year, the general manager, Jack Waterbury, left and I became acting publisher as well as editor, with an increase in salary from $85 a week to $100. One of the obligations that came with being publisher was making political contributions.

I learned that the county supervisors made the decision on where to place legal advertising, worth several thousand dollars a year to the *Enterprise*. But to get the advertising, we were expected to make a political contribution to the Democrats—we were clearly a Democratic paper. However, since corporate political contributions were illegal, I was expected to make the contribution on my own. One week's salary. Non-reimbursable.

I seriously thought about making no donation and writing an editorial about what I considered a corrupt practice, but I quickly rationalized that would be futile.

The *Enterprise* had revenue of about $250,000 a year and lost a few thousand dollars, so the income from the legal ads was significant. In my new role as publisher, to attack the system would have been to lose the advertising without any hope of changing the system. (On investigation I learned the practice was universal and so well known that no one in a position to change it would be in the least surprised by my revelation.) For once I kept my mouth shut. Fortunately, our cost controls had been sloppy enough that with a little bit of effort and attention I was able to put the paper in the black. It turned out this was the first time it had had an operating profit in years.

Starting as editor and ending up as editor and publisher was a pattern I was to repeat, and it created a learning opportunity that was crucial in starting *Maine Times* later. Although I loved my years in Saranac Lake and later considered returning when Jim Loeb wanted to sell the paper, by 1965 I was ready for a change in career and I wanted to fulfill my original ambition and return to Maine where a job was awaiting me.

Eight

Return to Maine for Good

In April 1965 I married Eunice Theodore, whom I had met when she worked summers at the *Lake Placid News*, and we set off for Bath, Maine, where I had been hired as editor of the *Bath Daily Times*. Unfortunately, no one had informed the existing editor of decades that he was being replaced. The general manager, Lou Estes, was the only one told I had been hired and he did not feel it was his responsibility to fire the old editor. So I told Cam Niven, the owner of the *Bath Daily Times* and the neighboring *Brunswick Record*, who had hired me, that I still intended to take the job and I would return to my parents' summer home for a week to give him time to resolve the situation in Bath.

At the end of the week, Cam said he had arranged a meeting with the editor, Ace Trueworthy, and we would discuss what each of our duties would be. At that meeting, I outlined what I intended to do—everything. The next Monday, I showed up for work and Ace didn't. For several years he came in every Friday to pick up his paycheck, the only severance he had after decades of keeping the paper going.[1]

And "keep it going" is descriptive. Despite some very talented people on the staff, the *Bath Times* was suffering from neglect. It was printed on an old flatbed press with poor reproduction, producing pictures so muddy it was sometimes difficult to tell what they were. The paper often missed its deadline, coming out too late for the 4:00 P.M. shift change at Bath Iron Works, which constituted a large portion of its circulation.

There were no local editorials, only canned opinion from a national

---

1. Cam Niven's method of replacing editors persisted for years. Although John Cole and I left of our own accord, as did the next editor, a string of new editors learned they no longer had a job when their replacements showed up for work, with no warning to them.

syndicate, and local news was a rarity on the front page. Local stories went on the back page. The top story on the left-hand side—the second lead—was "Weather Elsewhere," a wire service feature that told you what the temperature was in Portland, Oregon, and Calcutta, India. Because all the pages were laid out in metal frames (chases) at the same time, and there were usually only eight pages, stories continued (jumped) from page to page, almost at random. A story might start on page eight, continue on page six, and finish up on page seven. It took a persevering reader to follow this trail to the end.

Since there were no local editorials—the syndicated editorials were wishy-washy to appeal to the broad constituency using them[2]—writers tended to editorialize in their stories. This heavy-handed injection of what was clearly opinion into the news stories had left the paper in some disrepute among a portion of its readers.

The *Times* was small, about 3,500 circulation, and I came on with a reformer's zeal, bolstered by all I had learned at the *Enterprise*. I now knew how such an operation functioned, from top to bottom, and I immediately changed the deadlines and made sure they were all adhered to, starting with myself, and told reporters their work would not appear unless I had it on time.

Thanks to what Armand Amell had taught me, I had the shop foreman, Arthur Johansen, in my camp immediately. We worked on the front page together from the first day, establishing a friendship that continued for years.

By my second day on the job, I was writing local editorials and one of the first I wrote suggested that all the merchants on Front Street, the main commercial artery, get rid of their clashing signs and put up gold-lettered signs on a black background. Within half an hour of the paper's hitting the street, a delegation of merchants arrived at the office to tell me why this was a stupid idea. Almost forty years later, when I received an award as a "downtown visionary," I recalled this story and noted that Front Street could still use work on its signs.

---

2. I don't know how many newspapers still used these canned editorials in 1965. It had to be few. Now you see editorial writers with nothing to say picking up editorials from other newspapers.

Local stories were moved to page one, work by local artists of stature[3] appeared regularly on the editorial page instead of an editorial cartoon, and we again became the smallest paper in the country to have New York Times News Service. I modernized the page layout, giving it the horizontal look derived from the heyday of the *Herald Tribune* and very much in fashion at the time. In those years, the Ayer advertising agency offered a national award for page one design and the *Bath Daily Times* became a finalist, chosen for its clean look and its adherence to what the judges liked to see.

Even though I was warned that our readers were interested only in local news, I tried to give them a good balance. Our surveys showed that for many of our readers, this was the only daily newspaper they read, a daunting fact for someone like myself who believed in the necessity of an informed citizenry. I was supposed to keep them up-to-date on the major issues of the world with eight pages a day, an exercise in careful selection of the news that I took seriously.

Despite my belief in a newspaper's educational role and my own interest in world affairs, I was properly affected by the story I was told to illustrate the interests of Bath readers. According to this story, Charlie Burden, a local pediatrician and founder of the maritime museum, had gone off to Yale straight from Morse High School. Once there, another student came by his room in Vanderbilt Hall and asked Charlie if he wanted to subscribe to the *New York Times*. Charlie allegedly answered, "I don't think so. I don't know anyone in New York."[4]

The publisher, Cam Niven, had not wanted to change the editorship until after the hotly contested question of urban renewal was settled. With only a final referendum to be held shortly after I arrived, it was defeated. I refrained from commenting.

---

3. I was helped in this endeavor by Ernie Haskell, Jr., whose father had done wonderful etchings and who had attracted others, including John Marin, to paint in the area. Maine, of course, is proud of its art heritage and I soon had talented artists submitting work for publication, especially the types of prints that reproduced well once we went to offset printing.
4. Today you can buy the *New York Times* at the local convenience store and can even receive Sunday delivery at home. I consider delivery of the *Sunday Times* and the recent availability of first-rate, locally baked Black Crow Tuscan bread as the final signs that we live in a sophisticated state.

The *Times* had previously made clear its support for urban renewal and while I could plead ignorance as a rationale for not taking a stand only a few weeks after I arrived, I am not sure how I would have come out at the time. The people I would come to respect the most, people like Bill Haggett who was chairman of the city council and Charlie Burden, the pediatrician, were for urban renewal on the grounds that Bath's retail district was in bad shape and stood in danger of losing its anchor, Sears. Some historic buildings would have been torn down, and that didn't appeal to me. But I tended to favor federal programs then, and I had had no experience with how a town rebounded when a large portion of its downtown was eradicated or whether new businesses really would move in. Regardless of what urban renewal might have accomplished, the battle shook the established order in Bath.

A key figure in promoting urban renewal had been John Newall, president of Bath Iron Works, the dominant industry in the "Shipbuilding City." Newall's father had been legendary, keeping the shipyard from going bankrupt during the military slump following World War I and leading it into World War II when the company produced more war ships than the entire Japanese industry. While employment had slipped back to 2,500 from more than 20,000 in Bath and South Portland combined during the war, Newell was still the dominant industry personified. He did not hesitate to use his authority, even though he had been rebuffed in the past.

Only a few years before, in 1960, the local garden club had decided to beautify the park in front of the library with a statue by world-renowned sculptor William Zorach, who had summered for years in nearby Georgetown. A local school teacher had spread a false accusation that Zorach had been a communist and Newell joined the fray on the side of opponents to the Zorach sculpture, thus putting himself on the opposite side from the philanthropically minded segment of the community. Newell was always to prove enigmatic. He would in the 1970s forsake his industrial friends and turn from a supporter of nuclear power to an ardent opponent.

At the time of the urban renewal vote, when he headed the local authority, he made the double mistake of being inaccessible and of threatening that BIW executives would no longer live in Bath if its citizens did not do what he wanted. While much of the rhetoric had to do with federal coercion and tearing down architecturally significant buildings, the real question was whether the urban renewal project would keep the anchor stores in downtown Bath and help smaller local merchants. Although the votes in Bath were strung out over several years, there was already a plan to build the region's first shopping mall at Cooks Corner, between Bath and Brunswick. This had been the impetus for Cam Niven's tentative decision to merge the two papers his family owned, the struggling *Bath Daily Times*, and the healthy and growing weekly *Brunswick Record* that had more than three times the circulation. With a new shopping center midway between two towns that were less than 10 miles apart, the large advertisers, most notably Sears, would want to reach both communities efficiently. Despite the benefits of such a shopping center to the newspapers, Cam had allowed the *Times* to support urban renewal, whose goal was to block the shopping center's development.

Urban renewal's most visible opponent, Bud Shepard, who ran a small clothing store on Front Street, kept up on trends nationwide and was convinced, as history would prove correct, that the large retail stores were moving to shopping malls regardless of such local efforts.

Bob Cummings, the reporter who covered the issue for years and came to support it, had changed his mind two decades later when interviewed for a history of Bath.[5] "It was a totally blank check that they were gambling," Cummings told the historians. "People felt that . . . they could create a store like Sears. But in retrospect we were all dreaming. It would have destroyed the town . . . . My guess is that nothing would have come in."

With urban renewal dead, I campaigned to build on Bath's incredible depth of quality architecture and to refocus on the river, as had been suggested in the early urban renewal plans and then abandoned.

The Kennebec River that runs through Bath was very different from the comparative trickle that ran through Saranac Lake, and the Kennebec was the defining feature in the city's history. Famous as the route of Benedict Arnold's march on Quebec, for its pure ice,

5. Kenneth R. Martin and Ralph Linwood Snow, *Maine Odyssey: Good Times and Hard Times in Bath* (Bath, ME: Patten Free Library, 1988).

and for its now almost extinct salmon, the Kennebec had made Bath America's cradle of ships. For centuries its banks had been lined with shipyards and all the allied industries they spawned. The heirs to the great shipbuilding fortunes this created continued to keep a connection with the city, even if that meant only maintaining a summer home at nearby Small Point.

But in the days when Maine's rivers were turned into open sewers, the Kennebec became the collector for the six rivers that ran into it at Merrymeeting Bay. This included the Androscoggin, declared one of the ten filthiest rivers in America. The Androscoggin started in New Hampshire's White Mountains and was soon polluted by a large paper mill in Berlin, New Hampshire. From there, it just kept accumulating more toxins. The Kennebec itself began at Moosehead Lake and was the economic basis for several cities, including the capital of Augusta, which added its municipal as well as its industrial sewage. Much of this pollution also affected Merrymeeting Bay, one of the prime duck-hunting sites in the United States.

Ed Muskie's campaign to clean up the nation's rivers had just begun in the U.S. Senate and we were very aware of the problem. Bob Cummings focused on the Kennebec in his stories and one particular story had a startling quote. After learning that the local hospital straight-piped its waste into the river, Bob quoted a local nurse as saying, "If you think that's bad, consider what the funeral homes send into the river."

Cummings was a first-rate reporter and a committed environmentalist. He also knew the city of Bath inside out. Because he had led the paper through the urban renewal controversy, he had felt he should succeed Ace Trueworthy as editor. He may have resented my arrival on the scene but he continued to report in a professional manner.

A couple of years later, when we had merged the papers and John Cole and I began to contemplate leaving, Cummings asked me if he ever had any hope of becoming editor. I asked Cam Niven, who said, "No," and Cummings left the *Times-Record* for the Portland papers, where he became the featured writer in the *Sunday Telegram*, almost ten times larger in circulation. There he picked up on an issue he had begun to write about in the old *Bath Times*, Maine's public lots. A fellow named White Nichols believed thousands of acres under the control of the paper companies still belonged to the state since only the cutting rights had been ceded. Cummings made this his crusade, eventually stimulating the state to reclaim the land for the public. I don't think he would have succeeded without the *Telegram's* circulation. His promotion barrier at the *Times-Record* turned out to be good for him and for the state.

While my overriding concern was the editorial content of the paper, I never lost interest in graphics and the technical end of newspapers. As soon as Cam would allow it, we began to print the *Times* on Brunswick's new offset press, drastically improving its appearance. The fact that we created the paper in Bath and took page proofs 10 miles to Brunswick to be photographed and etched into printing plates, all without missing a deadline, indicated how technically easy the merger would be. It also made me realize that whether the press was 10 miles or 75 miles away made no difference except in terms of logistics, a key factor in the options we would have for printing *Maine Times* a few years later.

With the *Bath Daily Times* improved graphically and with the staff throwing itself into some of the state's most controversial environmental issues, we began to get noticed on the statewide level. In 1966 we won an award from the Natural Resources Council for the best environmental reporting, beating out the *Brunswick Record*, in whose shadow the Bath paper had been living for the past decade.

Cam Niven, who seldom visited the *Times*, decided to go to Augusta to accept the award for the paper, reinforcing my belief that the most useful function of awards is to keep one's publisher happy. In this case, there was the added pleasure that we had come out ahead of our sister paper, the *Brunswick Record*, which regularly won awards and was recognized throughout the state for its environmental coverage under John Cole's editorship.

Once again, I was thrown into the publishing end of the paper. The *Times's* general manager, Lou Estes, was the classic salesman, good-natured and free-wheeling. With the daily paper struggling, he had started a weekly shopper that was delivered free throughout the entire circulation area and that made money. But he also operated the business out of his back pocket and when an advertiser owed the

Times money, he was not averse to taking it out in trade, a common practice with small-town newspapers and radio stations. A conflict arose when Lou traded new tires for his car for an overdue bill. Since Lou used the car primarily for business, the practice could be considered legitimate but an absentee publisher had no way of knowing how many such transactions there were and how scrupulously they were reviewed. Lou Estes left, with the *Coastal Journal*, the shopper he had founded, and since the merger with the *Brunswick Record* was on the horizon, Cam asked me to take over the publishing duties temporarily.

After Lou left I looked at the accounts receivable and discovered one of his more innovative sales techniques. Dozens of advertisers owed bills for $8 that had never been paid and had been carried on the books for years. I did some research and found that $8 was what we charged for a signature ad, one of the more dubious promotions used by small-town newspapers. In a signature ad, twenty or thirty merchants are listed as supporting the local high-school basketball team or a civic event. The sales pitch is something like: "Hey, it's only eight bucks. Do you want to be known as someone who won't support the basketball team, even for a measly eight bucks?"

I telephoned some of the delinquent advertisers and learned that they had never been asked if they wanted their names listed. Then I called some of those who had paid and some of them said they hadn't been solicited either; Lou had just put their names on the ad and they had paid when they received the bills. It appeared that more than half who had been listed without being asked actually paid. Lou had refined the system. By listing twice as many merchants as were needed to pay for the ad, with 50 percent payment, he still covered the cost.

I wrote off the remaining $8 charges as uncollectible.

A confrontation occurred after Cam had put me in charge of the business operation. I noticed that the labor leader Ben Dorsky, my old acquaintance from the Coffin gubernatorial campaign, who printed the *Labor Record* in our shop, was putting the union bug on it, indicating it had been produced by a union shop. Of course, there were no union members in our operation; that's why we were so much cheaper and that's why Dorsky was there, to maximize the profits for a paper in which he owned a major interest, I'd been told.

So I confronted Dorsky and told him he could no longer use the union bug since we were non-union. He went to Cam and I'm not sure what Cam said to him, but I know Cam didn't like losing the business. However, Cam was above all a straight-shooter. He backed my position and Dorsky took his paper somewhere else to print.

But my primary interest then lay in getting the *Bath Daily Times* and the *Brunswick Record* merged as quickly as possible. Journalistically, I could not envision facing the limitations of the *Times*'s small readership indefinitely and there was not much hope for enlarging the circulation of the *Times* by itself. All of the changes I had made had no discernible impact. The only thing that created a jump in circulation was when we instituted home delivery in West Bath and obtained 250 new subscribers. Since they were not offered home delivery on any other paper, they took ours.

Cam wanted to merge the papers and the merger had been implicit in his decision to hire me, but he also saw the pitfalls and the probability that we could lose money in the first year; the existing profits from the *Record* far outweighed any losses from the *Times*. That we had been producing the *Times* in Bath and printing it on the offset presses in Brunswick should have swung the balance in favor of going ahead. The logistical problems had already been ironed out.

To make it even easier, we moved the editorial offices for the combined operation to Bath with John Cole taking the title of editor and my becoming managing editor.

John and I had discussed the merger for years and when Cam seemed to be balking, I had gone to John and pled with him to put pressure on Cam to go ahead. I looked to John as more than a friend; I saw him as a mentor and working side by side with him had tremendous appeal. Also our interests dovetailed. I loved the technical end of editing: coordination with production and layout, working one-on-one with reporters, and copyediting and writing headlines. John was a brilliant writer. At times his writing overwhelmed his reporting, but he was always engaging. John also had a gift for being able to conceptualize the big campaign and crusade for it.

Before the merger, John had championed the cause of L. M. C. Smith, a gentleman organic beef farmer who wanted to prevent Central Maine Power from spraying herbicides on the power line right of way that ran across his property. With John providing coverage and writing strong editorials, they won the battle and set a state-wide precedent. John had also led the campaign to prevent a single road that ran down the spine of the narrow Harpswell peninsula from being declared a scenic highway—on the grounds this would increase traffic and destroy the very qualities the project was supposed to make available to more people.

But perhaps most important was a journalistic philosophy John had developed, partly out of necessity, about how a local paper should serve its readers. Because the morning daily, the *Portland Press Herald*, also served Brunswick, the morning daily would always have a report on the previous night's town council meeting before the weekly or subsequently an afternoon daily could. Therefore, we had to offer something more than a rehashed report.

John would take an issue raised at the council meeting—or some other board meeting—and pursue it. Seldom do elected officials have all the information they need at the first public meeting; many of the questions they raise go unanswered, at least until the next meeting. John's style was to send a reporter out to answer those questions and any others an intelligent observer might have, then run a story explicating the issue in detail. Similarly, in covering town meetings, still a major annual event for communities in the circulation area, he would do most of the coverage before the meeting. Reviewing the warrant, he would pick out the controversial issues and do stories exploring them in advance. From this evolved a theory of journalism that it was a newspaper's responsibility to give its readers the information they needed to make sound decisions. As obvious as it may seem, this is still not a universal practice and it was in contradiction to a newspaper's traditional role of instantly recording history.

With the papers merged, we were allowed to hire a new reporter, Ken Morrison, who had worked for the Associated Press. John cared more about Ken's pieces than any others, and for good reason. Now he could turn someone loose on his story ideas and the results were impressive.

Ken wrote about injustices suffered by the Passamaquoddy Indians who lived in Washington County, a good five hours away. He wrote about mistreatment of the mentally handicapped. We did a series called the Forgotten Poor about a substandard housing development on the outskirts of town, and we exposed the fact that Maine still had a debtors' law and people were going to jail, after a hearing in a local official's kitchen, for not paying their bills. Primarily using Ken, we wrote about whatever interested us.

The actual operation of the paper fell pretty much to me and to Elizabeth (Buffer) Fine, who had been de facto managing editor and copyeditor at the old *Record*. Having worked in the past for such publications as the *San Francisco Chronicle*, Buffer was fast and professional. Between us, we handled all the copy.

But there was unrest at the top. Cam had always faced contradictory forces. When he took over the *Record*, he assumed control from his father, P. K. Niven, who had come into the position through marriage. His wife—Cam's mother—was the daughter of Frank Nichols, who had owned both papers but who had been proudest of the *Bath Daily Times* where a plaque memorialized the paper's contribution to the election of President James Buchanan.

P. K. was noted for his devotion to Bowdoin College and Central Maine Power, then a major reactionary force in the state. After the merger, P. K. still had an office at the paper although his official duties were non-existent. He gave John suggestions but I had almost no contact with him; indirectly, I felt his presence because when we wrote something he didn't like about the power company, he would make sure the vice president for public relations would take us to lunch and set us straight. John and I were never influenced by this tactic but the lunches, at the old Eagle Hotel which still had white linen tablecloths and was soon to make way for a supermarket, featured a good finnan haddie. The finnan haddie became something of an incentive for criticizing the power company.

Even in the last days we were at the *Times-Record* we would spot P. K. in his office marking names listed in an ad against the war in Vietnam. We were told he was particularly interested in Bowdoin faculty who subscribed to the ad. Both John and I were strongly against the war and said so editorially, but P. K. couldn't do anything about that. Cam was a good insulator. Although we would sometimes hear the complaints about the paper Cam had heard at the previous Saturday's cocktail party, we never received a "command" from Cam.

Sometimes the criticisms were valid but whenever we didn't like a suggestion, we stood up and defended ourselves and that was that. Since Cam was so involved with the community, often philanthropically, it could be said that he represented the local establishment, especially the business community, and his viewpoint may have been influenced by them. On the other hand, he never forced a position on us editorially. He made his case as he had every right to do. It was his newspaper. But he also valued our independence and unless we had done something he considered egregious, he drew a clear line of authority that he did not cross.

As good as Ken Morrison's stories were, there was an irrefutable argument to be made that they didn't sell extra papers. The stories were especially open to this criticism when they reported on something that didn't occur within our coverage area.

Ken was not the only frill, an example of our doing what we wanted to do as journalists rather than what we had to do. Another was my arts coverage. At least the art pages that I instituted on Thursdays were mostly local, with a few infusions from Portland, and they didn't cost anything because I edited them and wrote for them on my own time. John and I never complained about being overworked. We were delighted to have this forum and if we had to do the really interesting stuff by investing extra hours, we didn't care.

Then a greater problem arose. When we moved the editorial offices from Bath to Brunswick, we also moved the production staff, and those working in Bath had been paid less than those working in Brunswick. This might have been justified when the papers were separate because the *Record* was making money and the *Times* was losing money. But once Linotype operators were sitting side by side, performing the same work, with many of the Bath people having more seniority, the wage discrepancies became intolerable. Led by the Bath contingent, but with support from many of the Brunswick production people, the back shop threatened to unionize.

For Cam the central issue was never clearing up the wage discrepancy. He was fair and would remedy that. On the other hand, he did not do so in time. I suspect he had been poorly served by those to whom he had delegated authority, and a situation that could have been diplomatically handled had spiraled out of control. The issue for

Cam became control, and unionization meant lack of control. A strike was called.

The editorial staff stayed on the job, but John and I clearly sided with the production workers and tried to intervene on their behalf. Unfortunately for the Linotype operators in particular, technology was working against them.

We were printing offset and IBM had recently introduced a carbon ribbon, proportional-spacing typewriter that produced camera-ready copy that could not be distinguished from what had been set on a Linotype. Anyone who could type could now become a typesetter, producing work much faster than a traditional typesetter, and an IBM Selectric cost only about $1,200 as opposed to thousands for the complex and quirky Linotype. And we could lease them.

The union was voted down and everyone came back to work but two important things had occurred.

In an effort to justify Ken Morrison's salary, John and I had come up with the idea of turning his stories and my weekly art pages into a separate tabloid that would be contained in the Thursday *Times-Record*—the week's best-selling issue due to the grocery coupons—and would be sold separately in a broader area. There would be no extra editorial cost but there would be enough extra circulation to generate new advertising revenues that we thought would cover the extra press run. After the strike, that idea was put on a very back burner.

For years we had talked about a statewide weekly, first as part of several existing weeklies, later as a stand-alone. Cam had made his arguments against our extra coverage only too well. Daily newspapers were about local coverage, and local clubs and television listings and sports scores and bridge columns. We had been spending 90 percent of our time doing what we had to do in order to spend 10 percent doing what we wanted to do.

We now envisioned a statewide weekly that would report no fires or murders or traffic accidents, that would have no comics to worry about keeping in order, that would be freed of all the restrictions that so hampered us.

The *Times-Record* was through with its birth pangs. It was in good shape and the merger would prove to have been wise. It was time for us to move on.

Part 3

IT IS ONLY HUMAN for officials to feel that unfavorable news and critical comment is biased, incompetent, and misleading. There is no denying the sincerity of their complaints and there is no use pretending that any newspaperman can regularly give the whole objective truth about all complicated and controverted questions. The theory of a free press is that the truth will emerge from free reporting and free discussion, not that it will be presented perfectly and instantly in any one account.

—Walter Lippmann, "Today and Tomorrow" column, April 25, 1936

Nine

The Nuts and Bolts of *Maine Times*

On October 4, 1968, I was standing in a supermarket parking lot in Westbrook, the aroma of the sulphite paper mill wafting overhead, handing out copies of the first issue of *Maine Times*. My partner, John Cole, was back in Brunswick attending a celebration given by our backers, Kate and Jim Redwine, but I had more important things to do.

Part of my strategy for distributing that first issue had been to hand them out to workers as they left the major mills. We knew that the S. D. Warren paper mill in Westbrook had almost a thousand workers, but we did not know they were spread over several shifts. Based on our experience with Bath Iron Works (BIW), we thought they would all come out at once. They didn't, so I still had some 500 copies of the first issue to distribute.

Consequently, I was trying to foist them on shoppers who, because of another mistake I made, thought I was trying to give them a political handout.

Maine Times was a tabloid, and the only tabloids most people in Maine had seen before were political promotions. As for color on the cover: ditto. And there, taking up the entire front page, was Ed Muskie who was running for vice president. No wonder they thought it was a political tract.

Those mistakes were minor compared to all the other mistakes I had made. In doing my financial projections, I had not factored in inflation. For several years there had been almost none. And while I had come pretty close to estimating the amount of money we would lose before breaking even, I had miscalculated how fast we would lose it. I thought we would lose $150,000 in three years; we lost $174,000. But we lost $119,000 of that in the first year. To make these figures relevant today, multiply by ten. By my estimate, the cost of starting a similar publication would be at least $2 million.

Fortunately, our core, totally seat-of-the-pants supposition had been correct. There was an audience for a statewide newspaper that dealt with the issues that we wanted to cover. It was not as large as we had hoped, but it was large enough so that we would eventually survive.

To prepare for that first issue, I had left the *Times-Record* in August 1968 and set up shop in two upstairs rooms at an old bank building in Topsham, across the river from Brunswick. The rent was $75 a month. Cam Niven had allowed Buffer Fine, Ken Morrison, and John Cole to stay on at their jobs at the *Times-Record* until the last minute. An ad sales person, a production person, and a part-time secretary would round out the staff: seven people to start a new statewide newspaper.

Prior to publication, we had created our own mailing list of graduates of Maine colleges still living in Maine, culled from alumni registers by John's teenage boys and then stamped onto metal Addressograph plates. With a few hundred advance subscriptions at $5 a year that had come in response to flyers I had placed under car windshield wipers, we were going to sample 10,000 of the college graduates each week in four-week cycles. Through a combination of this sampling, free distribution at selected events, and newsstand sales, we intended to maintain a base circulation of 20,000, gradually reducing the free copies as they were replaced by paid subscribers.

We would print in Belfast, 75 miles away, sending the paste-ups of early pages by mail. On Thursday morning, I would drive an hour and a half with the final pages to arrive by 7:00 A.M. After printing, the copies to be mailed to subscribers and small newsstands were processed in Belfast and I carried the rest of the copies back to Topsham in my blue Plymouth Barracuda, usually arriving before noon. In essence, we were taking what we had learned when we printed the daily 10 miles from the editorial offices and applying it to our new venture. The only equipment we needed besides old typewriters were a single IBM Selectric typewriter and a Rube Goldberg headline-setting machine called a Typositor; we didn't own even these—we leased them for less than $100 a month.

We did not realize our good fortune then that local postmasters still had a lot of autonomy, and the modern hub distribution system, dictated by some hands-off executive in Washington, had not yet slowed down the mail. The postmaster in Belfast was the father of Mike Bryant, in charge of production at the Belfast printing plant, and a strong supporter. In Topsham, Charlie Payne was acting postmaster and he was willing to do anything to help us. He was soon succeeded by Bernie Pagurko who managed to be equally helpful while following the rules more strictly. These men still believed the U.S. Post Office was a vital communications service and they quickly invested in our success.

While we were sending out all those free copies, we had to use third class mail, which legally doesn't have to be delivered for three days. Some out-of-state readers did have to wait a couple of days for their paper, but in state, almost everyone received it the next day. Even though the labels said third class, every postmaster in Maine seemed to know this was a new publication and therefore time sensitive, and since they could process it more rapidly than required, they did so.

We met with similar cooperation in trusting our pages to the mail. We shipped the paste-ups from Topsham to Belfast in easily identified boxes that would occasionally get lost. When they did, our postmasters in both locations took up the hunt like the air force tracking a missile. They called their fellow postmasters and, operating through their own network, invariably found the pages in a matter of hours. Although there were some close calls, the printing of the paper was never delayed by lost pages.

Postal rates were also dramatically lower when we began, and we could mail our 10,000 subscribers their copies for about $120 a week. Rate increases would soon push that up to more than $1,200 but not before we were able to gain a foothold. The cost today would be higher again but if starting now, we would try to deliver electronically. The U.S. Postal Service has removed itself from the timely delivery business.

Those first heady weeks we were signing up more than 200 new subscribers a week and I was euphorically predicting that we would reach 10,000 by the end of the year. It turned out that subscribers did not continue coming in at the same rate and we barely passed 5,000 by the end of the first year.

Newsstand sales also ran well below my expectation, climbing to

5,000 a week and then holding steady. We had not even done the rudimentary research of checking how many copies of other publications sold on the newsstands in Maine. Our 5,000 figure turned out to be equal to sales of the Sunday *New York Times* and higher than such magazines as the *Atlantic* and *Harper's*. However, on a monthly basis, we were selling 20,000 copies, an important figure because it put us on a par with such best-sellers as *Playboy*, a fact my friend David Turitz at Portland News brought to our attention and that we were able to use to encourage other distributors to help us increase our sales.

If circulation was healthy but not earth-shattering, advertising was another story.

We had been able to get a few well-wishers to advertise in the inaugural issue, but that proved to be the exception. Typical was the ad from Ward Brothers, a high-quality department store in Lewiston, whose owner, Larry Ward, was involved in liberal causes. John, who had known Larry from peace-oriented political campaigns, had asked Larry personally for an ad and reported proudly to me that Ward's would be running a full page. "Just once or every week?" I asked. "Oh, I'm sure it will be every week," John had answered. Of course, it was just once but Ward's did continue supporting us through smaller ads.

Despite our sparse circulation, some of the initial advertisers had impressive results. Harpswell House, which manufactured specialty slate products, had a customer respond to their $40 ad by ordering a couple of $150 slate tables, beautifully trimmed in hardwood. A shop called New Cargoes at the Old Custom House in Wiscasset found that their small ad brought in customers who liked to spend a few minutes discussing the newspaper before they bought something. It was clear that the customer was joining the advertiser in supporting a publication he or she wanted to see succeed.

Some advertisers placed their initial ads with us because they wanted to help us—but it turned out to be a good buy. Not only did readers share an interest in the new paper but they felt, accurately it turned out, that our advertisers would have tastes similar to their own. One of the keys to our advertising success over the next twenty years was to match the reader and the advertiser, not to try to entice an advertiser who had a product that would not appeal to our readers. This limited the potential advertisers, but it also meant that those who succeeded were loyal and regular.

As I look back over that first year, I realize that most of the ads came from friends of the paper, including my uncle, Sam Goldsmith, who ran a clothing store in Old Town, and people who supported what we were doing. Some had a less obvious relationship.

One day in 1969 I was having a cream cheese and olive sandwich at the counter in Hays Drug Store, the flatiron building in front of the Portland Museum of Art that is now a Starbucks. A small man two stools down from me said, "You look like a Cox." I replied that I was, and we struck up a conversation about the new newspaper while we finished our lunches. Then he invited me across the street to his store which sold clothing for large and tall men and gave me an ad. I told him I wasn't sure advertising in *Maine Times* would do him much good and he held up his hand, palm outward, telling me I didn't understand. He wanted to support what we were doing. Not fully appreciating why he should care so much, I accepted the ad. It would have been impolite to reject it.

His name was Maury Drees and it was years later that I learned who he was. He had been a partner with my Uncle Morris when they had promoted small-time boxers across Maine. One Saturday night they were in Rumford, a mill town in the foothills, and their boxer, a certain Pinkie Silverstein, didn't show up. The other promoter said one of them would have to substitute. Maury Drees would not have bought anything at his own clothing store; he was short and slight. And my uncle, while larger and a former high-school basketball player, was not exactly a pugilistic type. They drew straws to see who would fight. My uncle Morrie lost. He stepped in the ring and as soon as the other fighter touched him, he went down for the count.

No wonder Maury Drees had a soft spot for his partner's nephew, a connection he did not mention to me although my uncle was still alive at the time. Maine is one of the few remaining places where such connections still count.

In spite of the sense of shared interest between readers and retailers that would give our ads much more pull than would normally be expected from such a small circulation, ads were scarce, even though a full page cost only $160 and the smallest display ad only $3.80.

With our single sales person struggling during the initial months, a man came in one day and said he had good contacts and was sure he could sell ads for us. At least he sold me and I agreed to give him a draw of $100 a week against a 20 percent commission on any ads he sold. After four weeks and $400 he hadn't sold a single ad, and I finally had to tell him I couldn't afford to keep him on. When I broke the news that he would no longer be getting the $100 a week, he began to plead with me that he needed the money to feed his family and he said he was about to sign a contract with a customer. How long was the contract and how large was the ad, I asked? It was a one-inch ($3.80) ad for four weeks. Our new salesman had to go. He wept and I had difficulty in not joining him.

We had begun publication with less than $30,000 in the bank. John and I owned all the voting shares. He had invested $10,000 and I had invested $11,000, so I owned the controlling interest. We had hoped to raise $40,000 in non-voting stock, something John felt would be easy with his connections.

We did manage to raise $5,520 in non-voting stock, the bulk of it $4,000 from John's friends Jim and Kate Redwine. We never did raise the rest.

Our fund-raising efforts were not helped by our determination that no one should invest who could not afford to lose the money. This is just what we told some of our friends—the photographer Tom Jones, rejected by me, invested in the failed *Brunswick News* and still reminds me of this policy. Bob Solotaire, an old friend of John's who became a great friend of the paper, invested $1,000, which he soon needed back and I had to scrounge to come up with an extra $1,000 that week. I would just as soon not have had it in the first place.

On the other hand, Buffer Fine put in $1,000 of her own money and as we needed more cash I put in another $5,200 in non-voting stock with money that my father had given my children. The non-voting stock was all repurchased ten years later for double what they had paid for it, not exactly a killing for the investors.

My father, who had died in 1966, had given me some stock, much of it in Bath Iron Works, and it had increased in value to $56,000 by the time we started *Maine Times*. I now began to dip into that money, soon plowing all of it into *Maine Times* to cover operating losses. Although John had inherited some money from his mother, he said he was not prepared to put any more in the paper. Our strategy was no strategy. When we ran out of money, we looked for more.

In our search for outside money, we turned next to L. M. C. and Eleanor Houston Smith, whom we both knew and for whom John had crusaded when the Smiths didn't want the power company to spray herbicides on the electric lines that ran through their organic beef farm.

The Smiths were astute entrepreneurial philanthropists, and they demanded a detailed financial plan for their accountants in Philadelphia to go over. So several months after we had begun publication, I was forced to do the kind of detailed financial projections I should have done before we started.

The Smiths accepted the plan and lent us $15,000 at 6 percent interest. A decade later, when interest rates soared, I wanted to raise the interest rate but they would not hear of it. And when I finally paid off the loan, Mrs. Smith wrote me that it left her with mixed feelings, because with the loan paid off she felt she had lost her special relationship with the paper. And a special relationship it was— total support without ever asking us to do anything, without even suggesting a story idea.

Six months after we began publication, I needed a major infusion of money and, swallowing my pride, I went to my mother. After I laid out the entire situation, she said she would lend me the money at market-rate interest but with a caveat: my own loans of $56,000 would need to be converted to voting stock and my ownership share would have to rise accordingly.

I took this message back to John, saying that he would now own about 12 percent but I would be willing to keep the old stock split if he were willing to invest more money of his own or raise more money from some of the people he had initially thought would invest. By this time, John was buying old buildings, fixing them up, and reselling them, and he said he could make much more money that way than he ever could with *Maine Times* so I could take the stock and be responsible for raising the money. Neither of us fully understood the ramifications of such a dramatic change in ownership.

John's building investments didn't turn out as well as he hoped, mainly because he didn't keep good records of how much he was putting into them, and the profits he thought he was making were eaten up in expenses. On the other hand, I was the one who had to worry about meeting payroll, not him. While John had never been good about money, what I had previously considered a minor flaw—his inability to consider the future cost of something he did—now became a major affront. John had always had the habit of spending money we didn't have without consulting me first. Now, having rejected taking an equal responsibility for the financial success of the paper, whenever he made a costly decision without my approval, my patience was minimal.

That first year we lost $119,000. We had raised $98,000, including the non-voting stock, the Smith loan, and subsequent small loans from both John and myself and my mother. But in the end, it was the loans from my mother, finally totaling $70,000, that carried us over.

We lost $32,000 the second year and $17,000 the third. Although we lost another $4,000 the fourth year before turning it around on an annual basis, by that fourth year we did not need to borrow any more money. I developed a compelling interest in losing as little money as possible. I was determined to stop borrowing. There were few stronger incentives to financial independence than having to ask my mother for money. Once we broke even, we never borrowed money again. I suppose I was too conservative, but borrowing had been so unpleasant, so demeaning, that even when I needed to invest in the paper for expansion, I made sure I had the money in hand before doing so. I never again spent money I didn't have.

Those start-up figures may seem tiny in today's world, but they were real money to me. In those first years, we were producing *Maine Times* for $2,000 an issue. When I sold in 1985, it was a much better staffed paper but it also cost more than $15,000 an issue. Postage costs were ten times what they had been and printing rates had risen five-fold.

When I went back to the paper in 1992, the weekly costs were at $20,000 an issue or a million dollars a year. That first year, our costs had been $192,000 and had dropped to $160,000 the second year.

In the years I was at *Maine Times*, other statewide publications and several Portland alternatives started and failed. Why did we survive?

Of course, we were lucky. We came out with the right product at the right time. Although it was not exactly the audience we envisioned, there was a large enough audience that was interested in the important issues facing Maine to make us successful.

I had also learned at the *Bath Daily Times* that creating a quality product is not enough to guarantee success. Back then, I had been able to increase circulation only when I opened up a new home delivery route that had not existed before in West Bath. It was a harsh but important lesson: no matter how wonderful you considered the product, you had to sell it to people. That I was prepared to do.

Also, thanks to my experience as reluctant publisher of those small dailies and my interest in the technology, except for running the press, there was not a job I could not do myself. With Linotypes replaced by IBM Selectrics and later by computers, I could set the type, lay out pages, and even strip the negatives. Because I was there, every press day for the first fifteen years, I knew enough about the press—and knew the pressmen well enough—that we always got a superior product. I constantly learned new techniques working side by side with Mike Bryant in Belfast, then Ray Greenlaw and Skip Stubbs at Brunswick, our two printers. I knew what it took to do each job and I was not lured into overstaffing. Partly because I worked side by side with everyone at *Maine Times* and so appreciated what they did, those who stayed were incredibly productive.[1] No one ever tried to slide along; it was contradictory to the culture.

As was common among liberals in 1968, we saw ourselves as the friend of the workingman and expected to have a large blue-collar following. That was one of the reasons we gave away samples of those first issues at the mill gates. And if we were such adamant supporters of educational reform, we were sure teachers would scoop us up; we spent thousands of dollars fruitlessly soliciting them. Most teachers proved incredibly apathetic about the world *Maine Times* covered.

On the other hand, education would be a factor in readership. This was the audience that read for information on which to base decisions. It quickly became clear that since our audience was highly educated, it tended to be high income. Politically, we split along traditional party lines with a third Democrats, a third Republicans, and a

1. Inflation and growth were not the only reasons for increased costs. Gradually, more people were hired to do the same amount of work. This was particularly true of editors.

third Independents. That was a time when Maine Republicans were primarily Rockefeller Republicans who grew up on the moderate conservatism of the *New York Herald Tribune*. They had sensitive social consciences and were strong environmentalists, the issue that we had not planned to make our centerpiece but which soon became the cornerstone of our identity. Environmental leaders in the legislature, such as Harry Richardson, Dick Berry, and Hoddy Hildreth, were Republicans.

Although we did not know it at the time, we were part of the alternative press movement. Out on the West Coast, Bruce Brugmann had founded the *San Francisco Bay Guardian* which would rise meteorically. The *Boston Phoenix* had begun but would split ideologically with the *Real Paper*, which called itself "the real alternative" and then died. The first wave of alternatives was issues-oriented and paid circulation, but within a very short time the free metro alternatives would start. The television program *60 Minutes* cited us as among the best of the "underground" press. I preferred "alternative" and wrote them a letter that they read on the air. It said: "We appreciate your mention of *Maine Times* and no doubt our readers, a third of whom are Republicans, were titillated to hear us called underground. But, Mr. Wallace, my mother will never understand."

Classic among the new breed of free-circulation alternatives was the *Chicago Reader*, founded by a group of Carlton College alumni, with Bob Roth as editor. It featured a well-written and well-illustrated cover story, supplemented by incredible listings and reviews. It had the best of the new cartoonists, including Linda J. Barry and Matt Groening. And it had classifieds. It was well written and when you read the *Reader*, you knew who you were. The *Reader* was distributed free and demographics were determined by where the paper was left.

Bob and I became good friends at a Ramada Inn in a cornfield in Columbia, Missouri, in 1974 and he was always trying to convince me to go free circulation.[2] I felt we could not do it because of the

---

2. We had both won Penny Missouri awards for special sections, the first time the alternative press had broken into those ranks. Peggy Fisher entered the contest for us, but the organizers insisted that I attend as they used the winners in seminars for paying students. That same year we won the only award *Maine Times* ever received that I considered important, a University of Missouri Honor Award. *60 Minutes* was another recipient that year. The Missouri Honor Award was not something you entered and I had not entered any awards

rural nature of our population and the fact that a quarter of our subscribers lived out of state, but he always made me think about what
we were doing.

One point Bob made that I utilized was that newspapers have two
sets of functions—reader functions and user functions. The stories are
reader functions. The entertainment listings, the ads, and most impor-
tantly the classifieds are user functions, and it is the user functions
that are more likely to attract an audience than reader functions.

Maine Times was a discretionary buy. You didn't have to have it to
find out what was on TV or what the school lunch was that day or
when your kid's team played next. We gradually built some user functions among those interested in the arts, but if you missed a particular
week's issue it was no great loss.

That meant people had to talk about our stories with their friends
so that if you circulated within a certain group, you had to have read
Maine Times that week to participate in the conversation. Our subscribers not only had to identify with us, they had to want to read
what we wrote.

We quickly made some sound business decisions about who we
were. We could not go after the large institutional advertisers—the
banks, the utilities, etc. Their advertising was mainly image oriented
and therefore totally discretionary. In general, they didn't like what
we wrote or what we stood for, so why should they support us?

Our natural advertisers were small, specialty shops who catered to
our clientele. As such, they did not worry about cost per thousand like
the ad agencies did—and our cost per thousand was astronomically
high in comparison to the Portland *Sunday Telegram*, which had more
than 100,000 circulation at the time. Our advertisers measured success
on whether an ad brought in more business than the ad had cost, so
we geared our rate structure to these people.

Instead of giving the largest discounts to those who ran the largest
ads, as was the general rule, we based our discounts on frequency and
the standard became the every-other-week ad. A boutique or a book-

competitions—Peggy had—since we won the A. J. Leibling Award as the best weekly newspaper in America. The award turned out to be a sham, run by a man who judged all the
papers himself. He argued that he still chose the best, and the year we won for weeklies, the
Christian Science Monitor won for dailies. They didn't seem as embarrassed as we were.

store or a restaurant might run an ad that cost only $8, but if they ran it every other week, they received a handsome discount. We, on the other hand, did not have to sell the ad every week and any changes came in from the advertiser. By the time I sold *Maine Times,* we could count on ten pages of these ads a week, half our needs. They ended up being so geared to our readership that our polls found that many people read the ads first.

How these ads were perceived was brought home to me when I met a young furniture maker whose parents asked how he was doing with his business. He had moved to Maine and his parents, summer residents, subscribed to *Maine Times.* When the young man said he was doing well, his mother replied, "Well, if you're so successful, why aren't you advertising in *Maine Times?*"

Our search for subscribers became equally selective. The first year we had been flabbergasted when we put an ad in the paper for Christmas gift subscriptions and received more than 500 of them. Our own subscribers were obviously our best source of new subscribers.

Consequently, we put a coupon in the paper asking subscribers to send us the names of friends they thought might be interested. The names poured in and the people who had sent them told their friends, without our asking, that they would soon be receiving copies of *Maine Times* at their request. We mined that vein for years.

Of course, we followed the normal route of trading lists with organizations that overlapped with us, but at first there were few such organizations and their memberships were small. So we had to be more inventive.

That a quarter of our subscribers lived out of state created problems. Almost all either summered in Maine or had strong connections to Maine; this was not the sort of publication one read for nostalgia. But when these readers were out of state, their value to advertisers was limited. As our circulation went up, regardless of where subscribers were located, our costs went up, necessitating an increase in ad rates. Too many out-of-state subscribers could lower the effectiveness, based on cost, of our advertising. So while I did not initially discourage out-of-state subscribers, I soon worked harder to get those in state. Later I would stop soliciting out-of-state subscribers.

For a publication our size—and we topped out at just over 18,500, subscriptions were 12,500 and regular newsstand sales 6,000—subscriptions paid for little more than the cost of printing, handling, and mailing the paper.

Newsstand sales were particularly difficult because there were so many Mom and Pop stores that carried only five copies. In the supermarkets, we were always competing for shelf space or getting covered up by another publication. Our best outlets were the traditional newspaper stores, a classic one being Day's Variety in Brunswick, run by Pete Ouellette.

I had known Pete since my days on the local paper, and I was one of those who reserved the Sunday *New York Times*, a group he viewed as chronic complainers. But we got along wonderfully and he was a great supporter of the paper, putting it on the counter by the cash register and selling more than 100 copies a week. Similar traditional newsstands—Victor News in Lewiston, Joe's Smoke Shop in Portland—gave us similar display and had strong sales in the early days. Gradually their sales eroded as the supermarkets carried more periodicals, especially the checkout counter tabloids, and convenience chains, like Cumberland Farms and Seven Eleven, proliferated.

Tastes and habits were changing as well, and as newsstand sales decreased at the traditional stores, other sales did not pick up correspondingly. Just maintaining newsstand sales became a perpetual battle and gradually eroded to less than 4,000 a week.

Each week, for the first ten years, I took the newsstand copies to a half dozen stores in Brunswick, including Day's Variety and the Bowdoin College Bookstore. These outlets were different enough so that this sampling gave me an instant indication of how a particular issue had sold. There were significant variations from week to week. These sorts of tasks sensitized me to the details that can mean life or death for a publication like *Maine Times*. On my route, because of the direction I was heading, I dropped the paper off first at Kennebec Fruit and then walked across the street to Day's Variety to deliver theirs. One day Pete Ouellette complained because a customer had told him Kennebec Fruit had the paper before he did and after all, he was our best outlet. The time difference could not have been more than 30 seconds, but after that, I always walked across the street and delivered Pete's papers first.

I had been extremely lucky that before we started publication I stopped in to see David Turitz, then head of Portland News, the largest distributor in the state, for advice. According to David, I was the only person starting a new publication who had ever sought his advice *before* starting. I left David's office with some crucial knowledge of how the system worked, with the beginning of a lifelong friendship, and with a recommendation for a movie critic, his friend Rob Elowitch.

Typical of the way David operated was an incident that occurred at least a decade after we had started publication. Someone on his staff found a clerical error that indicated *Maine Times* was owed $3,000. We would never have known about it if David hadn't sent a note of explanation along with the check.

As the first summer of publication approached, we realized we would have to put someone on the road to open new accounts that were only available in the summer. These accounts would be key to exposing summer residents to the paper and converting them to subscribers.

Through the life of the paper, we found that with good ads in the paper itself, 1 percent of the newsstand buyers converted to subscribers each week. Therefore if we sold 6,000 copies on the newsstand, we would get 60 new subscribers from the paper itself. These unsolicited subscribers compensated for the 2,500 to 3,000 who did not renew during the year.

We advertised for a student to travel the state for us, to visit existing newsstands, most often small operations that might carry only five or ten papers, and to open new ones, sometimes bookstores or restaurants that weren't covered by the distributors.

By far the best applicant was a Bowdoin student. He was intelligent, attractive, and very personable. There was only one other consideration: he was black.

How would people out in the boondocks accept him? Especially in the wilds of Aroostook and Washington Counties where we were already viewed as to the left of Chairman Mao, would he run into unfriendliness and be unable to get us the kind of display we sought? Finally, I said to hell with it. If *Maine Times* couldn't do the right thing and hire someone on his merits, who else could we expect to do the same?

He turned out to be incredibly successful, partly because he was black. Everyone remembered him and almost everyone was curious. Sometimes they were so curious they asked questions that might have buffaloed a person without his poise. Being on his own, traveling all over the state, he told me he had enjoyed the experience. He had also done an excellent job for *Maine Times*.

There was nothing sophisticated about the way I operated *Maine Times* and my own ignorance and simplicity were probably critical to our financial success. I could not have set up our books on an accrual basis if I had wanted to and I could not have understood them if someone else had. Instead, I had gone to our local accountant, Maurice Boucher,[3] and asked him what he needed to do our taxes, then made sure that information would be made available to him. For my purposes, accounting was strictly cash-flow.

A newspaper is a simple operation. There is income from only three sources: subscribers, newsstands, and advertising. Newsstand sales fluctuated little from week to week. Once we had subscribers, we knew they were going to renew at a rate of about 80 percent so we could count on that money, based on month-by-month fluctuations. October, the month we began, was a good month, as was December with all its Christmas gifts. April, tax month, was bad.

We could track new unsolicited subscribers as a percentage of newsstand sales, and we could predict new solicited subscribers, based on a return rate of 1.5 to 2 percent, depending on the mailing list we were using. Advertising was a little more unpredictable but showed steady increases.

Payroll accounted for 40 percent of our weekly expenses and printing and mailing made up another 35 percent. Both were easily predictable from year to year. That meant all other expenses—everything from rent, electricity, telephone, and supplies—were only 25 percent.

Each week, I dutifully recorded on sheets of graph paper the income and expenses. Although I would receive the figures on an

3. Maurice was another of those special people we dealt with for years. He was fascinated by what we were doing and liked understanding exactly what the figures represented. In our family manner, his daughter interned with us for a short time while in college. He always offered good advice and charged very little. The new publisher continued to ask for the adding machine tapes, showing actual cash flow, from our bookkeeper. She, like me before her, found they gave her a clearer picture of what was actually happening week to week.

adding machine tape, I insisted on copying them onto the graph paper myself. Actually copying those figures gave me a sense of their reality and a control that I would have obtained no other way. If we just turned down the heat a little and didn't talk quite so long on the telephone, I would have that much more to buy another freelance story. I thought in nickels and dimes.

My primitive accounting system also meant we were able to project extremely accurately a year ahead, something that was important because of the seasonal cycles of a newspaper. Like most retail businesses, a huge proportion of revenues came in because of Christmas. We also tended to do well during the summer, and once we had developed the Summer Guide which brought in revenues of up to $100,000, that became a shot in the arm. Then there was mud season, the three months from February through April, when the incoming cash could not match expenses and we would draw down the reserves we had built up from Christmas.

Since I refused to borrow, even short-term, the key was in predicting exactly how much cash we would need until we began to have a positive cash flow again in June and July. This was particularly important because of the profit-sharing plan we developed—Christmas bonuses.

Even though it would have been better for employees if we had put the money into a retirement plan earlier than we did, everyone loved the Christmas bonuses and realized that the bonuses were dependent on how the paper had done that year. I don't think the bonuses ever went down in aggregate, but some years some people received less if we hadn't done as well.

In a good year, many employees received the equivalent of several weeks' pay in their bonuses and it lifted their spirits. After I sold the paper, the new owner gave people raises and stopped the Christmas bonuses. They probably received more money during the year, but it didn't have the same psychological effect and all the old-timers complained to me about the cessation of the Christmas bonuses.

The bonuses allowed me to encourage the feeling among the staff that we were all in the project together. Salary structures reinforced the same message. Even though people are not supposed to know one another's salaries, in an operation of only twenty-two people, one should expect they do. My basic principle was to keep the salary structure as even as possible, a reflection of the fact that everyone's job was important to the paper's success. For competitive reasons we had to pay a reporter more than a bookkeeper, but it was not that much more. The ad manager, key to revenues, was normally the highest-paid person on staff, sometimes making more than me. I did not pay myself multiples of what others earned. I earned only marginally more than the lowest paid staffer since our priority was to bring everyone up to a decent wage.

One reason I could pay myself less was that I owned the building and the rent left me some extra income but the most I ever took in salary came after I had left and returned and was paid about $40,000.

Christmas became a signal event. The first year, we had held a Christmas party at my house for staff and a few friends of the paper. The supper was potluck except for a baked ham my wife, Eunice, prepared, an item that became a fixture at future parties.

In 1972, after we moved from the old bank building to a large Federal house on the hill in Topsham, the parties expanded. They were still potluck, with all the staff contributing, but now we could afford pretty good wine from Tess's Market and we had expanded into our multi-generational tradition. Included as well were people like Helen and Robert Dudley, my next-door neighbors, and my mother-in-law, Lucy Theodore, who had moved to Brunswick to be near us. Our house was only about a hundred yards from the office and Mr. Dudley took over projects at the office as well as at our home, where we raised chickens together and he taught Eunice how to putty windowpanes.

One person never to miss a Christmas party was Elliott Schwartz, our food critic, who was also a professor of music at Bowdoin and a well-regarded modern composer. His appetite was legendary and as soon as the food was laid out, someone would announce dinner was served by calling out that everyone should take what they wanted before Elliott got to the buffet.

Our production manager, Meredith Herzog (affectionately called Gidget), would stop work early the day of the party and set about decorating the central composing room. Everyone left a little early to go home and get dressed up. This was a family celebration, akin to the gathering of an ethnic clan with all the shared experience and identity. People routinely disappeared to reporters' rooms upstairs and anyone venturing that way would have noticed the distinct aroma of pot.

Even with small children and seventy-year-olds participating, a lot of wine was consumed. But no matter how one felt the next day, everyone showed up to clean the office and discuss the party of the night before, inevitably declaring it the best ever.

The culture at *Maine Times* was a reflection of the era and my personal preferences. Despite being career-oriented and obsessed with the success of *Maine Times*, I also believed in extended families and Eunice and I were always coming up with schemes to buy houses with our friends and live communally. Fortunately, none of those projects ever reached fruition.

But the office was communal and Gidget's boys and Margaret Campbell's daughter came to the office while still in bassinets. We put a gate in front of the stairs and the door to my office when they began crawling and when they could walk, they visited me, often playing on the floor in front of my desk in a way that did not bother me. Gidget or Margaret could see their children from their work stations in the composing room to respond if anything went wrong so I really had no responsibility.

During the summer I had a vegetable garden in the yard, where I would escape from time to time. Even fifteen minutes of weeding would help me relax and think more clearly. Once the vegetables were large enough, we would have a break at ten o'clock every morning when I would pick and slice cucumbers and carrots and tomatoes and place them on a large tray in the composing room. Everyone would share.

Of particular pleasure were summer mornings when I would walk the three minutes from our house to the office before anyone else arrived and cut fresh flowers from the garden that I would then place in vases on people's desks. Who received them depended on who appreciated them.

Late in the day, when I needed to get away from my desk for a while, I would mow the lawn. If someone came to visit me at that time, they were sent outdoors and had to yell over the noise of the

lawnmower to make themselves heard. In one of the annual staff photos, which we printed as a greeting in the New Year's edition, you can
notice, if you look closely, that I am not wearing shoes.

One of my favorite recollections is of a person of some self-importance visiting me in my office, which had an attached sun porch. It
was a beautiful, sun-drenched room, and I had installed in it my
father's partners' desk. The office was quite impressive if you didn't
notice the old pet stains on the rug.

While we were talking, there was a knock at the door and I said to
enter. In came Heather Davis—her mother Roberta had worked for
me back at the *Bath Daily Times* and had joined us at *Maine Times*
after a break for having children. Heather was two years old and riding her plastic Big Wheels tricycle. She pedaled up to the desk, said,
"Here's your mail, Peter," and pedaled back out, closing the door
behind her. My visitor was aghast.[4]

I tried to institutionalize the team culture with our Monday lunches that included the heads of all departments, even if there were only
two people in the department. By noon, I would have already met
with the writers and at this luncheon meeting I represented editorial.
Gidget would be there to represent production; Annice Dubitsky for
bookkeeping and newsstand sales; Roberta Davis for subscriptions; and
Cam Smith and then Karen Taylor for advertising. For the fifteen
years I held these meetings, they consisted of the same people.

The staff was not without its turf wars and rivalries, and these
meetings were a strong message that problems had to be solved and
cooperation re-established each week. Sometimes that cooperation
broke down during the rest of the week.

I had hired all the key people and I tended to hire strong personalities. Gidget in particular built her own fiefdom and whenever there
was an extra job to be done, she would volunteer. The more she did,
the more she controlled. After I left the paper, with her intuitive
understanding that knowledge is power she was able to control more
and more because no one else knew how to find file photos or upgrade
the computers.

---

4. Heather was to marry one of my son Tony's best friends, Steve Arnett, and in the summer
of 2003 they visited us with their new baby. I was touched.

Subsequently, the new owners moved to the old paper mill at the bottom of the hill, where they installed a lunch room with a microwave. Probably on the order of the new publisher, Anna Ginn, they installed a suggestion box, to which, of course, Gidget held the key. Betta Stothart later told me the story of putting a suggestion in the box and then coming back to see Gidget emptying the contents directly into a wastebasket. It's only hearsay, but if true, it was pure Gidget.

The Monday meetings were an effective method of exchanging information and it gave the non-editorial staff an opportunity to keep up-to-date on what was happening editorially. They did not try to influence what the writers wrote, although they were not reluctant to criticize a weak story. The ad department particularly liked being in the know about upcoming stories because it gave them something to talk to their clients about and gave advertisers a feeling they were part of an insider group. We were always careful of the barriers between advertisers and editorial content, but our ad department also nurtured the feeling that we all believed in the same principles.[5] The other staff enjoyed knowing what lay ahead editorially as well, and these discussions reinforced a message I believed in—that everyone's contribution to the paper, from the person answering the telephone to the person processing subscriptions, was important.

As much as I tried to solicit new ideas and to reach joint decisions, the Monday meetings were never totally effective in this way. Their greatest benefit was in preventing bad decisions, because what seemed a good idea to one department might have major drawbacks for another. So, while everyone was willing and eager to offer criticisms of someone else's suggestions, in the end, everyone believed it was my job to come up with the new ideas and make the tough decisions.

---

5. One day an advertiser called me to complain about a story, and while I knew the caller was an advertiser, at first the subject did not come up. I discussed the story with her as I would have with any reader until the person identified herself as an advertiser. When she did so, I said she had just ended the conversation because her identifying herself as an advertiser implied I should give her special consideration. I then hung up. A few minutes later Karen Taylor, our ad manager, came into my office, having just received a call from the same advertiser. Karen explained that the person was pleased I had hung up on her after she identified herself as an advertiser. "That kind of attitude is why I advertise in your paper," she had told Karen.

Ten

If You Run a Crusade You Attract Crusaders

From the beginning *Maine Times*, with a tiny editorial staff and heavy reliance on freelancers, was able to do what other papers didn't. Despite our low pay and total lack of prestige, even as a start-up we were able to attract first-rate talent. Our pool was twofold: Those who were frustrated by their careers in traditional journalism and were willing to trade money for opportunity; and those, particularly women, for whom the doors of traditional journalism were closed.

Our only full-time staff writer when we began was former AP writer Ken Morrison, who had come with us from the *Times-Record* where we had hired him to write stories of statewide interest, always a testy subject in what was essentially a local paper.

In the year he stayed at *Maine Times,* Ken wrote a good deal about the Indians, especially the Passamaquoddy near Eastport who were subject to constant outrages, including some white hunters who had come on the reservation looking for sex, killed an Indian, and gotten away with it. Ken also wrote vividly about land being bought up in Maine for bargain prices and then being sold to buyers in Boston, sight unseen. What the buyers didn't know was that much of the land could not be built on.

I never fully understood why Ken left us so soon, but several years later he told me one of the reasons was he didn't like the way John changed his stories, with the implication that in an effort to make them more dramatic, the editing had compromised their accuracy.

All editors have the impulse to jazz up stories, to make the lead as compelling as possible to lure readers. The trick is to create interest without distorting the story. Ken felt the line had been crossed.

Editors must respect a writer and enhance his work by adapting to the writer's talents and weaknesses. A good editor asks questions to fill in gaps and to test the trustworthiness of sources. When a story is on deadline, options are limited, but even then, the editor's role is to protect the writer and the publication by making sure the highest standards are met. Good editing is not an exercise in power; it is a colloquy.

When I later took over as editor, I made a point of returning stories to the writers whenever possible for them to read and approve my revisions. It was more difficult to go through this process with free-lancers, particularly in the early days when we were always starved for copy and could not wait several weeks to run a freelance piece that had been sent back for rewriting and editing. I wanted the writers to read the edited versions because the major reason an editor changes something is lack of clarity in the original, and if it is unclear to start with, there is a good chance the editor will misinterpret what the writer intended to say.

On the other hand, returning edited stories to writers can lead to arguments about the changes and I can understand, if not condone, why John wanted to avoid such situations. Unfortunately, they are part of the job.

In 1971 with John still in editorial control, we hired Bill Langley who had worked for the Portland papers and then moved to Florida. He had returned to the area to write for the *Brunswick News*, a competitor to the *Times-Record* that lasted only six months. Bill was extremely talented but quirky with lots of personal problems. When he was on, he was really on and did some fine stories for us, laced with his particular sense of irony. But Bill also had the unnerving habit of not showing up for work and offering no explanation.

For our next reporter, John, without consulting me, hired Bill's wife Lynne, whom Bill had married in Florida and who obviously wanted to move to Maine with him. I had no complaints about Lynne's credentials; I knew nothing about her. My reservation was that with only two staff writers, we were hiring the wife of a person who was already showing signs of serious problems.

But John had already made the promise and Lynne turned out to be a competent and hardworking reporter. Bill eventually left the paper and dropped out of sight, but Lynne stayed on for several years.

One of the best stories Bill ever did, in collaboration with Aimee

Gauvin who had brought it to us, was about the telephone company in a little town called Weld. The owner of the company monitored all calls, since they still went through an operator, and he berated people for making late-night calls because they woke up the person acting as operator, sometimes himself or his wife. He also insisted that before any emergency calls were put through to the fire department, he approve them. The Public Utilities Commission (PUC) files were full of complaints from citizens and from the fire chief about the emergency practice.

The failure of the PUC to respond to these complaints was to have terrible consequences. On Sunday evening, at 8:00 P.M., January 3, 1971, two space heaters exploded in the Jackson family home, causing a fire. A neighbor called the fire department, where the firemen were on duty and playing cribbage. The call was not put through to the station because the telephone company president was not on hand to approve the transfer.

Meanwhile, three children were trapped upstairs in the house. The neighbor called again and got the telephone company president's wife, who, after some discussion, contacted the fire department who immediately responded. The firemen believed that the 15- to 30-minute delay caused by not getting the first emergency call through had cost them any hope of rescuing the children.

The story put the blame not so much on the owners of the phone company as on the PUC, which had refused to act for so long in the face of so many complaints. John Cole said in his accompanying editorial: "[The PUC's] record is a mockery of public service; it serves instead the interests it was designed to monitor. If the Weld hearing is not the beginning of a more responsive PUC, then we suggest the men now on the commission be asked to resign, and that the governor replace them...."

The governor did replace them and the new PUC, headed by Peter Bradford, a former aide to the governor, led a campaign to make the commission responsive to consumers rather than utility owners. When we covered their first major case in detail, that of state Senator Richard N. Berry and the utilities he owned, Senator Berry sued us for millions.

The Weld story was one of our few true exposés and it did lead to changes in local practices, but it wasn't that difficult to do. Most of the material we needed was in the public files.[1] Despite all the complaints from the people in Weld, no newspaper had been interested enough to dig through those files and print the story.

When we offered our story to the Associated Press in advance of publication, they turned it down on the grounds that publishing something so critical of the PUC would destroy the PUC as a source, a clear indication of the mindset that allowed us to have such a clear field. The dailies seldom picked up on our stories, since to do so would be an admission they had missed something. On the other hand, individual reporters used us for leverage, allowing us to influence the mainstream agenda. Bob Cummings, my former colleague in Bath, said on several occasions that he had used the threat of *Maine Times* to force the Portland papers to let him do the environmental coverage he wanted to do.

The opposite side of the coin was that we were always looking for a new approach to a story, asking ourselves what major issues we had to cover even though the dailies were also covering them, what we had to say that was different. What new information could we bring to the readers?

To this day, the dailies let their coverage be determined largely by those publicly debating an issue and rely on the conflict between the two sides to uncover the facts. They are not driven by their own curiosity or sense that important stories are being neglected.

Not every story, no matter how enticing at the time, turns out to be as important as one first thought. The next exposé Bill Langley did illustrated the problem of overblowing a story that on the surface was juicy but in reality was not as important as we had believed.

One of our readers who lived in the mountains near Rangeley had a young man come to his door late one night in a rainstorm. He was lost and explained that he was on a navy training exercise that simulated escape from an enemy prison camp and had had to live off the land for several days. Now he had to get back, but he was lost. The reader directed him back and called us.

---

1. One of our role models was *I. F. Stone's Weekly*. He made a career of exploiting public documents no one else took the time to wade through.

With the tip from the reader, Bill Langley was able to find the camp and even photograph it from the air. It turned out to be part of the Brunswick Naval Air Station and men were taken there to learn what to do if captured in Vietnam. They simulated torture, according to some Bill interviewed but, in retrospect, the idea of teaching soldiers how to escape from a prison camp and live off the land seemed rational and hardly open to major criticism, even if the landscape in Maine and Vietnam offered different opportunities.

The military made its classic mistake. It denied the place existed, even to members of Congress whom we had asked about the camp when we ran into a blank wall with the navy. Later it did admit the facility existed and we found out that it was also used by military personnel as a hunting camp during season, a minor but enticing abuse. In retrospect, we overplayed the story.

One of our landmark stories came in 1977, due to the efforts of Myron Levin, a former reporter for the *York County Coast Star*, who wanted to do stories for us on a freelance basis. Typical of the *Maine Times* culture, Myron didn't care about the money as much as he did about the opportunity to spend more time on a story and to reach a statewide audience. His best piece exposed the practices at DeCoster Egg Farms in Turner.

Jack DeCoster was a born-again Christian who ran a classic industrialized egg operation with thousands of chickens crowded into poorly ventilated egg houses, all of them tended by migrant workers, mostly from Mexico, who lived in overcrowded trailers DeCoster supplied and where they faced sub-standard living conditions. What Myron uncovered was truly shocking, as was the fact that the migrant workers had been so unsuccessful in obtaining better working and living conditions. No one in government seemed to care.

That story became the most requested issue of *Maine Times* we ever printed, but essentially nothing happened. There were government inspections and a slap on the wrist and then everything went back to where it was before. DeCoster expanded into the DelMarva peninsula and his manure disposal there led to a plague of insects, which neighbors complained about to little effect.

A decade later, weekly reporter Gregory Davis was to cover DeCoster again, and what he uncovered was essentially the same as what Myron Levin had described in 1977 but this time OSHA, now under the direction of Secretary of Labor Robert Reich in the Clinton administration, took action, forcing a clean-up and starting a long game of cat and mouse as DeCoster created different companies and used other subterfuges to try to escape making the changes OSHA had ordered. This time the daily press picked up on the story and the public was aroused enough that many grocery stores stopped carrying DeCoster eggs. I presented an award to Davis on behalf of the Maine Civil Liberties Union.

DeCoster became for me a classic example of the limits of journalism. Only when a government agency finally decided to act did anything happen, and this took years despite lawsuits on behalf of the migrant workers and a general sense of outrage among the public.

We saw even less concern for longterm, bad conditions at the Maine State Prison. There, Peggy Fisher first uncovered the policy that the state essentially let the prisoners do whatever they wanted, including deal in drugs, so long as they maintained discipline themselves. Although the administration denied our stories, a few months later they locked down the prison on the grounds it had spun out of control under the system Peggy had described. But not much of the public—with the notable exception of the Maine Civil Liberties Union—cared what went on behind bars and until its last days, Maine Times continued its prison coverage, including the death of a prisoner only a few feet from the guards, with little result. There is a deep-seated conviction that people in prison are there because they are bad and if they suffer as a result, they deserve it. Cost alone has forced the state to begin looking at alternatives to the old incarceration system, but with the war on drugs and the mantra of zero tolerance, the trend toward more prisons and less prevention remains dominant.

We had become the court of last resort for people who felt they had been wronged by public agencies and each week we sorted the complaints that came to us to decide what merited coverage and our limited resources. Partly because of our reputation and partly because of our accessibility—I accepted all phone calls, as did reporters— we always had more people coming to us with stories than we could handle.

In those very first years, John Cole had spoken editorially about our role as watchdog in writing about the Weld telephone company. Fifteen years later, when I was interviewing the new president of Central Maine Power, a company with whom we had been doing battle since the beginning, he told me how someone had come to him with a complaint about being mistreated by a government agency and he had suggested the person contact us. I considered his recommendation a particular compliment.

There was so much that the other press did not cover, even when events occurred in their own backyards, that we had a free run on stories all the time. Editors at the dailies seemed not to read the other papers. We read most of the forty weeklies in the state and were often able to identify stories of statewide significance that had been covered only as local items, or we would spot trends when the same thing was occurring in different communities across the state. This was how we discovered a repeated hot-button topic, cell phone towers that created visual blight and angered local residents. Until we covered the issue, each group in each community thought it was alone and tended to repeat the experience of others without ever benefiting from it.

When I returned for two years as editor in 1992, I purposely took a different tone, influenced by what I had learned through my work in non-profits where we were often looking at the same policy questions from a different perspective. I had also begun to participate in the Eco/Eco Civic Forum which was geared to gaining consensus on environmental and economic issues through open discussion between business people, government employees, and environmentalists.

The focus did shift somewhat from uncovering malfeasance or sloppy policy to seeking solutions. The issues had also changed. No one was threatening any longer to build an oil refinery on the coast of Maine. Instead, we were being eaten away by sprawl, one small bite at a time.

The invasion was not from industrial polluters but from Wal-Mart killing off downtowns, who contributed to their own demise through complacency, with the connivance of local officials who kept offering the big boxes and strip malls tax breaks because they wanted the revenues a Wal-Mart would bring them even if it was doing so to the detriment of their own and surrounding communities.

In our Twenty-fifth Anniversary Issue in 1993 we recognized sprawl in all its forms, including homogenization and uglification of the landscape, as the primary issue of the future. It was to be another five years before the issue began to resonate on a statewide basis and only in 2002 did the people finally establish an umbrella non-profit, GrowSmart Maine, to fight sprawl comprehensively. (Having left the paper again by then and having approached the issue through various non-profits, I was part of GrowSmart's inception.)

The first element in determining what we covered and how we covered it was who became our reporters. Even from the earliest days good journalists wanted to work for us because of the opportunity and challenge. They knew they would be given much more freedom in what they covered—part of that freedom being relief from spending so much time on the classic accidents and fires. They also knew they would be allowed more leeway, have more time for each story, have more space, and be able to exhibit more writerly skills. What limited the job applicants was money. Even at a time when reporters weren't paid very well, we paid less. Gradually we narrowed the gap, and if we never caught up with the larger dailies, at least we offered a living wage and a sense of excitement.

Phyllis Austin, who was to be at *Maine Times* longer than anyone but Meredith Herzog, hired herself. An experienced AP veteran who was ready for a change, she came to me and said she wanted a job. When I did not have one to offer, she freelanced until there was an opening. By then she had impressed me so much with both her skills and her energy that there was no option but to hire her. Over the next three decades, she never lost her enthusiasm or drive. To her, the public's interest in the northern forest was a public trust, and she had a personal mission to keep an eye on it.

Edgar Allen Beem came to my attention because of a column he wrote for one of the short-lived Portland alternatives in which he made fun of *Maine Times* and its readers, terming us all Yuppies or Young Urban Professionals, one of the first uses of that label in Maine. I thought it was extremely well done and asked him to come see me, not realizing that we also shared a deep interest in Maine art. He had a long, controversial, and colorful career at *Maine Times* as art critic and cultural gadfly.[2]

When we hired Scott Allen, now a writer at the *Boston Globe*, we were in a different situation. We could offer more competitive salaries and we were inundated with qualified applicants. But I had one overriding criterion: I wanted someone who could think sequentially, who would ask each question based on the answer to the last one, and who would seek his next source of information to elaborate on what he had learned from his last source. Intellectual capacity interested me more than experience.

This criterion grew out of my own increasingly frustrating experiences. Most conversations I had with people went nowhere. Too many people came to any subject with a set of beliefs and preconceptions and never deviated from them. The conversations never synthesized the material and progressed. On the other hand, I had a few friends with whom I particularly enjoyed talking because they always asked questions that made me question my own preconceptions. They led me new places. I wanted this same characteristic in our writing and therefore in our reporters. So, instead of one of the more experienced reporters available, we hired Scott fresh out of Bowdoin College.

At first I put Scott under the supervision of my wife, Eunice, who not only reported but edited the shorter pieces. She came to me one day, frustrated because she felt Scott's opinions were getting in the

---

2. My mother harbored a deep-seated dislike for Edgar. She considered him a smart aleck and an ingrate. She was particularly galled by an article he wrote on the summer colony at Prout's Neck where he maintained that such people, who lived in physically and socially gated communities, only took from Maine and gave nothing back. We had been flooded with mail after the story, and one letter from a summer resident I respected said Edgar had been right on the mark. On her deathbed, my mother would blurt out requests. They always started with, "Peter, would you do me one favor before I die?" and my response would be, "What is that, Mother?" The first had to do with my car, the least expensive Subaru I could find.

"Peter, would you get rid of that Japanese grasshopper of a car you drive and get something that befits your position?"

"What is that, Mother?"

"A Buick Regal," she replied.

Another day she asked, "Peter, will you do me one favor before I die?"

"What is that, Mother?"

"Fire Edgar Allen Beem."

Her final question was, "Peter, would you do me one favor before I die?"

"What is that, Mother?"

"Get rid of that paper and do something worthwhile with your life."

---

way of his reporting, and I agreed to talk with him. When Scott came into the office I was in one of my brutal moods and told him that while he was at Bowdoin his professors were paid money to listen to and respond to his opinions. But now people were paying 50 cents each to read what he wrote and they didn't care about his opinions, they just wanted to know what had occurred. Scott accepted my comments with total equanimity and quickly developed into a first-rate reporter.[3]

What I told Scott, and wrote to him in a 1983 memo, is indicative of my struggle to balance the freedom I wanted the writers to have, with my feelings about letting opinions interfere with good reportage. Commenting on his conflicts between reporting and commentary, I noted his "gratuitous insertions on the rich" in a story about Northeast Harbor, saying the negative implications of his asides weakened the story.

"I don't care what your ideology is, but I don't want to see it distort your reportage," I wrote, making clear that I did not expect reporters to be intellectual eunuchs but wanted them to understand their own predilections and to control them. "A good story goes to the important issues and answers all the questions an intelligent reader would have.... Writing that, through style, tells a reader the reporter is coming at the story from a specific viewpoint, turns off the intelligent reader.

"You should be aware enough of language to immediately identify the words and phrases that are laden with ideological baggage. To use language properly, you must understand not only its primary meaning but its connotations as well. [My old Yale poetry professor, Cleanth Brooks would have been proud of this statement.] Frankly the language you used in the new lead on the food distribution story belonged in the college dormitory room debate and is best left there."

Taking loaded language out of stories is relatively easy. Making sure ideology has not distorted reportage is another issue, and that is what lay behind some of the toughest decisions I had to make about reporters over the years. The most basic premise of the editor-reporter

---

3. I thought it was equanimity. Years later Scott told me he had found the confrontation devastating.

relationship is trust, and sometimes the cause of fatal distrust is not meaningful distortion of the facts but a peripheral infraction.

In 2003 the *New York Times* wallowed in guilt over the Jayson Blair case, where the reporter had pretended to be places he was not and had otherwise misled his readers. The *Times* clearly aims for perfection, as do all the best newspapers, but there must also be a realization of the limits of a newspaper's institutional ability to prevent all infractions by a reporter. Jayson Blair's actions probably could not have been predicted wherever he was; perhaps, in a different working culture, he could have been uncovered sooner.

Daily newspapers do not fact-check daily stories. There just isn't the time. At *Maine Times*, we did not fact-check in any systematic manner. As editor, it was up to me to have enough institutional memory to spot potential dangers, to check names, and to confirm a fact, either with the reporter or with a telephone call, if it seemed suspect to me. When not relying on my own knowledge of the state, I was operating by intuition. After the story had been published, I was aided by my total accessibility. Word was out that a person could call with a complaint and talk with the editor. But this was after the fact.

The reality is that the editor must be able to trust his reporters and if that trust is broken, he must get rid of them. The indicators of bad reporting come slowly, seldom from the subjects of the reportage itself, since the victims tend to stew rather than complain. In a small office like ours, other reporters would pick up indications of bad practices, sometimes by something as simple as hearing one end of a telephone conversation. In our office, other reporters would have quickly learned if a Jayson Blair had gone where he said he had gone. I faced a similar situation at *Maine Times* and was given my first warnings in-house about a reporter using the telephone and then writing as if the interview had been face-to-face.

I have never seen a reporter consciously print a falsehood. The infractions are much more subtle, having to do with context and selection. Since we allowed reporters to be more writerly, to describe as well as to quote, we left more room for going astray.

One of my weaknesses was to put up with the first infractions, to try to explain to the reporter what I thought was wrong and to get him or her, in the future, to avoid what I considered a mistake. This could be as serious an offense as using a quote out of context, something a reporter could be immediately fired for. Not only did I think the reporters I had hired were redeemable, but I also realized that if I sacked reporters for a first offense, I would be facing an unacceptable rate of turnover. Running the gamut, from expressing opinion where one shouldn't to a misquote, everyone made a mistake from time to time, and it was my job to minimize them. In some cases, after I thought I had clearly outlined the parameters and had made clear to the particular reporter his or her sins, there would come an incident where I blew up because I felt betrayed and although the particular incident might have been minor, it was monumental to me. The unforgivable was to repeat something I had specifically said was not allowed.

In 1975 I had such a confrontation with a reporter whose work I was beginning to suspect because I was afraid he was using quotes out of context. I had already discussed the issue with him and thought he was being particularly careful as a result.

The blowup came when there appeared in a story a quote about a gay bar that had come from a letter sent to me. The letter had been on my desk and I had not offered it to the reporter but the reporter had seen the return address and picked it up from my desk, taken it out of the envelope, read it, and inserted the information in his story as if he had been the recipient. So the infractions ranged from going through my mail to false context.

Again, a memo I wrote at the time shows how I was groping with the problem.

"The goal of the story is to give the reader a clear picture of the reality.

"While I accept the fact that any intelligent reporter will make judgments on what he has seen or heard, I expect he is enough of a professional not to let his own opinions lead to distortion . . . . The reporter should not try to set up a situation within the story where a person's comments will come out in the worst possible light. This does not mean that a person who says something bad or stupid should be protected . . . it just means that what he says should be reported precisely and without any attempt to embellish.

"I must believe that a reporter is accurate and honest with himself. I was suspect when you told me [one time] that you didn't like [the subject of the story] and were going to 'get him' in the story. As you know, I cut out quite a bit of your description of him that I thought was uncalled for. I left in the quotes on the assumption that they were accurate, both literally and in context. In a subsequent letter, he charged they were distorted by context. I chose to believe you in this case, partially because his letter itself showed his biases; but I would prefer not to have any question in my mind at all.

"No matter how different *Maine Times* is from other newspapers, [fairness] is a canon of journalism to which I subscribe. We are not a weapon to be used against people.

"You seem to think that writing a clear, accurate, factual article is a waste of your talents. You refer to such stories as AP pieces in a derogatory manner.

"As far as I am concerned, every article in *Maine Times* should be clear, accurate, and factual. That is the first step. After that, it may be, indeed should be, well written (which doesn't mean over-written) and it may contain insights other reports don't carry.

"I consider these the major differences between us and other newspapers: We cover issues others don't; we highlight issues and events on the horizon, before they sail into the public domain; we take a clear viewpoint or focus where it applies and where it clarifies; we are more thorough and consequently more accurate in what we report; we strive to maintain a style that does not become a slant.

"I expect a reporter to exert his intelligence on a subject, not his personality or ego. (Except in rare instances, I don't want to know about the reporter; I want to know about the subject.)" This was written at a time when many national stories were about the reporter and how the reporter interacted with the story. Hunter Thompson and his Gonzo Journalism were the epitome of this, but the reporter as participant was widespread, moving from the alternative press to the mainstream, especially in magazines.

I continued, "By exerting intelligence, I mean that a story may lead logically to a certain conclusion. But it must be logical and it must contain or deal with arguments on the other side. We are not writing propaganda for a particular viewpoint; we are exploring ideas and issues. Without viewpoint, such exploration is a mess.

"I am not particularly interested in how a reporter asks a question nor am I interested in a disagreement that may have arisen with the subject.... In fact, while I sometimes [express disagreement] with a subject [during an interview], I don't do it to convince him; I do it to get a clearer picture of where he stands.

"It is not your job as an interviewer to convince anyone of something you believe (I thought this was a mistake you were making with Ed Muskie the other day and one reason you were having so much trouble getting information), but to find out what he believes. You are there to draw the person out and to get him to talk about specific topics which may be germane to what you are writing about.

"I am frustrated because when I try to make a point about style, you seem to understand, and then you do the same thing the next week. Considering all I had said about the need for absolute fairness in the Gannett editorial writing piece, I was amazed by the judgmental sentences and phrases I had to cut out."

Perhaps the greatest flaw in my attempts to bring this reporter into line was my belief that I could make such a change in him. But that was part of the challenge. We were going to hire talented writers, people with strong opinions, and try to work with them in developing a new kind of journalism, a work very much in progress. Some responded beautifully and some didn't. I thought that as editor I could control the process and prevent overstepping, and sometimes I could. Sometimes I couldn't.

Maine Times reporters did not have weeks to work on most stories. Due to our lack of resources, they had to be incredibly productive, turning out more copy in a week than many daily reporters. For a major piece, a reporter had only three or four days, including a day to write, so before starting, s/he would have to have a clear idea of just where s/he was heading and whom s/he was going to interview. This was developed in conversation with me, and I was expected to be well read on the subject and to offer good lead contacts, people who could tell us the right people to interview. As the story progressed, the reporter would often discuss it with me, telling me what s/he had learned and expecting me to discover gaps in information and make suggestions as to how those gaps might be filled. Sometimes my information would come from reports and other documents the reporter had given me to read. Phyllis Austin, especially, expected me to read everything she gave me and the assignment could be considerable. She then looked to me as a sounding board for her ideas on how to pursue the story.

For the more complex stories, a reporter would do more preparation before actually starting down the final stretch, working half a day or a day a week on research and interviews until s/he had enough material and focus to know where the story was going. To free up the time, I would mix in "you were there" assignments where the reporter focused on a meeting or a single interview that could be done in a day or two. So the reporter might be working on a complex subject for weeks and then come to me and say s/he was ready to wrap it up in the next week. We did not have the luxury of giving a reporter several weeks of producing nothing else while s/he worked on such a major piece.

We also let reporters learn incrementally, by covering the same subject over a long period of time. Sometimes, this began with coverage of meetings, perhaps the Maine Milk Commission to provide an introduction to milk pricing and the economics of dairy farming, or the Pesticides Control Board, a basically adversarial regulatory agency where the pros and cons of different pesticides and their uses were laid out. Other papers would go to these meetings when they were warned there was to be a particularly contentious confrontation, but we would staff them over a period of time when we thought the issue was ripe. Although each meeting invariably produced a story, it might be only a short one, what we called a News of the Week, but with each meeting, background expertise was accumulating and when the big story emerged, our reporter was not only there but was well informed on the details and context.

Our habit of sticking with an issue and covering it from multiple viewpoints also helped. While my wife, Eunice, covered the Pesticides Control Board, Phyllis Austin covered the chemical spraying of forests, a major contributor to the spruce budworm epidemic that hit Maine's forests in the '70s and that resulted in such outrages as the accidental aerial spraying of people's vegetable gardens with herbicides. The coverage of each informed the other and our readers as well, and the knowledge of forestry issues that Phyllis developed during those years formed the backbone for her reportage for another two decades.

This staying with a story could have its pitfalls, most notably becoming the captive of one's sources, as is the danger with any reportage. By working on the same area of coverage for several years, reporters developed contacts they relied on to be accurate and to put them onto other good sources, but sometimes this could cause a reporter to overlook new voices on the subject and have coverage determined by the source rather than by the subject's evolution.

One of the best sources we had over the years was Dick Barringer, who had come to Maine partly because of his relationship with John Cole in an early think tank called the Allagash Group. Dick had become director of the State Planning Office and conservation commissioner during the budworm epidemic. He then went on to teach at the Muskie Institute and to run for governor. He was one of the best informed and most acute thinkers in the state, but at one point Phyllis had begun to turn to him for information on so many stories that I told her, only half jokingly, that there would be a ban on any quote from Barringer for the next six months. She got the point and expanded her sources.

One of the weaknesses of too many daily reporters is that they don't read, partly because they are so busy chasing down stories, and partly because they have been taught that more important than the content of what is said is who says it. If a politician or public figure says something, it is news. If a mere informed citizen says the same thing, it is not news.[4]

For many of the types of stories we did, there was background material of much greater importance than what anyone could tell us in an interview. You could not do a good job if you had not read the literature.

No issue was more contentious than the use of pesticides and herbicides in forestry management. There was strong evidence that the reason we had had an epidemic of spruce budworm that threatened

---

4. But those citizens and their level of expertise should be described. Today new organizations crop up that may be little more than one person with an ax to grind and the press will cite him/her as director of an organization with an important sounding name without telling the reader why he/she should have credibility.

the entire forest industry was because we had developed an even-aged forest of the same species of tree, therefore making it susceptible to the pest. And this even-aged forest was the result of practices where large tracts were cut, to make it more economical to extract the wood, and allowed to grow back in the single, most valuable species, the competing species eradicated with herbicides. All kinds of scientific papers had been written on the subject, arguing the pros and cons of these practices, and they were just waiting for someone to read them, which we did.

By the 1980s people were writing books on controversial environmental issues of the kinds we covered, and these books proved invaluable in setting the stage for what we were doing. Sometimes I read the book first, sometimes the reporter did, but often we both read it.

The same was true of the hundreds of governmental reports that come out each year, almost all with a cover press release and summary that is often all the daily reporters read in their attempt to get the story out as quickly as possible. Our reading the entire report and making a few strategic phone calls would usually result in a drastically different story.[5] The trick was to find what was important in the report, not what those issuing the report wanted you to pick up, the latter being the subject of the accompanying summary.

I had also developed other sources of easy information. For some reason, we appeared to be the only newspaper that routinely read the decisions of the Maine Supreme Court—I did this myself. Hardly a month went by when we did not get an exclusive story from one of these decisions, all laid out and ready to be written because court decisions present the salient facts before they do their conclusions.

By the 1990s and my last stint as editor, I had become more concerned with background and the nuances of reporting. By this time I had participated in decision-making at a number of non-profits and I had seen many of the same issues from a different perspective than I had when viewing them through the reporter's lens. Whereas in the

---

5. In the 1990s I hit the jackpot with a telephone call about a long-overdue report on Freddie Vahlsing's career in Aroostook County. Since I called at noontime, there was no secretary and I reached the author of the report, who not only gave me important perspective but told me fascinating "war stories" about his encounters with Vahlsing. There's more about Vahlsing in Chapter Eleven.

past we had reported on what the decision was when it was finally made, I was now much more aware of how the decision had been reached and in many cases I found that process to be the more important story.

Our policy of having a single reporter stick with an evolving issue gave us an advantage over other Maine newspapers in that they were always looking for the easy confrontation and that was often just what people were avoiding when trying to reach a decision. Many of the most important stories, therefore, became "unreportable" by the daily press, partly because they would not allow a reporter the time to cover unproductive sessions and partly because many reporters do not know how to do an issues-based story rather than one based on confrontation.

Not that the daily press, especially the Portland papers, didn't try to do major "investigative" pieces, but most of their articles consisted of many people saying the same thing, as if repetition were the same as validity. And they were the purveyors of conventional wisdom, not that conventional wisdom was always wrong. Many times it was correct and the situations they called for to be corrected needed correcting, but the result was always predictable and not very enlightening to the informed reader. (It can be argued the function of the daily press is to inform the uninformed. The potential flaw is that the uninformed choose to remain uninformed and do not read such articles.)

After I left the paper altogether I became increasingly convinced that reporters had to be allowed to spend more time backgrounding. This became particularly apparent in our discussions about sprawl at Eco/Eco, where we would spend hours discussing the hidden incentives that led to dispersed patterns of development—zoning regulations, tax policy, utility costs, etc.—and then discuss ways to change those incentives without confrontation between the different constituencies represented. Indeed, under the Eco/Eco format and policy, participants were asked and forced by peer pressure to reject their roles as spokespersons for a particular interest and to use their specialized knowledge to approach the larger issue. Thus, the housing developers, who claimed that in the end they didn't care where they built houses just so long as they could build them, did not argue for relaxing standards so they could build more profitably. Instead, they enlightened the rest of the group as to what economic and other incentives made them act in the way they did, and how changing those incentives would change the way they acted.

This is a far cry from the old confrontational style of journalism and it demands a tenacity by reporters and readers alike to stay with an issue long enough to fully understand it. The critical point is no longer conflict; it is evolution.

I had already begun to sense this change in 1992 when I came back to edit *Maine Times* for two years, but even then I did not understand the depth of the change and the difficulties the press would have in covering issues in such a drastically different manner.

I think the press has become worse, more polarized, more driven by the special interests who want to keep the public focused narrowly, a tactic that has played into the hands of those politicians who simply mouth the code words to bring along a given constituency. Abortion, gun control, gay rights are all the wedge issues that no longer leave themselves open to sane discussion but become easy tests of a politician's loyalty to a particular group. At the same time, readers are frustrated by the more complex issues, such as global warming, because they do not see a solution.

When I am now asked whether the old *Maine Times* could have survived, both editorially and financially, I am emphatic in my answer: Yes. It would be different, of course; it would probably be more clearly defined in who its audience is; and it might have to admit that such an audience, one that reads for solid information on which to base decisions about the future, is constantly diminishing. But that audience, even in a state as small as Maine with its population of just over a million, is still large enough to support a publication, especially with cheaper ways of producing and delivering it to readers. Audiences are becoming fractionalized and therefore smaller, but the traditional press, in trying to dumb-down to reach the largest possible audience, is losing the really important audience, those who think and base their opinions on the facts. Those most likely to affect public policy are left without this source of state or local information.

As much as ever, the local mainstream press relies on others to raise and explicate issues, so if there is no organized opposition, the bad aspects of a proposal simply go uncovered. But to me the role of a newspaper editor was and is to act as the intelligent reader, to spot the questions that need to be asked, and to make sure his reporters ask those questions as a surrogate for the informed public. I still don't think it's such a radical idea.

In Pictures

My father, Oscar S. Cox, was best known as the lawyer who came up with the precedent to draft the Lend-Lease Act, the primary instrument for supplying our allies with armaments and other supplies during the Second World War. In March, 1941, President Franklin Delano Roosevelt signed Lend-Lease into law. That's Oscar, age thirty-five, standing behind him. To the far left is Representative Sol Bloom, the key member in the House for passing the legislation. Oscar was his tutor on the bill, anticipating questions and supplying answers. Second from the right is Edward Stettinius, former president of U.S. Steel, who became the first administrator of Lend-Lease and then Secretary of State. Oscar's title was General Counsel for Lend-Lease but he was the de facto administrator responsible for bringing together an exceptional group of men, including Phil Graham (later publisher of the *Washington Post*), Joe Rauh (civil liberties attorney), Lloyd Cutler (Presidential lawyer and Washington eminence grise), George Ball (Undersecretary of State and Vietnam war opponent), Walter Thayer, publisher of the international *Herald Tribune,* and Eugene Rostow (dean of Yale Law School). When Lend-Lease was disbanded at the end of the war, Oscar left government.

Right: During the 1940s, jobs were held simultaneously in Washington, so Oscar became Assistant Solicitor General while still involved with the war effort. When it turned out a group of Nazi saboteurs who had landed from submarines might be sentenced to only a few year in prison under civil law, Oscar once again came up with an innovative legal solution—trying the eight saboteurs before a military tribunal where they could receive the death penalty. The trial was under the direction of Attorney General Francis Biddle (right), but Oscar handled much of the case, sitting next to the legendary FBI chief J. Edgar Hoover every day. I am six

or seven, my brother Warren two years older. My mother, Louise, is wearing her favorite hat with the pheasant feather in it. My mother has tried to dress me properly, as she would keep trying for the rest of my life. My brother convinced me he should alter the camel's hair coat I am wearing, and by cutting off the sleeves and shortening it, made me a vest. Our mother was most unappreciative. During the saboteur trial, I recall picking up my father in the late afternoon and being impressed by the soldiers with their water-cooled machine guns behind sandbags. Biddle also called in my father—along with Joe Rauh and Ben Cohen—for an opinion on whether American citizens of Japanese descent could be interned on the West Coast. Their equivocal position is emblematic of my father's skill, as a young man, in finding ways to accomplish what his boss wanted. This was especially true when his boss was the President of the United States and has left me convinced that even today, a President sets the tone for staff opinions. Like my father, their instinct is to tell the President how he can do what he wants to do.

AFTER THE WAR, Oscar turned to international law and one of his most important clients was Fiat in Italy. In 1950, about the same time Oscar was locked in the Turin factory during a Communist strike, my parents visited Sestriere with Ginia Gargioni, executive assistant to Prof. Vittorio Valletta who ran the company until Gianni Agnelli was experienced enough to take over. Ginia looked out for my brother and me when we visited Europe. When, age seventeen, I went to Grenoble to study the summer of 1955, she had me met at the boat by a Fiat driver who warned me about French perfidy and bedbugs and advised me that the best cheap hotels were close to the train station. Almost a decade later, when I was able to make a spur-of-the-moment trip to Sestriere to ski, Ginia made sure we had excellent accommodations at the Fiat-owned resort. When I wanted photographs of European rivers to run as examples of what could be done in Saranac Lake, Ginia supplied them. She even got my brother a signed photograph of Gina Lollobrigida, the buxomy film star, after he expressed his admiration for her. Ginia Gargioni made me love everything Italian, so much so, that John Cole, my newspaper partner, used to say my great regret in life was that I was not born Italian.

I WAS TWENTY-THREE when I landed the job as editor of the *Adirondack
Daily Enterprise* in Saranac Lake, New York. That's me with the Napoleon
hat with the typographical error in the center of the back row. Bill
McLaughlin, the talented columnist who liked nothing better than to
make fun of me, is the tall one on the far left. The older gentleman, far
right, who like so many others came to Saranac Lake to cure his tuberculosis, is Ernest Rogers, a former Latin teacher who was the proofreader
and my tutor the first year I was at the *Enterprise*. Third from the right
in the back row is shop foreman Armand Amell who taught me how to
compose a page and who introduced me to type lice. His lessons formed
the groundwork for the technical knowledge I would further develop and
which would be so important in our ability to start *Maine Times*. In the
front row, looking like an owl, is Howard Riley, one of my closest friends.
He went from Linotype operator to managing editor and mayor of
Saranac Lake. I had breakfast with the composing room staff every morning after clipping the Associated Press wire. Eighteen people was not a lot
to run a daily, even a small one, but then we didn't have a lot of circulation (about 3,700) or a lot of money (annual sales of $250,000).

My surrogate mother in Saranac Lake was Bea Sprague, later Edward, who had been a friend of Jim Loeb who co-owned the paper. If there was anyone interesting visiting the area, Bea would make contact. That's why she invited Charles Jackson, the author of the classic novel about alcoholism, *The Lost Weekend*, to dinner. His kinkiness was more than we reckoned for. Recently, I was visiting my brother in Washington and there was a letter by the telephone from Outerbridge Horsey—the seventh, I think. Bea collected unusual names and the diplomat Outerbridge Horsey, the third, was one of her favorites. She would have been pleased by the coincidence. Because I was not married and had no family responsibilities when I lived in Saranac Lake, I made some of the most lasting relationships of my life. It was Bea who introduced me to Janet and Fritz Decker, to whom I turned when I learned I had cancer.

If BEA SPRAGUE was my surrogate mother, Libby Donahue was my surrogate maiden aunt. As administrative assistant to Congressman Frank M. Coffin, she kept promoting me during the 1960 gubernatorial campaign in Maine. Libby had had a distinguished career, as women's White House correspondent covering Eleanor Roosevelt for the national newspaper, *PM*, and as a speechwriter for Adlai S. Stevenson when he ran for president. Libby, along with her friend Joe Rauh, kept pushing me to write about my father and she loved introducing Eunice and me to her wide circle of accomplished friends as well as her bright relatives of our generation. Libby had deep Maine roots and was a great supporter of *Maine Times*, writing a series for us on the planned construction of a nuclear power plant in the early '70s. You could never tell when Libby would show up in Maine for the summer; it was a natural phenomenon, an impressive force of nature. Our children grew up knowing the highlight of summer was Libby's arrival.

I MET JOHN COLE when I worked for him and Sandy Brook at the *Kennebunk Star* during the summer of 1957. I was still in school. Later I came to the *Bath Daily Times* as editor and John and I joined when that paper merged in February 1967 with the weekly *Brunswick Record*. This is the second issue, with the logo designed by George deLyra who would also design *Maine Times*. The classic layout and the heavy emphasis on local news were typical. Ken Morrison, who came with us to *Maine Times*, wrote the series on local housing problems (lower right) and John wrote the weather story. As editors, we wrote articles, editorials and columns as well, not worrying about the work load but only too happy to have the opportunity to do what we wanted. Despite complaints from a later editor of the *Times-Record*, publisher Cam Niven was exceptionally fair and allowed us great latitude. He also protected us from his much more conservative father, his predecessor as publisher.

MAINE TIMES MAINE TIMES MAINE TIMES MAINE TIMES CENTS 20

Volume I, Number I   Friday, October 4, 1968

THE UNION IS DISSOLVED

Muskie in '72
p.4, pp 8,9

EDITORIALS
pp.6,7

Teachers in revolt
pp. 2,3

30 minutes to Lebanon
p. 15

THE FIRST ISSUE of *Maine Times*, October 4, 1968, unfortunately looked a lot like a political handout, something I learned as I tried to give copies away at a shopping center in Westbrook, just outside Portland. Senator Edmund S. Muskie was on the cover, the vice presidential nominee running with Hubert S. Humphrey. The fellow next to him is Hannibal Hamlin of Maine, Lincoln's first vice-president. We liked the "what if" he had stayed on for Lincoln's second term. The repeated *Maine Times* logo was George deLyra's idea and we were to stick with it in some form for more than twenty years, until the new owners decided a redesign would spur subscriptions. It didn't.

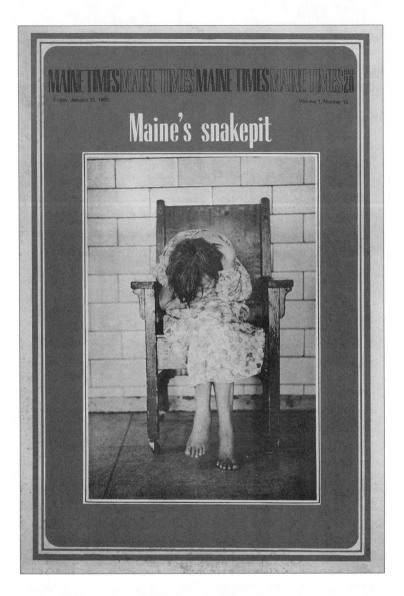

SOON WE IMPLEMENTED a distinctive color mask to take better advantage of the limited use of color our presses allowed. I got the idea from a British publication illustrated in a Swiss magazine. Although newspapers, including the *Times-Record* under our editorship, had written before about the institution for the retarded, Pineland, at *Maine Times* we presented the story much more strikingly and we did not let go of it. Years later, after a class action law suit, the clients were mainstreamed. Today, Pineland is a home to cattle raised for Wolfe's Neck Natural Beef, a project I have worked on for years. In Maine, everything comes around eventually.

A YEAR AFTER *Maine Times* started, *Time* magazine published a flattering piece in its press section. To make us worthy of national coverage, they made it seem as if we had accomplished more than we had in that first year but who were we to complain? A friend made up this birthday card with the hint we should not take our press clippings too seriously. The background reads: Nothing TIMELY, Nothing New. John was forty-six and I was thirty-two when we began. John quickly became the public face of the paper and I was grateful, a situation that was to change after our ownership positions were drastically altered.

It SEEMED NATURAL that we would do a Women's Issue in 1971. That's where our sensibilities lay and we had the women on staff to do the job. Lucy Martin, seated far left, had applied for a job as a typesetter, not telling us what a fine writer she was, something we learned from her work on the Women's Issue. She then became a full-time reporter. Other staff members putting it together were, left standing, Lynne Langley and Eunice T. Cox, writers. Seated, Roberta Davis, subscriptions, Pat Arbour, production and art, Betty Rubin, office, and Meredith Herzog, production. Standing right are writer Peggy Fisher and advertising rep Cathy Guild. *Maine Times* had a disproportionate number of female writers in the early days, partly because we offered an opportunity to highly skilled women who could not work full-time because they were raising families. Throughout my tenure, *Maine Times* reflected changing staff interests that were fortunately matched by changing reader attitudes. As so often is the case with such a personally driven publication, our readership aged with us.

FINDING NEW TALENT was one of the most enjoyable aspects of running *Maine Times*. We had never had political cartoons because we could never find a political cartoonist good enough. Besides, good political cartoons are often mean and Maine is too small a state, with everyone knowing everyone else personally, for meanness to thrive. But when Doug Coffin (yes, he is the son of Frank Coffin) came along, I couldn't resist his strip, "Cronies." It caused a good deal of controversy because it made fun of much of our readership, including the classic summer resident and the new arrival who thinks she knows all there is to know. People who have seen this cartoon hanging in my house have told me they don't know what a short cord is but if you buy firewood in Maine, you'll soon learn. Doug went national with his cartoon but had to water it down too much. He continued to make suggestions to me about the paper's graphics and introduced me to new ideas well into the '90s.

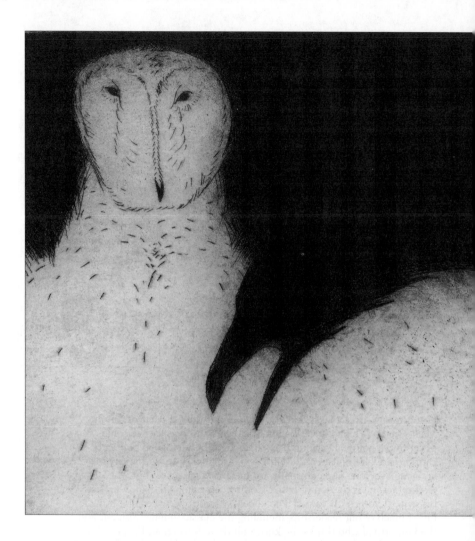

If Doug Coffin's cartoons could prove difficult for some, Robert Shetterly's drawings, which ran on the editorial page for years, baffled a good portion of our readership and they let us know. Of course, that did not keep us from using his work. Why not make your readers think a little, even exercise their imaginations? Visual puzzles have always pleased me and after this one ran, I bought a copy for my wall, so that I could admire the owl and the raven, white and black, positive and negative images. It is part of a Shetterly series based on William Blake's *Proverbs of Hell* and the inscription reads: "The crow wish'd everything was black, the owl that everything was white."

By 1984 WE HAD GROWN from a staff of seven to twenty-two, and each year, at New Year's, we ran a group photo in the paper. At this time, we had the dynamic trio in the ad department, Karen Taylor, Marg Watts, and Sarah Harper, who deftly matched advertisers to our audience and made *Maine Times* the place to be for a specific group of advertisers. When I run into any of the people pictured, we immediately launch into conversation as if it had been only a day or two since we last saw one another. Eunice and I are still in touch with many old staffers. After she had left *Maine Times*, Annice Dubitsky told me she would never again work at a place where she felt what she did was so important. Left to right, standing: Evariste Bernier, Annice Dubitsky, Roberta Davis, Eunice Cox, Ellen Grant, Meredith Herzog, Jeff Clark, Chris Ayres, Karen Taylor, me, Nancy March, Tom Jones, Barbara Feller-Roth, Sarah Harper. Seated, Susan Winn, Kathy Brawn, Margery Kelly, Edgar Allen Beem, Phyllis Austin with Scout, Marg Watts, and Beth Webster Fenwick.

WHEN I MARRIED EUNICE, I became a part of her family. In 1965, on our return to Maine, her sister Kathy, then twelve, came to spend the summer with us as she did most summers through college. Kathy and I have remained particularly close, and when we visit New York, where she lives, she scopes out the best new restaurants. Like many adopted New Yorkers, she relishes the city and knows its neighborhoods intimately. Her interest in food and art coincides with ours as well. What Kathy and I are inspecting here is definitely not museum quality.

Then there is the Greek side of the family. The nephews of Eunice's stepfather came to Lake Placid when they were teenagers and both, Chris and Gus Theodore, have become successful, Chris as a stockbroker and Gus as a restaurateur. Both also adopted me into their family. In 1985 I visited the family village of Demati for the first time, and Gus masterminded a trip by taxicab through Greece, leading us places I never would have seen otherwise. With us on that trip were his wife Sheran and their daughter Athena, then a precocious three-year-old, whose fondest memory of the trip is when a bee bit me on the rear end. Athena graduated from Yale in 2004 and we now recite the opening lines of *Canterbury Tales* together. One day, at an engagement celebration in Philadelphia, I asked Gus how many of the hundreds of people there, on both sides, were in some way connected to Demati. If you included marriage, he said, all of them. I included myself. As for all the Greek weddings I have attended—well, there's a movie still to be made.

HOWARD RILEY DELIGHTED me by coming to my retirement party in 1986. Here he is with me and Eunice and he looks older than we do. Anna Ginn, the new publisher, arranged the party and she was a great party arranger. Libby Donahue came up from Washington; Kathy Theodore from New York; Sue Scheible from Boston. Shep Lee told the story about how I wouldn't take orders when he was Frank Coffin's campaign manager, and David Turitz did a real roast, as requested. He shocked some of the audience but I was amused. The party was a tribute to our sense of extended family and shared mission. A few years later, we had an alumni gathering at our home in Georgetown. When it is time to do so again, Roberta Davis will arrange it all.

Even though I spent several summers with my cousins in Bryson City, North Carolina, when I was very young, rarely did I see members of my mother's side of the family once I grew up. Before our family moved to Washington, when I was in the third grade, my best friend was my first cousin Little Fisher who grew up to be Fisher Black who would have won the Nobel Prize for economics had he not died prematurely of cancer. In 1997 we had a Black family reunion in Tampa, Florida. My brother, Warren, and his wife, Claire, also attended. Warren, who lives in Washington, D.C., is one of the nation's leading contextual architects, meaning he designs buildings to harmonize with the existing architecture, an important goal when the existing buildings are significant. One of the best things my brother ever did was bring Claire into my life. I always look forward to seeing her and we have so much that we enjoy talking about it is hard to shut us up. She, too, shares the art and food combo. Their two children, Alexandra and Sam, are exceptional.

A Tom Jones family portrait, 1997. Our daughter Sara is a potter, and our son Tony became a ski instructor at Jackson Hole after college (how I would have liked to ski as he does), then returned to Maine where he is now in business with his wife, Heather. Lucy Theodore, Eunice's mother, came to our house almost every weekend for two decades where she and I could debate the day's events over breakfast as we read the newspapers. Lucy's idea of nirvana was eating pickled hering while watching Lawrence Welk, a moment I chose to disappear. Lucy died in 2004 at the age of ninety-three. Buddy, the lab, is eight years old in this picture. It was Eunice's idea to get him, but because I spend more time at home, he sticks with me. When she goes away, Buddy comes to bed with me, gradually working his way up from the foot of the bed until his head is on her pillow, where he thinks it belongs. Eunice is seated; I am standing.

SARA'S WORK IS DEFINED by her exceptional sense of color. She and I have long shared an interest in art and from the age of six, she accompanied me as I reviewd art shows for *Maine Times*. In 1985, when I broke my leg skiing, Sara took advantage of the circumstances by pushing my wheel-chair when we visited museums in New York, placing me before paintings she preferred, more Basquiat than Breughel.

WHEN TONY AND HIS WIFE, HEATHER, came to Cervinia, the Italian side of the Matterhorn, with us in 2001, it was a relief because he had her to teach skiing so he could leave me alone. Soon he will have his children to teach, starting with Anna, born in 2002. Olivia was born in 2004.

LIKE HER GRANDFATHER, Anna likes to drive lawnmowers.

Eleven

What Made *Maine Times* So Different?

We had done no market research prior to starting *Maine Times*. We had done no research at all. Instead, the idea of starting a new statewide newspaper, an idea that had found early germination in our living room in Kennebunkport in conversation with my father, was a gut reaction. Had we done accurate research we would have been startled by the reality, that there were at most 20,000 buyers at any given time and many of them lived out of state. That would have seemed low to us, too low to have taken the risk. As it turned out, those numbers were enough for us to succeed.

Nor did we do any objective analysis of what the public wanted. We knew what we wanted to write about; we knew what we considered important. Our job was to convince enough other people they shared our interests and concerns, not to try to meet some inchoate demand that few could articulate because they had never seen such a paper before. And we certainly didn't want to emulate the pattern dailies followed to please their readers. We wanted to escape the world of bridge columns and TV listings.

The most acute analysis of our editorial success came years later from Bill Dunfey, a member of the New Hampshire hotel family who was a newspaper junkie and a sympathetic observer of *Maine Times* since its inception. He was in an excellent place to understand what was going on next door to him because as a Democrat and a liberal, he felt particularly isolated in a state where journalism was dominated by the bullying *Manchester Union Leader* under the vitriolic William Loeb. In that state, anyone who had the temerity to stand up for the underdog, to espouse civil liberties, and especially to oppose the United States' Cold War policy, was quickly labeled a pariah and isolated. It was Dunfey who suggested that we had succeeded because we showed a significant group of people in Maine that there was a community of like thinkers, and now they had some way to communicate with one another. We told them they were not alone.

Some of the stories we featured in the initial editions of *Maine Times* were not really new. We had covered the Pineland Center for the retarded back at the *Bath-Brunswick Times-Record* and there had been other press coverage, but now we had a statewide audience and the tools to increase our impact. We knew that there were those within the system who thought the conditions were as atrocious as we did, but the legislature wasn't willing to put up the money to remedy the situation. There was then, as now, a general feeling that if a problem remained hidden, it did not exist. Newspapers that raised such issues without the means to implement a solution were troublemakers. Although their editors may have shared our concerns about conditions such as those at Pineland, other papers did not seem to share our sense of outrage, and the dailies of Maine did not campaign. Covering a situation once and letting it drop was enough; follow-up stories were old news. Whether intentionally or not, the Maine press fostered the apathy that occurs when injustice remains unexposed. Those who wanted change were often discouraged by the lack of public support. *Maine Times* provided them an incentive to continue by giving them a conduit to the public and to the policymakers. The latter were forced to read the paper because they had to know what we were saying.

Our first Pineland cover for *Maine Times* pictured a girl in what looked like an electric chair and carried the headline: "Maine's Snakepit," a reference to a 1947 movie about the horrors of an insane asylum that would still be recognizable to our readers. It cried out for action. The retarded, many of them functional enough to have participated in normal society, were being warehoused at best. At worst, they were restrained with torn sheets in pools of urine.

John and I fully expected that our exposés of sordid conditions would result in a public outcry and an immediate remedy of the situation. They seldom did.

Eventually conditions at Pineland improved, and it was finally closed as such institutions became obsolete and the clients were mainstreamed. But the decisive force was not us; it was a class-action suit brought on behalf of the former inmates, led by poverty agency lawyer Neville Woodruff, who persevered for years. Our moral support may have encouraged him to keep going, but we did not cause the change; others did.

Sometimes change takes even longer or there is no change at all. Only in the last decade were efforts made to implement the basic reforms at the Boys' Training Center that we had outlined almost thirty years before. Even as this is written, there is a new investigation of the institution because boys were still being placed in solitary confinement for days rather than hours as the rules stipulated. The rules may have changed but the attitudes have not. The core values of the state corrections department have remained the same and still focus on punishment rather than rehabilitation. While there is an emerging unrest about the almost total emphasis on incarceration in our penal system because of the escalating cost and stable recidivism rate, there has been no real change in the underlying philosophy and so new buildings are built and new regulations promulgated but the children are treated the same as they always were. You could have taken that same story and republished it today, and the essential picture would have remained accurate.

It took us a long time to understand that a newspaper alone could not bring about the change we wanted. We believed it was not a newspaper's job to become involved in the politics of reform but only to point out the unacceptable conditions that cried out for reform, and if there were proposed solutions, to describe them as well. We were correct about the limits of journalism, but we did not understand that public outcry alone will not drive actual reform, for public outcry will eventually die down. There must be someone within the bureaucracy who wants to pursue the same goals, or there must be an individual whose persistency borders on the fanatic to carry on the crusade for years before there is meaningful action. Perseverance is an overlooked necessity in effective social reform.

During the first two years of *Maine Times*, the issue that emerged to dominate all others was the environment, especially on a statewide basis.

Back in the days of the *Times-Record*, we had become aware of a man named John Harris who wanted to build a breeder nuclear power plant in Maine and couple it with an aluminum smelter, an absolutely mind-boggling combination of danger and pollution. A byproduct of aluminum smelters is fluoride in quantities that can etch a car windshield.

Harris needed to sell his idea to a community because he planned to finance it with tax-free bonds that only a public entity could issue. So in 1969 he took his scheme to Trenton, a small village at the entrance to Mt. Desert Island and Acadia National Park.

The only other statewide paper, the *Sunday Telegram*, treated it as a local story, as did the large dailies and the wire services, which left the field pretty much to us. John Cole did the coverage and in a piece of new journalism in which John left no doubt where his heart was, he painted an epic of Wall Street villains as "the men in the dark suits" against the good folks of Trenton. It wasn't just locals against those from away. John wrote: "The moderator, Wayne Libhart of Brewer, and the town counsel, was curt with his instructions about who would be allowed to speak and who wouldn't. As it turned out, the [project's backers] got the floor firstest with the mostest, and Mr. Libhart made sure the voters kept quiet. Indeed, he insisted." I had forgotten all about this vignette a decade later when Libhart showed up as the lawyer suing us for libel on behalf of a state senator.

On the other hand, Dr. Freddie Homburger, "speaking in a loud, clear, and spirited voice with a trace of a Swiss-German accent" was eloquent in his opposition. John wrote that in response "the audience that had been politely silent for more than four hours jumped to its feet with a spontaneous outburst of cheers, applause, whistles, and yells that made up a great, explosive, unanimous demonstration of support for preserving what's good and small and true in Trenton, and keeping out what's big and strange and threatening, even though the monster does have money."

John's style in this article, written and edited by him in 1969, was not replicated by anyone else and once I became editor, I tended to edit him very lightly. As overly one-sided as it seems today, some readers regretted our move to more balanced reporting and recalled these first issues with admiration.

I don't think there was any question Trenton would have turned the idea down. The project had been presented in a way that would raise the wrath of almost any community in Maine, and Trenton trounced it—to our readers, we had been the reason for this stunning rejection. We not only reported on such events that were important to those who saw Maine as a unified state, as a way of life, almost as a mystique, we took sides and we won—on their behalf. We were their personal watchdog.

When we reported early the same year that the Baxter Park Authority was about to allow snowmobiles in the "forever wild" enclave, we did a cover story and John wrote an editorial urging readers to call the Authority's chairman and listed his phone number. Our outraged readers phoned as requested, almost driving the commissioner from his office and setting off a furor that ended in a reversal of the decision. The situation proved unique—a single story generating such an instant reaction—but the circumstances were perfect. There was an avid constituency for protecting Baxter Park, and snowmobiles were still perceived as noisy, fume-spewing intrusions. The Authority must have known it was treading on thin ice by allowing them in the first place, and the public outcry was enough to tilt the scales the other way.

Then came the oil refineries. Governor Kenneth Curtis had brought to state government his own brain trust of bright young men and one of the proposals that emerged was a free trade zone in Machias, with an oil port to be run by Occidental Petroleum under Dr. Armand Hammer. (Only much later were books to be written about Hammer and his dubious relationships with the Soviet Union.) The citizens of Maine were told that if we did not allow an oil refinery, we would see our home-heating oil and gasoline prices soar beyond the rest of the country; the slogan developed in Texas was "Let them freeze in the dark."

(This past summer, thirty-three years later, when gas prices soared across the nation, Maine, still without a refinery, soared as well but retained one of the lowest pump prices in the country.)

The proposed refinery became a moveable feast, migrating next to Casco Bay, then to Sears Island in Penobscot Bay, which brought a flood of donations from establishment summer residents. It then moved to inland Sanford which, having lost its backbone textile industry, was a much more receptive site,[1] and finally uttered its last

1. Because it was thought to be so desperate, Sanford was chosen as the site of a proposed Indian gambling casino in 2003. It failed statewide at referendum.

gasp in depressed Eastport. The refinery was never built. Our opposition was strong and our coverage thorough at all the serial sites. We did learn that while our opposition to the site in Penobscot Bay brought us new subscribers, it did not do so in Sanford. The summer residents in Penobscot Bay relied on our paper to learn what was happening when they were gone for the winter, and they also realized that the oil refinery would not be the last industrial project to threaten their summer Eden.

Although other newspapers had been covering Freddie Vahlsing, whose roots in Maine went back to 1963, the tenacity with which we followed his exploits was both typical and unique to us. Vahlsing had needed to declassify a small river, Prestile Stream, freeing it from water pollution restrictions, in order to operate his proposed sugar beet refinery, touted as the saving alternative for Aroostook County where the ubiquitous potato crop was suffering. He had managed to give the impression that Senator Ed Muskie supported him, and with only a handful of dissenters (who later wore their dissent as a badge of honor), the legislature went along with the Prestile declassification, allowing its total pollution, and the state, willing to prostitute itself in the name of economic development, guaranteed $17 million in loans to build a sugar refinery. Much later the operation was to go bankrupt, and it was disclosed that Vahlsing had made a healthy profit by contracting with companies he formed to build the refinery, even though the sugar beet operation itself failed.

In 1968, our first year of publication, the Canadians dammed the Prestile Stream at the border to prevent the pollution from coming into their country; at *Maine Times*, we kept up with every major Vahlsing move for the next two decades.

That same year, a young counter-culture attorney named Don Gellers instituted the Maine Indian Land Claims case, which may have been a factor, we reported in a story, in his arrest for possessing marijuana. The following year Gellers was convicted, which led to his disbarment. He jumped bail, fled the state, and was replaced by Tom Tureen who won the case for the Indians and three decades later represented them in their attempts to open a gambling casino in Maine.

In 1969 we also made our first mention of Joey Aceto, a sixteen-year-old who, on the advice of a psychiatrist had been placed by his mother in the Boys' Training Center. There, he told our reporter, he had been sprayed in the face with chemical Mace and locked, naked, in a bare cell for two days.

One never knows where a particular story is going to lead, but because of my memory of this incident, every time Joey Aceto showed up, I made sure he was covered.

That first year, Aceto's charges against the director of the center—who would later become commissioner of corrections—were dismissed and he was sent on to the minimum security Windham Correctional Center for adult offenders. He didn't show up again until 1973, four years later, when we reported he had been convicted of assault with intent to kill and sent to the maximum security prison at Thomaston. In 1975 Aceto was paroled from Thomaston and we reported that he had taken up with a radical group, headed by Raymond Luc Levasseur and Thomas Manning, which intended to foment revolution with armed robberies and bombings. Levasseur had started as a prison reformer and we had previously covered his exploits. What we did not know at the time was that Aceto was probably a law-enforcement plant in the radical organization.

In 1976 Aceto admitted participating in three bank robberies and agreed to testify against his former cohorts. A year later, Aceto was the star witness against Dicky Picariello in his trial for politically motivated bank robberies. We staffed the trial and covered it in detail. After the trial, Aceto took a new identity and disappeared into the witness protection program. In 1983 Joey Aceto, still in the witness protection program, participated in the murder of another inmate in an Arkansas prison. The victim was stabbed seventy times and beaten with a hammer.

Then, a year later, Aceto was once again the star witness in a trial against a politically motivated bank robber; Aceto was also sentenced to twenty-five years for the Arkansas murder.

A discerning reader could have tracked Joey's evolution from screwed-up kid to brutal prison murderer, with a stint as government witness along the way.

Often we were the first to pick up on an emblematic person. Thus, we did our first profile on Scott and Helen Nearing, the gurus of the back-to-the-land movement, in 1969 and in our Twenty-fifth

Anniversary Issue in 1993, Helen Nearing was profiled for her analysis of both the past and the future. We were the first publication to spot what we called the "inmigration" of young people into the state, part of the back-to-the-land movement but also broader, as young people sought the quality of life and sense of community Maine had to offer. Everyone else was so busy being negative about Maine, decrying the loss of the textile, shoe, and then poultry industries, that they didn't understand the state's attractions were actually enhanced as the major polluters left. For us, lifestyle was what Maine was all about. We could have lived anywhere we wanted and we had chosen Maine. We knew why these people were moving to Maine—for the same things we were celebrating in *Maine Times*. And our crusading for a better Maine—socially, economically, and environmentally—was a banner of optimism, a belief in the ultimate perfection of where we had chosen to live.

In 1971 the women on the paper came up with an idea they presented to me and I approved—a women's issue, produced entirely by the women on the staff and their friends. John didn't like the idea. Although he supported such causes as the Equal Rights Amendment, he still didn't understand why some visitors to the office complained about the *Playboy* calendar on his desk. (The women on the staff knew him well enough that they had stopped trying to argue with him about such things.)

John may have seen the Women's Issue as me and the women ganging up on him, and not without some cause. But it was a natural for us, not just because the issue was so ripe and so in keeping with our overall message. It was natural because we had such a deep pool of female talent: Women were willing to work for what we could pay; there were then few openings for women with the responsibility we were willing to bestow; and many of our women contributors were trapped housewives with good educations and work experience who because of family obligations could only take part-time work.

I worked on the issue in an advisory capacity and was allowed to proofread but the range of knowledge among the participants— including all of our production staff and advertising staff—was enough that they didn't need any help. We knew of no other such Women's Issue in the nation, and our readers were proud of what we had done.

In this case as in most others, we didn't copy what others did. We did a Women's Issue because that's where we were in our lives; that's what we cared about, and fortunately, that's what our readers cared about.

Our own interests, spurred by what we read, what we observed, and whom we talked to, drove our coverage from the first day and for the next twenty years. We didn't just respond to special interests but tried to define the larger issue.

Consequently, we often identified a major emerging issue before others did. From the beginning we had covered the sea urchin story as emblematic of the problem with fisheries, the conflict between those wanting to extract as much money as possible as quickly as possible from the resource and those wanting to make sure the resource was harvested in a controlled manner so that it would last forever. With sea urchins, we lost. The harvest quickly rose from a gross of $4 million a year to $28 million, and it collapsed just as quickly due to over-harvesting. We didn't stop with sea urchins.

In the late '80s, after I had left as editor, Phyllis Austin asked to work with me on a major series on the depletion of ground fish stocks and what could be done about it. The continuity was such that no one minded this arrangement and Phyllis produced a comprehensive series on ground fish that effectively predicted the issues and the debate that would occur for the next fifteen years. We were ahead of our time because we chose to write about the issue when we recognized it was important. We did not wait for a public official to declare it important, nor did we wait for the key agency, the Department of Marine Resources, because it was caught in a political bind that immobilized it.

As recently as the '90s and my last tour of duty as editor, we were the first to write comprehensively about non-point pollution, the runoff from parking lots and lawns, and about the emerging issue of sprawl. We alone tracked the invasion of some nineteen Wal-Mart stores in two years and we looked at other states, especially Vermont, to see how they had dealt with problems similar to ours, including the revitalization of downtowns.

The stories thirty years after *Maine Times*'s founding and under a different editor may have been less strident than those first articles, but they were essentially similar in that they went beyond what officialdom was saying to identify emerging issues and to stick with continuing problems. If *Maine Times* were still publishing today, I like to think it would still be playing the role of the curious observer, asking the questions no one else in the press is asking. It would be doing stories on how federal budget cuts affected state programs and the state budget; on how war-on-terrorism money that has become a pork barrel allocation is being used by those receiving it in Maine. I like to think *Maine Times* would be documenting the effects of the hardening of political polarization, the futility of highway bypasses that are allowed to become strip developments, and the need for new approaches to land protection since we cannot simply buy all we need to preserve. Because we loved nothing better than finding the flaws in projects we supported, I like to think *Maine Times* would relentlessly critique passenger rail service, the public financing of political campaigns, and term limits.

When we began publication, the targets were relatively easy and well defined. We and our friends had protested the war in Vietnam, holding candles on the Brunswick mall. Boys were being kicked out of school for wearing pants that were too tight—in one school the test was to drop a golf ball down the front and see if it came out at the ankle. Other school children marched with wooden rifles in high-school ROTC. Add the conditions at the Boys' Training Center and Pineland and a sense of outrage became inevitable.

The tone of *Maine Times* did change. It evolved from the purely confrontational to the solution-oriented. But so did we, and so did many of the people making policy in Maine. However, in its essentials, in its own understanding of its journalistic mission, *Maine Times* did not get softer. It just got better and the perception it was best its first decade is only a perception blurred by time and filtering out all but the recognition something dramatic had arrived on the Maine journalism scene in 1968.

From the first issues, lifestyle and culture were part of *Maine Times*'s character. These softer stories contributed to the feeling of shared interest. A full 20 percent of the paper was devoted to our arts coverage—John used to joke that the reason we had so much arts coverage was that the publisher (me) was also the arts editor. The arts community was one of the already established statewide communities. They all knew one another from years of struggle and they were our natural supporters; they had waited years for someone to show an appreciation of what they were doing.

We reviewed contemporary art shows and wrote profiles on artists across the state. We reviewed theater and dance seriously and by high standards. We printed poetry. And we did extensive listings of art and cultural events. One reader commented that an outsider, not realizing most of the venues were 50 miles apart and that a consumer would have to travel hours to attend them all, would think Maine was the cultural mecca of the nation.

In some ways, Maine was a mecca, a least for visual artists. There is a universal pride in the quality of Maine art and even people who care little about art know that Winslow Homer and Andrew Wyeth painted here. Many of the existing galleries in 1968 were the direct descendants of earlier and more famous groups.

The Barn Gallery in Ogunquit grew directly out of the old art colony that had made Perkins Cove famous as a bohemian enclave (and where as a college student I had gone to some pretty wild parties).

The Maine Art Gallery in Wiscasset was being run by Adolph Ipcar, married to Dahlov Ipcar, a well-known and well-respected artist and illustrator. Dahlov was the daughter of William and Marguerite Zorach who had long summered at Robinhood Cove in Georgetown and were part of a neighborhood that included sculptor Gaston Lachaise and photographer Paul Strand.

Willard (Bill) Cummings was trying to drum up local support for the Skowhegan School of Art, of which he was one of the founders. The South Solon Meeting House, where he participated in painting its frescoes, was a Maine landmark. The Skowhegan School, financed by New York patrons, remains on the cutting edge of contemporary art.

Crafts people migrated to Haystack at Stonington, and aspiring young conductors spent their summers learning from Pierre Monteux in Hancock. New galleries and colonies seemed to continually emerge and many towns, particularly those on the coast, had their own art associations with galleries.

I used to have long conversations with Adolph Ipcar about the need for galleries such as his in Wiscasset to evolve from membership organizations to selective, juried shows. These galleries were associations that guaranteed their members exhibition space and as such were supported by the members. There was not yet enough of an art-buying public to support the galleries on their own.

Maine's summer artists were internationally famous and Andrew Wyeth headed the contemporary roster. There were others then or emerging: Alex Katz, Neil Welliver, Robert Indiana, and others. The first award from the newly formed Arts and Humanities Commission went to the photographer Eliot Porter.

Our focus was on contemporary, year-round artists and if the galleries were associations that were reluctant to sift out the best, our task was just the opposite. George deLyra, John Laurent, and DeWitt Hardy were artists I singled out from the beginning and whom we would continue to write about for years. Bill Manning at the Portland School of Art led the indigenous abstract contingent.

A small group within the art community already knew who the best artists were but until I started traveling the state, I didn't know and I was able to transmit a sense of discovery to other readers. In those first days, we—*Maine Times* writers and readers alike—were sharing our discoveries.

In the late 1970s, I hired Edgar Allen Beem as our cultural writer and he began to review and write profiles of the leading painters and sculptors in Maine, the result of which was a book, *Maine Art Now,* published in 1990. Some of the artists in the book are the same ones I reviewed in the first days of *Maine Times,* but the list kept growing, and while it included the nationally recognized who worked in Maine, it was dominated by people doing world-class work who were not yet known outside the state. The talent pool was and remains deep.

We brought the same sense of discovery to our travel pieces. During the 1960 gubernatorial campaign, Frank Coffin had used his old copy of *Maine, A Guide Downeast,* the WPA (Works Progress Administration, a New Deal agency) guide edited by Dorris Isaacson, to glean unusual historical facts about each town we visited. He would then include a tidbit in his speech, sometimes surprising his audience with the information, always impressing them with how much he knew about the state.

An incident during the campaign served as an inspiration for *Maine Times*'s approach to the state's more obscure history. One day we were going door to door on Beals Island, off Jonesport, and almost no one was answering our knocks. Later, we were told that many of the people were reformed Mormons and we had been campaigning on Saturday, their Sabbath. My curiosity had been aroused and for years I had wanted to learn more about these people. Almost a decade later, I had the incentive to do so at *Maine Times.* Led by a charismatic preacher, a group from Beals had sailed for the Holy Land to establish a colony. Many of them had died when they were in dire need of water and their leader said manna would come from heaven and he refused to put into port. All of this was related to a temple at Shiloh, far from Beals Island in Durham, that still stood. These stories were not new; most had been told before. But at *Maine Times* we approached them with our own brand of naïve freshness. Our readers shared not only our curiosity but our sensibility about what was interesting.

A combination of satisfying curiosity and the search for excellence defined our dining reviews and food writing. No one had ever written dining reviews in Maine before and for good reason. Most restaurants were terrible.

There was one first-class restaurant in the state, Le Domaine, in Hancock, which located there because of the summer music school led by Pierre Monteux. Elsewhere in the state one could find an occasional good American meal—roast beef and fluffy biscuits or perhaps an exotic finnan haddie—but it was more typically the land of soggy vegetables. You could get a great steamed lobster and steamed clams at any number of wharves where you sat at picnic tables and pounded them with mallets; and the fried clams at several stands—my favorite still being the Clam Shack at the bridge in Kennebunkport, site of my youthful excesses—were excellent. But in the winter, the pickings were slim except for rituals like the roast beef Sunday lunch at the Jed Prouty tavern in Bucksport.

I didn't do all of the reviews but all of our reviewers were like me— they had eaten well somewhere else.[2]

2. I can still remember trout amandine straight from the Isère River, which I had in Grenoble at the age of seventeen, and my first salade Nicoise, on a terrace overlooking the Mediterranean in Nice in 1959. Or the paella we ate endlessly in Pamplona because it was cheap. Or the risotto Milanese my father's Italian friends introduced us to.

We praised the simple, the great strawberry pies at Helen's in Machias or the biscuits at Moody's Diner in Waldoboro, but we also had no mercy on the pretentious new restaurants opening in Portland, especially one that thought it was chic to charge you for tap water since, they claimed, that's what the French did.

When we praised a restaurant, it would experience an immediate surge in business. What our readers lacked in numbers, they compensated for in enthusiasm. The dining reviews were such a success that I stopped doing them after receiving numerous calls from readers who wanted to know where to take visitors for a meal. They would call me at home as well as at the office, and my entire identity was becoming that of a dining guide. Also, my wife was getting tired of eating bad meals, as most of them were, so I happily relinquished that particular duty.

Ideas for new features came from every direction. Early on, we published a centerspread called "Times One" that was an exchange of information, such as how to get rid of ants without using pesticides. Readers sent in questions and we either found the answers or sought answers from other readers. When that ran out of steam, I picked up on an idea from Paul Hazelton, a Bowdoin professor and friend from the Coffin campaign, and began the "Weather Report," which told readers what had happened the previous week across the state—when the ice went out of lakes, first and last frosts, the spotting of migrating birds. In a state as large as Maine, you could be skiing at Sugarloaf or sunning at Popham Beach on the same early May day. Barbara Feller-Roth was the perfect staff person to implement the project, letting the individual correspondents emerge so that readers were personally connected to the weekly natural happenings at Pocomoonshine Lake. When she left, I turned it over to an initially reluctant Jeff Clark, who grew to like it and excelled. Once, when I tried to discontinue it, we received such a flood of letters and phone calls that I was forced to reinstate it.

We also allowed idiosyncrasies. One summer, partly to amuse myself while sitting with the kids at the beach, I did Maine-related crossword puzzles. Only one person, Annette Elowitch, the wife of our first movie critic and a good friend, ever expressed interest in solving them.

We had instituted a feature called Back of the Book to allow both staff and reader essays on personal rather than issues-oriented subjects, and reporter Don Kreis used it to call for the replacement of Public Radio's most popular feature, "Morning Pro Musica" with Robert J. Lurtsema. He unleashed a cascade of opinion on both sides that washed through our pages for several months.

Along the way, there were parallel failures but for the staff, *Maine Times* was a constant adventure and new ideas, not all of which were implemented, were daily sustenance.

Even today people will tell me that they discovered *Maine Times* in the 1970s and were astounded that such a publication could exist in Maine. Many have volunteered that it played a role in their deciding to move to Maine.

I don't think it was just because of our engagement with public policy, although most of the people who have said this to me shared our social consciousness. I think it was because of what Bill Dunfey said about identifying a community of like-minded people.

Our graphics at *Maine Times* defined us. We had asked George deLyra, a talented graphic artist as well as a painter, to design the layout for *Maine Times* the summer before we started. Our readers were not put off by the tabloid format and they were impressed by the black and white photography. We used drawings by Maine artists and integrated my fledgling sense of design into the paper.[3] Only a couple of years after we started, the Maine Arts and Humanities Commission gave us an award not for our arts coverage but for the way we integrated design into the paper. When I used color to bring life to a Robert Indiana LOVE that we published in anticipation of an Indiana show, I received a letter from the artist saying he liked what we had done even though it was entirely different from any actual rendition of the LOVE series.

From the beginning, we had a staff photographer and we used photographs boldly, playing them large and demanding that they not be

3. I continually educated myself about graphics and found a Swiss publication called *Graphis* invaluable. The idea of a color mask on the cover came from a British publication illustrated in *Graphis*, and many of the ideas I played with in those first years were adaptations of what were being done internationally at the time.

mere illustrations but devices for communicating the story on a different level. Tom Jones's pictures of Pineland were more devastating than any prose could have been. Steve Nichols did memorable portraits, and when Phyllis Austin wrote an article on the five most influential men in Maine, Steve, at my suggestion, used Richard Avedon as a model and photographed the subjects with stark directness. Later, Chris Ayres was to create, in weekly collaboration with Edgar Allen Beem, an archive of sensitive portraits of Maine artists.

I enjoyed photography and the photographers knew it and trusted my judgment. I appreciated subtle strengths and differences, such as Chris Ayres's uncanny sense of composition when taking aerials or Don Hinckley's ability to highlight the contrasts of snow or Scott Perry's panoramic eye. Through experience, I learned what would reproduce best—sometimes, unfortunately, not the best photograph—and because I oversaw the pressrun every week, I would constantly call for ink adjustments to try to bring the photographs closer to what I had initially chosen.

We also had staff artists. Margaret Campbell's and Jon Luoma's distinctive drawings came to define the paper's look. Many others participated on a freelance basis, with top artists willing to do a cover for $100 because they enjoyed the challenge and the exposure. Robert Shetterly's enigmatic drawings teased the readers on the Op-Ed page.

Doug Coffin, whose cartoons made sly fun of our readers, kept me constantly on my toes about graphics and introduced me to the work of Edward R. Tufte and his criticism of visual clutter. I tried to implement some of his suggestions about the visual presentation of ideas.

Even though our lifestyle coverage was important in establishing the sense of shared interest, it was our serious coverage of issues that really mattered to us and that mattered equally to our readers. While the lifestyle material was just frosting on the cake, we tried to keep that frosting piquant. We never had to worry about running out of serious issues. There would always be more than we could handle with our limited staff and resources.

Twelve

A Judge Criticizes Advocacy Journalism and Criticizes Us

Our libel trial taught me a lesson about the very nature of journalism: reputation is everything. A state senator sued us because he thought we had unfairly damaged his reputation. His suit angered me because I thought his accusations were a slur on our reputation. The years it took for the case to run its course constituted for me an emotional roller coaster and in hindsight, I am sure the senator's emotions were similar to mine.

The trial raised core issues about the role of journalism in general and advocacy journalism in particular. It also made me think as I never had before about the natural overlap between public policy and the personal actions of a public figure.

We ended up with two adversaries in the case, the senator suing us and the judge publicly evaluating our journalism. And two issues were being tried: our integrity and our brand of journalism. The suit revolved around our stories about State Senator Richard N. Berry and how he operated five small public utilities he controlled. Was what we said about him accurate, or did he deserve the $5 million in damages for a litany of inaccuracies his attorney presented?

Just as important to us, if not to the general public, was what became a debate with the presiding judge over advocacy journalism and fairness. The judge, an intelligent and independent observer, commented as much about our brand of journalism in his decision as he did about the salient facts of the case.

While I have never had any illusions about being loved for what I do, I do have aspirations to be understood—in this I was like the senator we were accusing. He felt misunderstood and unfairly depicted. There is an almost eerie similarity between this case, which took place thirty years ago, and the contemporary corporate fraud cases, such as Enron and Tyco. The greatest difference is that vastly larger sums of money are involved in the current cases. But the defenses are the same—the executives were just doing what everyone else did.

We decided to write the stories not because of the particular senator involved. Indeed, we had previously praised him for his environmental stands and although he was a Republican and we were Democrats, he had every reason to believe we were friendly toward him. Although Senator Berry was to see himself personally as the target, our interest in him was coincidental. He became the focus of our coverage because we were interested in the performance of the Public Utilities Commission (PUC) and had been ever since our stories on the Weld Telephone Company, where children had died in a fire because of a failure of PUC oversight.

By 1975 the PUC had assumed a stronger regulatory role and by the time the hearings on the utilities controlled by Senator Berry began, a new, aggressive chair of the commission, Peter Bradford, had taken over.[1] Our reporter, Phyllis Austin, got wind this would be a landmark hearing, the first time the PUC had actually questioned the management of utilities under its regulatory control.

Berry, a powerful and effective state senator, was a major stockholder and chief operating officer of the five utilities.[2] As such, he paid himself salaries that were out of proportion to what the executives of larger utilities in the state earned. He made loans to himself from corporate funds. He charged personal expenses to the companies. He formed a new corporation, owned by the wives of his sons, and then made a sweetheart deal with it so that it effectively funneled money to his children's families. The added costs of operations that these practices incurred were passed on to the ratepayers, who had no place to go and no recourse unless the PUC acted on their behalf.

That the owner of a small, closely held business operated in such a way was not new. That such a company was subject to regulatory review and that the regulators were turning tough was new.

The story would play out at the PUC hearings for anyone who

1. Peter Bradford, like Andy Nixon and Neil Rolde, had been brought to Maine as part of Governor Ken Curtis's young brain trust. He was later to become a member of the federal Nuclear Regulatory Commission.
2. Family members were other major stockholders.

cared to attend, and we were the only ones who did attend on a regular basis. It was a ready-made story about the role of the PUC and how small utilities had previously operated for the benefit of the owners but at the expense of consumers.

The libel suit was filed in 1976 and was not decided for six years. The intervening years were trying. Being sued for so much money is a trauma. This was especially true for me as the person who continued to deal with it during all those years. Phyllis Austin, the other key person involved on our side, was not directly involved for years at a time. Our lawyers changed, even though our final lawyer, Angus King, was consumed by the case almost as much as I was when the trial became imminent.

Once the suit was filed, we learned that Senator Berry had been shopping for an attorney. His companies had previously been represented by Roger Putnam, one of Maine's leading establishment attorneys, and Severin Beliveau had recently represented him before the PUC. Beliveau was a leading Democrat and lobbyist who was himself to run for governor in the future and be crippled by the lobbying he had done for the tobacco industry. Although I personally liked him and admired him in many ways, I was to oppose his candidacy on the grounds that as governor you could not play both sides of the fence. He had supported the tobacco industry when he had been paid by them. I argued editorially that he either believed the companies' position that tobacco was not harmful, in which case he rejected overwhelming evidence to the contrary, or, if he didn't believe anything he said previously, all of his positions were unreliable. While Beliveau did not take on the libel case, his participation did have ramifications, since our initial attorney's firm was merging with his and they decided they would have to drop one of us as a client since our interests were in conflict. Much to our consternation—we liked our attorney, David Cohen, very much—we were the ones dropped. The firm's decision was not a commentary on the merits of the case but a calculation of which of the two parties might bring the firm more business in the future. Such a conflict was inevitable in a state as small as Maine where one's relationships are seldom isolated to a single encounter.[3]

3. When Beliveau ran for governor, John Cole worked for him.

Senator Berry did not have the disadvantage of many libel plaintiffs, that they must seek a lawyer on a contingency fee basis, and he hired Wayne P. Libhart, who struck us as an ideologue who disliked the press in general and the liberal press, of which we were the leading example in Maine, in particular. Although I did not make the connection at the time, John Cole's rough and unflattering depiction of him as the moderator at the Trenton hearings in 1969 could not have left him with good feelings about us. He tended to bluster and threaten, and his attempts at intimidation sometimes worked. Our new attorney, Angus King, who was only thirty-two in 1976 and for whom this was a case of major scope and importance, seemed susceptible at first but soon stood his ground. (Both Phyllis and I were taken aback as well and did not recover as quickly as did Angus.) Angus ended up doing an excellent job, exhibiting the analytical and logical skills that would later serve him well as governor.

The original charge against us was impressive in its length, the obvious point being that there were so many errors that they, prima facie, were indicative of reckless disregard of the truth, a prerequisite for "actual malice," which forms the basis of a libel case.

I had a good understanding of current libel law because most of it had been established during my career as a journalist and I was in the habit of reading U.S. Supreme Court decisions that were printed in the *New York Times*. After we were sued, I also went to the Bowdoin College library and read all the major libel decisions that formed the basis for current law. The key decision was *New York Times v. Sullivan* (1964), which contained the "public figure" and "actual malice" definitions. Libhart would argue that while Senator Berry was clearly a public figure as a member of the state legislature, his actions as president and chief stockholder of the small utilities were those of a private individual. I believed that the PUC hearings themselves left Berry a public figure because he was the focus of matters of public concern, but that was unnecessary. The presiding judge, Morton Brody, had made it clear from the beginning that he would probably consider Senator Berry a public figure and in his decision, he did not beat about the bush, quoting the Supreme Court that the question was whether the activities reported on concerned "anything which might touch on...[the] official's fitness for office." Judge Brody further said, "The business activities being investigated by the PUC did raise ethical and legal questions about Mr. Berry's conduct as president and chief stockholder of the various utilities." There is some irony in this definition offering us the added protection that comes with a public figure designation, because our primary interest was piqued not by his being a state senator but by the new aggressiveness of the PUC. We were focused on the issue rather than the individual.

Once a person has been declared a public figure, "actual malice" must be proved for a libel suit to carry. Actual malice is difficult for people unfamiliar with the case law to understand because they think it is a reflection of ill-will, when it refers only to the publication of information with the knowledge it is false or with reckless disregard for the truth, meaning that either the person publishing the statements knew them to be untrue or there were clear indications and warnings that the information was incorrect. As the ones doing the stories, based largely on public hearings before the PUC, we knew no such case could be made but proving actual malice, especially before a jury, is more a matter of circumstantial evidence. Animosity can be shown as an indicator of reckless disregard, and language can be shown as an indicator of animosity. Libel trials before a jury are tricky, since the commonly understood definition of malice is contradictory to the legal definition. A jury might decide the newspaper was being unfair and its stories were erroneous and want to reward the plaintiff, although this would not be in accordance with the law. Unintentional error and animosity are not enough to establish libel, if the person claiming libel is a public figure.

We were surprised when the Berry forces agreed to a trial before a judge without a jury. Even though we felt the judge lacked familiarity with current libel law—we thought he should have awarded us a summary judgment based on the facts as presented—we were confident that he would understand the subtleties of the law once he researched it more thoroughly, as he would during trial. Of course, he did, even though he sometimes indicated dismay over the difficulty for a public figure to prove libel.

The charges against us, as made in the original plaintiff's brief, were intimidating, partly because there were so many of them and partly because while they charged falsehood, they never said what they purported to be the truth. In other words, they were saying we had erred but not telling us specifically how we had erred.

Typical of this tactic, and at the top of their list of charges was the truth or falsity of a headline that said, "Berry Fined for Rangeley Loans." Later, the judge also indicated he thought the headline was inaccurate.

During depositions, Senator Berry's attorney, Libhart, questioned me at length about this headline and I kept asking what was inaccurate about it. I was genuinely baffled but his technique was not to clarify. It was to make me as uncomfortable as possible and he was succeeding.

The first paragraph of the story read: "A Superior Court judge has slapped a $2,000 civil penalty against Rangeley Power Company for illegally allowing its president, Senator Richard Berry, to borrow money from it."

I finally understood that they were claiming the headline to be false because Rangeley Power and not Berry personally had been fined. In writing the headline, I had been conflating Berry with the company since he was the individual who made the decisions that resulted in the fine. This disagreement over definitions proved to be at the heart of the case. They were not claiming that the totality of facts as we presented them was erroneous but that our characterization of those facts was wrong.

Only later, when Angus went over every individual allegation of falsehood and documented the source of our statements, were we able to outline this pattern of claims. This briefing book made the case for the accuracy of the stories and explained the few inaccuracies that did appear. It was the ultimate fact-checking report and I felt we came out very well, better than I might have expected considering the potential pitfalls of writing under deadline on a subject with technical aspects that were often new to us. However, at the start of the depositions, we were somewhat intimidated, as our adversaries had intended.

The first three years after the case was filed went by without much activity, but after the first depositions in 1979, which ranged over six months, Angus went into a minor panic because Phyllis Austin, like myself, had balked at Libhart's tactics. She was incredulous that she was being hauled into court for doing what she considered her job, and she initially reacted with animosity and a wariness that came across as evasiveness.

Phyllis's reaction at the deposition—it was to improve at the trial, where she did fine—reinforced my attitude about letting reporters respond to criticism of their stories. Despite their toughness about others, most reporters are thin-skinned when their own accuracy is challenged and quickly lose their ability to practice objective self-analysis. Put more simply, when they think their integrity is on the line, they get their backs up.

After this experience, I issued orders at the paper that whenever a person called with a complaint about a story, the call was to be referred to me as editor. I would then evaluate the complaint and check any factual allegations with the reporter. Since I was likely to be less defensive and therefore more sympathetic in tone to the complainant, it was easier for me to resolve the problem. Sometimes, it was just a matter of listening.[4]

The grievance is seldom about the recounting of the facts themselves. It can be a headline, an illustration, a characterization, made either by the reporter or by someone else quoted in the story. This is, after all, what set the senator off.

A complainant is calling because he feels personally hurt, and some newspaper stories do hurt people emotionally. Even without the threat of a libel trial, editors should be sensitized to their ability to inflict collateral pain and make sure the story truly contributes to the public good. There is no excuse for the gratuitous infliction of personal pain, although all newspapers are guilty of committing that sin at one time or another just because the information is so titillating, not because it is important to the public weal. Despite the rhetoric of journalism that we just print what is there, judgments about what to print are being made all the time and for a variety of reasons. (In writing this memoir, I have felt a constant tension between the need for personal revelations to illustrate the points I am trying to make and the privacy of my friends and colleagues over the years.)

---

4. The worst response and the one most likely to get you into further trouble is to be curt and say, "Write a letter to the editor." If the complainant merely wanted to write a letter to the editor, he would have done so without calling.

Angus had a better reason than Phyllis's edginess to panic. Libhart had told Angus he could produce a witness who would say Phyllis had said she wanted to "get" Berry. Phyllis said she had never made such a statement to anyone. For complex personal reasons, the witness never appeared.

Animosity, even as claimed in this circumstance, is not evidence of "actual malice." On the other hand, I had listened to her—and other reporters—enough to know how their conversations can take on an adversarial tone when they think they have "caught" a public official acting in an unethical manner. Good reporters are motivated by their sense of ethical outrage. They see themselves as the keepers of moral standards in the public sector. So Phyllis could have easily expressed the opinion that Senator Berry was acting improperly and that the PUC for the first time was calling him, and others like him, to task. Other reporters had made such statements to me in private and they could be rash in their choice of words. I subsequently lectured all our reporters never to say anything negative, even to me, about those they were covering. Phyllis had never made any such statements about Senator Berry to me. I had worked with her closely and I knew that even if she felt someone had been a "bad guy," she would never let these feelings taint the rigor of her reporting. She would never write something she knew to be untrue. However, my total confidence in her integrity did not change the fact that such a witness could create a negative impression in jurors' minds.

I have always argued that it is best to know the worst case scenario in any situation before making a decision, and Angus was certainly laying out the worst case scenario. I didn't like it. I wanted bucking up from my attorney. Instead, I found I was bucking him up. He was clearly shaken but fortunately he was shaken only temporarily.

The most worrisome problem to me was that our own attorney found the very number of alleged errors persuasive, when I had reviewed enough of them to find them unpersuasive as examples of error. (Of course, Angus was not really saying he found them persuasive but that a jury might find them persuasive, a distinction that I was in no mood to make at the time.) But Angus's skepticism paid off. I would have been much more cavalier in my dismissal of the claims than he was and in reviewing my deposition, I find my attitude of dismissal all too typical of myself. One of the key claims I have mentioned and that Justice Brody included in his written opinion as a strike against us was equating Senator Berry with Rangeley Power when the court levied a fine against the company. Thus the headline: "Berry Fined...." I summarily dismissed the charge by saying that I equated Senator Berry with his utilities because he totally controlled them. All the rest was mere technicality and therefore unimportant as far as I was concerned. The judge considered such a technicality important.

Angus researched every claim of error made by the plaintiffs and prepared a document that later became a forty-six-page appendix to our brief. His research, not our mere recollections, formed the basis of our testimony. He not only reread the stories but where necessary went back to the original PUC record and did further research, for instance, on what had appeared elsewhere in the press. We had underestimated the amount of coverage in the dailies, which did report the conclusions of the PUC and the courts even if they did not cover the process as we did. This parallel coverage was to work to our benefit in several ways, first because it was evidence that even if *Maine Times* had been absent, Senator Berry's reputation still would have been challenged by the PUC hearings, and second, because the daily press used some of the same language for which we were sued and they were not being sued.

Angus's entry on the "Berry fined" allegation illustrates not only where our defense lay but also the wisdom of his more dispassionate approach. He was thorough and convincing, much more convincing than I had been or would be with my own underlying sense of outrage. I could not conceal my emotion and, like Phyllis, I felt we were being hauled into court for doing our job in alerting the public to a regulated company's exploiting flaws in the system—poor oversight by the PUC— at the expense of consumers. Even though I like to think that, as editor, I was much more dispassionate and willing to see our own shortcomings than reporters were, I shared our reporters' attitude that we were the crusaders in the public interest. I didn't just share the attitude, I reinforced it.

The full text of Angus's approach to the fifty-first allegation in the plaintiff's complaint is indicative of his approach.

Article Date: September 12, 1975

Quote: "Berry Fined for Rangeley Loans" [headline]

Source: The story for which this headline was written.

Comments: The very first sentence of the article puts the headline in context and makes it clear that a civil penalty was imposed against Rangeley Power for the loans made to Senator Berry. Since Senator Berry was the principal owner, chief executive officer, and was, by his own admission, in charge of all activities of the company, and especially because these loans directly involved his activities both in the making and the receipts of the monies, this headline is essentially accurate. Any inaccuracy or misunderstanding created by the headline would be rectified by the first sentence of the story and the remaining information of the story which detailed the transaction.

Much was made at trial of the labeling of the judgment of the court as a "consent judgment." Other than the title of the document, however, this was not a consent judgment as that term is usually understood. In a normal consent judgment or consent agreement, the defendant admits no wrongdoing whatsoever, but simply pays an amount, or, as is more usually the case, promises not to do a certain action in the future, and the complaint is dismissed. In this case, the defendant, as is stated in the judgment itself, did not deny the violation of the statute, but only denied that the violation was willful and intentional. The complaint was not dismissed; a finding of violation was made, and the ultimate civil penalty was levied by order of the court. It is unclear from the testimony whether either Phyllis Austin or Peter Cox were familiar with or fully understood the legal implications of the denomination of the judgment as a "consent judgment." Again, the testimony of both Phyllis Austin and Peter Cox indicated unequivocally that any misunderstanding or misstatement in connection with this matter was unintentional.

Much was made at the trial of the use of the word "fine." Extensive argument would seem unnecessary that to the common mind (and according to the dictionary) this term simply means a sum of money paid for some violation of law, exactly what happened in this case. It is relevant that in every other newspaper account of this event (*Portland Press Herald* 9/6/75; *Bangor Daily News* 12/9/75, 2/19/76) the penalty is referred to as a "fine."

While Angus in his brief wiped away most of the charges of inaccuracy, there were some technical errors in the stories. One company, Winter Harbor, was repeatedly referred to as owned by Senator Berry although he had transferred ownership to his wife, a fact that would not show up in its annual report—the source for our stories—until after the stories had been published. We also thought a woman named Winnifred Berry was an ex-wife. Although Berry had been married before, she was not an ex-wife. To this day, I don't know who she was, but the error was typical in that it was minor, non-defamatory, and no one on the Berry side ever attempted to correct it.

By our calculation there were no significant, substantive errors of fact in the stories. Again and again, the plaintiffs took a quote out of context and tried to show that it mixed Senator Berry up with one of his utilities. We argued throughout that because Senator Berry so thoroughly controlled his utilities, a decision by him was a corporate decision and consequently a reprimand of that decision was a reprimand of him. At the same time, it was always clear that we were talking about his companies. The plaintiffs would take a line and isolate it. For instance, "[Berry] has filed for bankruptcy in federal court, which has tied up the utility's assets." They argued that it was the company that filed for bankruptcy and that it was Chapter 11 and not straight bankruptcy. Subsequent sentences in the story made both clear.

The best argument that Senator Berry could make, to my mind, was that the PUC had changed the rules and that it was examining his utilities with a scrutiny it had not used before. Berry argued throughout that he was following standard business practices and he may well have been—for an unregulated business. Many businessmen write off their personal expenses to the company and no one is the loser, except perhaps the Internal Revenue Service. Many small businessmen rent themselves space and equipment and take as much money out as possible in salary rather than dividends so they will not be taxed twice on it.[5] It is not uncommon in a company where the owner is also the boss for him to take advances on salary—what Berry claimed the Rangeley loans were—but let an employee do the same and it is called embezzlement.

5. I rented the building I owned to *Maine Times* albeit at fair market value.

Thirty years later, the issue of corporate executives using their companies as personal resources has become a major national issue. One of the most notorious was L. Dennis Kozlowski, former chairman and CEO of Tyco International, about whom the *New York Times* wrote: "The accusations against Mr. Kozlowski...are relatively straightforward: he and a codefendant, Tyco's former chief financial officer, are accused of reaching into the corporate cookie jar to pay for everything from Mr. Kozlowski's apartment on Park Avenue and homes in Boca Raton, FL, to jewelry from Harry Winston and Tiffany."[6] Kozlowski was running a private company, so the only ones he was taking the money from were his stockholders, but otherwise his case and the Berry case were similar, except that Berry was dealing in peanuts and Kozlowski was taking real money, in the millions.

My conviction in our own purity—some might call it arrogance— would backfire. My efforts to "enlighten" the public and subsequently the judge on the issue of objectivity and bias would be used against us. In an editorial, I had tried to deal with such terms as bias—save us from Yale English majors who are taught that the meanings of words often change with their context—and the judge took us to task. This was the other half of the trial where we were under fire.

In his decision, Justice Brody wrote in part: "The Court's examination of the articles and editorials in question...leads it to conclude that the instances of clear factual falsity are relatively rare. While not finding many significant falsehoods in the articles, however, the Court does note that the facts are often presented in less than an objective light. Without question, the *Maine Times* followed the involvement of Mr. Berry with the PUC [Public Utilities Commission] with a bias, one which the paper admits and characterized as 'practicing advocacy journalism' in an editorial aptly entitled 'The go-getum image,' January 30, 1976."

The judge then quoted from the editorial, written by me:

"When we decided to start covering the story [of Richard Berry and his public utilities] a year ago, we did so with a bias. We suspected the facts would show that the ratepayers were being exploited. We think further investigation proved this to be true and we think we accu-

6. *New York Times*, 29 September 2003.

rately documented the case. Rather than call that a bias, we would like to call it a conclusion, based on concrete evidence.... But we can say to our readers that we admit there is no such thing as being totally objective. While the myth of objective journalism is more detrimental than beneficial to solving society's problems, journalism can be both fair and accurate. That's what we try to do."

Justice Brody continued his critique: "The Court is satisfied that the bias or slant of *Maine Times* in this series of articles and editorials did, in some respects, treat the plaintiff unfairly. The Court will cite a few egregious examples, which certainly could not be characterized as 'fair and accurate' or 'objective journalism.'"

Having been invited by what I had written, and taking an opportunity to show his sympathy for Senator Berry, whom he was going to rule against, Judge Brody went on to cite examples not of inaccuracy but of lack of fairness. All of the examples were items the plaintiffs had claimed were inaccurate and therefore indicative of libel.

The judge started with a headline "Senator Berry does well with his mini utilities empire" on a story detailing how several small utilities owned by Berry and his family were used to make loans to him and benefit family members, including the wives of his sons. Although Senator Berry was an important member of the legislature and had a serious time commitment there, he paid himself more, when salaries from all the utilities were added together, than the president of Central Maine Power, the largest utility in the state with at least twenty times as many customers. The story documented how, in addition to this salary, he made himself loans, drew consulting fees, and set up the companies and satellites to benefit his children and their spouses.

Related to the same story, the judge cited as unfair a line in an editorial headlined "Senator Berry has learned how to bleed the system" in which I contended, based on PUC testimony and conclusions of the commissioners, that Senator Berry had benefited himself and his family through operation of the utilities to the detriment of the consumers. These practices led not only to higher rates for utility users but were the proximate cause of some of the financially weakened utilities having to be sold at bargain prices.

The offensive words, both to Senator Berry and to the judge, were "fleecing" consumers and "bleeding" the system. Both were contained in an editorial, and by law and by good journalistic practice, the facts on which an editorial opinion are based must be accurate. The judge was not contesting the underlying facts but only the boundaries of fair comment, even on the editorial page.

I took the judge's rebuke to be severe, and it made me question what other thoughtful readers must think about what I wrote. Had I gone too far?

Here is what the editorial said:

"If Senator Richard N. Berry owned five small businesses and made the income he does for working part time, he would be considered one of the world's greatest businessmen.

"But the fact that his businesses are public utilities puts his high income in a different light.

"For his role as president of the five utilities, Senator Berry pays himself more than the president of Central Maine Power (CMP) receives. (His annual total, exclusive of stock, is at least $50,651; CMP's president gets $43,104.) Of course, CMP's stockholders would probably complain if their president's salary were as relatively high. However, Richard Berry is not only president but dominant stockholder in all of his utilities, so there's no one to complain.

"Senator Berry bought the Woodland utilities for $7,500 and pays himself more than $17,000 a year for his limited services to those utilities. That's a pretty good deal when you double your investment in salary every year.

"And Senator Berry takes care of his family. They're the ones who lease Rangeley Power Company $62,000 worth of equipment for $36,000 a year. And Rangeley pays insurance, taxes, and maintenance. Therefore, the second year the family business had a clear profit of $10,000 and each year thereafter the equipment lasts they have a clear profit of $36,000.

"In private business, this would all be fine if the business could get away with such practices and remain solvent. But the competitive factor would make that possibility slim. Some other company president would take a little less salary and charge the consumer a little less and take away business.

"But utilities are, of course, monopolies. It is the role of the Public

Utilities Commission (PUC) to exercise on behalf of the consumer controls which normally are exercised by the competitive factor.

"In the past, this has not been the case. The PUC tended to accept the utility's cost figures and merely added a fair profit figure. But, as the hearings on Rangeley Power and other Berry utilities indicate, the PUC is no longer going to play such a docile role in the fleecing of the Maine consumer. It's pretty clear that one of the reasons the Rangeley consumer pays 60 percent more than the CMP customer and that Rangeley is on the brink of insolvency is because Senator Berry has learned how to bleed the system.

"It is up to the PUC to end the abuse."

The facts underlying the editorial had faced scrutiny at trial, with Senator Berry's attorney claiming some of them were inaccurate or distorted. The comparative salary figures for the Berry utilities and CMP were uncontested. At trial Senator Berry claimed his investment in Woodland was larger but the additional investment had not been his personally; that investment had been funded with bonds for which the corporation, Woodland, was responsible. They argued that to call the money from the equipment lease profit was false since it did not account for depreciation. In my description, I accurately noted that the company leasing the equipment paid back its full cost in two years and the leasee paid all other costs, such as insurance and repairs. Only after that did I compute "profit." There was a good deal of argument over bookkeeping practices, such as depreciation and length of amortization regarding the equipment lease, but the cost of the equipment and the amount of the lease were uncontested. If the company had chosen to amortize it over two years, the cash amount going to the daughters-in-law would have been as stated. I should have been more sophisticated in my description and not used the term "profit"; the wording reflected my own preoccupation with cash flow.

Senator Berry's attorney contested the average bills. We had based the comparisons on the cost of 500 kilowatt hours for abutting users in the CMP and Rangeley areas, which represented an almost 70 percent difference. Berry's attorney wanted to compare average annual bills instead. This would have looked better for their case since many of the Rangeley users were seasonal and thus the comparison would have been for part-time usage by Rangeley customers and year-round usage by CMP customers.

At trial, I found the comparative bills argument particularly galling since it was such a clear indication how the other side was juggling figures in an attempt to mislead the public, something it was our job to counter. Yet in countering it, we were being attacked as unfair.

The judge's criticism focused not only on editorials but on headlines. He would have had no sympathy with a newspaper's need to draw a reader into the story. He would undoubtedly see that as an indication of why headlines are by definition slanted, especially the magazine-type headlines we used.

So he cited as another example of unfairness the cover headline: "How some Maine people made political contributions, bet on horses, rented an apartment, etc., without ever knowing it." The story was about how these expenses were passed on to the consumers rather than being picked up by the owners and stockholders. The cover showed a mock bill, labeled "hypothetical electric bill" with the notation it was pro-rated on the basis of 2,500 ratepayers. Although the total of contested expenditures was more than $86,000, the amounts per customer were very low, the largest—liquor expense in Augusta—being only 2 cents per customer. The small size of these figures was therefore on the cover as well. The fact that the amount was so small was part of a later Maine Supreme Court decision overturning a PUC order, a fact the judge used against us. *Maine Times* had made clearer than the hearings how small the amounts were, pennies per customer. Our point was not the amounts but the principle. In retrospect, I can see how there would have been a good argument for not playing the story as prominently as we did, but that would have been purely a matter of editorial judgment. Nor do I think the story's location would have mitigated the judge's criticism.

On the other hand, there were more egregious actions described in the story, including a blatant violation of federal law where, I would argue, the amount involved was irrelevant. The story contained an illustration of a $100 contribution to a political fundraiser in Augusta, whose solicitation bore the warning: "Because of federal law, corporation checks cannot be accepted." Berry paid with his own personal check, which was marked "reem" for reimburse, and a corporate check, also illustrated, was drawn to reimburse him for the amount of his contribution. There could have been no more willful disregard for the law. Did the fact the amount was so small change that conclusion?

Although civil penalties were assessed against one of the companies and even Lincoln Smith, the PUC commissioner who sided most with Senator Berry, called some of his practices in running the utilities "deplorable," Justice Brody had a much higher opinion of Senator Berry and cited the Supreme Court case that threw out some of the PUC sanctions on the grounds that the PUC had overstepped its authority. The Maine Supreme Court had written: "The Commission exceeded its authority and acted without due process in instigating the investigation and hearings." The court elaborated that Berry had been required to explain expenses dating back five years, "a time the Commission's counsel admitted had been arbitrarily selected." It also found that in one instance Berry had been denied the opportunity to fully present his case when the Commission decided it had "heard enough" and closed the meeting at 5:30 that afternoon. It also found "evidence" of an ex parte communication between one commissioner and a staff attorney that was "inconsistent with their respective roles of judge and advocate" and it criticized the Commission for issuing press releases that "created unnecessary controversy and [were] at best indiscreet."

The dissent by Commissioner Smith, which was quoted in *Maine Times*, predicted the later Supreme Court decision and may have been part of the basis for it. He said that because the probe went back five years, it was "arbitrary and unreasonable," exactly the key element in the court's ruling. Smith also said he believed the case was "prosecuted with crusading zeal and unfortunately became a cause célèbre. The record betrays undue bias and irregularities in spots. The case must be decided, however, by analysis of the record, regardless of slanted coverage from segments of the communications media." We were undoubtedly the slanted media in question.

Smith said many of Berry's actions "were deplorable and reprehensible, transgressing my professional ethics but not always [transgressing] generally accepted business practices." This may have been the basis of Justice Brody's later statement about accepted business practices in his ruling on the libel case.

Commissioner Smith also focused blame on the PUC itself when he said the senator did not violate commission regulations because "as yet we have no codes. Some political expenses clearly were improper. In areas of a twilight zone, the commission's attention for misconduct more than three years ago appears patently unreasonable. To me, part of the decree attempted to superimpose a phantom code of ethics now in embryonic stages within the agency."

"The Plaintiff," Justice Brody wrote in his opinion in *Maine Times*'s favor, "obviously is a man who has made significant contributions to his business, his community, and his state. His management of the utilities was, for the most part, ultimately vindicated as a legally and ethically sound business practice. The Defendants could have been more thorough in their research [the stories were based primarily on the quasi judicial PUC hearings] and reporting, and more balanced in their treatment of the Plaintiff and thereby minimized the degree of condemnation undeservedly suffered by the Plaintiff and his family. On the other hand, fairness is not the standard by which a libel allegation is judged."

Judge Brody's conclusions were clearly his own although he implied they were based on the Maine Supreme Court decision which did not exonerate Berry's practices but instead was critical of PUC procedures.

The only substantive issues the Supreme Court addressed were the payment of personal expenses by Rangeley Power and the establishment of Berry's salary as president.

Concerning the expenses, it found those that should not be allowed so small—only $600 in a total of $86,000—as to be negligible in determining proper management. Similarly, it said, "The Commission's intrusion into areas largely reserved for independent business judgment, such as the establishment of salaries and the comparative economy of motel versus apartment accommodations, based solely on notions of what is in a commissioner's opinion, 'just and reasonable' cannot be approved." The Supreme Court was saying that the fact the combined Berry salaries were higher than the salary of the president of CMP was irrelevant. This is the closest the Supreme Court came to "approving" Berry's business practices.

Underlying both Justice Brody's criticism of *Maine Times* and the Maine Supreme Court's criticism of the PUC was an unease with the changes taking place in what was evolving as a much more aggressive regulatory climate. The PUC, under Peter Bradford's leadership, had gone back several years because that's where the evidence lay that they thought represented the mismanagement of publicly regulated utilities. They were indeed setting new rules for acceptable behavior because no rules had been set in the past. It was all most ungentlemanly.

Senator Berry said he was pleased with the decision, even though it went in favor of *Maine Times*. Obviously, he felt that Justice Brody's written opinion had repaired his reputation, and that's what this and, I think, most libel cases are all about—not the facts, but characterizations, and therefore reputations. That's why Senator Berry did not sue other newspapers which carried some of the same stories and even some of the same alleged "errors." It was the very consistency and longevity of the coverage that angered him—as did the PUC, whom he obviously thought to be the culprits but whom he could not sue. And I am sure he thought *Maine Times* was acting as the agent for the PUC and especially for Peter Bradford, its chairman.

Judge Brody gave Berry the satisfaction of saying his management of the companies was ultimately vindicated as legally and ethically sound. With the exception of the corporate political contribution, he may have done nothing illegal at the time.

We never claimed that Senator Berry was a bad senator because of his utilities. In fact, he was a good senator. Nor was there evidence that he tried to use his political influence to benefit his companies. That was not the point. The point was that small utilities had gone largely unregulated due to the laxity of the PUC. A new era had begun and the ratepayers would benefit. If covering such stories is not the role of the press, I don't know what is.

Subsequently, Angus King wrote an Op-Ed piece for us in which he argued that the characterizations in our editorials, so much under attack at the trial, were necessary for the public to fully understand what was happening. Without clearly stated opinions, particularly on matters such as business ethics, there can be no meaningful debate and consequently no improvement of policy.

I think Senator Berry was so personally affronted that he never focused on what the PUC investigation was all about. That Peter

Bradford, chairman of the PUC, or *Maine Times* might be motivated by genuine concerns about fairness in utility regulation rather than some kind of ill will toward him seems not to have been considered.[7]

Despite the fact that subsequent PUCs followed a similar course and by the time the case came to trial, specific legislation was passed to make some of his past practices against the law, Berry indicated at trial and in his brief that he still thought he was caught in a web of personal animosity. And his only way to strike back at this personalized, unfair treatment was to sue us.

I can understand and even empathize with Senator Berry's feelings of being the subject of personal vilification. I have never met a public official who thought criticism of him was fair. Everyone self-justifies. What I have just written about the libel trial can be seen as nothing more than my own extended self-justification.

But after the trial I was even more careful about how we characterized the actions of anyone we were writing about, and I was careful to separate their actions related to public issues from the purely personal. Fortunately for me, I was pretty much out of journalism by the time even the most sober and self-critical of newspapers felt it necessary to publish irrelevant personal scandal just because everyone else was doing so. In the Internet age, there is no longer any filter or any barrier to irresponsible personal allegations. The libel laws will not work against an individual who has nothing to lose by being sued even though that person can send false and even intentionally malicious accusations to hundreds of others with the push of a button. I do not have an easy answer but this is an example of where the law must adapt to technological change. The framers of the Constitution could not have been expected to foresee such developments.

The victim of unfair press coverage does need recourse. The U.S. Supreme Court has erected a strong wall of protection around the press where a public figure and public policy are concerned because the public figure has a platform from which to correct what he considers erroneous, something Senator Berry inexplicably refused to do in our case. He would not even respond when approached directly by us

7. Peter Bradford and I did have personal contact, occasionally playing tennis together. However, we never discussed the substance of the Berry hearings while they were taking place.

and asked to do so. Despite our offering the opportunity, he never brought our attention to our "inaccuracies" until he sued us.

There is no doubt the libel trial had a chilling effect on me. That effect was good where it made me more careful about fact-checking inflammatory accusations and personal characterizations. It was bad where it made me more hesitant to take on important public issues.

It took me years to get over Justice Brody's criticism of advocacy journalism.[8] I took it to heart and have thought about it again and again. In the final analysis, I have decided that the judge was wrong, that we cannot thrash out all important policy issues at the level of politeness he seemed to be advocating. We must make value judgments in this life and that's what we were doing in the Berry case and that in the end was why we spent all those years fighting for what we believed in.

8. Angus King, our former attorney, likes to tell the story that after I first read Judge Brody's decision, I said I wanted to appeal, and he replied, "You can't appeal. You won."

Thirteen

The Partnership Plays Out

Unseen by our readers, by 1971 when we were less than three years old, a major change was playing itself out at the paper. As co-founders, John Cole held the title of editor and I publisher, and the public perceived those roles in traditional terms. *Maine Times* was seen as the editor's paper.

When we had worked together at the merged *Times-Record*, there was more than enough for both of us to do on the new daily. In those days, an editor of a small paper took on a much heavier workload than one does today and we would never have thought of non-writing editors or a separate editorial page editor. Both John and I wrote news stories; both of us had columns; both wrote editorials, John doing the lion's share but with me writing about Bath to maintain its interests on the editorial page. John came up with ideas for coverage and participated in discussions of story placement. I did the daily layout, and shared the line editing with Buffer Fine. It was a wholly satisfying working relationship, without friction.

When the time came to give up on the *Times-Record* and start *Maine Times*, I needed John. If nothing else, I would not have had the courage to go it alone, and John's disregard for the financial realities was probably a benefit. We didn't know enough to understand how poor our chances for success were.

John was the face of *Maine Times*. He was forty-seven when we began the paper, and I had just turned thirty-two. He did most of the public speaking. His resonant voice and irreverent and colorful comments were enormously entertaining, and they usually served our shared ideals. I, too, was an admirer, and I was used to him attracting attention; even as he gave the distinct impression that he alone "owned" *Maine Times*, he was also garnering positive publicity for us.[1]

---

1. His original share had been 49 percent; when we needed more money and he opted out of helping raise it, his share dropped to about 12 percent.

While John was a great conceptual editor, he was not a line editor. He liked thinking up the ideas for our next area of coverage and he was a brilliant writer, able to mobilize our readers emotionally and turn them into a political force, as he had with the snowmobiles in Baxter Park. His lack of interest in other aspects of editing created tension.

The crucial incident causing the change in editorship occurred in the most mundane manner. I was reading a story on the page—this was the final proofreading before going to press—and the writing began to disintegrate halfway through, becoming redundant and unfocused and seriously in need of editing. I took the page to John and told him my opinion and he replied, nonchalantly, "Oh, I agree with you, but I just got fed up with editing it and put it through as is."

I shouldn't have been surprised. When we worked together at the *Times-Record*, he had left the line editing to me or to Buffer, who had come with us to *Maine Times* but had died of lung cancer. With Buffer gone, John had been left with a job he didn't like and his response was not to do it.

My answer was simple. "If you aren't going to edit the stories, I will." This was fine with John, since he saw himself as getting rid of an unpleasant task.

John kept the title of editor but in fact became editor of the editorial page. He also wrote more—we all wrote when we had the time. But John's writing was exceptional and freeing John from many editorial duties benefitted the paper because it allowed him to cover the legislature as it had never been covered before. John did not limit himself to core issues; he would describe a legislator seeming to fall asleep at a committee hearing only to rouse himself to compare coyotes to Indians, as in the only good one being a dead one.

When Jim Longley became the Independent governor in 1974, John took him on as no other journalist dared and exposed his more bizarre actions. The Cole–Longley battle came close to open warfare, and our circulation reached its historic high.

In my first months as defacto editor, I tried to establish a tradition of collegiality with the writers, instituting Monday morning meetings at which we discussed story ideas and critiqued the previous week's edition. Writers were encouraged to propose their own assignments and to make suggestions for others. All proposals were open to question. I had so many things I wanted done that reporters knew they must be prepared to pit the importance of their ideas against mine. Usually there was consensus, since most of my assignments derived from what the reporters had already been doing or from ideas they brought to the meetings in the first place.

John thought these meetings were a terrible idea and a waste of time and after participating once, declared he would not return. Alone among those reporting, he determined his own story ideas, which he shared with me for logistical reasons, and I never tried to set his priorities. Of course I edited his pieces, but that was a pretty routine matter. I don't recall our ever having a major disagreement about his coverage.

Despite this change in how *Maine Times* was edited, I didn't change my own title until later, when I added managing editor to publisher on the masthead. Still, right up until the time he left *Maine Times* in 1978, John was known to the public as the editor of *Maine Times*. The title gave him the position he wanted and the setup gave me editorial control.

We didn't pay ourselves much at *Maine Times*, but as long as we were both there, I paid us both the same. Then in the mid-seventies, John asked to sell his stock. I told him that there was no real market for it since I was the only potential buyer and suggested that it was the one good investment he had made and he should hold onto it. Despite my advice, he took my offer of $20,000 for the $10,000 he had invested less than ten years before, and, I am sure, he remained convinced I had taken advantage of him. Had he held on until I sold the paper in 1985, another ten years, his share would have been worth about $70,000.

Our relationship had followed a classic pattern for partners. When I was in college, I had worked summers for him and had been smitten. John was a man of incredible charm. As long as you were on the same side, he was great fun to be around. He had great, grand ideas but also an unnerving disregard for how they would be executed or financed. Over the years, the workload and responsibility became uneven and, as I assumed more of both, the partnership became unbalanced.

It would be disingenuous of me to pretend I was not sometimes irritated by John's self-promotion or his making promises for me to keep. But these are the normal pitfalls of partnership and the pursuit of a common goal rendered them minor. Truly undermining our relationship was John's gradual relinquishing of responsibility for the future of *Maine Times*—both editorially and financially. When John's role as my day-by-day collaborator disappeared, our close bond of more than a decade began to unravel.

The dissolution of our partnership was painful. John and and his wife, Jean, had been very kind to Eunice and me. John needed more income than I could justify pulling from *Maine Times*, and John's free spirit could not relate to the pressure I felt to keep *Maine Times* financially afloat.

Once we were no longer working together, John and I naturally drifted apart. John wrote more as a freelancer, regularly appearing in national magazines, from *Audubon* to *Life*. Essentially, we established an arm's length working relationship, and our daily relations remained cordial. He later kept an office in our building in exchange for writing his column.

After John left *Maine Times* in 1978 to run *WorldPaper*, which was to be an international version of *Maine Times*, there were two incidents that temporarily severed our relationship.

John had become close to Pritham Singh, previously named Paul LaBombard, whom John had taken under his wing as a teenager. Pritham had worked in our circulation department when he was still in high school. Later Pritham made a lot of money in real estate and would eventually redevelop the old Truman winter White House in Key West.

In the early '80s, John, with Pritham, decided to start a new publication to compete directly with *Maine Times*. To staff the new paper, John and Pritham turned to *Maine Times*. Our longtime photographer, Steve Nichols, came to me apologetically and said John had offered him so much more money he could not refuse. I sympathized with Steve and did not hold it against him.

But I was bothered when John hired Ellen Grant to take on the role of publisher. I had hired Ellen soon after college and had tried to train her to take over my business duties. At the time John hired Ellen, we had just finished a major survey of our readers and Ellen was privy to important proprietary information. No one knew more about the financial workings—and weaknesses—of *Maine Times* than Ellen or I. I attributed Ellen's accepting the offer to inexperience and she was later to tell me it was one of the major mistakes she had made in her life. I was not so forgiving of John and Pritham, who would be benefitting from her insider knowledge of *Maine Times*. Their publication never got off the ground.

The second incident occurred in 1985, when I made it clear I was thinking about selling the paper. A recent graduate of Bowdoin showed up on the scene. We spent the day together and he presented himself as having a father who was willing to underwrite the purchase. He turned out to be an unacceptable potential buyer. Since he had gone to Bowdoin when John was teaching a journalism course there, I asked John if he knew the young man, and he said no.

A couple of years later, when *Maine Times* staff reporter Edgar Allen Beem was interviewing John about something else, John said the young Bowdoin graduate had been a front for him and Pritham, who wanted to buy back *Maine Times* for John. When Edgar said I would be upset to learn that, John said: "Why? If Peter had known it was Pritham and me behind the inquiry, he would have refused it out of hand."

In later years, John and I became cordial again and I didn't blink an eye when in the 1990s someone would mention *Maine Times* and refer to it as "John Cole's paper." I did sometimes laugh to myself when people said over the years that the paper was not as good as it had been when John Cole edited it. I wanted to ask, "Oh, when was that?"

When I learned in December 2003 that John had cancer, I called him and he was as charming as ever in his acceptance of the inevitable. I told him I also had terminal cancer—I was not expected to last the year—and he was reassuring in his own gruff way, not offering sympathy but saying we both had had good and productive lives. John died the next month.

Fourteen

Worn Out, Hiring Help, and Thinking of Retiring

By the early 1980s I was feeling worn out from being both editor and publisher. I was now in my forties and simply didn't have the energy I used to. Plus, the workload had increased as the paper became more successful, demanding more stories each week and more attention to finances. We were finally in a financial position to hire someone to help me, although not at a high salary. The portion of my job I wanted to spin off was publishing, so I started looking for a general manager.

Because I was offering only entry level pay, I was recruiting people who needed to be trained. That didn't bother me because I wanted them to be trained for *Maine Times* and for no other publication. I would not admit it but I wanted to clone myself fifteen years younger. I also hoped I could find someone who would be motivated not by the money but by the cause.

My initial efforts were disastrous. Even though I was spinning off part of my job, I was not relinquishing control and I tried to oversee the person too closely. One of the best candidates, Sandy Neilly, came to me after a few weeks on the job and said it was not going to work; she and I were just not cut out for each other. Years later Sandy and I worked well together on some projects at Maine Audubon, but she had been quicker than I to recognize that we were not going to be effective at *Maine Times* and I have always respected her for being more astute than I was.

The closest I came to success was Ellen Grant, a young and very energetic Colby graduate. She was smart and a quick learner. And she stood up to me.

But it also became obvious that as much as she enjoyed working at *Maine Times*, this was not going to be her life. Although she relished the responsibility I gave her, she also wanted to earn more money. If she stayed at Maine Times, she was always going to be earning less than friends of similar ability.

It would be hard for anyone to maintain my admittedly obsessive commitment to Maine Times. One morning we both arrived at the office at the same time, before anyone else. As we walked to the front door, there was a piece of trash paper on the ground. She walked by it and I picked it up. "Why didn't you pick up that piece of trash?" I asked. "I'm not paid to pick up the trash," she replied. "Neither am I," I said. "Yes, but you own the paper," she said. I answered, "And that's why you'll never own it," I replied, proving I could be a total pain.

Sporadically, competition to Maine Times emerged. We referred to such endeavors as "muddying the water" because none was run by people who really knew what they were doing and most were so drastically under-capitalized they were doomed before they started. But they were competitors for advertising, and we had to cope with them while they lasted.

Maine Magazine, a slick lifestyle magazine somewhere between Down East (not really a competitor) and ourselves, had come on the scene and immediately found itself in financial trouble. We were not yet ten years old and I was not considering selling Maine Times when I received a telephone call that led to one of my more bizarre experiences. Fortunately, I had the good sense to write myself a memo about it the next day.

In the last days of September 1977, Everett Ellin, who was running something called the New Enterprise Institute and about whom we had written, contacted me to say there was a group interested in buying Maine Times and that I should at least talk with them. Of course, I was always interested in someone who wanted to buy Maine Times, if only to find out how much they thought it was worth. There's nothing better for the ego.

Ellin was quite mysterious about who the group was but told me that they wanted to meet the next day at the home of Gerry Miller in Falmouth. I agreed and by 4:30 that afternoon, having made a few phone calls, I had found out that Gerry Miller was the financial backer of Maine Magazine.

When I arrived at the house, Ellin was already there with Miller and his wife, Nan. There was to be no one else. This was the group.

Although the Millers had arrived in Maine eight months previously, they had not yet unpacked and while the den where we met was furnished, I could look into the living room full of unpacked boxes. Just as we were sitting down for a first glass of Scotch, one of their dogs urinated on the bare floor and I noted in my aide-mèmoire that "the urine ran across the hardwood like incoming tide on a hard-packed beach."

Nan Miller came and went while the three of us kept sipping drinks and talking. I asked Gerry Miller why he wanted to buy *Maine Times* and he launched a 45-minute answer, starting with what a successful business person he was. He said he came from Buffalo and indicated his family was moneyed; from Buffalo he went to Toledo, where he ran a furnace company and sold it, making even more money. Then, having summered at Northeast Harbor, he moved to Maine where he worked with Ellin and "associated" himself with the stock brokerage of H. M. Payson.

When *Maine Magazine* began, he told me, he put up $40,000, which bought him a 36 percent interest. The initial investments were all gone by the second issue and he put in more, increasing his share to 70 percent, and from then on, he "called all the shots." Based on my own experience, the story rang true.

To illustrate his assumption of power, he said he was the one who forced them to hire a circulation manager from Time, Inc. They had just done a mailing of 30,000 and had received back 600 subscriptions the first week. If his figures were correct, that was a good return and I said so. He might even go as high as 1,000 or about a 3 percent return. But since they had spent $9,000 on the mailing and 1,000 subscriptions would only bring in $10,000, they were essentially buying subscriptions. When, after a quick mental calculation, I mentioned this, he changed the subject. He was the kind of person who was so enamored of his own "expertise" that he would tell you things he should not have or that had ramifications he had not thought about. When the downside was brought to his attention, he was offended.

Miller said the combination of *Maine Magazine* and *Maine Times* could be the foundation for a communications system for the state. He would own the parent company and bring me in to get things in shape. I replied that I wasn't interested in taking on a start-up publication, especially not one whose goals I didn't share, and I thought he had his hands full with *Maine Magazine*.

I was on my second drink and I began to nurse it, realizing it might be quite a while before we sat down to dinner. I don't know what my reaction would have been if there had been an attractive buyer, but I knew immediately I didn't want to sell to Miller. However, I remained resolutely polite. After all, it was his house.

Whenever I tried to explain why I wasn't interested in his proposition, he would go off on a 15-minute monologue about why I should sell to him. After a couple of hours there would be long pauses in his conversation as he lost his train of thought. At first I tried to speak during these pauses but quickly gave up when I learned that as soon as he remembered what it was he was planning to say, he would pick up where he had left off without having listened to anything I had said in the meantime.

We went in to dinner and switched to wine, a Nuits St. George that I considered a treat and drank more of than I should have. But I tried to remain cordial even when he made such comments as "*Maine Times* needs new blood, it's getting dull." If he thought I was dull, why did he want to hire me to run his magazine? But I kept my mouth shut.

Halfway through dinner, I didn't keep my mouth shut any longer. I raised my voice. Okay, I probably yelled. I told him to shut up for a minute and I would tell him why I didn't want to sell to him.

The only reason I would even consider selling, I said, was to be free of the headaches, and taking on an ailing *Maine Magazine* would put me under even greater pressure. What he was really talking about was a merger where the weaker publication would bleed the stronger one, and I didn't want *Maine Times* to be bled. If he couldn't get *Maine Magazine* on its feet, why should I expect *Maine Times* to do any better under his leadership? I told him that if he wanted to save his investment, he was going to have to roll up his shirtsleeves and step in and run *Maine Magazine*.

About this time I realized I was venting and I made some placating remarks, saying that while I would not sell to him, I would help him if he wanted me to. His wife began to play the mediator, repeating my

Worn Out, Hiring Help, and Thinking of Retiring

offer of help even if he didn't buy *Maine Times*.

Miller then asked me if I would be more interested in his buying into *Maine Times* if he didn't already own *Maine Magazine*. Trying to be gracious, I said yes, even though I didn't mean it. He asked if I thought I could work with him, if I thought he was a good guy. I said I thought he was a nice guy but I didn't know how well I would work with him since I had known him for only six hours. It was a lie, of course. He was the stereotype of a person who had come into too much money and thought that was a sign of his innate talent.

Then the tone of the conversation changed again, reverting to its ugly edge. My problem, he said, was that I was small time. "Don't you have ambition to do bigger things than *Maine Times?*" he asked. It was nearing midnight and the wine bottles were all empty.

Gerry Miller looked across the long table at me and said: "Well, in fact, *Maine Magazine* and *Maine Times* are in competition and if you won't sell to me, I'll put you out of business. And I can do it because I have the money to do it."

I stood up. "Okay, give me a price," I said, trying to sound face-tious. I then turned and walked out of the room with an air of right-eous indignation. I didn't have a coat so I headed for the front door. Unfortunately, the first door I opened happened to be a closet but no one else seemed to notice. When I found the proper front door and opened it, the cold air felt good on my face and I drove home, very carefully.

That evening dampened any desire to sell for another seven years. But by 1984, I was seriously considering selling because I was tired and had been unable to find the perfect assistant. This time I had a price in mind, $1 million including the building.

Some good people in Maine made inquiries, but the price was too steep for them and I didn't want to hold a mortgage. If I was going to get out, I wanted out free and clear.

My attempts at selling weren't going too well. Jim Ottaway, my old schoolmate from Exeter and Yale, got in touch to find out if *Maine Times* was something he might be interested in. Dow Jones had bought out his family chain of dailies and he was still an executive with the company. I wrote back and said that financially it would not fit in with their other publications.

Business reporter Frank Sleeper called from the *Portland Press Herald* and asked if it were true that I was considering selling. Against my wife's advice, which was to say nothing, I replied that I would sell to the right buyer for the right price, a disclaimer I thought was broad enough to make my answer meaningless.

The next day my picture was on the front page of the *Press Herald* under the headline: "*Maine Times* for Sale." At least it was a flattering photograph.

I soon got a call from Roger Conover. Roger was a Bowdoin graduate who had been a sternman for a Hemingwayesque lobsterman named David Pulsifer and was a longtime reader of *Maine Times*. He was presently editor of architectural books for MIT Press, and he knew someone who might be interested. He was clearly a person who understood what *Maine Times* was all about so I answered his questions and he passed on the information.

His potential buyer was Dodge Morgan who had bought some electronic equipment that others couldn't sell and started a very successful high-tech company, making the miniaturized communications systems used by the Secret Service and radar detectors for automobiles. He had just sold out to a larger company; the figure bandied about was $35 million.

Roger's wife, Anna Ginn, was Dodge's assistant. Anna had come to Maine to attend Bowdoin College for a year from Mount Holyoke, and her brother, Bill Ginn, had been executive director of Maine Audubon and was running an alternative energy company.

Perhaps Dodge's greatest attraction to me was that Anna would come in as publisher and work with me for a year of transition. Anna and I hit it off immediately, and my first impression would later prove correct. I was to work with her two different stints at *Maine Times* and I enjoyed every minute of the relationship.

Dodge loved playing the role of bad boy, and he was certainly fun to be with. He had Maine connections, including owning a summer home on Chebeague Island. I later learned that his first wife had come from Augusta and they had sailed together to Alaska, where he had worked for a newspaper.

Dodge was not going to edit the paper himself but use it as his base in Maine. I was hopeful that his ready cash would benefit *Maine Times* and allow it to do some of the things I had always wanted to do but had been unable to afford—to hire more staff and to produce ancillary publications such as dining and travel guides that would reuse material that had appeared in the paper. I did not want to sell to someone who would try to wring the last drop of profit from *Maine Times*.

I met with Dodge and his financial heavy in Gloucester, where Ted Hood was building the boat in which Dodge intended to sail around the world, alone, without touching land. His guided tour of the boat, especially his enthusiasm for adventure, was infectious.

Negotiations first fell apart, but then we settled on a price. He didn't want the building, so that took off $250,000, bringing my asking price down to $750,000. We ended up at $600,000 up front and a $75,000 non-compete contract. They would also continue to rent the building for an indefinite period and I would receive $5,000 a year and medical insurance benefits as a member of his board. There was nothing left worth haggling over and he had been straightforward. As far as I was concerned, he was meeting my original asking price even though it was not a straight cash deal.

Besides, my mother had died the year before and left me with enough money when combined with what I would receive for the paper that I wouldn't have to worry. Without touching principal, I would have an income of $80,000, more than Eunice and I had ever taken out of the paper in a given year. (That income was later to drop as interest rates went down from their historic highs in the mid-eighties, but the remaining income has still proved adequate since I just cut back on expenses. On the other hand, everyone asking me for money assumed I had more than I did.)

When I sold the paper, the first thing I did was give $100,000 to key, longtime employees. Some received $10,000 zero coupon bonds that were paying 13 percent interest. It was my attempt at social engineering, saying in effect I wanted this for their retirement. Most quickly sold the bonds and spent the money; I'm not sure anyone kept them the fifteen years to maturity when they would have been worth $33,000.

With Dodge setting off for his around-the-world voyage and with every employee receiving a free radar detector for his or her car, the transition was smooth. Anna and I worked well together. She was devoted to the paper and in keeping with tradition, underpaid herself. I got a raise and only had to do half the work I had been doing. Anna was the publisher I had sought but had never succeeded in finding.

When I sold the paper, revenues were around $900,000 and holding steady despite the long recession. I don't know if they made or lost money that first year; I didn't need to know.

Fifteen

The Search for New Editors Begins

After the sale of *Maine Times* I participated in the hiring of a new editor to replace me at the end of my year of transition. We chose Dave Platt whom we had known from his years as chief environmental reporter for the *Bangor Daily News*. Dave was bright, affable, and well liked.

When Dodge returned from his highly publicized singlehanded sail around the world, Dave was in place as my successor. Dave had never been an editor before and he had inherited a headstrong staff, all hired by and loyal to me. Dodge began to express reservations about Dave, feeling he didn't lead the staff assertively enough. There was merit to Dodge's complaint. The situation was difficult, but, I thought, not impossible. I kept arguing that Dodge should tell Dave specifically what he felt his shortcomings to be so that he would have a chance to remedy them but that did not take place, and Dave kept going the way he was, thinking everything was fine when it was not.

The editor of *Maine Times* had to work closely with his five reporters, the photographers, and the production staff led by Gidget (who epitomized the dilemma). Gidget was incredibly talented. She had come to the paper very young, with little experience but with a natural eye for design and an ability to work at breakneck speed. It would have taken several people to replace her and she left her mark on the design of the paper, staying there longer than any other person, coming the first year and departing a decade after I did. Her contribution to the success of *Maine Times* was considerable. While she and I worked extremely well together, if given the chance, she would exert the authority given her, sometimes to the consternation of others.

My relationship had been distinctive with each writer but since they were all such strong personalities, we had numerous tugs of war. Reporters like to do the same stories over again, stories with which they are comfortable, and the editor has to move them on to something else. There are even times when a story is unprintable. It's not like spiking a daily story on which the reporter has spent a few hours and which one can claim the paper didn't have space for. Not to publish a story a reporter had been working on for several days or even weeks was like a thrust to the heart, with the same reaction.

With a paper like *Maine Times*, which doesn't *have* to publish anything in particular, there must be a sense of direction set by the editor. Certainly there is consultation and interplay with the rest of the editorial staff, but the paper must be something more than what the writers felt like writing about that week. In its simplest form, to let the writers go off on their own runs the risk of having a bad mix of stories any given week. In a more subtle way, it invites redundancy.

You couldn't just tell *Maine Times* reporters what to do without establishing that you were in charge. Dave had been a good reporter and was a good person, but the staff quickly sensed his managerial inexperience and tentativeness, and they were merciless. The decision was made to bring someone in over Dave. (After Dave left *Maine Times*, he became communications director for the Island Institute and editor of their annual, *Island Journal*, and their monthly, *Working Waterfront*, which he slowly turned into a first-rate niche publication, a must read for anyone in Maine interested in coastal issues.)

To supersede Dave, Dodge announced he would do a national search for a world-class editor. Only the best for the best. I suppose such talk was good for my ego but it was also garbage. What we needed was not a big name but someone with talent who was willing to do the work of several people. As we announced our world search, no one asked how much the paper could afford to pay.

Dodge quickly found his man, Matt Storin, who had been the editor of the daily *Chicago Sun-Times*, which he had left after a dispute with the publisher. Matt's ambition was to go back to the *Boston Globe* as editor, an ambition he subsequently fulfilled.

Matt came to *Maine Times* in 1988 and was paid about $70,000 a year, almost double what anyone had received before. And Dodge helped him buy a home in Arrowsic, on the Kennebec River.

Then the money really began to flow. A top Boston designer was hired to redesign *Maine Times* and he did a polished job, even though the paper ended up looking like other papers he had designed but the readers didn't know that nor did they seem to particularly care one way or the other. Anyone who thinks a redesign will have a significant impact on circulation is dreaming. More important, Dodge and Anna poured money into circulation, a place where money could bring results, and results were needed to justify Matt's salary. Since Dodge had the capital, he could afford to invest it in the hope that he would get a good return. This was the exact opposite approach from mine which was only to spend money that was already on hand. At the time, I would have agreed that *Maine Times* needed an infusion of capital even if I would have used it differently.

Although I did not realize it then, it was during this period that the goal of 50,000 circulation was laid down and each week reporters were notified of the increase in circulation, which came in disappointing numbers.

When I had sold the paper in 1985, it had a little more than 16,000 paid circulation. In the year and a half Matt was there, it climbed to 19,000, slightly above our previous peak of 18,500 in 1976. That circulation didn't climb farther was not Matt's fault. He was a strong editor and handled the writers with easy authority. As an experienced professional, he was more connected with circulation problems than Dave Platt, who had come from a reporter's background.

The staff respected Matt and even though his knowledge of Maine was scant, theirs was considerable and he knew how to channel their talents.

However, Matt's lack of involvement with Maine was not without its drawbacks. Reporters said he sometimes was reluctant to write editorials about specific Maine issues where he felt he did not have adequate background. Reporters were accustomed to editorials that complemented their stories. He gave the impression he was networking for his next job. *Maine Times* was a stopover.

I was beginning to realize Dodge had unrealistic expectations for *Maine Times*. When he had mentioned boosting circulation to 50,000 in the past, I had demurred, noting that the *Maine Sunday Telegram*, the largest paper in the state, had a circulation of only 120,000. I said that to reach the proposed numbers, *Maine Times* would have to be a different kind of publication, one that reached a mass audience, and I added, facetiously, that he had better put in TV listings and comics and a sports section if he wanted to reach those kinds of numbers.

Recognizing the limitations to *Maine Times*'s circulation growth, I had hoped Dodge would use his capital to spin off other publications. Years before we had done a gardening book based on our articles and it had taken a decade to pay for itself. I had felt that if there had been several *Maine Times* books or guides, all reusing material we had already paid for, he could build a small but profitable publishing company. That was not in the cards. Dodge was not interested in incremental growth.

Nor was Matt. In fact, he seemed only marginally interested in *Maine Times*. He left after two years to become editor of the *New York Daily News* and four years after that became editor of the *Boston Globe*, where he remained until the *New York Times*, which bought the *Globe*, brought in their own editor. When he left *Maine Times*, Matt said that his heart was in daily journalism.

While Matt was editor, Dave Platt had stayed on as executive editor and they even hired another person with a title of managing editor, but when Matt returned to the world of dailies, the job reverted to one person. The new editor was Jay Davis who had founded the *Waldo Independent*, a weekly that went into competition with the *Belfast Republican Journal*, our old printers.

A few years previously, a freelancer had submitted a story on the competition between the two Belfast papers and I had sent it back to him, asking him to delineate more clearly what the differences were between the two papers. He replied that there were no great philosophical or journalistic differences except that they didn't like each other. Jay had had a fight with his old publisher and started a competition paper, dooming both of them to a constant struggle to stay alive.

Jay was a strange mixture for someone who had started a news-paper. His commitment to communalism made me look like a robber baron and although, as editor, he was part of management, he professed a reluctance to fully participate in management, telling us during his interview that as a matter of principle he would side with reporters against the owners.

Dodge and Jay connected philosophically, at least initially. Dodge liked being the iconoclast so much that he must have liked having an anti-management manager. Because he never fully understood that the basic problem for Dave Platt had been exerting control over the staff, something Matt Storin had remedied, he did not foresee the problems that would arise when Jay Davis consciously chose not to lead the staff.

Jay was under pressure from Dodge to be more outlandish and under pressure from the staff to do its bidding, the combination of which resulted in an unfortunate cover headline: "The Last Honest Man in Augusta." It had been suggested by the reporter and referred to the current attorney general. Unfortunately, it implied that everyone else in Augusta was dishonest and the reaction was predictable

When Jay replaced Matt, Anna was left without an editor as ally and helper in her attempts to boost circulation. It wasn't that Jay didn't want more circulation nor that he didn't come up with suggestions; it's just that Anna felt he treated circulation as Anna's problem, not his.

A convergence of problems that were beyond Jay's control caused the circulation problems. First, Dodge and Anna stopped pumping money into increasing sales. Second, because the emphasis had shifted to special editions, the regular editions had less advertising and therefore a smaller news hole. That meant there was less to read.

I have a stack of memoranda from this period and later in which there is constant second-guessing about the editorial content of the paper, blaming the editors for not attracting more readers. While there is some validity to the criticisms, they all miss an essential point—lack of space made the editor's task more difficult.

The bottom line was that *Maine Times* was for people who liked to read and the editor was the chief reader. The writing was superior to anything else in Maine and often was on a par with the best nationally. Over the years, we had the food writing of Leslie Land who you will now find in the *New York Times*, and the nature writing of Susan Shetterly, whom I put on a par with Annie Dillard. Even though I was not a fan of modern dance, I always found June Vail's dance reviews so well written that I enjoyed reading about something I never intended to see. All of the staff reporters were good writers; that was one of the key criteria for hiring them.

The year before I sold, the paper routinely carried five major articles plus short pieces and reviews. A subscriber had choices and even reading only half of what was available would still have an hour or two of material. With smaller papers, the options were fewer. Now, a subscriber would have to read a higher percentage of what was available to get the same amount of material he could choose in the past. It was an impossible task.

That task was exacerbated when the staff took power again. Once more, the paper reflected what they were interested in, when they were interested in it. Issues that *Maine Times* should have been covering were missed because no reporters took the initiative and no one told them they had to cover the story. This increased the problem with mix, as did the special issues themselves, which demanded a reader be interested in the theme or pass on that issue.

Then, in 1993, seven years after I had left, Anna came to me and said she needed my help. Circulation was slipping. She said she needed someone she could work with or she could not solve the financial problems that had evolved, largely to meet expectations that were never fulfilled.

During the seven years of my absence, Anna and I had stayed in close contact, partially through Dodge's "board," of which we were both members. There were also—during Dave's and Jay's tenures but not during Matt's—many rump sessions over drinks that included Anna, Dodge, and myself. I understood the problems she faced and had confidence in her abilities. I had enjoyed the year we had worked together and now I was rested. But I did not want to become the permanent editor of *Maine Times* again, nor did I want to be the reason for Jay's leaving.

Anna assured me that she only wanted me to sign on for a few months while she looked for a new editor. I asked her what she would do regarding Jay if I did not agree to come aboard. She assured me that she would replace him anyway. I don't know if she effectively convinced me of this or if I just wanted to be convinced.

I still am not sure what Dodge's attitude was toward Jay at this point. He had certainly participated in the criticism of the paper under Jay but then there was a tradition of criticism of the paper no matter who was editing it. I could lead the parade when it came to criticizing issues of the paper I had edited myself. Based on the inexplicability of later events, it is possible Dodge never approved of Jay's leaving and my being brought back. On the other hand, I have a memo in which Dodge suggests that I be brought back.

Certainly a factor in Anna's wanting to get me back was that Dodge had finally issued the order that *Maine Times* had to break even and break even soon, and Anna saw no way that she could accomplish that without the active cooperation of her editor. I was even more conscious than she was of the necessity to bring *Maine Times* back to break even. Although Dodge had often scoffed at the lack of retained earnings under my ownership, his massive losses, running into the hundreds of thousands of dollars a year, made my small but consistent profits more attractive.[1]

So there I was back at *Maine Times* in the spring of 1992, having agreed to take a salary of $40,000, slightly lower than Jay's but higher than Anna's and higher than I had ever paid myself. I was energized and most of the staff still consisted of people I had hired and with whom I had worked. My return was like a homecoming.

I intended the first issue to be a statement. I wrote the cover piece on Jonathan Reitman, who had successfully led the discussions that resulted in effective Worker's Compensation reform. The message was that *Maine Times* was going to be less confrontational and more concerned with seeking solutions through consensus. I was going to bring to bear all I had learned in almost a decade of trying to solve problems through my work on non-profit boards, the focus of my public policy efforts in the years away from *Maine Times*.[2]

Advertising revenues were still healthy, although a dangerous trend had begun to show itself—special issues were getting out of hand. There were now four seasonal guides, spring and fall having been added to the winter and summer guides existing when I left. And there were special theme issues at every opportunity. Although this made it easier to sell advertising, much of the advertising had simply been switched from regular issues to the special ones. What *Maine Times* covered was being determined by advertising potential rather

1. When I sold the paper, I had bought back the non-voting stock and paid off the loans, with the exception of those from my late mother.
2. When I went back, I resigned most of my board positions, based on any potential conflict I would have in writing about issues on which they had taken public positions.

than editorial merit. Someone should have analyzed whether the paper was just switching ads from regular issues to more advertiser-popular specials but in the quest for more revenues, no matter how they were attained, the pressure was to do just the opposite. Long-term policy was in danger of being compromised by short-term returns. Although I commented on it, this was now Anna's responsibility and, as editor, my only insistence was that we do special issues only when we had something special to say and when the editorial content could meet our standards.

Although we had done special issues from the early days of *Maine Times*, I did not fully appreciate at the time how little readers like them. As a reader, I disliked special issues in other publications. I was always disappointed when the *New Yorker* did a special issue and there was less of interest for me to read than in their regular editions.

Circulation had dropped below 16,000, slightly less than where it was when I had sold the paper eight years before. It was a loss of 3,000 from the heyday of 19,000 under Matt Storin and from our old high of 18,500 back in the mid-1970s.

I felt we needed more physical effort and had my eye on Anna's special assistant, a bright young woman named Diane Kew. Diane could bring faster, concrete results by putting more effort into the advertising side, but in the long run, I felt it was important to build circulation again, not to some unrealistic high, but to its natural peak of around 18,000.

We did try one all-out effort, when we wrote a cover piece on how the Cook's Corner shopping center, halfway between Bath and Brunswick, had decimated both downtowns. The theme of the story was how this had not been a single, planned decision but the cumulative effect of a number of independent decisions which reinforced one another. I knew the issue well, having been editor in Bath when the shopping center was first built and having subsequently become a student of urban sprawl in Maine. Although we did not use the term, it was one of the first major pieces in Maine to be done on the effects of our particular brand of sprawl.

For our promotion, we tried something new. Typical of me, it was not a big bang solution with unrealistic expectations. It was instead a test of an incremental strategy that, if successful, we hoped to use elsewhere. Diane visited downtown merchants in both Bath and Brunswick, explaining what the story was going to be about. She offered the retailers free copies of the paper to have on their counters but also asked that they place a copy, with their compliments, in the shopping bag of any customer they thought would be interested in the story. In other words, we were asking them to identify those among their customers who might like to read *Maine Times*.

It worked beautifully. The store owners felt we were giving them something of value and the customers felt they were receiving something of value. We experienced a surge of subscriptions from Bath and Brunswick in the weeks after the story ran.

At the same time we had concentrated on Bath and Brunswick, we had maximized our trade-out radio advertising and increased our point-of-sale posters. Whether it was the promotion or the nature of the story itself, newsstand sales in southern Maine surged—a couple of thousand extra was a surge. It was one of the most encouraging signs in recent years. I wanted to keep repeating the model but was limited in being allowed Diane's time. Doing what we had done in Bath and Brunswick was highly labor intensive and even the best results would be slow.

While Anna and I agreed on the need to focus on circulation, we kept tightening the budget to meet Dodge's demand to break even. I lost a reporter for other reasons but did not seek a replacement. Office staff was pared. The figures indicated that with letting go one person, who expected to lose her job anyway when a new computer system was installed, we could break even. We were only $40,000 off the mark, already a victory for a publication that had been losing hundreds of thousands of dollars a year in recent years.

After a family visit to Canada, Anna came back with one of the best ideas anyone had proposed in years and one that could have led us in a new direction. She proposed that we put out an edition of the Summer Guide in French.

The Summer Guide had continued to prosper, running more than 120 pages and grossing more than $100,000 or 10 percent of annual revenues.[3] On her trip to Canada, Anna had been struck by how

3. The Summer Guide was also a contradiction to the premise in all those memos that only

everything in Quebec was in French and although thousands of Quebeçois came to Maine for the summer, there was nothing published on this side of the border in French. Since we had already done all the research and writing, translating the editorial material into French would be relatively cheap. We would then sell ads catering to this clientele. It might not be as large as the English edition but the cost would be almost entirely the cost of printing.

Anna had previously published a *Maine Almanac* that made money, and we were now saving material we used in a feature called "Just the Facts" for use in a future almanac. Indeed, we were selecting much of the material we used in that feature with an eye toward reusing it. Computers made such multiple use more attractive.

Anna took the idea of the French Summer Guide to Dodge but met with total indifference. We talked about doing it the next summer, but for Anna and me that next summer was never to come.

Feeling a certain amount of desperation at the lack of commitment to a clear course and sensing the mixed messages coming from Dodge, I knew something was wrong and I tried to corner Dodge one day when he was in the office by telling him we had to give more priority to circulation and we should sit down and talk about it. He clearly wanted to avoid me. All he wanted to talk about was consolidating *Maine Times* and *Casco Bay Weekly*, an urban Portland free weekly he had bought, in a Portland location. Dodge saw the merger and move as the salvation and nothing was going to convince him to look at alternatives.

I suspect that by now he thoroughly disapproved of Anna's having brought me back—I was certainly not making it easier to move to Portland. Later, he would pass on to me a letter from Matt Storin in which Matt described my latest editorship a "disaster." It was unclear from the letter itself exactly what he meant but it was clear that he was responding to something Dodge had said or written. I had become like those other editors with whom Dodge was unhappy but who would never learn the specifics of his unhappiness. At this point, I

controversy sold. The "Summer Guide" was selective and offered a unique perspective on enjoying the state, but its attraction was that it was large and comprehensive, and that it stayed on the newsstands for a month. It sold four times as many copies on the newsstand as a regular edition.

didn't care and his attempt to insult me with Matt's comment fell on deaf ears.

In early 1994 Dodge announced he was moving *Maine Times* to Portland because *Maine Times* was still losing money. The long honeymoon—or more accurately, the era of mixed messages—was over. Not only would *Maine Times* move, but Anna would have to get rid of most longtime employees and hire new people to do the same jobs for less money.

Anna balked at firing the employees, arguing correctly that they were worth what they were paid and that the inefficiencies of new hires would far outweigh the cost savings. What it was that set off Dodge's reaction is not clear; it could have been the failure to break into the black; it could have been reluctance among almost the entire *Maine Times* staff to merge with *Casco Bay Weekly*; it could have been Anna's refusal to fire staff. Whatever the cause, Dodge fired Anna. On the spot. She was to be out of her office by the end of the week.

This was the person who had come to *Maine Times* as Dodge's vanguard, the person who had been his special assistant for several years before coming to Maine. She was a person of such loyalty to Dodge and with such obvious affection for him that the rumors persisted they must be having an affair. It was a rumor I never believed.

In all the years we had worked together, in all the time I had known her, I had never heard Anna indicate in any way that she had any greater priority than pleasing Dodge. That may have ultimately been her downfall.

Anna left without a whimper and with no recriminations. Even when we discussed it later, her only emotion was a slight bewilderment. She had been so close to breaking even after all those years of huge losses, most of them incurred trying to reach the unrealistic goals Dodge had set. As for the staff, she was proud of her pride in them. She was proud they respected her and worked so hard for her.

It was a message perhaps only I could understand because she had taken that staff over from me and she had managed to perpetuate the *Maine Times* culture. Maybe there were no longer fresh vegetables from the garden at 10:00 A.M.—the office had moved down the hill to the old mill where there was no room for a garden. But it was still an operation where everyone worked for the paper as if it were a crusade and they all knew that what they did mattered; everyone believed he or she was crucial to the paper's success.

After Anna's departure Dodge brought in Bill Rawlings to whip both *Maine Times* and *Casco Bay Weekly* into financial shape and to merge the two of them in Portland. I had previously been cool to the move, saying that any savings would be negligible and far outweighed by the heightened perception of *Maine Times* as not only a Southern Maine paper but now a Portland paper.

Dodge had met Rawlings when the two were serving on another board and had found in him an amenable hatchet man. Rawlings was a type I had seldom met except at cocktail parties, where after a few words of conversation he would have sent me scurrying across the room.

Rawlings had been an executive in several major corporations, including Gillette, and saw himself as infallible. He had recently moved to Kennebunkport and, in his sixties, was suffering from cancer and expected to live only a short time. To keep busy, he was helping Dodge.

When Rawlings arrived at *Maine Times* where he was going to spend a couple of days a week, advertising director Karen Taylor had just about firmed up a promotion with a chain of gasoline stations where patrons would receive free copies of the paper. Karen, in return, would use this additional free circulation to try to boost advertising sales. The idea had been germinated when Anna was still in charge and had fallen into my lap. I had serious reservations about such gimmicks and whether they worked, but it was not something I wanted to get in a battle with Karen about.

With Anna gone, I asked Bill to look into the situation before any final commitment. Who would be receiving the papers and how many would there be? Was this our demographic group? How much would it cost us? Was this the best way to spend the money? And how would we gauge its effectiveness and monitor it?

Of course, Rawlings said. Anyone would answer those questions before going ahead. He then proceeded to do nothing. Only later did I learn that the free papers were to be given exclusively to people who used high-test gasoline—which meant they drove big American cars—and probably few were potential readers. No one ever found out how many papers were actually delivered into the hands of potential readers and how many found their way to the trash. Because there was no coding, we could not learn if any of them subscribed and it had no effect, one way or the other, on newsstand sales. It also appeared to give no boost to ad sales.

I quickly learned that Rawlings knew nothing about newspapers and had no intention of learning anything. Whatever his business experience, at *Maine Times* he had no impact except to leave the business side leaderless.

I was initially friendly with him and made a point of having lunch with him on his days at *Maine Times* and discussing our problems. He was cordial enough even if not particularly engaged.

One day, on returning from lunch, we were discussing a subject we wanted to continue and so went upstairs to my office. In the adjacent office, through which we had to pass, Edgar Allen Beem was interviewing Buzz Fitzgerald, president of Bath Iron Works, the state's largest employer.

Fitzgerald was about as down home as one can get, and we had known each other in Bath when we were both in our twenties and he was a young lawyer. Our greeting was therefore quite informal and I introduced him to Bill Rawlings by his name alone. We then went through to my office and closed the door.

"Who was that?" Rawlings asked me. I repeated that it was Buzz Fitzgerald. "What's he do?" Rawlings asked. He was not familiar enough with the state to actually identify the name of one of its best-known business leaders. "He's president of Bath Iron Works," I said. Rawlings immediately got up and went back to the other room, interrupting Edgar's interview and telling Buzz that during World War II, he had been on a ship the same time as Admiral Arleigh Burke—after whom the current class of destroyers the Iron Works was building was named. Standing behind Rawlings where he could not see, Edgar raised his eyebrows and I returned to my work.

It didn't take long for me to realize that Rawlings had only two clear tasks: to oversee the move to Portland and to get rid of as much of the current staff as possible.

Dodge actually participated in finding the new building in Portland and in a fruitless rebellion, I insisted that the upstairs, windowless room the *Maine Times* editorial staff would occupy be decorated properly.

Business side staff were told they would not be compensated for the extra drive to Portland or for the parking space they would have to buy there. Some were simply advised to look for new jobs.

I had already said that I would soon be leaving *Maine Times*; I had been back for more than a year. With a modem hookup, I could edit much of the material from home and would not have to make the hour drive into Portland more than once or twice a week. In the meantime, we would speed up the search for my replacement.

What I did not foresee was that we would use a freelancer to deal with the new computer needs, mostly a modem connection that my editing from a remote site would entail. This was before local Internet hookups were available. Whoever designed the system did not understand what we would be using it for and since we had hired him on the cheap, he was not available when the system did not work as planned. My initial attempts at editing long distance were a disaster, and since I do not have much patience with unreliable technologies, I was quickly frustrated. Under the new management structure, no one cared and I didn't have the authority to solve the problem myself.

In the search for my replacement, we had already done some interviewing and had found two excellent candidates—Sandy Marsters at the *Biddeford-Sanford Tribune* and Doug Rooks at the *Kennebec Journal*. With the current situation bordering on chaos, I had suggested that we not hire a new editor from outside at a time of such uncertainty. I could not in good conscience have asked anyone to leave a solid job to come to *Maine Times* at that point. Instead, Randy Wilson, a thoughtful reporter who liked to edit, would take over many of the editing duties as I pulled back.

At the time, I did not realize how I was inwardly seething. We were being thrown into a secondary role with *Casco Bay Weekly*, which controlled the front office and the advertising departments. Their staff had nothing but contempt for us. We were the old fogies to their vital youth. The front office itself was packing-crate collegiate. Their ad department had been bad-mouthing *Maine Times* for years as they competed for our downtown advertisers, and now they were being asked to sell for us as well. Circulation had been turned over to the person who drove the truck for *Casco Bay Weekly* (which was free distribution); he hadn't a clue about what was involved with paid circulation.

We were working with and sometimes for people who didn't know anything about how *Maine Times* functioned and could care less. Rawlings's system for planning the move was to have Gidget do it. There was no thought given to what was thrown out and what went down to Portland. One day during the move, I happened to be in the old office and saw crates of valuable materials that were being taken to the dump rather than make the trip. I was too discouraged at that point to lodge a complaint.

Rawlings had not even taken care of such basics as dealing with the post office, so our third class mail, which included all subscription renewals, continued to arrive at Topsham. In the beginning, Roberta Davis, one of our best and longest-term employees, picked up the mail every day on her way from Topsham to Portland but her future at the paper was doomed and she soon found a good job at Bowdoin College.

A month and a half after Roberta's departure, Seth Sprague, who was acting as publisher, stopped Anna on the street and told her that something was wrong and that *Maine Times*'s cash flow was well below what it should have been. It turned out that no one had been picking up the mail in Topsham and the subscription renewals had been piling up. When this was discovered, after some six weeks, not only were thousands of dollars in checks waiting to be sorted and deposited, but help had to be brought in to update the subscriptions that normally would have been done by existing staff on a week-by-week basis. That was just one situation I heard about later; there must have been many more, each of them costly, that took place because they had systematically fired everyone who knew what was going on in his or her departments.

Shortly after the move I was driving into Portland with a box of materials I needed. There was no place to park in front of the building in spite of the fact I had suggested that Bill Rawlings go to the city and ask that a couple of spaces be designated 15-minute parking so that customers could drop off ads or other material. There were no empty spaces in the lot behind the building—the spaces *Maine Times* had reserved were not for the likes of me. So I spent a half hour finding a parking space, at a garage a few blocks away, and lugged my box to the office. This was particularly irritating to someone who had been accustomed for years to walk to the office. On the way out of the garage, I asked the attendant if there were any special rates as compared to the 75 cents an hour I was paying. He told me that the garages all made deals with companies that allowed their employees to park at reduced rates and even to have designated parking areas.

By the time I got to the office I was in a terrible mood—a combination of my growing sense of guilt over participating in the demise of the *Maine Times* staff, the move into a hellhole of an office, and that morning's inconvenience. After depositing my box upstairs, I went looking for Rawlings.

I found him with his feet up on his desk, drinking coffee, and talking with an employee I did not know. I let him have it. I said I had asked in the past that he deal with the parking situation and I had just wasted a half hour because he never got out of his chair and did anything. So why didn't he do something now? I then left.

A few minutes later he came up to my office and said that he didn't mind that I criticized him, but that I should not have done it in front of another employee. I replied that was all he cared about, appearances, but everyone in the place already knew he was incompetent.

He said I couldn't talk to him like that, and I said then why didn't he fire me. I said he didn't have the guts.

The next day he sent me a letter suggesting that I speed up the process for my departure which I took to mean he had fired me, and Randy took over editing the paper.

The fall of *Maine Times* was precipitous. The reporters stayed but they had been put on a freelance basis. In the business, advertising and production departments, only Gidget remained and even she would leave in several months. *Casco Bay Weekly* took over ad sales and the classifieds were combined, most notably the personals.

That combination was indicative of everything that was wrong with trying to combine the two operations. *Maine Times*'s personals were of the let's walk on the beach, sip wine, and listen to Mozart variety. *Casco Bay Weekly*'s were full of one-night stands and group experimentation. The new personals must have scared the bejesus out of the old users.[4]

People who used the personals felt safe and they even sent back testimonials. Several got married. It was the epitome of the people-like-us syndrome. Readers of *Maine Times* tended to be like each other and sexual predators did not fit our demographic profile.

However, no one is ever safe and in the mid-1980s, a woman who had used the personals disappeared. It was suspected that the day she disappeared, she might have been going to meet someone she had made contact with through our personals. The police called us; we cooperated. We worried. We debated whether we should discontinue the personals.

Soon it was discovered the woman had simply been overcome by her responsibilities and had moved to Florida where she intended to start over. She was alive and well and we were relieved. Our personals could survive that blow, but they could not survive a *Casco Bay* ad that read "Well-built young man seeks adventuresome couple for fun and games."

Display advertising plummeted. This was due partly to the fact that the people now asked to sell for *Maine Times* had only contempt for the paper and partly to the fact that customers who had been visited regularly by our staff were now being serviced only by telephone. Advertisers outside of Portland were neglected and Portland advertisers who did not already advertise in *Casco Bay Weekly* were told that paper was a better buy than *Maine Times*. Soon editions that would have carried twenty pages of advertising were carrying only ten.

Newsstand sales, now totally neglected, also dropped. And, since 1 percent of those who bought at the newsstand subscribed, subscriptions also began to fall off. Dodge had always argued that *Maine Times*

---

4. *Maine Times*'s personals had started spontaneously back in the 1970s, and we had debated whether to carry them at all. We decided to go ahead but to censor them, something we were careful not to do with any other advertising—except for the libelous or obviously false. We appointed Maria Parker of the ad department, who was easily offended by bad taste, as chief censor and we told the public of our decision. A few wags immediately set out to fool our resident censor, the most successful being Robert Skoglund of St. George, who was developing his persona as the Humble Farmer. He sent one in that flew right by Maria into print: "Christian gentleman seeks female companion to assume missionary position." That was as naughty as they got.

subscribers were so loyal it would be impossible to lose them; he was now proving that was untrue.

Randy Wilson left for a new job and Dodge hired Doug Rooks, the editorial page editor from the *Kennebec Journal,* to be the new editor. Depleted of staff, Doug, in a burst of energy, seemed ready to write the entire paper himself—editorials, a weekly column, and often the lead story. With smaller papers, now routinely only twenty-eight pages, the number of stories available to readers decreased again. Doug understood the old *Maine Times* and he shared our basic outlook, so the editorial thrust remained the same. The core of the old editorial staff remained as well. What ensued was not an editorial failure but a business failure.

Advertising continued to drop and soon there were only about two pages of paid advertising in each issue, a revenue loss that could add up to more than $500,000 a year. Dodge had already experienced a large loss the year of the move, partly because the move had been so badly handled—indeed, not handled at all—that it was much more expensive than it had to be, but mostly because of the plummeting advertising. Now he was facing increased losses with no hope for a turnaround.

Before the move to Portland, Anna and I had both encouraged Dodge to sell the paper. We sensed his loss of interest and we felt he should sell while it was still worth something. He rejected the idea. Now Dodge said he would sell the paper and donate the proceeds for its continuation.

Most notable among the new investors was Sherry Huber. She had been an unsuccessful candidate for governor and previous head of the state's waste management agency. Sherry's commitment to environmental issues was long and substantial, and she had the financial resources to make it work. The other principals were Sandy Marsters, the newspaper editor whom I had considered seriously for the editorship but had put off because of the uncertainties; Neil Rolde, a former U.S. Senate candidate with broad knowledge of the state; and John Buell, a resident of Mt. Desert Island with ties to College of the Atlantic.

Although I ran into Sherry once right after her investment was announced, I was surprised that she never asked me anything about the paper. We had known each other since we were teenagers and lived across the street from one another as summer residents in Kennebunkport; my wife, Eunice, had worked for her husband, Dave; she had been president of Maine Audubon; and she had been a major backer of a Maine environmental think tank. Our paths had often crossed and even though she had told me she was disappointed when I didn't endorse her when she ran for governor, I certainly felt on amiable terms with her.

I did talk with Doug Rooks during this period and asked if they had come up with any business plan. He said they hadn't. I knew that without a business plan that treated *Maine Times* as a new start-up operation, there was no hope of success, no matter how good the editorial content. It had sunk so far its ad revenues were down to about what they had been our first year of operation. Circulation revenues were only higher because the rates were higher.

The purchase figure I heard was $300,000, the amount they would have paid Dodge and he would have returned for operating expenses. Dodge's only gain was to be out from under the heavy losses.

They could easily lose $300,000 in a year and that's about what it took—a year—before *Maine Times* was on the market again. This time Doug Rooks appealed to subscribers, who sent in some $40,000, but he didn't really have a plan for what to do with the money and publication had already ceased.

That plea was indicative of two things—reader loyalty to *Maine Times* and Doug's being naive about the financial end of the operation.

Suddenly, out of nowhere, Chris Hutchins stepped in. Chris was the son of Curtis Hutchins, the founder of the Dead River Company and one of the real movers and shakers in Maine in the 1960s and '70s when only a few corporate titans exerted tremendous control. An article we did on the five most influential people in Maine during the '70s included Curtis Hutchins.

But Curtis did not turn Dead River—which had already begun diversification from its land holdings into oil delivery—over to his children. Instead, he put in charge Andy Nixon, who had come to Maine in the '60s as an aide to Democratic Governor Ken Curtis.

I had met Chris Hutchins in the early '70s when I was doing a story on a Dead River development near Sugarloaf Mountain but had not had any contact with him since. He had been receiving income from his holdings in Dead River and had started a business of his own, which proved to be very successful; he was rumored to have plenty of money to invest in *Maine Times*.

Even though Sherry Huber and her group had ceased publication, once Chris Hutchins came into the picture they tried to recapture some of their investment and the negotiations turned testy. Apparently the key bone of contention was the remaining subscriptions and their value. In any case, Chris Hutchins decided that instead of fulfilling the unexpired subscriptions, he would offer everyone a new subscription at a reduced rate and drop all subscribers who did not take the offer.

By this time, subscriptions had dropped to about 5,000, half the level they had maintained for more than thirty years. Only half chose to take the new offer; the other half, who considered they still had valid, paid-up subscriptions, went away mad.

Chris Hutchins did return the money Doug had raised from subscribers, telling Doug he was a wealthy man and couldn't expect the subscribers to subsidize him. He also moved the entire operation to Brewer from Augusta, where it had relocated after the first sale. Hutchins lived in Bangor and later moved the paper there. He took the title of editor even though Doug continued to run the editorial end of the paper.

When the dust cleared, *Maine Times* had only 2,500 subscribers and newsstand sales of about 1,000, lower than even our first week of publication thirty years before. Advertising was still about two pages a week, down from twenty, and Hutchins decided to drop all classified advertising, the most profitable sector.

With new staff and new direction, advertising began to pick up but circulation remained slow. The new ownership clearly did not recognize how difficult it is to get new subscribers, and to have cut off half the existing subscribers and left them angry at the paper made the job even more difficult. *Maine Times* was not only starting over; it was starting over with self-imposed handicaps.

Not unexpectedly under the circumstances, *Maine Times* began to lose its sense of mission. Once again, selection of stories seemed to depend on the interests of the writers and no one knew how to develop and stick with an issue. While there were some stories that fulfilled the old function of representing viewpoints that had no other outlets, the stories became more and more Sunday features, about dog sled racing or small press publishers or other interesting activities taking place in Maine, while giving no coherent coverage to important trends. Without *Maine Times* to offer such coverage, no one was there to offer it.

The only hope was to reinvent *Maine Times* from scratch, possibly using the Internet for distribution, and coming up with a new business plan and a new editorial mission.

But there was no one to look at reinventing *Maine Times*. Jay Davis came back as editor and the direction was enough the same so that die-hard subscribers held on. Why Chris Hutchins, who was clearly conservative, was so willing to pay good money for the name of the premier liberal publication in the state always baffled me, but in all its iterations, he never turned the editorial content conservative, only soft and lifestyle oriented.

Hutchins also articulated no coherent business plan, according to those still in touch with me, and the paper continued to hemorrhage money until Hutchins finally closed it down, only to revive it several years later as a slick, lifestyle publication in competition with *Down East*. The slick *Maine Times* hired a high-powered staff and went out of business in six months.[5]

During its short life, the new publication was so far from what we had intended that if anyone asked me whatever happened to *Maine Times*, I told them it no longer existed and left it at that.

---

5. In the meantime, *Casco Bay Weekly* had continued to lose money as well. Dodge gave it to his ex-wife to run, but she could not save it and it, too, went out of business as an alternative weekly.

Part 4

I, FOR ONE, AM NOT DISPOSED to blame the politicians and the businessmen. They govern the nation, it is true, but they do it in a rather absent-minded fashion. Those revolutionists who see the misery of the country as a deliberate and fiendish plot overestimate the bad will, the intelligence and the singleness of purpose in the ruling classes. Business and political leaders don't mean badly; the trouble with them is that most of the time they don't mean anything. They picture themselves as very "practical," which in practice amounts to saying that nothing makes them feel so spiritually homeless as the discussion of values and an invitation to examine first principles. Ideas, most of the time, cause them genuine distress, and are as disconcerting as an idle office boy, or a squeaky telephone.

—Walter Lippmann, A *Preface to Politics*, 1913

THE PROBLEM IS ONE for which public remedies are most likely to be found by choosing the more obvious issues, and tackling them experimentally in various communities. The commissions of study which will no doubt be set up are likely to be more productive if they can study the effects of practical experiments.

—Walter Lippmann, "Today and Tomorrow" column September 7, 1954

Sixteen

Ask Me for My Brain and I'll Give You My Body and Soul

My father's death at the age of sixty-two from a stroke spurred my decision to retire early and by the time I turned fifty, I had left *Maine Times* to garden by the sea at our new home in Georgetown and to write novels. However, I could not give up my desire to participate in public policy and I needed a new way to do it. I chose non-profits.

I thought about running for the state senate but once I seriously considered what would be entailed if I should win, I dropped the idea. I was not prepared for the long hours spent on the irrelevant, on the hearings which were too often inflated by long speeches from the special pleaders or the uninformed, the constant compromising so crucial to legislative effectiveness.

Another option was the executive branch. Even if anyone would have appointed me, I was not deeply interested in a position with a particular department. My range of interests is broad and I am consumed by how problems interlock. I needed a different venue to express my public policy ideas.

So when I retired as editor in 1986, I tested a new realm.

My first foray was to join the board of the Maine Civil Liberties Union. It was an organization with which I had total affinity, believing as I do that the real genius of the U.S. Constitution is the protection of the minority from unfettered majority rule. Coincidentally the MCLU had been founded in 1968, the same year as *Maine Times,* and by our attorney Louis Scolnik. Over the years, its causes had often shown up on the pages of *Maine Times,* a natural confluence of interests.

After some rocky years, the MCLU was being run by Jean Sampson, an exceptional woman whose wisdom I always appreciated. I had met her during the Coffin campaign and followed her efforts trying to reform the state university system and to find ways to place women back in the labor force after they had raised their children to school age.

The state board was committed and sophisticated. At the time, we had to deal with the backlash from supporting the right of Nazi sympathizers to march in Skokie, Illinois. The American Civil Liberties Union's position that the right of free speech extended to those whose ideas we found abhorrent, while at the core of the organization's mission, had cost members. Defending the free speech rights of Nazis was too much for some.

The big issue in Maine turned out to be censorship. First, a high-school library had banned a book about Vietnam, *356 Days*, and a student had sought to have it restored. With the help of the MCLU, he succeeded. Shortly after that, the Christian right sought to pass a statewide ban on pornography, with all of the vagaries that entailed. We led the opposition in a statewide referendum and won, and, of course, were labeled as supporting pornography.

The MCLU, by its very nature, was doomed to be misunderstood by much of the public, including the President, a summer resident, who talked with scorn about "card-carrying members" of the American Civil Liberties Union.

When we opposed random searches of canoists on the Saco River, the vituperative criticism from the *Bangor Daily News* was typical of the know-nothing approach that purposely presented us as only interested in making life easier for criminals.

In an editorial, they wrote:

"The Saco River searches were devised as the only effective method of cutting down on the rowdy, drunken, pot-puffing antics of the lowlife who unfortunately comprise a rather inescapable fraction of the vacationers who course the popular river . . . . It is the rights of this wretched group that the civil liberties contingent, with its offended dignity and phobic apprehension of creeping authoritarianism, now rushes to serve."

Drunks on the river had been a problem, and it would have been easy enough to arrest those who showed signs of drunkenness, just as it is with drunk automobile drivers. The courts have been quite clear that massive searches without probable cause are acceptable only when the threat to society is great, such as when the police are warned someone is driving into the city with a massive bomb in his car and they search all cars as a precaution. A drunk in a canoe did not constitute such a threat, a consideration that was part of our decision-making process. The tone of the Bangor editorial implied that some lowlifes are not entitled to constitutional protections, disregarding that what can happen to a lowlife can happen to an upstanding citizen, and that normal, law-abiding citizens have a right to go about their business without being stopped and searched for no proximate cause.

The judge who heard the case, Donald Alexander, adroitly stated the principle:

"If the search here can be justified, then a stop and search of every car crossing the Kittery Bridge [the major southern entry to Maine] could also be justified on the hope . . . that a few violations of liquor importation laws and perhaps some occasional contraband substances may be found.... Certainly such would be efficient and expedient...the rule of law remains that in the United States more than a balancing test of expediency is needed to invade one's house, detain one's person, or even search one's canoe."

Of course, the civil liberties union spends its time defending the unpopular. The popular is almost never the victim of government overzealousness. The irony, not lost on board members, is that those who oppose us often end up coming to us for help when they are the victims of the majority.

In April of 1988 alone, the MCLU was asked to look into the following situations:

• Insurance companies classified homosexuals as a distinct and separate group for coverage purposes.

• Although it had no policy regarding teacher/student relationships, the University of Maine at Presque Isle threatened a professor when it was found she was having a lesbian relationship with an older, nontraditional student. The relationship had existed before the woman became a student.

• A citizen complained that the issue of church and state was raised by the town's using tax money to plow a church parking lot and allowing the church to use town property.

• Two complaints raised the issue of whether a state law that allowed women but not men to petition the court for paternity tests denied men the ability to gain custody of a child born out of wedlock.

One of my favorite cases, and one I wrote about in the newspaper, involved our old attorney, Louis Scolnik, who, after some opposition because of his civil liberties connections, had been named to the Maine Supreme Court. The case had been decided while I was still editing the paper and before I joined the MCLU.

The defendant, Hartley Armen, had been trying to get a meeting with then-Representative Olympia Snowe to express his disagreement with her position on Nicaragua. Her staff kept putting him off. After visiting her Presque Isle office and speaking from there with her Washington office, he still received no satisfaction, so he announced that he was going to sit in as a protest of the congresswoman's "persistent refusal" to meet with him or anyone else in his group—whereupon, he was immediately arrested for criminal trespass.

The majority of the Maine Supreme Court said Armen had had his say and his threatened sit-in was disruptive. Judge Scolnik, in lone dissent, said Armen's sit-in was protected by free speech but he also cut to the heart of the matter, writing: "Elected representatives and their employees in the field must expect and tolerate dissident expression." He went on to say that Congresswoman Snowe was elected to represent all the citizens of her district, not just those who voted for her and agreed with her. The image of elected officials having those who disagree with them arrested was not as compelling to the general public as it was to me.

I also served on the national board for a short period, an unforgettable experience. Meetings were held in New York City and the board consisted of some eighty individuals, all of whom were deeply committed and some of whom were downright doctrinaire. A young black firebrand was always accusing everyone else of being racist, a sure way in such company to stifle dissent even among chronic dissenters.

The board president and moderator was Norman Dorsen, the most skilled meeting chair I have ever witnessed.[1] He managed to keep the eighty civil libertarians civil with one another and to further the dis-

---

1. I learned some years later that Dorsen had been a summer intern in my father's law office.

cussion to a point of resolution even when board members were ready to argue for hours over a minor distinction. We not only debated endlessly how many angels could dance on the head of a pin, but argued over what their ethnic and sexual distribution should be.

Even at its best and most effective, the civil liberties union is by definition a reactive organization. It spends its time keeping bad things from happening or at its most proactive, trying to overturn bad laws or regulations that were implemented in times of public hysteria.

Several years later, in 1994, when I joined the board of the Portland Museum of Art, I could not have linked up with a more different group of people and a more different culture.

Art is to me a vital part of everyday life. I am interested by the art, good or bad, in people's homes; I regularly visit galleries; I notice how avant garde art filters into everyday design. When I go on vacations, my itinerary is art museums and good restaurants. I have visited most of the great museums in the Western world and have come to recognize that the history of art is the history of culture. The Portland Museum of Art is clearly Maine's premier art institution, and with a new building recently constructed, it was in search of a more well-defined mission. The question for me was how to redefine the provincial museum so that it was merely provincial in location, not in viewpoint. Counterintuitively, I thought one way to make the museum important, not only locally but nationally, was to make it the premier showplace for Maine's own artistic traditions.

In 1987 Tom Crotty, a fine painter and gallery owner who was intensely involved in Maine art, had called together an ad hoc group to look at the role of the museum and had asked me to attend. Tom had long recognized that no matter what we wrote about art in *Maine Times*—and he often disagreed with it—we were committed to art in Maine as few other organizations were.

Representatives of the museum attended as well, and although they were unwilling to admit the museum was a socially exclusive organization, they would at least allow there was a public perception that it was, and that this perception needed remedy. There was a good deal of discussion about how specific and dominant the Maine focus of the museum should be and DeWitt Hardy, an artist who had also curated at the Ogunquit Museum of Art, raised the issue of putting Maine art in historical perspective. This is where such discussions had led in other venues, and it dovetailed with my own thoughts about art as cultural history.

That and several other concepts I was to support later came up at that meeting. Peter Sheldon, who was on the museum's collection committee, noted that the museum did not have a clear collections policy. The group generally agreed there should be more highly curated small exhibits related to current events in Maine and that the Portland museum should become the focal point for all Maine collections. The point was not to limit the focus to Maine but to use the strength of the Maine art tradition to reflect broader concepts.

Nothing concrete ever came of that meeting but when I was to join the board seven years later, those ideas were still in the back of my head. In the spring of 1994, Dan O'Leary had just been hired as the new director and the museum was ripe for charting a new course. I immediately hit it off with O'Leary and found him both easy to talk with and receptive to my ideas. On the other hand, he was a consummate diplomat and never, to my knowledge, offended the board, undoubtedly an element in his success. The three years I spent on the board were to become an exercise in frustration but an important learning experience.

When I was being solicited for the board, members told me they were interested in my ideas and not just my financial contributions. But I was to learn almost immediately that this board was all about raising money. Any discussion of the role of the museum was to be in the vaguest mission-statement type terms.

The very composition of the board created a dilemma. Since fewer than six of the thirty trustees were seriously interested in art and art museums as specific institutions, to have solicited their participation in operational matters would have been to open the door to uninformed second-guessing. It was my impression that the curatorial staff did not trust the art-related judgment of the board and therefore wanted to keep the board from active participation. Informing the board would have invited meddling. So the circle was complete: The board was uninformed and so could not be brought into policy matters. If the board learned more about operations, it might insist on making decisions beyond its competence. I was to witness similar situations on other boards and to conclude that the dilemma is endemic to non-profits governed by the marginally informed.

I should have been tipped off by a retreat held in early December of 1995 at the Portland Country Club. The guru-in-chief and facilitator at that meeting was a corporate management expert—the president of the board was an expert in "governance"—who told us it was the responsibility of the board to hire and fire the executive director and otherwise stay out of the operation of the institution. This was a view of a board's role that was then gaining preeminence in corporate America and that would soon lead to catastrophe, but in raising the objection that board members should be more involved, I not only ended up a minority of one, at least in terms of speaking out, I was clearly going against the grain. I had that queasy feeling I was in the wrong place at the wrong time, the guest who was mistakenly invited to join the club where everyone else was comfortable with the unwritten rules.

Just how out-of-step I was with the rest of the board was illustrated by an incident that took place a few years later at a committee meeting. I had recently viewed a photography show at the museum in which there was a picture of two young women and a young man, all naked. The women were injecting a drug in their veins, and the man was sitting between them with an erection. I was talking about it with fellow board member Jim Moody, one of the state's leading corporate executives, and I suggested that we should have a policy about how we displayed such pieces and how we might react to complaints about them. In the case of the photograph, it was hung in a cul de sac with a guard at the entryway. I suggested that the guard could be instructed to say to any adult coming in with children that the adult look at the pictures first and then decide if they were appropriate for the children.

Without discussing the merits of what I was saying—whether or not, for instance, this was unacceptable censorship—Moody said that was not a concern of the board.

I replied that I thought the board acted *in loco parentis* and was expected to exercise such oversight on behalf of the public. I then asked him what he would do if a reporter called him as a board member and said he had been contacted by a woman who had attended the museum with her children and claimed her children had been exposed to pornography. Moody replied that he would say the reporter should talk to the director of the museum, since he didn't know anything about it.

Of course, most board members would not have known anything about it. I suspect they seldom attended the shows except for the opening receptions. But as a journalist, I was shocked that Moody thought he could so easily avoid what I considered one of his roles as a trustee. I admit the problem was thorny and I did not have an easy answer, but I also thought it was precisely the kind of question the board should consider.

Typically, I inundated Dan O'Leary and other board members with my suggestions. I had opinions about the upgrading of the museum café, the collections policy, possible exhibitions, linking with other museums, and the refurbishing of the small library. The curators were all new to Maine. I felt they did not have broad knowledge of the recent history of Maine art and that I could offer some of the insights I had developed in covering the Maine art scene, first as a reviewer and then as an editor, for the past thirty years.

Underlying all of my suggestions was a consistent theme—art should be part of the ordinary life of interested Maine citizens and the museum should be the focal point of all Maine art. Part of fulfilling that task was to make the museum attractive to visit, on every level.

I wanted the museum library to be a gathering place, much like the Phillips Gallery in Washington, where in 1959 I had seen people adopt it as their own art-lined living room. Or like the Yale Art Library, where I had chosen to study because of the diversion of bound volumes of *Life* magazine. I suggested that this could be a meeting place with regular programs where interested people would gather, before going home, to discuss pertinent topics with someone well-informed on the subject at hand. The library was significantly upgraded, at least for a while, but the idea of the museum as a meeting place never received much support. To other board members, it was a place you visited once every few months to see an exhibition, not a place you habituated.

My ideas for exhibits combined my interest in art as a cultural reflection with my own experiences. Purposely selecting a topic that had been resolved so that I could not be accused of promoting a particular political agenda, I suggested that at the time of the state referendum against pornography, the museum could have mounted a small exhibition on censored art, using reproductions. I thought such an exhibit would inevitably demonstrate that the desire to censor depends entirely on the taste and standards of the period in which the censors are living. What is considered sacrilegious or pornographic can soon become so commonplace it loses its power to outrage. I thought such an exhibit at a time when the issue was in the public mind would be educational as well as interesting.

Another of my ideas was an exhibit on Ben Shahn, who had a major Maine connection because he had taught at the Skowhegan School of Painting and Sculpture where his wife, Bernarda, still went every summer. His daughter, Abby, had become one of the best and best-known painters in the state, as well.

What particularly interested me about a Shahn exhibit was the tension between art and content. When I was in college, I had written a paper on Shahn's murals at the U.S. Dept. of Health and Welfare in Washington, which contained some of his most famous images. Largely because Shahn was considered left-wing rather than because of the content of the paintings, the government had decided in the 1950s to cover the murals with large curtains that would be drawn back only on request. Shahn had made his reputation on such paintings as those of Sacco and Vanzetti, when the trial and execution of the two anarchists accused of murder had split the nation. Shahn's paintings of the defendants, the judge, and the president of Harvard, had been devastating, and even though Shahn had moved more toward abstract work as he grew older, the political content of his work was still important.

I had once shown some of my son's friends, then high-schoolers who knew nothing about either art or history, the Sacco and Vanzetti paintings and they had immediately recognized the gist of the message even though they did not know who any of the principals were. They then asked me to tell them about the case, so for them the artistic rendition came first and piqued their interest in the history surrounding the paintings.

I thought a Shahn show, because it would be so accessible, would

Ask Me For My Brain and I'll Give You My Body and Soul

offer an opportunity to examine the nexus between art and politics. My own prejudice was that Shahn, once extremely popular and esteemed by critics, had been unfairly dismissed as an artist because of the political content of his early work. This coincided with my belief that Robert Penn Warren's fine novel, *All the King's Men*, was often dismissed as being mere political history. Today, in both painting and literature, we freely mix the two and see political allusions as a legitimate layer of art.

No one at the museum shared my enthusiasm for a Shahn show enough to discuss it further although a major retrospective, which I did not see, was later done at the Jewish Museum in New York. I am sure that the Portland staff looked askance at a trustee even venturing to offer an opinion on possible exhibits. Of course, it could have been a bad idea. A few years previously, the president of the board had instigated a show on the art of useful objects, ranging from toasters to roadsters, and while I thought it interesting, it had flopped with the public.

I also asked to be allowed to sit in on the meetings of the Collections Committee, headed by Charlton Ames who later became president of the board and was one of the few members who had a genuine interest in art. Some of the ideas I expressed he later picked up in his own manner with his own modifications. A few were so obvious as to remove any pride of authorship. For instance, I suggested that the museum identify what it wanted, learn if anyone in Maine or connected to Maine (lots of summer residents) owned pertinent works, and then cultivate those people by asking them for loans with the hope they would eventually donate some of the desired works to the museum. To carry out such a plan, the museum would need a clear list of priorities for its collection. This concept was later included in one of Ames's recommendations, but whether it was ever acted on I don't know.

The debate over a collections policy proved I had not lost my counterproductive, undiplomatic characteristics and put me into conflict with a new curator, Kenneth Wayne, Ph.D. Wayne had been hired because in giving her major Impressionist works to the museum, Joan Payson Whitney had stipulated a special curator. The most famous painting in the collection, Vincent Van Gogh's *Irises*, had not come to the Portland museum but had been auctioned for the benefit of the family and came in at about $64 million, at the time the highest price ever paid for a painting at auction.

Wayne preferred the honorific of Doctor in respect to his recently received Ph.D. from Stanford (1994). I must admit that anyone who uses the title Doctor and is not a medical doctor causes me to twitch.

Wayne had studied and worked on the West Coast and was given the task of drafting the collections policy. His suggestions were a grab-bag of the nineteenth and twentieth centuries, including a good deal of Dada and Surrealism. My feeling about many of the Dada icons was that their cleverness was everything and once you had seen them, you had no need to see them again, whether a fur-lined shaving cup or the Mona Lisa with a mustache. The objects were just as meaningful in a book as in a museum because they had no visual depth. The clever idea was the whole point. I felt the list he had compiled showed no perspective on creating a sense of uniqueness for the Portland Museum of Art.

The collections policy was made more difficult by the fact that the acquisition budget was so low, less than $20,000 a year, that during my tenure on the board two major works, a Marguerite Zorach painting and a Louise Nevelson sculpture, had both been purchased by subscription. Other major works were usually given to the museum by a benefactor.

Doctor Wayne's first pitch for acquisition was for a Dali lobster telephone. Salvador Dali had created ten of the telephones, old circular-dial, black phones with the receiver a red plastic, life-sized lobster.

In his memo citing the relevance to the Portland Museum's collection, Wayne wrote:

"After Picasso, Dali is probably the best-known artist among the general public. This acquisition would give us our first major Surrealist work. The lobster imagery ties it to Maine and would, hopefully, help stir up enthusiasm to purchase it. The lobster makes it an object with special resonance for us. Our visitors would find the Lobster Telephone to be especially enchanting."

The price was $145,000.

The Collections Committee had told him that while this was not a priority for them, if he felt he could raise the money for the purchase, he should go ahead and do so. The idea was quickly and diplomatically dropped. However, I was unable to let go.

At the first board meeting after I had heard of the suggestion, I was discussing it over a sandwich with another board member, when Wayne walked by and overheard me. He said nothing was going to happen because he didn't think he could raise the money. I replied that it was a bad idea anyway and that his suggesting it showed how out of touch he was with the possible mission of the museum.

I chose not to serve the automatic second term on the museum board and it was a good lesson to me: just because I cared about an institution and thought it had great potential didn't mean I could have any meaningful impact on it. Nor would it ever be easy to make board members agree that their role was not just to support an organization but to broaden the range and impact of that organization. I could not understand that many people join boards because they are satisfied with the status quo and feel no compulsion to change anything.

At the same time I was experiencing such frustration on the museum board, I was involved with another organization, Eco/Eco, whose title was meant to reflect a concern with both the economy and the environment (ecology). The idea, initiated by Ed Kaelber of College of the Atlantic, who had also been instrumental in my setting up the Maine Public Policy Scholars, was to bring together business people, government officials, and environmentalists to discuss problems of common interest in a non-confrontational manner. The group was not asked to review a solution to a stated problem. Instead, it was asked to analyze the problem, utilizing its collective experience to help others in the group to understand it. Although many of the participants represented a special interest, they were asked to leave their advocacy instincts at the door and not argue from any institutional perspective. Thus, a person from the Chamber of Commerce or from Audubon was to put aside whatever position his or her organization might have on a particular issue and look at it freshly.

Eco/Eco held some large meetings, one of which was moderated by Angus King before he ran for governor, but its most effective method was relatively small dinners, usually twenty to thirty people. This may have also reflected the preference of Ted Koffman who had taken over operation of the organization and was later to name me co-chair. I am not sure there was another co-chair.

Ted was then at College of the Atlantic and was permitted by them to spend considerable time with Eco/Eco, which he developed into the closest thing Maine had to an effective, non-partisan think tank. Ted has since become a state legislator and quickly emerged as one of the most astute voices in Augusta, a judgment I may be prejudiced in making, because over the years we worked together we also became good personal friends.

As a group, the Eco/Eco participants came to realize that we all shared basic values or we would not have been there in the room together. We all cared about the future of Maine. We all felt an obligation to serve the state. And we all believed in the state's role to serve the people. The differences came in our experiences and perceptions. I learned that at the corporate level, there had been a tremendous change in the three decades since we had started *Maine Times*. Many of the values and concepts that earlier executives had either rejected or simply not considered in their actions were now commonly accepted, especially by middle management and the younger, upcoming executives. Most notably, environmental concerns were now accepted as the norm. While the pendulum would swing toward the past with the administration of George W. Bush, I continue to believe than in a state like Maine, the environmental ethic is so imbedded that we will never abandon the gains of the last four decades. At Eco/Eco, no one was arguing for a laissez-faire policy. We could all agree on what needed to be done and even what the priorities were. (We self-filtered the hard-liners who stood fast on the non-existence of global warming. Nor did we have anyone who advocated creationism.) The discussion turned instead to how to do what remained to be done most effectively and focused on such issues as who should pay for environmental cleanup. Should it be only the industry that created the pollution or should it be the taxpayers who needed protection from the consequences of the pollution? And when it was public demand that created the problem in the first place, should the purchase price of a product or service include the cost of future cleanup?

Our sessions were often revealing in an unexpected way. I recall a presentation by Kevin Gildart from Bath Iron Works when he explained how difficult it was to get shipbuilders to obey some of the new safety regulations, such as wearing masks while painting, when they had done without for years and were convinced they had not been physically damaged.

One concept most of us came to share was that we had to get people to take more individual responsibility for their own polluting habits, from wasting electricity to driving gas-guzzling automobiles. If industry should be responsible for removing pollution from its processes, then individuals should do the same. The easiest part of controlling industrial pollution, especially air pollution, had been accomplished, and cleaning up the remaining pollution would be expensive. Put simply, cleaning up the last 10 percent would be more expensive than had been cleaning up the first 90 percent. On a cost/benefit scale, improving consumer habits was more effective.

Thus, in 1993 when the state instituted CarTest, we all agreed it was a good idea. Under the program, every automobile would be tested for emission controls, at a cost of $12 every two years, in a sophisticated special station. We thought this was instructive for individuals and a significant step in their taking responsibility.

Unfortunately, the public thought otherwise and the program was extremely unpopular, quickly becoming a hot political issue. Angus King, then running for governor, opposed it and we howled to ourselves. In retrospect, if Angus has supported CarTest, he probably would have lost, but he won and the program was disbanded. So much for our political acumen.

The big breakthrough for Eco/Eco came in 1997 when we decided to hold a statewide conference on sprawl, just then beginning to emerge as a significant issue and very much on the agenda of Angus King's thoughtful director of the State Planning Office, Evan Richert.

The conference, held at College of the Atlantic in Bar Harbor and organized by Ted Koffman, took a tentative approach, calling itself "The Paradox of Sprawl." The name was an effort to project neutrality on the issue even though we had a strong belief that this was an imminent and important problem.[2] The conference made clear that

2. An earlier environmental priorities project, partially funded by the federal EPA and including several Eco/Eco participants, had identified Maine's top emerging problems. At the

the effects of sprawl were stimulating widespread concern, even though many of the people bothered by it did not fully understand it as sprawl and even fewer understood its causes. People simply saw the Maine landscape being eaten up by unattractive development.

There were a few who insisted sprawl was a sign of growth and therefore good, that the people in Southern Maine might not like it but those in Northern Maine did. This viewpoint was fostered by an incredible provincialism, a belief that what happened elsewhere could never happen in a particular part of Maine, and a total obtuseness to what was actually happening. Downtown stores and services were being abandoned or migrating to strip and mall developments on the outskirts of towns, a process that was not only destroying traditional communities but was also costing taxpayers lots of money. It was this second focus, the economic impact, that we eventually took.

At the conference, participants were given considerable information about what was going on in Oregon and Maryland, the states leading the anti-sprawl movement, but both of them employed much stronger government intervention than was felt possible in Maine.[3]

Although there was broad support for decisive action among the participants at the Bar Harbor conference, the dissenters there—those who denied there was any problem—could not be overlooked. Unless we convinced them and those who shared a similar viewpoint, we would be doomed in our efforts. Subsequent events have proved that while there is general public agreement that sprawl is a bad thing, once solutions are proposed, such as greater density in housing, effective opposition emerges.

The next step following the conference fit with the procedures of Eco/Eco which were not to propose solutions prematurely but to let the solutions evolve from an understanding of the problem. Because of the governor's approach, the problem would be defined in econom-

head of the list was global warming, but with it came the understanding that there was little the state could do by itself. Sprawl ranked in the top echelon of problems.
3. The direction Maine would follow was set by Governor King, who said the state must act before it is too late, but the mechanism would not be heavily legislative. Instead, it would be market driven. However, he stated, "The market isn't working...because of all the hidden incentives that aren't being taken care of." Buttressing the governor's position, State Planning Office Director Evan Richert noted that "many state policies promote sprawl," and cited changing those incentives as a first order of business.

ic rather than aesthetic terms, even though the public's sense that the beauty of Maine was being destroyed in the process was a powerful underlying motivation. It was, however, a factor that did not need reinforcement.

To start building a grass roots constituency for action, Ted Koffman and Evan Richert, under the sponsorship of Eco/Eco, an independent, government-free organization, took the discussion on the road, holding public forums the length and breadth of the state. Such forums attract those already interested in the issue, and few people showed up who didn't agree sprawl was a problem. On the other hand, the meetings received good local publicity, bringing the issue to the forefront in areas where it had not been discussed, and elucidating issues that would not have been raised otherwise. This was especially true in the parallel meetings Koffman and Richert held with local officials.

I sat in on one meeting where the director of the local public works department explained why the spread of residential housing to what was previously farmland was so expensive. Before such residential development, the roads led only to farms and, after snowstorms, had not had to be plowed until later in the day, but once residences were built, people expected the roads to be plowed in time for them to go to work so everything had to be open by 7:00 or 8:00 A.M., creating a demand for more plow trucks and more drivers. This expense was never factored into the cost of the new residential development.

Richert was also able to introduce the audiences to information his department had collected in an earlier pamphlet called *The Cost of Sprawl*. The pamphlet was replete with pertinent facts but as is always the case, for a concept to really move forward, there must be at least one example that is emblematic, resonates with the public, and is simple enough so it gets repeated and therefore spreads to those who have never seen the statement in its original context. The data that became the symbolic centerpiece for discussion was that Maine had spent $350 million to build redundant schools during the past twenty-five years, due to population relocation, while student population had actually decreased by 27,000. The problem was partially met by the governor's recommendation, subsequently implemented, that state funding be made available for school renovation as well as new schools, which were almost invariably located outside the core community.

The interest Eco/Eco and Planning Office efforts created dovetailed with the legislature's creation of a task force that recommended more state money for the so-called service center communities, those that provided key services such as hospitals, schools, and courts that drew people from outlying areas. The service providers themselves did not produce tax revenue. The task force also agreed with the governor's proposal to change school construction financing and supported more funding for downtowns. In unison with the governor, it supported efforts to keep state office buildings in existing downtowns.

While legislative and executive groups were stepping right into concrete proposals, the Eco/Eco Civic Forum, which had become the SmartGrowth Forum, began monthly meetings in Augusta to discuss related issues and to uncover the hidden incentives the governor had referred to at Bar Harbor. The forum was open to anyone interested and consisted of an array of individuals ranging from developers to environmentalists as well as representatives of concerned state departments. The housing developers said they were willing to build anywhere and in any manner, depending on what the public wanted and what state regulations allowed. They did not have a particular interest in preserving the status quo—which was driven largely by the two-acre minimum lot size, meant to reduce density. The homebuilders pointed out that because federal mortgage underwriting programs placed a limit on the cost of land for new housing, such loans could not be obtained to build in existing communities where prices for large lots were too high, even where they were still available. Therefore, the combination of mortgage policies and minimum lot sizes made building in the countryside, often converting farmland, inevitable.

The Eco/Eco discussions revealed a range of such factors causing sprawl. For instance, it had been policy that when a person built outside the current power system and had to be added on, everyone using the system paid equally. Subsequently, this policy was changed, assessing the new connector for part of the added cost and theoretically acting as a disincentive to such add-ons.

While there was consensus among the Eco/Eco group that traditional neighborhoods with their smaller lot sizes and mixed uses, more conducive to pedestrian traffic, were desirable, there was concern whether enough people wanted to live in such neighborhoods to make their building economically feasible.

As the Eco/Eco discussions were taking place, the planning office published its study on housing markets. It disclosed that a third of potential home buyers would prefer to live in traditional neighborhoods but such housing was unavailable. Planning Director Richert launched a campaign to get such a development, known as the Great American Neighborhood, built as a model.

A number of people involved with the Eco/Eco discussions became involved in what was to be the landmark project, called Dunstan Corners, located in the fast-growing Portland suburb of Scarborough. Representatives from Scarborough had appeared at our Augusta meetings to tell us how they were being inundated with the demand for new residential development because of their proximity to Portland, but that the average new home caused a $12,000-a-year tax deficit, mainly because of associated school costs.

With strong backing from the State Planning Office and the determination of some thoughtful developers, Dunstan Corners proposed much greater density than the current zoning of two-acre lots would have allowed. It also called for mixed housing—condos and one-bedroom apartments as well as full family houses—with commercial development to fill the needs of the immediate neighborhood and thus reduce traffic in and out. The alternative design would have produced dramatically more tax revenue without a significant increase in the number of school students, thus ameliorating the problem the town had faced previously with new residential development and which had led many people to oppose such development altogether. For opponents of the project, the overwhelming negative was traffic. The greater the density, the greater the traffic on an already congested road system. Dunstan Corners was soundly rejected in voter referendum in 2003.

But the idea of such high-density, mixed-use developments persisted and others have been planned. Only after they are built will anyone know if a successful model can reduce the opposition that density itself has come to foster.

Eco/Eco functioned not only as an incubator for ideas and a review forum to identify flaws in proposals and to make modifications to meet legitimate objections, it also became a significant lobbying group, made more effective, I like to think, because it was not allied with any special interest. Since we had reached our decisions through consensus from a broad and knowledgeable group, we understood the issues, even those we had not necessarily developed ourselves. Several of the ideas had to go through the legislature.

Spearheaded by Adrian Wadsworth, a dairy farmer from Turner who could see the larger issues and had a long-term commitment to preserving agriculture, we supported reducing the penalties of withdrawing land from farmland preservation in the hope this would encourage more farmers to seek the tax break and guarantee their land remained in farming. The measure passed the legislature.

We also supported a proposal by Transportation Commissioner John Melrose to protect Maine's arterial roads from being reduced to congested connectors. An arterial is a road that supports through traffic at speeds of 50 mph. Because there was no control over the number of curb cuts (driveways) that could access the road, drivers entering and exiting the arterial were forcing down the allowable speed. When speeds were reduced to connector road standards, about 25 mph, there was a demand to build new arterials to replace the old ones. Commissioner Melrose argued that aside from the issue of using up land and causing new sprawl, the state could no longer afford to build parallel roads.

Melrose was one of Governor King's best appointments, a man with a new vision for a department that had been trapped in the myth that the only form of viable transportation was the automobile, who could actually get his new ideas to filter down through the ranks of his department. Melrose was friendly to an organization like Eco/Eco, despite its lack of official standing, and made presentations himself. Several members of his staff were regular and effective participants in the long-term discussions of the SmartGrowth Forum. It was because of people like Melrose who understood the ideas behind the positions Eco/Eco was taking that the organization was able to transmit those ideas into concrete action.

We operated in almost the opposite manner as the legislative process. The legislature tends to pinpoint a single manifestation of a problem and then seek a way to remove the manifestation without necessarily dealing with the underlying cause. We identified a problem, tried to understand why the problem had occurred—often it was the unintended consequence of previous, well-meaning legislation—and tried to remove the underlying cause. We searched for the incentives, both hidden and overt, both negative and positive that caused a chain of events leading to the unacceptable manifestation. Our analysis sometimes made legislation unnecessary because changing incentives accomplished the goal.

Our method was not widely replicated. Many bills come from constituents who are driven by sincere emotion but have never tested their ideas in the arena of open debate, and lawmakers routinely introduce bills to placate constituents. Fortunately, most of those bills die.

More often a bill will come from a well-defined constituency where the measure at least attempts to accomplish what that constituency wants, whether it is business or environmentalists or someone else. These measures are positive for those introducing them, but have specific negative effects on those who oppose them.

Many bills are purely ideological, representing a philosophical viewpoint it is impossible to prove or disprove. Much legislation regarding education falls into this category—there is no way to prove what is proposed is going to work or not work, but it matches a particular set of beliefs. Much legislation to improve "the business climate" is similar.

If we could have introduced the Eco/Eco decision-making process into the mainstream of government, it would have been a signal victory. (In all fairness, some legislative task forces and some executive research efforts do try to follow this ground-up procedure, with varying success.)

One proposal emanating from Eco/Eco—and being sympathetically and concurrently considered both by the legislature and the executive—was the Maine Downtown Center, devoted to enhancing downtowns as a way to preserve an important Maine resource and to fight sprawl. Many elements of downtown revitalization that were proposed by the governor and legislators swirled around the concept. These included locating government offices downtown, incentives for owner-occupied apartment buildings, affordable housing, and building code reform to make it less expensive to rehabilitate historic buildings.

Our small subgroup at Eco/Eco sifted through all the ideas on the table, constructed an organizational model, and decided the backbone of the effort would be the Main Street program from the National Trust for Historic Preservation. Maine was one of only six states not to have used the program, which encourages downtowns to compete directly with malls by hiring a downtown manager whose job is to promote the interests of downtown alone and to organize downtown interests into a cooperative and cohesive action group.[4] No one else was looking out specifically for downtowns. Chambers of Commerce, which tend to be regional, need all the members they can get and cater to mall occupants as much as downtown interests. Town managers and planners are pulled in other directions as well, often in an endless quest for new tax revenue, no matter where it comes from.

I came to the Main Street program from two directions that represented a potential conflict but that turned out to be reinforcing. Before we had come up with the actual plan for the Downtown Center, I had agreed to become one of two advisers from Maine to the National Trust for Historic Preservation, and one of the first things the Northeast Regional director, Wendy Nicholas, asked me to do was bring the Main Street program to Maine.

I told her I would look at the program more carefully and only if I thought it was a good fit for Maine would I advocate for it. I did look and I did come to agree it was the best program available. My decision was influenced not only by a general approval of the program by others working on the Downtown Center concept, particularly those from the state preservation office, but also the efforts of two key downtown revitalizers from Bath, Bill King and Jayne Palmer. They had long been in the trenches in a community I knew well and had continued to follow since my days as an editor there in 1965. If they

4. The four basic points of the Main Street program are: Broad-based local organization, including not just merchants but users of downtown; restoration of historic facades; development of downtown promotions; and the attraction of new businesses that complement what exists and cumulatively increase the attractiveness of the whole. It is a self-help program, and a local community in Maine would be expected to raise from $60,000 to $120,000 per year as its share of running the program.

thought Main Street was the best alternative available—and they were very knowledgeable on the subject, having visited and studied Main Street communities, particularly in New Hampshire—it was a powerful argument in its favor.

What I learned through my National Trust involvement had more impact on what I did in Maine than my Maine experience had on the Trust. At a Trust meeting, I learned about rehabilitation codes and became an advocate for similar reform in Maine, an effort as yet unsuccessful but thanks to Ted Koffman not dead, that grew out of Eco/Eco as well.[5]

While many contributed to the Downtown Center concept, our Eco/Eco group took on the task of bringing it to reality and much of the practical implementation fell to me. The original legislative proposal called for an appropriation of $250,000 and a new position at the Department of Economic and Community Development (DECD), the state's primary economic development agency that had gone through many iterations and that I had scrutinized since the first days of *Maine Times*. It quickly became apparent that the money was going to be a lot less than $250,000 and when it became obvious there would not be enough to create a new position at DECD, the agency and its director lost interest. This was fine with me as I had always conceived of the center as a public-private alliance, located outside state government itself but receiving help from government agencies. I also believed the backbone of the funding had to come from the participating communities and they had to find it valuable enough to want to pay for it.

I persisted in getting the Downtown Center started and found strong support and creativity in Evan Richert, who called a meeting of the potentially involved state agencies to see if we could dig up operational funding. The idea was that each agency would give us a little bit from its own budget, ranging from $1,000 to $5,000, to cover the initial operating costs of an office, and it would have representation on the board. Part of the Downtown Center's mission would be to

5. Even where there are no building codes, those advocating new buildings instead of rehabilitation often cite costs based on bringing the old buildings up to new building standards. This can include such factors as the width of corridors that may have little to do with actual safety but which can drive up costs dramatically.

coordinate their efforts in the field, a job a state task force, under Jim Nimon of DECD, was trying to do but that could easily disappear with a change in administrations.

Evan called a meeting at his office and representatives from the key agencies appeared, along with me. Everyone except DECD indicated they would like to contribute but no one made an actual commitment, and I left the meeting disappointed.

I discussed the impasse with Evan, and he suggested that I see if I could get help from the governor. A few days later, I was talking with Angus—he had a summer home about a mile from where I live year-round—from whom I had never asked anything in his role as governor. I told him I needed help and when he asked what it was, I replied that I needed him to give something from his contingency fund to help start the Downtown Center, with which he was already familiar because of his own interest in revitalizing downtowns and his leadership in the anti-sprawl movement. He asked if $10,000 was enough. I said that was just fine and the conversation was over in about three minutes.

I called Evan to tell him, word quickly spread, and suddenly the other departments found the money. A three-year commitment was made by the State Planning Office, Maine State Housing Authority, Department of Transportation, Maine Historic Preservation Commission, Department of Environmental Protection, and the Finance Authority of Maine. The Department of Economic and Community Development offered no money although it probably had the most available, including Community Block Development Grant (CBDG) funds totaling $17 million, some of which could be used for downtown revitalization. The commissioner, Steve Levesque, said instead they would offer in-kind help, which never developed beyond the participation of some DECD employees.[6] Levesque became co-chair of the Center's board, along with me, and left me with the impression that his main interest was in keeping tabs on what we were doing.

We still needed an appropriation to provide services to the participating communities, and the chairs of the committee we were

6. The agency's role did gradually increase, and several years later the DECD representative to the board instigated a level of cooperation that significantly increased the center's effectiveness.

approaching were Representative John Martin and Senator Sharon Treat, both of whom I had known for years and both of whom I had had disagreements with in the past. However, both are extremely professional and overlooked any personal feelings about me.

John Martin was particularly engaging. He had been the longtime and somewhat autocratic speaker of the house when one of his key aides got in trouble over a voting scandal, the impetus for driving Martin from office. I was still at *Maine Times* and used Martin as a poster child for term limits (I have later come to realize that term limits were a bad idea). Term limits passed, he was out; he got re-elected, and he was back. Martin was and is an excellent legislator. He does his homework and he asks questions in a firm, sequential, and professional manner. You had better be prepared for Martin's questions before you appear before him at a public hearing.

With the budget crunch emerging, we feared for any appropriation, but Martin and Treat got us $100,000, to be funneled through the State Planning Office.

The Downtown Center was housed at the non-profit Maine Development Foundation (MDF). It had been around for a decade and its board was largely business people, representing banks and major corporations. As such, the foundation thrived by giving the impression of civic involvement without ever doing anything that would rock the boat. Typically, it established a set of economic indicators and then kept track of them, publishing a nice booklet each year, but there it stopped. Any comprehensive approach as to what might improve the indicators was missing.

The greatest problem I had with the Downtown Center was trying to prevent it from becoming another window-dressing organization and nothing illustrated the pitfalls, and my failure, better than our initial small grants project.

At the suggestion of Evan Richert, with whom I heartily concurred, we decided to make small grants of about $4,000 each to participating Main Street communities to allow them to jumpstart innovative local projects that would act as models to other communities in how to focus on downtown improvement.

The sort of hands-on approach I envisioned had been contained in a speech at the first downtown conference by one of the principals at

Reny's department stores, a small, locally based chain that had bet on downtowns and become the anchor for several communities. John Reny had made four points about what downtown merchants needed: Be open for business when customers want to shop, i.e., evenings and on weekends, not when shopkeepers prefer to be in the stores; reserve on-street and adjacent parking for customers, not employees; have bathrooms available; and bring in recreational food vendors such as ice cream carts.

I had met with some of the downtown managers and suggested seeking grants for such things as getting merchants to make their restrooms available to the public and using the grant money to hire someone to monitor and clean the bathrooms.[7] Another idea I floated was an electronic kiosk with a computer where anyone wanting a particular item downtown could type it in and find out who carried that item. This was before Maine supermarkets instituted a similar feature to help customers find the proper aisle for a product.

The applications contained no new ideas. Instead, we received proposals for buying banners to put on light posts, a project that was not only mundane but that would soon become a cliché. When we reviewed the proposals, I suggested that we not fund any of them but go back to the communities and help them develop better ideas. I argued that to fund such mediocre projects was to reward low expectations and to waste our money. But I was told that the towns had been informed they would receive the money no matter what they proposed and had, in fact, been told not to expend a lot of time or energy on their proposals so that to not make the grants would be a breach of faith. I later talked to the downtown managers and learned that this analysis was correct; all of them agreed they would be very upset to have to come up with new proposals.

I did lose the battle, but, I hope, not the war. I tried to convince others on the review committee that to support the mediocre was to preempt the first-rate and that by making the grants based on even distribution rather than on excellence or innovation would make us just another government agency that was more interested in satisfying defined constituencies than in getting anything meaningful accom-

7. In Europe, of course, public restrooms with attendants that one tips are commonplace.

plished. In accepting the state appropriation and in being housed at a foundation that was so dependent on government approval, the Downtown Center had taken on unwanted baggage. Merit would sometimes seem secondary to making sure each town was treated the same—except for towns represented by a powerful legislator who should be treated a little better.

It did become clear that the Downtown Center would have to move eventually from the Development Foundation, and I subsequently became involved in the foundation of a new, statewide smart-growth umbrella agency, called GrowSmart Maine and spearheaded by Alan Caron. The possibility of the Downtown Center moving there remains open.

My experience with the Downtown Center as a concrete result of our theoretical discussions at Eco/Eco reinforced my belief that non-profits could actually make things happen, especially in a state like Maine where channels to government, as indicated by my ability to participate in an ex officio manner, are relatively open.

The Downtown Center happened because a lot of other people believed in the same concept; the role I played was in persevering and not letting the idea die or get sidetracked. After the center was established, I realized we faced a whole new set of problems that I was unable to deal with, largely due to the fact my illness limited my time and commitment.

At the peak of my non-profit activity, I had become an informal liaison among several groups, able to cross-pollinate ideas, promote cooperation, and increase effectiveness. I was president of the Wolfe's Neck Farm Foundation that was trying to preserve open space through farming, the natural counterpart to downtown revitalization in fighting sprawl. I pulled in wildlife habitat protection through my board membership at Maine Audubon, proper use of the marine fisheries resource through the Conservation Law Foundation, and new approaches to forest protection through Manomet. With my cumulative viewpoint, I was optimistic about the increasing role of non-profits in driving public policy, not just in their usual adversarial role in preventing bad things from happening but in a newly creative role of incubating ideas and developing models.

With my medical diagnosis of cancer in the early winter of 2003, I cut back drastically on all my non-profit activities, saving most of my energy for Wolfe's Neck Farm, where I had been involved the longest and where there was the opportunity for the most dramatic success.

Seventeen

The Wolfe's Neck Farm Experiment Finally Works

Erick Jensen, the executive director at Wolfe's Neck Farm and the driving force behind our natural beef operation, had organized a day-long meeting of the board to discuss how to cope with success. It was October 6, 2003.

For the past sixteen years I had been involved with the farm, and through all those years we had wrestled with how to fulfill our mission of helping to revitalize Maine agriculture while staying alive economically. The 680-acre farm, spectacularly running along the shores of Casco Bay in Freeport, the shopping outlet capital of Maine, had turned out to be a white elephant for the University of Southern Maine, the original recipient of the property. After a decade, the university threw up its hands at the losses it was incurring and returned the gift. I was involved not only in the return of the farm but in trying to make it work economically where it had failed before.

Our small, minimally endowed foundation had taken control of the farm in 1997 and in 2001, after suffering our own unacceptable losses, we had established the Foundation for Agricultural Renewal (FAR), a separate non-profit under the control of the Wolfe's Neck Farm Foundation, to run the new business Erick Jensen had conceived. We would sell natural beef—without growth hormones, antibiotics, or animal feed supplements—raised throughout Maine to our strict standards. Through luck and ad hoc problem solving, we had almost instant success and were being looked to as a national model for farmland revitalization. Somewhat unexpectedly, at least to me, we were making money after only two years and we had to decide how to use that money. Even though we were a non-profit, members of the parent board were split on what we should do next. Some wanted to replenish our endowment; one even suggested selling the rapidly growing operation to a venture capitalist. Others wanted to rehabilitate the buildings that had suffered from years of deferred mainte-nance. Erick, aware that our early success was still tenuous and that problems we had never foreseen were emerging, wanted to plow more back into the business.

I had my own distinct ideas about where the money should go, and while I was sensitive to the needs of the parent foundation—I was president of that board when the new operation was being conceived and developed—I also remembered our past failures. I wanted to make sure we did not kill the golden goose by trying to take more from the natural beef marketing operation than it could afford.

In the two short years we had been in business, our cattle operation had grown to use 12,000 acres. Within five years, we hoped to in-crease the herd to effectively use 54,000 acres of Maine land, compa-rable to the venerable but troubled potato industry.

With 100 percent growth rates in the first two years and now ship-ping 100 head a week, we needed more cattle than were currently produced in Maine. It was not a problem we had foreseen. Conse-quently, we had begun to buy more cattle from across New England and subsequently would go even farther afield to meet the demand. Initially, we had thought we would buy out of state only to preserve the market for Maine farmers while they increased the size of their herds. While Maine was our first priority and we would continue to try to increase the herd in Maine, we now realized that we would have to be at least New England-wide to meet the demand we had created. In addition, we would have to become more involved in stim-ulating the supply, opening ourselves to new levels of risk.

There are three stages to raising the cattle. The first is the cow/calf operation, those who breed the animals and raise them until they are weaned. This operation involves a myriad of skills, including knowl-edge of animal husbandry.

The second stage is backgrounding, where the cattle are brought up to weight, gaining 500 pounds by grazing on grass for the summer. Maine has excellent grasslands but a short grazing season. It also has a lot of potential grazing land, starting with what the economically endangered dairy farmers own. Additionally, people who have bought old farms for residences still have fields they would like to keep open but have difficulty getting mowed because there is no longer a market for the hay. Such landowners have shown interest in cooperating with us in using their land for cattle grazing and therefore keeping it scenic. Although grazing cattle demands little care or expertise, the problems are still considerable, the most critical one being financial—who owns and therefore pays for the cattle while they are being grazed?

The third stage is the feedlot, where the cattle are fattened and take on the marbling, a nice name for the fat that runs through the meat and enhances the flavor. The longer you feed the cattle, the better the grade and we had decided to market only USDA Choice.[1] At the time of our discussion we already had six feedlots in Maine, one in Vermont, one in Pennsylvania, and one in Western New York.

At the feedlot, the cattle, particularly those in Aroostook County, eat potato peels and other non-organic products. Because of this final feed, we cannot market the beef as organic but only as natural.[2] In the meantime, the feedlots are expanding. It is our hope that they can increase their profit margin by selling us their cattle at a premium price whereas before they were selling them for whatever they could get on the commodity market. Because of our protocols, there are added expenses in raising cattle for us.

The commodity market has played a major role in killing local agriculture. A commodity is essentially a no-name product, interchangeable over a large region if not nationally. Milk is the typical commodity, with a Maine supermarket not caring whether its milk comes from Maine or Wisconsin. Only price matters, and when there is an oversupply, prices plummet for everyone, allowing only the larger and better financed operations to survive. In Maine there has been a classic attempt to use brand identity to overcome the commodity market in milk. Oakhurst Dairy advertises as a fresher, Maine-based product and has been able to buck the trend and survive because people in Maine want to support local agriculture. Oakhurst was also sued by Monsanto, a major producer of growth hormones, because the dairy

1. USDA grades are Select, Choice, and Prime. Prime is used only in a few restaurants and many want only a few cuts.
2. We hope some day to offer an organic option, at a higher price. While organic feed is prohibitively expensive at this point, we hope our established demand will create a market for organic grain that will convince Maine farmers to grow it.

advertises that its milk does not contain artificial growth hormones, apparently a significant selling point. Monsanto claims this is false advertising because there is no proof milk without growth hormones is any different than milk with hormones. Oakhurst does not say growth hormones are bad, only that its milk has none. The implication is clear, however. Those who try to distinguish themselves as more healthful because they do not use the new technologies being promoted by the agribusiness conglomerates will be punished. In the end, Oakhurst settled with Monsanto by changing its labelling somewhat. While Monsanto suffered a public relations disaster in Maine, it had successfully fired a warning shot. We heard the shot but have not changed our own labels, which note our non-use of growth hormones.

Wolfe's Neck Natural Beef needs more land to graze the additional cattle we hope others will breed. The land is there but how do we bring it into our program? In 2003 Erick Jensen increased our own herd at Wolfe's Neck Farm, buying extra calves and grazing them for the summer. The calves gain more than a pound a day and consequently increase in value, netting up to $200 a head at the end of the grazing season, all from eating the grass that is growing anyway. As intended, the farm has become our own laboratory where we will develop a complete cost analysis and a program that can be replicated by anyone with ten acres or more who wants to graze cattle for us. We hope to have these satellite farms all over the state, each with a large sign that says, "We proudly raise beef for Wolfe's Neck Farm." These farms will make our product more visible and bring aboard a whole new grower constituency that will not only promote what we are doing but will be highly visible on the local level. They will be the living proof and constant reminder of how we are saving open space.

Erick describes this as a particular vision of mine, but he has shared it from the beginning and I find it is one of the most appealing aspects of the program for the outsider who may know little about raising beef. As anxious as I am to forge ahead, Erick has said we are not yet ready, reversing the roles we have played in the past few years where I have so often been the one to counsel Erick not to try to move faster than the conditions allow. Based on my own experience at *Maine Times*, I have been acting as a mentor to harness Erick's entrepreneurial zeal.

We have operated on a shoestring, actually financing the start-up with $238,000 in grants but as of this meeting, we have made a profit for the past six months and have more than $100,000 cash on hand. The business is still run by Erick and by David Ordway, in charge of sales, with help from Dawn Downs as part-time office staff. A consultant made the astute comment that the business consisted of "two guys and a fax machine." It has been the classic entrepreneurial start-up, totally dependent on the people and the sweat equity involved. It is an anomaly, an entrepreneurial venture run by a non-profit board. I claim that we have been more efficient and effective because of our lack of capital and the need to be innovative, to say nothing of the work ethic both Erick and Dave display, Erick heading north for the five-hour drive to Aroostook at the first indication of a problem or David heading south the four hours to Connecticut or New York to explore new markets.

The beef operation started because we needed to make the farm self-sufficient. It also fit our social purpose. But now that there is money, there is competition for it, and I keep reminding people that our goal is not just to make money. Making money allows us to pursue our social purpose. Even within a non-profit, the sudden availability of money, even when its continued flow is far from certain, changes attitudes.

There are three legitimate demands on that money. The first is what goes back into the business, to fund expansion and to compensate the principals, to give them some kind of long-term benefit that rewards their entrepreneurial efforts in a business in which they will never be allowed to own an equity interest.

The second is what will be returned to the Wolfe's Neck Farm Foundation, to cover its operating deficits and to upgrade its buildings. Later, there will be grants for projects the farm foundation wants to fund.

The third is direct return to the farmers, both as an incentive to raise more cattle and as a part of our self-declared status as a de facto cooperative. We are committed to share the profits with our producers in an effort to make farming more profitable and therefore to protect farmland as open space.

As I was sitting there, listening to this discussion, I alone was aware of how far we had come since I first became involved with the farm in 1987. This was not only the culmination of our efforts to make the farm self-supporting and a model for agricultural revitalization, but it had been the crucible in which I had forged my ideas about supporting non-profits through earned income, about non-profits as an incubator of new ideas and the creator of models to test those new ideas, and finally about non-profits as the instigators of what I had come to call market-based environmentalism. The basic concept of market-based environmentalism was finding ways to reward producers in the natural-resource-based economy for responsible environmental practices. It was already emerging in forestry with the concept of green certification, where retailers would label wood products that had been harvested according to strict environmental standards. I also envisioned it in fisheries, using as an example shrimp that were trapped rather than dragged. Not only are trapped shrimp less damaged themselves, but trapping obviates the scraping of the bottom and the unwanted bycatch associated with dragging. Would people pay enough of a premium for such shrimp to compensate for the added cost of trapping? If shrimp were like beef, the answer could be yes.

My path to this day of coping with success went back beyond 1987 and the fact that I came to know Lawrence M. C. Smith and Eleanor Houston Smith in the 1960s because of their environmental interests. They created Wolfe's Neck Farm and gave it away in the hope that such a course would be more beneficial to the state than just passing it on to their heirs. The Smiths had been investors in Maine Times, lending us $15,000 at a crucial time. They also invested in what was to become Tom's of Maine, a successful Maine company specializing in healthful toothpaste and cosmetics. In another of those connections that always seems to crop up in my life, my father and L. M. C. Smith worked together on military procurement projects in World War II.

In the 1940s the Smiths had bought the Stone House as a summer home and had gradually purchased more contiguous land and houses until they owned a massive tract in Freeport, a highly developed region of Maine.

In 1969 they had given the state a large parcel in the middle of the farm to become Wolfe's Neck Woods State Park. Nearby they had operated a public campground, Recompence Shores, keeping the prices artificially low and the sites primitive. Recompence fit into their overall scheme of making more of the Maine coastline accessible to the general public.

Typical of the Smiths was their behind-the-scenes preservation of what was to become Popham Beach State Park, a massive sand beach at the mouth of the Kennebec River, and one of the jewels of the state park system.

The state had expressed interest in acquiring the beach as early as the 1950s but did not have the money and would have had to float a bond issue to purchase it. The bond issue itself might have had the negative effect of pushing up the price of the land and encouraging sales for development. So the Smiths stepped in and quietly began buying the land, more than 350 acres in all, mostly shorefront and rare sand beach, and held it until the state was in a position to purchase it for the park. That occurred in 1968, when the Smiths sold the land to the state for less than the appraised value, basically what they had paid for it, and took the difference as a tax credit. Far-sighted philanthropy and hard-headed economic thinking were combined.

L. M. C. Smith, known in his Washington days as Alphabet Smith, died in 1975 and his wife continued their joint vision, in 1984 giving the rest of the farm and their former summer home, the Stone House, to the University of Southern Maine, a project she would not live to see fulfilled as she died two years later. Although the Smiths' six children each received shorefront property, there was still a feeling among some of them that she had given away the farm that was part of their heritage, a feeling that was to color future developments.

The driving university force behind the gift had been Robert L. Woodbury, then president of the University of Southern Maine, but he soon became chancellor of the entire university system, leaving the farm in the hands of administrators who did not share his vision. At the time of the gift, Woodbury spoke of the Stone House as a site for summer institutes on Maine history, arts, and literature and a retreat center of international importance. The farm would continue its role of experimenting in alternative agriculture.

When giving the farm to the university, Mrs. Smith had funded a separate foundation, the Wolfe's Neck Farm Foundation, to oversee operations and had endowed it with less than $500,000, half of which was in land that could be sold. The board was made up of members of the family, members of the university, and members of the public, a third each. It was through this board that I entered the scene in 1987 at the specific behest of two of the daughters, Mary Minor Smith and Meredith Smith, to look at the possibilities for the farm, which was already floundering under university control. A year later, I was to join the board.

I noted in my first memo, after preliminary meetings with the key interested parties, that "the university doesn't care what I do so long as it does not directly conflict either in fund-raising or in academics. I am basically going to try to make the farm self-supporting with demonstration projects which will lend themselves as teaching tools." That goal has never changed and was a reflection of what I thought Mr. and Mrs. Smith would have wanted.

The relationship with the university can only be described as strange, and it became even stranger when Woodbury moved two hours away to Bangor as chancellor. The university had some real interest in the separate gift of the Stone House as a conference center, but except for Woodbury, university officials viewed the farm itself as an albatross. Even though others in the university may have been cool to Woodbury's vision, the gift was too attractive to cast aside, being only twenty minutes from the Portland campus and close to L. L. Bean, which attracted some 4 million customers to its store annually. The university's goal, once Woodbury left, was to keep the operating deficits as small as possible and to recover as much of the loss as possible from the foundation's endowment. The visible deficits tended to run about $35,000 a year and this was more than 10 percent of the liquid endowment, an obviously untenable situation since it would soon obliterate the entire endowment. The actual deficit was much higher because so many of the costs were pooled with other university expenses, including such things as insurance and whatever maintenance was done.

Along with the foundation, the initial organization had also included an advisory board of people interested in agricultural policy. When I interviewed them, I found "its members share an understanding of the policy considerations as well, one of the most important to them being the preservation of a viable agriculture in Southern Maine as a way to preserve open space in a productive manner." A good decade before it was to become a visible issue, these people had identified the danger of sprawl and predicted what would eventually become a key method of combatting it: productive alternatives to housing and commercial development.

The advisory board also agreed that whatever the farm did to demonstrate alternatives to current agricultural practices, the nonprofit had to show it would be profitable on a working farm without the kinds of tax breaks and underwriting Wolfe's Neck enjoyed. Although the advisory board members had a vision that proved prescient and they knew a lot about practical farming, they were cut out of the loop, reflecting the university's lack of interest in what they had to say. This lack of interest in the ideas of those who really cared about the real world of agriculture in Maine was—and unfortunately still is—typical of the university—and, I am sure, of many universities. The University of Southern Maine, at that time, was catering to the local business community that wanted trained personnel, especially engineers. Down deep, it still saw itself as producing skilled employees for an identified job market, a high-level technical school in disguise. And like everyone else, it had jumped on the high-tech bandwagon, overlooking the potential in Maine's resource-based economy.

The farm itself had been something of a hobby under the Smiths, and much about it remained a hobby. The university was not the organization to change that. Each month, Charlie deGrandpre, the longtime farm manager, drove as far as Connecticut to deliver the meat to loyal customers. With transportation costs and Charlie's time factored in, there was no way this practice was going to do anything but lose money. Of course, no one made those calculations. This was the way it had always been done and the desire was to fulfill the wishes of the tiny but loyal group of consumers.

Charlie was succeeded in 1989 as farm manager by his son David deGrandpre, and we formed a small management committee consisting of myself, Mary Minor and Meredith Smith, and Donna Somma from the university to help him reduce the deficit.

David was given a job without a vision, with the immediate goal to hold the operation together with baling wire and duct tape. But he was also smart and understood some of the deeper problems we faced, pointing out that much of the grazing land the farm had been able to use for free had now disappeared to development, and that the farm could make more money selling organic beef grown by other farmers than it could by raising and selling its own. With the herd remaining at its current size, he argued, there was no hope of erasing the deficit. Years later a team of MBA students would reach the same conclusion.

While those of us on the management committee dove into the minutia of the operation and tried to help David solve his very practical problems, we also recognized that we were dealing with much larger issues facing the agricultural community in Maine and elsewhere. We never lost sight of the larger public policy issues regarding the loss of farmland to development.

One alternative David studied was a massive cow manure composting operation that could be a profit center but that would result in heavy truck traffic and was rejected out of concern for the neighbors. Other attractions, such as an animal petting area, raised problems of dealing with the public in a farm environment.

We contemplated bringing in a visionary, such as Eliot Coleman, who was then developing an agricultural plan for a school in Vermont that raised its own food. Coleman, an early associate of Scott and Helen Nearing in Maine, was to become the guru of off-season crop farming in northern climates.

Basically, we wanted the university to give David more autonomy to run the farm itself and to use every means possible to offset the deficits, a change it was ready to accede to if only by default. Sadly, David was killed in an accident when he hit a live power line, and at this point the university decided to take over the farm operation as well, hiring a farm economist named Guy Hutt to run the operation and causing the deficits to soar to as much as $250,000 a year if all the costs were attributed. Behind the changes and in charge of the operations was Sam Andrews, the university's vice president for administration, essentially its money man. Guy Hutt didn't believe the farm could ever be self-sufficient, and he seemed to offend most of the neighbors, testing what had always been an excellent relationship. Hutt was correct about the profitability under current conditions and, as a university employee, he had neither the desire nor the incentive to change those conditions. The university was in a perpetual holding pattern with the actual farm operation, a situation that put it into conflict with the family and the non-university members of the board.

The relationship between the university and the foundation began to seriously deteriorate with family member Sam Smith, president of the board, going public with the foundation's concerns that the university was mishandling the gift. His letters to the press upset the university administration. Recognizing not only the truth of what Sam was saying but also the necessity to say it, a majority of the foundation board backed Sam. The board voted to no longer deplete the endowment just to fund the university's deficits. Endowment funds would be used only for specific projects that fulfilled our agricultural and educational missions. Since the university never proposed any innovative projects, we froze the endowment.

Sam Smith's public complaints led to a meeting with university officials and trustees, held on the porch of the Stone House one chilly afternoon. At that meeting Richard Pattenaude, who had taken over as president of the University of Southern Maine long after the critical situation had evolved, told the trustees present that everything was going well at the farm and that all problems would soon be solved. This resulted in an outburst from me in which I said that the trustees were at the mercy of whatever information university officials spoon-fed them, information that in this case was dead wrong.

As with other boards on which I served, trustees were not well enough informed about the actual operations to make the kinds of policy decisions they should have been able to make. After Sam Smith's detailed complaints and the meeting, the trustees looked at the operation with a more jaundiced eye. The trustees, of course, did not do anything meaningful to change the situation. They relied on the administration to come up with alternatives. None was forthcoming. By the mid-1990s, even the ever-optimistic Pattenaude had to recognize that there were deep troubles that could not be solved under the current structure, so he suggested that the university divest itself of the farm.

I was given the task of negotiating the return and figuring out who would run the farm after the university left. Because the gifts had been separate, the university would keep the Stone House, which was already evolving into a self-supporting conference center.

Under the original gift, American Farmland Trust held the easements on the property but, recognizing it as the economic black hole it was, the trust did not want to be responsible for its operation. Although it had a representative on the board at the time, it had little commitment to solving our problems and its interest was to further diminish.

If no one could be found to operate the farm, the deeds said the land would revert to the state as part of Wolfe's Neck Woods State Park and the state would be responsible only for mowing the fields. They could even tear down the buildings whose maintenance was a major cost burden. When I called Herb Hartman, head of Parks and Recreation and an old friend, to tell him the state might inherit the farm, he was taken aback. He noted that the state would have to agree to accept the land, something it might be reluctant to do without the funds to maintain it. Only a few years later the state would float bonds to buy such land to preserve, and today for the state to own such a unique tract so close to Portland would be considered a coup.

It became clear that the only entity that could take over the property if we wanted to continue farming it in any way was the foundation. Although the liquid endowment had been pushed down to about $250,000, we did have rapidly appreciating land we could sell to replenish it, to as high as $700,000. Since members of the foundation board did not want to give the state the endowment as well as the land, I began to develop in my own mind a rationale that if we used all of the endowment in an effort to make the farm self-supporting or at least reduce the operating deficits to a level we could handle, we would be no worse off than if we accepted the only alternative to our ownership, reversion to the state. I am not sure whether the family members not on the board realized how close the farm came to going back to the state and what this would have meant to them as owners of summer homes abutting farm property.

At the time, we discussed the matter at a board meeting and the others seemed in agreement about using the endowment as a last ditch effort to save the farm as a farm. Once the transition was made and the endowment began to decrease as we used it to cover deficits, board members, especially the family members, worried about the potential loss of the endowment. My goal was to use the endowment to make the project work and if we failed and lost the money, then we were where the board had said it wanted to be—giving the farm to the state without any money in the endowment. When the situation looked hopeless and it seemed we might have to let the state take over the farm, everyone was in agreement about gambling the endowment. During the ensuing years, the board approved spending down the endowment once again to cover operating losses as we tried one experiment after another to reduce the losses or to find a way to increase earned income. Six years later, in 2003, after allowing the endowment to be used as collateral to obtain short-term operating capital for the natural beef operation, the board began to back away from its earlier position. In 2004, with Wolfe's Neck Natural Beef picking up enough of the operating costs so that the foundation no longer had to dip into the endowment, the board began to balk at using the endowment for collateral, even though the exposure was slight. Once the imminent threat was gone, risk avoidance took control.

Of course, the endowment could have been replenished through fund-raising, but no one was talking seriously about a major capital campaign. Most of the non-family members on the board were there for reasons other than deep pockets or the desire to raise money. While some of the family members were continuously generous, others indicated they had no intention of putting significant amounts of new money into the farm. Without the financial leadership of the family in a capital campaign, we would have had to find new lead donors and I saw none on the horizon. Alternative agriculture and working farmland are not sexy to potential donors.

In 1996, having been given the task of negotiating the return of the farm from the university, I spent up to thirty hours a week on the project. I believed we could yet realize the farm's potential, and it was an interesting and mentally stimulating project. That I was not getting paid had no effect on my choice of how I used my time. E-mail allowed me to correspond with the principals involved on a daily basis without having to travel all over the state. It also provided written documentation of the negotiations, a fact I found very useful when someone would subsequently try to alter a position.

Because we had had an engineer's report done on the farm, we knew the university had neglected maintenance during its ownership. The university agreed to some projects, such as extremely expensive repairs to the Mallet Barn, the second-largest post-and-beam barn in Maine, which stood as a landmark near the Stone House. But we accepted a certain amount of deterioration and were willing to take the farm back, minus wear and tear, as the university had received it, including the cow herd.

Then one day Sam Smith called to tell me the cows had disappeared and he had learned they had been sold and were in feedlots in the Midwest. This was a staggering breach of faith.

Until this point, the negotiations between the foundation and the university had gone smoothly. The university wanted to get rid of this huge, money-sucking property and was willing to spend a little more and make a few concessions in the short term to be freed of much greater costs in the long term without a lot of adverse publicity. It was not good for the university's reputation that it had returned such a valuable gift because it could not handle it, and it certainly did not want to publicly expose the animosity that had developed, particularly with the family members.

Although the relationship between those running the farm and the board was bad, there was goodwill between the university president and myself and between me and the university system attorney, Vendean Vafiades. I had known Vendean when we had both served on the board of the Maine Civil Liberties Union and I knew her to be a fair-minded and extremely ethical person.[3]

So when I learned of the missing cattle, I contacted Vendean and she contacted Rich Pattenaude, who immediately set up a personal meeting with me. When I arrived at Pattenaude's office in Portland, Sam Andrews was just leaving and he didn't look happy. Clearly, the cattle could not have been moved without Andrews's knowledge and consent.

Pattenaude immediately said the cattle or their equivalent would be returned to the farm. He did not want to discuss how their removal

3. Her father represented us, along with Angus King, during our libel trial, but this had no bearing on my relationship with Vendean.

had happened. I was not only curious; I wanted some admission that the university had acted underhandedly. The most I could squeeze from him was how even he was kept out of the loop. He told me that sometimes people under his direction operated to a different agenda than the one he had set. As an indication of what made him such a good university administrator, Pattenaude refused to discuss with me how the cattle had disappeared in the first place or to say who was responsible. He chose glossing over for the sake of future harmony within the organization, where I would have chosen bridge-burning confrontation.

In taking back the farm, we needed someone to run it and we ended up with two prime candidates, Rick Kersbergen, a cooperative extension agent with a good feel for alternative agriculture and those in Maine who were on the cutting edge, and Erick Jensen, who had worked at the farm under Guy Hutt, and was currently selling feed in the Midwest. Kersbergen turned down the job because it was so chancy and Erick accepted.

Our decision to hire Erick is what ultimately saved the farm. We thought we were just hiring a farm manager, someone to care for the cattle and keep the buildings in minimal repair. We expected to participate with him in reducing the deficit, although we had only the most rudimentary plan to do so. We did not foresee that we would soon call on him to manage an increasingly complex operation.

Erick was young. When we hired him in 1997, he was thirty-one years old. Before he even arrived, we had made a deal with Americorps to run an educational program at the farm that would bring us net revenue and help us repair some of the facilities. We also cut a deal with Bob Smith, a local entrepreneur who specialized in resort management and a committed partisan of the farm, to run the campground and guarantee us a net of $25,000 a year from it. Then we would sell the properties left to the foundation and push the endowment up to $700,000, giving us 5 percent or $35,000 a year to cover our operating deficit.

As usual, our optimistic financial projections were wrong and we vastly underestimated what Erick would be called upon to do as manager of the farm and the person ultimately responsible for its success.

Once we began to operate the farm ourselves, we realized how much the university must have actually been losing, and even with our best cost control efforts and the fact we did not have to pay the union scale wages they did, we discovered that the natural deficit for the operation was between $100,000 and $150,000 a year. There was no way we were going to cover this out of the endowment, and even with the added income from the educational programs and such minor projects as a university ropes course that paid us rent, and a tent for weddings, we were still not going to cover the gap.

Erick tried to exploit every possible source of revenue. When the Portland Public Market opened in 1998 and solicited us to run the fresh meat operation, we jumped at the chance. The financial projections we did showed it could be profitable and we hired David Ordway, who was willing to give up a good job at L. L. Bean, to run the market operation. David was excellent but our figures were not. Even when we were making money on paper, the cash flow was not showing the same result because we were never able to accurately determine the cost of goods. Added to this were the seasonal fluctuations. There were just not enough customers.

Ted Spitzer, the person chosen to run the market, had been hired as a consultant to make plans for the market and was knowledgeable on what had happened in places like Seattle. However, he had never run such a market himself. He had developed a set of rules he would not break. For instance, he would not consider having vendors sell prepared foods at the market since he did not want it to become a food court. Because he had managed to antagonize local farmers through his lack of sympathy with their particular problems, they never participated in the Portland Public Market but continued their successful farmers' market a few blocks away. Having local farmers selling their own produce is the core attraction of such a market and, if included, they would have brought their loyal clientele with them. Instead, those customers continued to patronize the farmers' market, largely to the exclusion of the Public Market.

I had tried to convince Spitzer that he should offer incentives to other well-known specialty vendors, such as Harbor Fish, the premier fish market in Portland, and Micucci's, a successful Italian wholesaler that was expanding its retail operation, to open branches at the Public Market. When I later talked to the owner of Micucci's about why he did not go to the Public Market, he said it was not attractive enough. During the first years of the Public Market, Micucci's went through a rapid growth spurt at its retail store a few blocks away even though Micucci's did not have the advantage of nearby food vendors and so had to be a destination stop. When the Public Market did bring in a similar operation, it could not match Micucci's in either price or range and quality of product, and even if I had not been loyal to Micucci's, I would have been forced to continue shopping there to buy what I needed. Such competitive realities were disregarded.

As market manager, Spitzer was a theoretician and did not possess the hands-on, solve-all-problems attitude so necessary in a start-up operation. The market, supported by the Libra Foundation, with Maine's deepest pockets, was underneath an entrepreneurial challenge without an entrepreneur to run it. I had been personally involved in discussions among those interested in farm policy prior to the opening of the market, and the Wolfe's Neck Farm Foundation's judgment in entering the market was no doubt influenced by my enthusiasm for the idea. But no matter what we did, we kept losing more money so we finally gave up the project as a lost cause.

The Portland Public Market venture was to be one of those projects to solve all our problems. Not only did it not work as we had planned, but the scatter-shot approach of everything else at the farm was creating new problems.

While I had negotiated the return of the farm to the foundation and the agreement with Americorps, I began to pull back after Erick took over and he was left with conflicting interests. Steve Niles, who directed the educational programs and Americorps, saw himself as a separate authority, since his funding was channeled through a state agency. He quickly expanded his programs to include on-site classes for children and a massive summer day-camp. Both were very popular within the community and generated desperately needed revenues.

Erick was juggling everything else, trying to bring the finances under control; the Public Market losses had sent the deficit soaring once again past the $100,000 mark, quickly eating into the endowment even with the added principal we had obtained through land sales and a soaring stock market.

We added new projects, including Friends of the Farm, a membership organization that generated net revenues and also acted as a pool of committed volunteers who worked on needed projects around the farm.

Despite all the activity, we were back to our old practice of trying to hold the operation together with duct tape and baling wire, trying to reduce the operating deficit through cost-cutting and nickel-and-dime new projects.

When we took on the role as ad hoc rescue shelter, accepting animals their owners did not want and trying to integrate them into our educational programs without proper planning and oversight, we began receiving complaints, some filed with the state animal welfare officer, that we were abusing animals on the one hand and were running an unlicensed petting zoo on the other. The subsequent inspections exonerated the farm and Erick's management, but we learned that if we were going to invite the public to the farm, we had to meet the standards the most exacting member of the public demanded, and took action accordingly.

With my approval, Erick left the educational programs pretty much alone, assuming the program was being monitored by the state agency funding it. Our assumption was false in several ways. It turned out that the parent state agency had criticized some of Steve's periodic reports and asked for more information. Although we later learned we were accountable for these reports, we had never seen them or the state agency's response. Our neglected responsibility came out in a federal audit that caught us totally by surprise. Fortunately, there had been no malfeasance, only sloppiness, and we were left alone, sadder but wiser.

This all came to a head when we had to cope with the fact that the funding for Americorps would run out in the fall of 2003. Steve wanted to continue the programs and came up with a plan to do so without the previous funding. His financial projections left the foundation board uneasy and Steve took his ideas elsewhere.

Although I was in a minority on this issue, the educational program for grade-school children never impressed me. It did contain some good basics on the interrelationships between farming and the environment, but almost all of what was taught could have been taught in the classroom with visits to the farm. It struck me as a feel-good project, and I was not impressed by the fact that the local school administrators liked it, a reflection of my belief that the schools were not very rigorous in their standards.

I believed that our unique mission was in educating farmers and adults, an area we were neglecting due to lack of resources. I had initiated the Americorps project for two reasons: it took little oversight from us and it would generate net revenue to the farm while fulfilling an educational responsibility. Now we were ready to move on.

After almost forty years of interest in the subject of small farm viability, I had come to the conclusion that a key flaw was the disconnect among farmers between what they produced and the consumer, especially the sophisticated consumer. This was becoming more apparent as the interest in food in America reached new highs. But no one was dealing with this disconnect, at least not in Maine. It was not only a particular concern of mine but one which I felt I had the background to help remedy.[4]

One of my long-term goals for Wolfe's Neck Farm was to have it teach local farmers how to produce specialty products that would demand a premium price from the increasingly sophisticated American food consumer. For years, Maine cheesemakers had been trying to produce cheddar, an oversaturated market if there ever was one. When I first learned, back in the 1970s, that some Maine farmers—actually back-to-the-land types rather than traditional farmers—were making their own chevre, a soft artisanal cheese from goat's

---

4. I grew up at a time when Wonder Bread was the standard of excellence, and from my earliest memories in the 1940s I had watched the deterioration of the quality of food we received. When I was a child my grandfather kept chickens and killed the Sunday bird, letting us watch it run around, spurting blood from its neck, after he had chopped off its head with an ax. At home, in a suburb of Washington, D.C., we still bought our own chickens at a farm and the butcher shop actually cut meat. As a teenager I had been exposed to European food. The summer I spent in Grenoble, at the age of seventeen, may not have perfected my French, but it improved my palate. In the 1950s Italy was still a mecca of regional cuisine. I learned that while they ate manufactured spaghetti in the south, they ate soft pasta in the north. I had my first risotto Milanese—firm arborio rice infused with saffron—at the Galleria in Milan. I learned that real Parmesan was a protected name, with the cheese produced by artisans on small farms to rigid specifications in a narrow region. Gorgonzola cheese got its distinctive blue mold from a cave in which it was cured, in the town of Gorgonzola, and only that cheese could bear the name in Italy. The best prosciutto came from Parma, and if you wanted the classic Florentine steak, it had to come from Chianina beef.

milk, I took a sample to my friends at the Department of Agriculture. They thought it tasted funny.[5]

Under my dream plan for the foundation—to teach farmers how to make such high quality products—we would send them to Europe to learn the techniques and they would come home and teach other farmers how to do the same. Erick and I still share the dream, but realize it is a number of years off.

The positive side of the problems that emerged during this transitional period was that Erick and I began to work together much more closely and we developed an excellent relationship. It was a natural collaboration. Erick had the classic entrepreneur's talents. Because of my experience in starting *Maine Times*, I understood much of what he was going through, including the isolation that occurs when you alone are responsible for such an operation.

While Erick had managed to bring the operating deficit down to a manageable level of less than $50,000, he recognized that the severe budget cutting and the consequent pressure on staff could not last. He needed a way to generate new revenue. That's when he came up with the idea for Big Beef, as we initially called the natural beef marketing project, and made contact with Common Good, a set of serendipitous events that were to lead us out of the wilderness.

Erick had learned of an operation on the West Coast called Oregon Country Beef, a cooperative of small ranchers who pooled their resources to provide meat for the natural foods market at a premium price. From this he developed a plan for doing the same thing in Maine, with the key difference that we would not be a true cooperative but only act like one. This peculiar role emerged from the combination of Erick's and my experiences.

Erick, despite his strong entrepreneurial streak, also had a strong belief in his need to make life better for farmers, in particular to develop ways in which they could continue to farm. He often cited the case of his own father who had to give up farming because of rising land values and sell the land to cash in and to be able to retire.

5. For me, chevre was like Proust's petite madeleine, the pastry that set off his chain of memories. I had had my first taste of chevre on a mountainside above Grenoble in 1955, and to taste it brought me back to that farm-created meal under a shade tree, high in the Alps.

In my own journalistic experience, I had seen cooperatives fail again and again in Maine. Usually they had been started by young idealists who were looked down on by the traditional farmers who were in the commodity market anyway, whether producing potatoes or animals. For years in the potato industry there had been truly boom years, when farmers in Aroostook County especially made big money, and they did not want to give up that chance even though the lucrative years were becoming more scarce. We were to find that the same take-it-while-you-can attitude created difficulties with Aroostook beef farmers when we tried to convince them to take a longer range view.

Maine potatoes once dominated the national market. But largely due to the resistance of Maine farmers to embrace strict quality control, they are now considered an inferior table product. Potato growers pin their hope for the future on processed french fries for fast food chains. Maine potatoes became a commodity, indistinguishable from potatoes grown elsewhere and considered inferior to the same product from Idaho or California.

Similarly, the apple industry made the decision to cut down its older and more difficult to harvest (they're taller) apple trees and replant exclusively with Macintosh. This happened almost simultaneously with the introduction into the market of crisper eating apples, such as Granny Smiths, from the Pacific Northwest.[6] The relatively mushy Mac suffered. As local dairies with name recognition went under, Maine milk also became a commodity, being sold under various store brand names, and the dairy farms began to disappear at a rapid rate. Except for a few pockets, this pattern dominated Maine agriculture.

We set up the Foundation for Agricultural Research (FAR) as a de facto cooperative because it needed the participation of many small farmers. Our budgeting was predicated on paying the farmers even if our efforts failed. When we had failed at the Public Market, farmers who supplied us were never affected and we hoped our past record

6. One of the trees cut down was the Northern Spy, a crisp and tart apple that is harvested as late as October. It is my favorite apple. One day in the early 1980s at the Fairway Market on the upper West Side in New York City, I was watching the produce manager pile up his apple display and I asked him if he ever had Northern Spies. He said they were difficult to get, but if he could get them, he could charge a whopping premium. By this time, Maine orchardists had few Northern Spies left, even if they had known how to exploit such a market.

would inspire confidence in our integrity.

Both Erick and I believed that we would have to assume most of the risk and gradually bring the farmers into our program. As we became financially successful, we could set up a profit-sharing system that was the same as a cooperative. But one of the attractions to me was that Erick's proposal required the existing Maine beef farmers to do very little differently than they were already doing, since most did not use antibiotics in the feed or growth hormones or animal-based feed supplements. Even with the changes we were asking them to make, we believed they would increase their profit margins. In the long run, we would have to make it clear to them how they were benefitting specifically from our program. We thought that just getting a better price for their product would not be enough. We were more correct than we knew.

When our application for FAR went to the IRS, the person reviewing it sent back a list of pertinent questions, the most important of which was why this had to be a non-profit. Why couldn't the same thing be done by private enterprise? The implication was that we would be a traditional venture start-up in disguise. The tax expert we had advising us was a little taken aback by the question but our long-time attorney, Peter Plumb, could see immediately that I was anxious to respond and so I was given the task of explaining to the IRS why this project could be undertaken only by a non-profit. It was an opportunity for me to explicate much of what I had learned over the years and for the first time to make my case for market-based environmentalism. No one believed more than I that non-profits can take a leadership role in shaping public policy and accomplish what neither government nor private enterprise can.

In responding to the IRS questions, I wrote, in part:
The private sector is leery of agriculture in general and perceives it as a dying economic sector. It is also extremely risky. Farmers are notoriously independent. Banks know nothing about the technical issues—raising quality beef takes broad knowledge about feed regimens, genetics, and even meat cutting. The risk involved far outweighs the potential profits, 2 percent profit being the industry standard. Banks will finance a tractor with valuable land as collateral, but neither banks nor

the more venturesome lender is interested in being involved in a start-up such as this.

Government cannot do such a project, based as it is on selectivity, not equality.[7] We are helping only one segment of agriculture, and we are offering inclusion only to those who meet our quality criteria. While anyone could participate, many will choose not to under the circumstances we impose—raising cattle on unsprayed pasture, with no growth hormones, no antibiotics in the feed, and no animal by-product in the feed (the assumed cause of mad cow disease).[8] And they must constantly document their procedures and agree to be reviewed by us. State agencies cannot do the same. They must help all in a similar category equally. To select even on the basis of quality would be seen as discriminatory and is politically unfeasible.

In our political system, government agencies are constantly pressured to consider factors other than merit or quality alone.[9] Finally, in times of tight budgets, the state tends to focus on existing programs with strong constituencies. If agriculture is to make a turnaround in Maine—farmland and farmers are declining dramatically—it will have to come from elsewhere than private enterprise or government.

The Maine Department of Agriculture has already given up on much of its development and marketing function, due to lack of funding. Similarly, as farming continues to decline, our land grant university has cut back its own experimental farm activities. Although FAR is in no position to take over these important government functions for all of agriculture, we have stepped into one sector and replaced previous taxpayer expenditures.

While it would appear that the premium price we offer could be replicated by private enterprise, it is not being done and because a goal of private enterprise is to maximize their own

7. Our lack of success in securing USDA grants we have applied for, despite the impact we have already had on Maine agriculture, proves my point about government support. Others on the board find my satisfaction in this point disconcerting. I, too, would rather get the grant. It would make life easier.
8. When mad cow disease struck in 2004 our sales actually increased. We also had never killed "downer cows" (those that couldn't walk to their own deaths) and adhered to the latest in humane killing techniques.
9. This was brought home by my experience in making grants at the Downtown Center.

profits, it is never likely to be done.

Farms are disappearing in Maine. In 1954 there were 23,368 farms. The most recent census puts that figure at less than 5,000. The number of farm managers dropped correspondingly, making it the greatest loss in any sector other than telephone operators. Farmers have the lowest wages after retail workers.

While some private enterprises might act as we do, we can think of none that would combine all the characteristics listed below:

Our financial records are open to the public. We harbor no trade secrets and freely share what we have learned.

We operate under a set of ethical standards, toward the land, toward the animals, toward the people with whom we deal. If there is conflict between those standards and "profit," profit becomes secondary.

We are committed to supporting small farms even though large farms might be more "efficient."

Our goal is to develop ways to make small farming, practiced responsibly, profitable, not to be profitable by following the path of least resistance.

The operation may never be sold. No individual may take advantage of any equity that is built up.

The IRS approved our non-profit status and we started in business, using a relatively small Boston distributor, and trying to reach a variety of small markets. From the beginning, Whole Foods, a company totally in tune with our objectives, bought our meat and marketed it under its own label. Gradually, it increased its order and at all times it proved a helpful partner, guiding us through some of the pitfalls of the competitive national market we were entering. Whole Foods acts as something of an early warning system for us. In its annual report, it predicted increased consumer focus on the humane treatment of animals.

Erick had combined idealism and practicality in setting up the original operation. Since our primary goal was to help Maine farming, we always gave preference to Maine operations and started with feed-lots in the state. However, we had to seek a slaughterhouse outside the state, Moyer Packing in Pennsylvania. We simply could not be competitive by using the small operation we had previously used when we killed only four steers a week.

The slaughterhouse ran our cattle through the first of the day when the equipment had been cleaned and was free of any possible contamination. It would not run a lot smaller than 80 head so we had to adapt our system. We were helped by the fact that it wanted to develop a natural beef line—it processed 1,700 head a day so our 80 every other week, when we started, were hardly a profit center for it. Despite Moyer's size, it was a sympathetic partner and the relationship has both grown and flourished.

We were not so lucky with out initial distributor, Oxford Trading.

When we began the operation, we were already hoping to get a supermarket chain and were cultivating Hannaford, one of the major chains in Maine and New England. It had been carrying Coleman natural beef from Colorado and wanted to continue to supply the niche market if only to preserve it should it ever expand into becoming really profitable. We had the added benefit of being local and supporting small farms, an ideal to which the top management at Hannaford was sympathetic. A phone call Governor King placed to the president, urging him to consider using the Wolfe's Neck product, helped get us a hearing.

In the long run, while I was correct that there would be a lot of logistical hurdles to overcome with Hannaford and that the purity of mission would never be determinative, having to deal with the realities of the supermarket world was good for us and we would have been unlikely to find a traditional supermarket more sympathetic than Hannaford.

We did have immediate problems that I had never foreseen, mainly selling the whole cow. Hannaford was taking steaks, mainly ribeye and sirloins, and Whole Foods was taking better cuts, such as tenderloins. The question was what to do with the rest of the animal.

Erick hired David Ordway, who had worked for us at the Portland Public Market, to do sales and he traveled all over New England looking for outlets that would take the less popular cuts at a premium price, but because we could not learn from Oxford, on a week-by-week basis, exactly what it was selling and what it was discounting, we decided to switch distributors. Again, taking advantage of the system we were forced into if we wanted to go regional, which we had to in order to succeed, we contracted with Empire out of Rochester, New York. Empire was extremely cooperative and while it did not aggressively promote our product over others it carried, it kept us up-to-date on all sales and eventually hooked us up with their computer system so David could check inventory at any moment and know what he needed to sell to minimize the discounts. This technology played a significant role in our profitability. We eventually dropped the amount of discounted product from 7 percent to 1 percent, a crucial figure in a business where profit margins are less than 2 percent.

Throughout the start-up we had had help from Common Good, a new non-profit founded by Warren Cook and run by Kristin Majeska. The idea behind Common Cause was that it would help non-profits develop income-generating operations to enable them to fulfill their charitable missions without always having to ask for money. Common Cause helped with raising the start-up money. Even more important, it constantly reviewed our figures and acted as financial consultants, developing real knowledge of our operation and holding us accountable. Nothing is more valuable for a start-up than to have someone doing reality checks and preventing the entrepreneurs from believing their own wishful thinking.

I had long been an advocate of earned income for non-profits and had come to believe that wherever possible non-profits should become self-sufficient. Much of this philosophy had derived from conversations with Marion Kane, the past president of the Maine Community Foundation, of which Common Cause was at first a subsidiary. Marion, who was the second president of MCF, was a great believer that too many charities simply propped up failure instead of replacing failure with success.

We were also lucky in the emergence of another non-profit, Great Bay Foundation, whose mission was to fund the start-up of socially beneficial businesses. Its initial problem seemed to be finding good projects, ones that not only brought social benefit but that were run in a professional enough manner to have a good chance of success.

Later, we were to receive help from the Libra Foundation, the major fund established by Betty Noyce with her share of Intel. After her untimely death, it was run by Owen Wells and we gradually developed an excellent relationship with Libra, primarily through Craig Denekas who sat on both boards. As it turned out, our visions were similar and our greatest asset was Erick's combination of farmer and entrepreneur.

We had created a natural tension within the operation of Wolfe's Neck Natural Beef by starting a classic entrepreneurial enterprise within a non-profit organization, ultimately overseen by the parent board, some of whose members brought a more traditional business approach and most of whom heard about the actual operation only on a quarterly basis.

The FAR board itself was informed in greater detail, reviewing the nuts and bolts of the operation on a monthly basis at three-hour meetings, as well as participating in projects such as grant writing and trouble-shooting as the need arose. I was often called on for my memo writing and this, combined with my close relationship with Erick, kept me well informed.

The two boards came to represent the classic differences in boards on which I had served. Whenever the board has scant knowledge and exercises minimal informed oversight, the executive director takes more authority both because the onus is on him to perform and because he begins to distrust the judgment of his board, which is not close enough to the operation to make sound decisions at the management level. There is an ever shifting line, depending on the organization, that determines just how much board officers or committed board members should become involved and how much knowledge they should develop.

In the case of FAR, there were sound reasons for a high level of individual involvement, if for nothing else than to act as an effective sounding board for Erick and to ask him intelligent questions or make sure he had reviewed all the pertinent data as he made new proposals. Wolfe's Neck Farm Foundation, on the other hand, had to rely on FAR's detailed oversight, since it could only maintain superficial knowledge.

No one can ever predict what will happen with a start-up venture. Something always goes wrong and a business's success depends in equal parts on luck and on the key person's being able to adapt on an almost daily basis. Erick not only had the adaptability but he was ready to do whatever was needed to solve the problem at hand. Such ubiquitous concern may be a management weakness in a more mature organization where authority must be delegated, but it was essential at Wolfe's Neck Natural Beef where, if Erick didn't do it, no one else was there to do it for him. Erick's knowledge of beef farming and his intelligence were keys to success. So was his determination to make the project work and his willingness to do whatever was necessary.

Erick's and my relationship was helped by the fact that we saw eye-to-eye on the larger mission of the farm as a catalyst for the revitalization of agriculture in Maine. I brought the additional focus of how this fit into the anti-sprawl movement and exemplified an alternative approach to developing the resource-based economy. Knowing that the farm could play such a major role in key public policy issues facing the state gave us both incentive.

While I deferred to Erick on technical matters, I did learn more about beef than I had ever intended, and we did have numerous sessions where I and other FAR members helped frame the questions to be asked about the next steps. But with the exception of a few personnel matters where I simply told him he could not act as precipitously as he wanted—another entrepreneurial trait is impatience—Erick made the decisions.

This was a new role for me and one I came to enjoy. Erick was in the driver's seat and I was just going along for the ride, but we were accomplishing everything I had hoped for. And we had a knowledgeable and committed board.

A key element of that accomplishment, and one I had a difficult time getting others to see, was how a non-profit could be a leader in public policy by developing a model of market-based environmentalism, a term that is now, unfortunately, being used by the Bush Administration to describe something quite different. Our goal was to get a premium for our product because it was raised in an environmentally sound manner. And that premium became an incentive for farmers to use such methods. I had arrived at this point incrementally, over decades, as I had found limited success in instituting deep environmental change by both private business and government.

After sixteen years, Wolfe's Neck Farm had actually reached the stage where it was becoming self-supporting and contributing to the revitalization of Maine agriculture. I would never have guessed it would take so long. Nor would I have guessed its impact would be so forceful. Nor would I have ever expected that one of my major contributions to the future of the State of Maine would involve a bunch of cows.

Summing Up: Maine Was an Important Choice

Shortly after we began *Maine Times*, we received a cartoon, anonymously, in the mail. The sender had altered it slightly, labelling the two men perched on a camel "Cole" and "Cox." In the first panel, a spectator is saying, "Look at the two assholes on that camel." In the second panel, the two men have dismounted the camel and are raising his tail to inspect his rear end.

Although the role of humor in puncturing self-importance and pretense is universal, I like to think it is more acute in Maine and I like to think it reflects part of a uniquely Maine culture. One way Maine humor exposes pretension is to take literally what a person is saying figuratively. Especially people from away often ask a question in an indirect manner, probably out of politeness, and part of the Maine tradition is to take that indirection, that euphemism, at face value and turn it back on the questioner. Thus we have the Maine classic where the summer visitor comes back in July and sees his neighbor Jake. "Jake," the summer visitor says, "I heard you buried your wife last winter." Jake replies, "I had to. She was dead."

There are literally hundreds of such jokes but I didn't fully understand their implications until I became both the perpetrator and the subject of one.

In the early days of *Maine Times*, we printed in Belfast, an hour and a half from our offices in Topsham, and on the way home I loaded my car with papers, making a rendezvous in Augusta to drop off several thousand for the newsstands, and taking a few hundred more back to the office. Once the print run was finished, I was always in a hurry to make my transfer so the papers would be delivered on time.

One day, I was on Route 3, about halfway between Belfast and Augusta, when I spotted a cow walking toward me on the opposite side of the road. I slowed down, hoping I would not have to stop and do something about the cow. Then I saw two men working on a culvert only a few yards farther down the road so I pulled onto the shoulder and rolled down the window to talk to them without getting out of the car.

Once I had their attention, I asked, "Did you see that cow in the road?"

"Yup," one of them replied.

"Where do you think she belongs?" I asked.

"Probably that farmhouse up the road," he said, gesturing to a house only a hundred yards behind me.

"Well, shouldn't someone tell them their cow is loose in the road," I asked, digging myself in deeper as I tried to hint that they might do something since I was not volunteering myself.

"Yup," the workman replied.

"Can you do it?" I asked, biting the bullet and finally getting to the point, however obliquely.

"When we get there, we'll tell him," the workman said.

"Well, what happens if a car hits the cow before then?" I asked.

"If a car hits that cow," the workman replied, "there's going to be a helluva mess."

There is a good deal of talk about the Maine culture and the clash between natives and those from away. There is always talk of those who are attracted by a place to which they migrate and then begin to change, destroying the very attributes that attracted them in the first place. I think the conflict occurs not based on where one was born but on how one relates to other people and how well one understands a set of traditions rooted in time and place.

The first standard is egalitarianism. I don't claim Maine is unique in its strong sense of egalitarianism, but the idea that everyone follows the same rules runs strong.[1] Anyone who tries to pull rank is quickly put down. On the other side, people respect the privacy of the well known and many appreciate being left alone. That balance was struck

1. The oft-told and probably apocryphal story about Martha Stewart illustrates the unwritten rule. It is related that Martha Stewart was visiting a summer resident enclave where she went to the general store and asked to use the telephone. When she was told that the public used the pay phone outside, she replied, "Do you know who I am?" To which the person standing behind her said, "Do you know who I am? I'm David Rockefeller, and I use the pay phone outside."

perfectly at the Five Island Wharf where everyone in Georgetown went for lobsters and clams on picnic tables. I was on hand several times when Governor Angus King was also present. As a local resident, Angus personally knew many of the people there at any given time and everyone would say hello but not make a big deal that he was governor. Other Maine residents who recognized him would either smile, or come over to shake his hand and say something quietly, but it was clear they did not want to disturb his lunch with his family.

Angus, who is "from away," has an intuitive understanding of Maine culture and often told a joke about how he was commonly mistaken for a television personality named Bill Green, whom he resembles. You never assume that someone knows who you are, even if you have every reason to expect they do. But it is all right to play the game of not knowing while knowing.

Shortly after we bought the house in Georgetown, I went to the post office to get a mail box. Because the property was well known—and expensive—I could expect that I would be known. This was reinforced by the fact that the post office at the time was the social hub of the community and the two postmistresses knew everyone and were a reliable source of information about anything happening in town. Not only that, but the head postmistress, Jackie Drake, was related to the hermit who had originally inhabited the property we bought. So when I asked if there was a post office box available and she asked how long I planned on staying in Georgetown, I replied, "Until I die." Jackie did not apologize for not recognizing me, nor would I have expected her to. Her answer had perfect pitch: "You got me."

On a more practical level, anyone who wants something done in Maine treats the person performing the service as a peer. I think this is a throwback to days when many services were traded. If you needed a new roof, you didn't hire a roofer but your neighbor came over and helped you, a favor that was soon repaid by mowing a field or hauling wood. Even in the most impersonal city, it is a good idea to develop a personal relationship with your plumber or electrician but in Maine it is an accepted tradition based on a respect for the person's skills, not just an attempt to have the service person come when needed.

In any rural environment, interdependence increases. Where I live, even if I did not like my neighbors as much as I do, I would remain on cordial terms with them. In the middle of the winter, there is no one else to call on if your car needs to be jump started. Actually, there is someone else to call—a service 15 miles away but who would ever rely on that?

Another tradition is sharing the land. In the days when we regularly visited Matinicus Island, 23 miles off the coast, we would use the paths that cut across private property, often running within feet of someone's house. You were welcome to use the path but you didn't so much as pick a wild blackberry on someone else's land.[2]

One day I was playing tennis with a newcomer who had moved to Maine year-round. He told me he was surprised to learn that clam diggers regularly went across his property to reach the flats and asked me what he should do about it. I said he should offer them a cup of coffee and a parking place the next time he saw them.

I explained that clam diggers had probably been using that access point for generations and they considered it their right to do so. In return, they would respect his property rights and keep an eye out for his house when he was not there. As long as the clam diggers had an interest in the property, I explained, they would consider it their responsibility. Should he deny them access, on the other hand, if the house caught on fire, instead of calling the fire department, they would roast hot dogs over the flames.

Because Maine is less mobile than many states and because the towns are smaller, there is greater inter-generational continuity. When our daughter, Sara, lived in Portland, she enjoyed the fact that she carried an identity as the great-grandchild of people who were still occasionally remembered. As might happen anywhere, Eunice's and my friends were quick to patronize her pottery shop when she opened for business. But she also had customers who knew about her grand-

2. Matinicus was a time warp we visited often when the children were young, replicating my own childhood experiences. We stayed with our friend John Ladley at an old dance hall with no electricity and with pumped water and an outhouse. Only residents had cars, so we walked everywhere. Days were spent at the beach, fishing in the harbor, and picking berries. If we were lucky, John Mitchell from across the way would come over in the evening and tell stories. Otherwise we would play games with the children until it got dark, and then go to bed at 9:00 P.M., knowing everyone would rise at first light the next morning.

father and greatgrandparents. When our son Tony and his wife Heather moved back to Topsham to rehabilitate what had been a major eyesore on the main street, they were welcomed not just for the project but as people with roots—and a reputation—in the community.

There is a more important aspect to one's not being able to escape one's past actions; you are responsible for them.

One day in Bath, back in the 1960s, a reader, referring to my editorials, said to me that he hoped I did not have the last-one-off-the-bus syndrome. He explained that too often the newest arrival in town thought he knew everything about how the community could improve itself and made all kinds of suggestions about how to do so, but never stuck around to personally experience the consequences of his proposals. The message was that if you stick around, if you don't move somewhere else when things don't seem perfect, you learn to live with the consequences of your own decisions, and by doing so, perhaps you are a little more humble in realizing that you may not be right about everything.

Maine culture derides pretense, pretending you know more than you do, pretending you are more important than someone else. It reveres respect, respect for the intelligence, skills, and hard work of others, recognition of others as individuals, and acceptance of the beliefs and opinions of others, even when one disagrees.

I like to think I chose to live in Maine because I understood all this, but when I was a teenager and first fell in love with the state my father had always held up as ideal, I certainly could not have rationalized my feelings.

As it turned out, we were a good match. I not only respected Maine's traditions but its traditions reinforced and honed my own instincts and core beliefs.

I believe in social responsibility, that we are all in this world together and must look out for one another and help one another. This belief lay behind the very concept of *Maine Times*, that there were shared values binding residents of the state, no matter where they lived. I cared about all of Maine, not just where I resided.

My belief that some people are better educated, more thoughtful, and more rational than others led others at the office to label me an elitist, a bad word ever since the 1960s. It is an epithet that I long ago stopped rejecting. There are people who through talent and training are capable of making better decisions and they should be the ones called on to do so. When I seek advice, I go to the person who will anticipate the possible consequences of various courses of action, not the person driven by an ideology.

I have even dared to say—in private—that I am not particularly interested in trying to get people uninterested in the issues to vote. To me this is a logical, if politically incorrect, extension of my belief in an informed electorate.

I believe right and wrong are not relative. The decisions in my life that I have regretted have involved fudging for expediency. Whenever I have let the call for pragmatism outweigh a core principle, I have regretted it.

Maine's somewhat conservative, highly individualistic culture may make it more difficult to initiate thoughtless change, but if you are willing to put in your time, do your homework, and earn the respect of others, change in Maine is actually more easily accomplished than in other states.

My experience with the Downtown Center was a case in point. Without any organized political constituency behind me and therefore without clout, I was able to meet with key commissioners and others based solely on the validity of the idea. There are few states where this would have been possible.

Because relationships are multi-faceted, they are allowed to be complex. Although I attacked what I considered John Martin's autocratic style when he was speaker of the Maine House and I promoted the term limits which forced him out of that position, I always admired his skills as a legislator. And I found him personally engaging. Martin also became a devoted participant in the Maine Public Policy Scholars, and we have continued to cross paths because of that joint interest. At a recent meeting of that program, he presented me with a citation from the legislature, obviously written by him with a knowledge of my background that surprised me a little. Our sense of shared commitment to the state and long association in the fields of public policy outweighed any specific differences. Because we shared the Maine ethic, I have been lucky enough to have similar relationships with others, with whom I disagreed more fundamentally .

Although newspapers inevitably focus on confrontation, I appreciated that the conflict of ideas could be framed by personal respect. Max McCormack, a professor at the university, espoused forestry practices that we opposed at *Maine Times*. At a meeting I was attending in the early '80s, he criticized *Maine Times*'s coverage of him as unfair and cited specific examples, some of which I considered valid points. So later at the same meeting, I said from the podium that he was correct and I publicly apologized. He subsequently invited me to speak to his graduate students to explain our position and our relationship, even though we never came to agreement on forest practices, was cordial. Being able to argue about issues without personal animosity is an ingredient of the Maine concept of respect and is unfortunately becoming increasingly rare.

While I was genetically and environmentally programmed to be a reformer, to love public policy, and to be involved with my state, Maine has also reinforced my belief in personal relationships. This has been multiplied for my children who have chosen lifestyle over careers of public influence. Both my children now live in the country and are attempting to build their own utopias, with strong commitment to their local communities.

Eunice is better than I am about observing the traditional amenities of small town life and her projects have included a shelter for the homeless, where she worked weeks with fundamentalist church people whom she liked and respected for their down-to-earth, unpretentious sense of obligation to others. Unpretentious herself, Eunice takes pleasure in her job at an elementary school where she has worked enough years to view the long-term growth of her students and to develop lasting relationships with her fellow teachers.

When we both worked at *Maine Times*, Eunice was a binding force within that extended family. Even when she was not working there, she was my critic and sounding board, the person to whom I turned more than anyone else for informed judgment. Her intimate knowledge of the paper, both from having worked there and from my having brought the problems home for discussion from day one, kept me on an even keel.

In this memoir, I have hinted at the interconnections and longevity that enabled me to accomplish whatever I have accomplished. My concept of market-based environmentalism emerged from forty years of thinking and testing ideas that related specifically to the Maine situation. In serving on all the boards I have, including several not mentioned here, I was able to see how different people and different groups approach a problem. Some of my most important insights came from being at the right place at the right time, and I was only there because of my involvement with civic groups. As a journalist who viewed such participation as a conflict and as an editor who expected people to come to him, I would not have otherwise experienced these incidents that enlightened me to unexpected motivations behind public policy decisions.

In a meeting between Audubon trustees, of which I was one, and the hunting lobby, Sportsmen's Alliance of Maine, someone from Audubon suggested there was a concurrence of goals, particularly related to non-game wildlife, and that the two groups could cooperate in strengthening the fiscally starved Department of Inland Fisheries and Wildlife. George Smith, the executive director of SAM who was often accused of dictating department policies, made it clear he did not want Audubon to help the department in ways that would force his group to share its influence.

Over the years, I not only came to understand opposition viewpoints in some complexity, but I became a one-person liaison on a broad range of environmental issues. If Audubon concentrated on wildlife habitat and if the Conservation Law Foundation focused on stopping the depletion of the marine fishery and if Wolfe's Neck Farm was trying to preserve working farms, I could not only piece them together but I could suggest where each might cooperate with the others to increase their joint effectiveness. And sometimes I could help fill in the blanks, as with helping to start the Downtown Center as an antidote to sprawl-inducing commercial development that destroys farmland and causes marine pollution through runoff.

Maine has taught me perseverance. Not only have I been around long enough to experience the consequences of my ideas, but I have learned that the most enduring change can come slowly. It took me more than fifteen years of involvement at Wolfe's Neck Farm before we came up with the natural beef project that combined so many of my goals in a single project. Along the way, my theories were refined, based on experience and the crucible of debate with knowledgeable people. And when the convergence of ideas and people to carry them out occurred—personified by Erick Jensen—I was on hand.

Much of what is so important to me about Maine is summed up by a New Year's group that we were asked to join some fifteen years ago. The connection goes back to the Coffin campaign of 1960, and we gather several times a year to reminisce and to discuss ideas. Once we start, there is no stopping us and our New Year's Day breakfast lasts hours as the conversation links one small group then another in a free-for-all of informed discussion and deep commitment to Maine and to the nation. It is a well-credentialed group and our accomplishments are indicative of a profound compatibility.

Frank and Ruth Coffin form the backbone. After he lost the 1960 election, Frank headed the U.S. Agency for International Development in Paris and became chief judge of the First Circuit Court of Appeals. His incisive mind is matched by his self-deprecating sense of humor, and he and Ruth share an exceptional personal warmth that trumps personal accomplishment as a recommendation for friendship.

Jean and Dick Sampson have both died. Jean's social commitment went back to the early days of the NAACP and in Maine to the university system where she and Frank worked together on one of the better but still unsuccessful attempts at reorganization. I came to know Jean best through her direction of the MCLU and deeply respected her thoughtful advice. She had gravitas. Dick was a legendary math professor at Bates College and his sense of humor always made me avidly anticipate getting together. Dick was also a great lover of women, a talent he lavished on Eunice among others.

I did not know Irving and Judith (Jutka) Isaacson until we joined the group. Irving is the most conservative member and, in his eighties, the most enthusiastic. He isn't doctrinaire and when we discuss farming, which he approaches very differently from me, I go away with gratitude for what I have learned. Jutka was born in Hungary and sent to Auschwitz, which she not only survived but about about which she wrote a fine book.[3] Despite this experience, she has an unmitigated optimism about life that is infectious.

3. Judith M. Isaacson, *Seed of Sarah* (Urbana and Chicago: University of Illinois Press, 1991).

With Shep Lee, I share an interest in a broad array of state issues. Like me he is an avid civic participant, although his extensive board membership is quite different from mine, a situation that leads to lively conversation. With his wife, Candace, I discuss our shared interest in Italian food and culture. Shep pretends he is only Maine's largest automobile dealer but he is really an American ideal, the extremely successful businessman with a deep sense of social responsibility and the willingness to step into the fray to carry it out. One day I was talking with him about the fact that Maine has a high tax burden because we offer so many social services for such a poor state, to which Shep replied, "That's a positive recommendation, isn't it?" Not many businessmen these days so willingly pay taxes to benefit the rest of the public. Shep is also deeply involved with politics and is a good friend of George Mitchell, the former Senate majority leader, and consequently always has good, insider stories to tell his fellow Democrats.

Good friends. Long-term friends. Shared interests, starting with the State of Maine. A genuine love for the state in which we all live. Wanting to make a difference and trying to live one's life in a way that benefits others. Deep concern for one another. These traits and more bind our little group. And the group epitomizes why I am so content that I chose to live and work in Maine.

Index

Numbers in italics are for photos or illustrations.

Bradford, Peter, 187, 245, 362–33
Bradlee, Ben, 116
Brandeis, Louis, 14
Brandeis University, 67
Brawn, Kathy, *219*
Brennan, Justice William J., 54
Bretton Woods, 65–67
Brody, Judge Morton, 247, 249, 355–64
Brook, Alexander Bacon "Sandy," 107–12, 212
Brooks, Cleanth, 87, 89
Brown v. Board of Education, 305
Brown Hotel, 114
Brunswick Record, 109
Bryant, Mike, 167, 173
Bryson City, North Carolina, 11
Budge, Don, 77
Buell, John, 295
Buffum, Imbrie, 131
Bunche, Ralph, 77
Burden, Dr. Charles, 152
Busbey, Congressman Fred, 48
Bush, President George W., 4
Bush, Vannevar, 48

Cadwallader, Wickersham, and Taft, 14
Camp Pocono, 67–69
Campbell, Margaret, 182, 243
Cantwell, Tom, 138
Caracciolo, Nicola, 21
Caron, Alan, 326
Carter, President Jimmy, 14
CarTest, 314
Central Maine Power, 160, 191
Chace, James, 45
Chambers, Whittaker, 65
Chard, Ernie, 122
Chicago Reader, 174
Chiang Kai-shek, 44
Chicago Tribune, 31

Churchill, Winston, 23
Ciechanowski, Jan, 5
Clark, General Wesley, 9
Clark, Jeff, *219*, 241
Clawson, Clinton, 117
Coffin, Doug, 218, 243
Coffin, Frank M., 54, 117, 311; campaign for governor, 117–22, 222; and Ruth, 365
Cog Railway, 65
Cohen, Benjamin, 7, 31
Cohen, David, 246
Cohn, Roy, 42
Cole, Cynthia, 107, 109
Cole, Darragh, 107
Cole, Jean, 268
Cole, John N., 107–09, 155–56, 158–62, 165–66, 168, 170–72, 186, 187, 191, 200, 208, 212, 215, 231, 232, 235, 247, 265–69
Cole, Marshall, 107
Coleman, Eliot, 337
Columbia Country Club, 12
Collins, Donald, 76
Common Good, 347, 353
Conservation Law Foundation, 326
Conant, James, 48
Conover, Roger, 275
Conrad, Joseph, 83
Cook, Warren, 353
Cooper, Dick, 104
Copland, Aaron, 20; visa denied, 48
Corcoran Gallery, 75
Corcoran, Tommy, 7
Corl, Doug, 135
Corl, Glen, 134
Corl, Natalie, 134
Cox, Alexandra, 223
Cox, Anna Walker, 226, *227*
Cox, Anthony Oscar, 73, *224*, *226*, 360–61

Koffman, Ted, 312–14, 316, 322, 324
Kozlowski, L. Dennis, 255
Kreis, Don, 242
Krock, Arthur, 26

Labor Record, 157
Lachaise, Gaston, 238
Ladley, John, 360n
Lafayette Hotel, 119
LaFountain, Bea, 136
LaFountain, Jimmy, 137
Lake Placid News, 125
Lamont, Corliss, 53
Landon School, 75–77
Land, Leslie, 282
Langley, Bill, 186–89
Langley, Lynne, 186, *216*
LeDomaine, 240
Lee, Candace, 366
Lee, Shepard, 119, 222, 366
LeMay, Peter "Hawkeye," 137
Lend-Lease, 3, 6; drafting, 23, first
    administrator, 26
Leonard, Sheldon, 85
Levasseur, Raymond Luc, 234
Levin, Myron, 189
Lewinsky, Monica, 142
Lewis, Fulton III, 55
Lewis, Fulton, Jr., 55
Lewiston Sun Journal, 118
Lexington, Kentucky, 114
Libel trial, 244-264
Libhart, Wayne P., 231, 247, 249
Libra Foundation, 344, 353–54
Life Magazine, 23
Lily, 11
Lindbergh, Charles, 25
Lippmann, Walter, 8; Walter and
    Helen, 81
Lisbon Enterprise, 54
Locke, John, 93
Loeb, Ellen, 126

Loeb, Jim, 55, 125–27, 210
Loeb, William, 53, 228
Long, Senator Huey, 89
Longley, Governor Jim, 266
Louchheim, Don, 88
Louisville, Kentucky, 114
Luoma, Jon, 243
Lurtsema, Robert J., 242

Maine Democrat, 122
Maine Civil Liberties Union, 190,
    301–05
Maine Community Foundation
    (MCF), 95–96, 353
Maine Downtown Center, 320–26,
    362
Maine Indian Land Claims, 233
Maine Magazine, 271–74
Main Street, 321
Maine Times, 19, 165–204, *213,
    214*
Majeska, Kristin, 353
Maltby, Dick, 90
Manomet, 326
Manchester Union Leader, 53, 228
Manhattan Project, 47
Manley, Prime Minister Michael,
    67
Manning, Thomas, 234
Mao, 44
Marble, Harry, 121
March, Nancy, *219*
Market-based environmentalism,
    333, 349
Marsters, Sandy, 291, 295
Martin, John, 324, 362
Martin, Lucy, *216*
MIT, 19
Masters of Deceit, 57
May, Marjorie Merriweather Post
    Davies, 142–43
Mayer, Joseph "Pancho," 85